Daily Light *on the* Daily Path

DAILY LIGHT

on the

DAILY PATH

THE CLASSIC DEVOTIONAL BOOK
FOR EVERY MORNING AND EVENING
IN THE VERY WORDS OF SCRIPTURE

FROM THE HOLY BIBLE
ENGLISH STANDARD VERSION

CROSSWAY®

WHEATON, ILLINOIS

Daily Light on the Daily Path

Copyright © 2002 by Good News Publishers/Crossway Books

Published by Crossway
>>1300 Crescent Street
>>Wheaton, Illinois

All rights reserved. No part of this publication may be reproduced, stored in a retrieval system or transmitted in any form by any means, electronic, mechanical, photocopy, recording or otherwise, without the prior permission of the publisher, except as provided by USA copyright law. Crossway® is a registered trademark in the United States of America.

Scripture quotations are from the ESV® Bible (The Holy Bible: English Standard Version®), copyright © 2001 by Crossway, a publishing ministry of Good News Publishers. Used by permission. All rights reserved.

Cover design: Jon McGrath, Simplicated Studio

First printing 2002

Reprinted with new cover 2012

Printed in Colombia

Hardcover ISBN: 978-1-4335-2997-9
PDF ISBN: 978-1-4335-1328-2
Mobipocket ISBN: 978-1-4335-1329-9
ePub ISBN: 978-1-4335-1635-1

Library of Congress Cataloging-in-Publication Data

Bible. English. English Standard. Selections. 2002.
>>Daily light on the daily path : from the Holy Bible.
>>>>p.   cm.
ISBN 1-58134-435-X
1.Devotional calendars. 2. Bible—Quotations. I. Crossway
Books. II. Title.
BS390   2002
220.5'208—dc21   2002010152

Crossway is a publishing ministry of Good News Publishers.

NP		33	32	31	30	29	28	27	26	25	24	23
16	15	14	13	12	11	10	9	8	7	6	5	4

DAILY
LIGHT
on the
DAILY
PATH

MORNING

*but one thing I do: forgetting what lies behind...
I press on toward the goal for the prize of the
upward call of God in Christ Jesus.*

Father, I desire that they ... whom you have given me, may be with me where I am, to see my glory that you have given me. ...I know whom I have believed, and I am convinced that he is able to guard until that Day what has been entrusted to me. ...He who began a good work in you will bring it to completion at the day of Jesus Christ.

Do you not know that in a race all the runners run, but only one receives the prize? So run that you may obtain it. Every athlete exercises self-control in all things. They do it to receive a perishable wreath, but we an imperishable. ...Let us also lay aside every weight, and sin which clings so closely, and let us run with endurance the race that is set before us, looking to Jesus.

Phil. 3:13-14; John 17:24; 2 Tim. 1:12; Phil. 1:6; 1 Cor. 9:24, 25; Heb. 12:1-2

EVENING

*"It is the Lord who goes before you. He will be with you;
he will not leave you or forsake you."*

And he said to him, "If your presence will not go with me, do not bring us up from here." —I know, O Lord, that the way of man is not in himself, that it is not in man who walks to direct his steps.

The steps of a man are established by the Lord, when he delights in his way; though he fall, he shall not be cast headlong, for the Lord upholds his hand.

Nevertheless, I am continually with you; you hold my right hand. You guide me with your counsel, and afterward you will receive me to glory. —For I am sure that neither death nor life, nor angels nor rulers, nor things present nor things to come, nor powers, nor height nor depth, nor anything else in all creation, will be able to separate us from the love of God in Christ Jesus our Lord.

Deut. 31:8; Ex. 33:15; Jer. 10:23; Ps. 37:23-24; Ps. 73:23-24; Rom. 8:38-39.

MORNING

But one thing I do: forgetting what lies behind, . . .
I press on toward the goal for the prize of the
upward call of God in Christ Jesus.

"Father, I desire that they . . . whom you have given me, may be with me where I am, to see my glory that you have given me."—I know whom I have believed, and I am convinced that he is able to guard until that Day what has been entrusted to me.—He who began a good work in you will bring it to completion at the day of Jesus Christ.

Do you not know that in a race all the runners run, but only one receives the prize? So run that you may obtain it. Every athlete exercises self-control in all things. They do it to receive a perishable wreath, but we an imperishable.—Let us also lay aside every weight, and sin which clings so closely, and let us run with endurance the race that is set before us, looking to Jesus.

Phil. 3:13–14; John 17:24; 2 Tim. 1:12; Phil. 1:6; 1 Cor. 9:24, 25; Heb. 12:1–2

EVENING

"It is the Lord who goes before you. He will be with you;
he will not leave you or forsake you."

And he said to him, "If your presence will not go with me, do not bring us up from here."—I know, O Lord, that the way of man is not in himself, that it is not in man who walks to direct his steps.

The steps of a man are established by the Lord, when he delights in his way; though he fall, he shall not be cast headlong, for the Lord upholds his hand.

Nevertheless, I am continually with you; you hold my right hand. You guide me with your counsel, and afterward you will receive me to glory.—For I am sure that neither death nor life, nor angels nor rulers, nor things present nor things to come, nor powers, nor height nor depth, nor anything else in all creation, will be able to separate us from the love of God in Christ Jesus our Lord.

Deut. 31:8; Ex. 33:15; Jer. 10:23; Ps. 37:23–24; Ps. 73:23–24; Rom. 8:38–39

MORNING

Sing to the Lord a new song.

Sing aloud to God our strength; shout for joy to the God of Jacob! Raise a song; sound the tambourine, the sweet lyre with the harp.—He put a new song in my mouth, a song of praise to our God. Many will see and fear, and put their trust in the Lord.

"Be strong and courageous. Do not be frightened, and do not be dismayed, for the Lord your God is with you wherever you go."—"The joy of the Lord is your strength."—Paul thanked God and took courage.

Besides this you know the time, that the hour has come for you to wake from sleep. For salvation is nearer to us now than when we first believed. The night is far gone; the day is at hand. So then let us cast off the works of darkness and put on the armor of light. Let us walk properly as in the daytime, not in orgies and drunkenness, not in sexual immorality and sensuality, not in quarreling and jealousy. But put on the Lord Jesus Christ, and make no provision for the flesh, to gratify its desires.

Isa. 42:10; Ps. 81:1-2; Ps. 40:3; Josh. 1:9; Neh. 8:10; Acts 28:15; Rom. 13:11-14

EVENING

Let my prayer be counted as incense before you, and
the lifting up of my hands as the evening sacrifice!

"You shall make an altar on which to burn incense. . . . And you shall put it in front of the veil that is above the ark of the testimony, in front of the mercy seat that is above the testimony, where I will meet with you. And Aaron shall burn fragrant incense on it . . . And when Aaron sets up the lamps at twilight, he shall burn it, a regular incense offering before the Lord throughout your generations."

Consequently, [Jesus] is able to save to the uttermost those who draw near to God through him, since he always lives to make intercession for them.—And the smoke of the incense, with the prayers of the saints, rose before God from the hand of the angel.

You yourselves like living stones are being built up as a spiritual house, to be a holy priesthood, to offer spiritual sacrifices acceptable to God through Jesus Christ.

Pray without ceasing.

Ps. 141:2; Ex. 30:1, 6-8; Heb. 7:25; Rev. 8:4; 1 Pet. 2:5; 1 Thess. 5:17

MORNING

He led them by a straight way.

"He found [Jacob] in a desert land, and in the howling waste of the wilderness; he encircled him, he cared for him, he kept him as the apple of his eye. Like an eagle that stirs up its nest, that flutters over its young, spreading out its wings, catching them, bearing them on its pinions, the Lord alone guided him."—"Even to your old age I am he, and to gray hairs I will carry you. I have made, and I will bear; I will carry and will save."

He restores my soul. He leads me in paths of righteousness for his name's sake. Even though I walk through the valley of the shadow of death, I will fear no evil, for you are with me; your rod and your staff, they comfort me.

"And the Lord will guide you continually and satisfy your desire in scorched places and make your bones strong; and you shall be like a watered garden, like a spring of water, whose waters do not fail."—This is God, our God forever and ever. He will guide us forever.—"Who is a teacher like him?"

Ps. 107:7; Deut. 32:10–12; Isa. 46:4; Ps. 23:3–4; Isa. 58:11; Ps. 48:14; Job 36:22

EVENING

"What do you want me to do for you?" He said,
"Lord, let me recover my sight."

Open my eyes, that I may behold wondrous things out of your law.

Then he opened their minds to understand the Scriptures.—"But the Helper, the Holy Spirit, whom the Father will send in my name, he will teach you all things."—Every good gift and every perfect gift is from above, coming down from the Father of lights.

The God of our Lord Jesus Christ, the Father of glory, may give you the Spirit of wisdom and of revelation in the knowledge of him, having the eyes of your hearts enlightened, that you may know what is the hope to which he has called you, what are the riches of his glorious inheritance in the saints, and what is the immeasurable greatness of his power toward us who believe, according to the working of his great might.

Luke 18:41; Ps. 119:18; Luke 24:45; John 14:26; James 1:17; Eph. 1:17–19

MORNING

"For you have not as yet come to the rest and to the inheritance that the Lord your God is giving you."

For this is no place to rest.—So then, there remains a Sabbath rest for the people of God.—Behind the curtain, where Jesus has gone as a forerunner on our behalf.

"In my Father's house are many rooms. If it were not so, would I have told you that I go to prepare a place for you? And if I go and prepare a place for you, I will come again and will take you to myself, that where I am you may be also."—With Christ, for that is far better.

"He will wipe away every tear from their eyes, and death shall be no more, neither shall there be mourning, nor crying, nor pain anymore, for the former things have passed away."—"There the wicked cease from troubling, and there the weary are at rest."

"But lay up for yourselves treasures in heaven, where neither moth nor rust destroys and where thieves do not break in and steal. For where your treasure is, there your heart will be also."—Set your minds on things that are above, not on things that are on earth.

Deut. 12:9; Mic. 2:10; Heb. 4:9; Heb. 6:19–20; John 14:2–3;
Phil. 1:23; Rev. 21:4; Job 3:17; Matt. 6:20–21; Col. 3:2

EVENING

"O death, where is your victory? O death, where is your sting?"

The sting of death is sin.—He has appeared once for all at the end of the ages to put away sin by the sacrifice of himself. And just as it is appointed for man to die once, and after that comes judgment, so Christ, having been offered once to bear the sins of many, will appear a second time, not to deal with sin but to save those who are eagerly waiting for him.

Since therefore the children share in flesh and blood, he himself likewise partook of the same things, that through death he might destroy the one who has the power of death, that is, the devil, and deliver all those who through fear of death were subject to lifelong slavery.

For I am already being poured out as a drink offering, and the time of my departure has come. I have fought the good fight, I have finished the race, I have kept the faith. Henceforth there is laid up for me the crown of righteousness.

1 Cor. 15:55; 1 Cor. 15:56; Heb. 9:26–28; Heb. 2:14–15; 2 Tim. 4:6–8

MORNING

For we who have believed enter that rest.

They weary themselves committing iniquity.—But I see in my members another law waging war against the law of my mind and making me captive to the law of sin that dwells in my members. Wretched man that I am! Who will deliver me from this body of death?

"Come to me, all who labor and are heavy laden, and I will give you rest."—Therefore, since we have been justified by faith, we have peace with God through our Lord Jesus Christ. Through him we have also obtained access by faith into this grace in which we stand, and we rejoice in hope of the glory of God.

For whoever has entered God's rest has also rested from his works.—Not having a righteousness of my own that comes from the law, but that which comes through faith in Christ, the righteousness from God that depends on faith.—"This is rest; give rest to the weary; and this is repose."

Heb. 4:3; Jer. 9:5; Rom. 7:23–24; Matt. 11:28;
Rom. 5:1–2; Heb. 4:10; Phil. 3:9; Isa. 28:12

EVENING

Set a guard, O Lord, over my mouth;
keep watch over the door of my lips!

If you, O Lord, should mark iniquities, O Lord, who could stand?—For they made his spirit bitter, and he spoke rashly with his lips.

"It is not what goes into the mouth that defiles a person, but what comes out of the mouth; this defiles a person."

A whisperer separates close friends.—There is one whose rash words are like sword thrusts, but the tongue of the wise brings healing. Truthful lips endure forever, but a lying tongue is but for a moment.—But no human being can tame the tongue. It is a restless evil, full of deadly poison. . . . From the same mouth come blessing and cursing. My brothers, these things ought not to be so.

But now you must put them all away: anger, wrath, malice, slander, and obscene talk from your mouth. Do not lie to one another, seeing that you have put off the old self with its practices.—For this is the will of God, your sanctification.—And in their mouth no lie was found.

Ps. 141:3; Ps. 130:3; Ps. 106:33; Matt. 15:11; Prov. 16:28; Prov. 12:18–19;
James 3:8, 10; Col. 3:8–9; 1 Thess. 4:3; Rev. 14:5

MORNING

Let the favor of the Lord our God be upon us, and establish the work of our hands upon us.

"And your renown went forth among the nations because of your beauty, for it was perfect through the splendor that I had bestowed on you, declares the Lord God."—And we all, with unveiled face, beholding the glory of the Lord, are being transformed into the same image from one degree of glory to another. For this comes from the Lord who is the Spirit.—The Spirit of glory and of God rests upon you.

Blessed is everyone who fears the Lord, who walks in his ways! You shall eat the fruit of the labor of your hands; you shall be blessed, and it shall be well with you.—Commit your work to the Lord, and your plans will be established.

Work out your own salvation with fear and trembling, for it is God who works in you, both to will and to work for his good pleasure.—Now may our Lord Jesus Christ himself, and God our Father, who loved us and gave us eternal comfort and good hope through grace, comfort your hearts and establish them in every good work and word.

Ps. 90:17; Ezek. 16:14; 2 Cor. 3:18; 1 Pet. 4:14; Ps. 128:1–2;
Prov. 16:3; Phil. 2:12–13; 2 Thess. 2:16–17

EVENING

The apostles returned to Jesus and told him all that they had done and taught.

But there is a friend who sticks closer than a brother.—Thus the Lord used to speak to Moses face to face, as a man speaks to his friend.—"You are my friends if you do what I command you. No longer do I call you servants, for the servant does not know what his master is doing; but I have called you friends, for all that I have heard from my Father I have made known to you."

"So you also, when you have done all that you were commanded, say, 'We are unworthy servants.'"

For you did not receive the spirit of slavery to fall back into fear, but you have received the Spirit of adoption as sons, by whom we cry, "Abba! Father!"—But in everything by prayer and supplication with thanksgiving let your requests be made known to God.—The prayer of the upright is acceptable to him.

Mark 6:30; Prov. 18:24; Ex. 33:11; John 15:14–15;
Luke 17:10; Rom. 8:15; Phil. 4:6; Prov. 15:8

MORNING

Remember [me] for my good, O my God.

Thus says the Lord, "I remember the devotion of your youth, your love as a bride, how you followed me in the wilderness."—"Yet I will remember my covenant with you in the days of your youth, and I will establish for you an everlasting covenant."—"I will visit you, and I will fulfill to you my promise. . . . For I know the plans I have for you, declares the Lord, plans for welfare and not for evil, to give you a future and a hope."

"For as the heavens are higher than the earth, so are my ways higher than your ways and my thoughts than your thoughts."—"I would seek God, and to God would I commit my cause, who does great things and unsearchable, marvelous things without number."—You have multiplied, O Lord my God, your wondrous deeds and your thoughts toward us; none can compare with you! I will proclaim and tell of them, yet they are more than can be told.

Neh. 5:19; Jer. 2:2; Ezek. 16:60; Jer. 29:10–11; Isa. 55:9; Job 5:8–9; Ps. 40:5

EVENING

"I will not leave you or forsake you."

Not one word of all the good promises that the Lord had made to the house of Israel had failed; all came to pass.—"God is not man, that he should lie, or a son of man, that he should change his mind. Has he said, and will he not do it? Or has he spoken, and will he not fulfill it?"

"The Lord your God is God, the faithful God who keeps covenant and steadfast love with those who love him."—He remembers his covenant forever.

"Can a woman forget her nursing child, that she should have no compassion on the son of her womb? Even these may forget, yet I will not forget you. Behold, I have engraved you on the palms of my hands."

The Lord your God is in your midst, a mighty one who will save; he will rejoice over you with gladness; he will quiet you by his love; he will exult over you with loud singing.

Josh. 1:5; Josh. 21:45; Num. 23:19; Deut. 7:9; Ps. 111:5; Isa. 49:15–16; Zeph. 3:17

MORNING

***And those who know your name put their trust in you, for
you, O Lord, have not forsaken those who seek you.***

The name of the Lord is a strong tower; the righteous man runs into it and is
safe.—"I will trust, and will not be afraid; for the Lord God is my strength and
my song, and he has become my salvation."

I have been young, and now am old, yet I have not seen the righteous
forsaken or his children begging for bread.—For the Lord loves justice; he
will not forsake his saints. They are preserved forever, but the children of
the wicked shall be cut off.—"For the Lord will not forsake his people, for his
great name's sake, because it has pleased the Lord to make you a people for
himself."—He delivered us from such a deadly peril, and he will deliver us.
On him we have set our hope that he will deliver us again.

And be content with what you have, for he has said, "I will never leave
you nor forsake you." So we can confidently say, "The Lord is my helper; I will
not fear; what can man do to me?"

Ps. 9:10; Prov. 18:10; Isa. 12:2; Ps. 37:25; Ps. 37:28;
1 Sam. 12:22; 2 Cor. 1:10; Heb. 13:5–6

EVENING

And in their mouth no lie was found, for they are blameless.

"In those days and in that time, declares the Lord, iniquity shall be sought in
Israel, and there shall be none, and sin in Judah, and none shall be found, for
I will pardon those whom I leave as a remnant."—Who is a God like you, pardoning iniquity and passing over transgression for the remnant of his inheritance? He does not retain his anger forever, because he delights in steadfast
love. He will again have compassion on us; he will tread our iniquities underfoot. You will cast all our sins into the depths of the sea.

He has blessed us in the Beloved.—In order to present you holy and
blameless and above reproach before him.

Now to him who is able to keep you from stumbling and to present you
blameless before the presence of his glory with great joy, to the only God,
our Savior, through Jesus Christ our Lord, be glory, majesty, dominion, and
authority, before all time and now and forever. Amen.

Rev. 14:5; Jer. 50:20; Mic. 7:18–19; Eph. 1:6; Col. 1:22; Jude 24–25

MORNING

*You have set up a banner for those who fear you,
that they may flee to it from the bow.*

The Lord Is My banner.—For he [the enemy] will come like a rushing stream, which the wind of the Lord drives.

May we shout for joy over your salvation, and in the name of our God set up our banners!—"The Lord has brought about our vindication; come, let us declare in Zion the work of the Lord our God."—We are more than conquerors through him who loved us.—But thanks be to God, who gives us the victory through our Lord Jesus Christ.—The founder of their salvation.

Finally, be strong in the Lord and in the strength of his might.—Falsehood and not truth has grown strong in the land.—"Fight the Lord's battles."—"Be strong, all you people of the land, declares the Lord. Work. . . . Fear not."—"Lift up your eyes, and see that the fields are white for harvest."—"Yet a little while, and the coming one will come and will not delay."

Ps. 60:4; Ex. 17:15; Isa. 59:19; Ps. 20:5; Jer. 51:10; Rom. 8:37; 1 Cor. 15:57;
Heb. 2:10; Eph. 6:10; Jer. 9:3; 1 Sam. 18:17; Hag. 2:4–5; John 4:35; Heb. 10:37

EVENING

"But one thing is necessary."

There are many who say, "Who will show us some good? Lift up the light of your face upon us, O Lord!" You have put more joy in my heart than they have when their grain and wine abound.

As a deer pants for flowing streams, so pants my soul for you, O God. My soul thirsts for God, for the living God.—O God, you are my God; earnestly I seek you; my soul thirsts for you; my flesh faints for you, as in a dry and weary land where there is no water.

Jesus said to them, "I am the bread of life; whoever comes to me shall not hunger, and whoever believes in me shall never thirst." They said to him, "Sir, give us this bread always."—Mary . . . sat at the Lord's feet and listened to his teaching.—One thing have I asked of the Lord, that will I seek after: that I may dwell in the house of the Lord all the days of my life, to gaze upon the beauty of the Lord and to inquire in his temple.

Luke 10:42; Ps. 4:6–7; Ps. 42:1–2; Ps. 63:1; John 6:34–35; Luke 10:39; Ps. 27:4

MORNING

And may your whole spirit and soul and body be kept blameless at the coming of our Lord Jesus Christ.

Christ loved the church and gave himself up for her . . . so that he might present the church to himself in splendor, without spot or wrinkle or any such thing, that she might be holy and without blemish.—Him we proclaim, warning everyone and teaching everyone with all wisdom, that we may present everyone mature in Christ.

And the peace of God . . . surpasses all understanding.—And let the peace of Christ rule in your hearts, to which indeed you were called in one body.

Now may our Lord Jesus Christ himself, and God our Father, who loved us and gave us eternal comfort and good hope through grace, comfort your hearts and establish them in every good work and word.—Who will sustain you to the end, guiltless in the day of our Lord Jesus Christ.

1 Thess. 5:23; Eph. 5:25–27; Col. 1:28; Phil. 4:7;
Col. 3:15; 2 Thess. 2:16–17; 1 Cor. 1:8

EVENING

"But will God indeed dwell with man on the earth?"

"And let them make me a sanctuary, that I may dwell in their midst."—"There I will meet with the people of Israel, and it shall be sanctified by my glory. . . . I will dwell among the people of Israel and will be their God."

You ascended on high, leading a host of captives in your train and receiving gifts among men, even among the rebellious, that the Lord God may dwell there.

For we are the temple of the living God; as God said, "I will make my dwelling among them and walk among them, and I will be their God, and they shall be my people."—Or do you not know that your body is a temple of the Holy Spirit within you, whom you have from God?—In him you also are being built together into a dwelling place for God by the Spirit.

"Then the nations will know that I am the Lord who sanctifies Israel, when my sanctuary is in their midst forevermore."

2 Chron. 6:18; Ex. 25:8; Ex. 29:43–45; Ps. 68:18;
2 Cor. 6:16; 1 Cor. 6:19; Eph. 2:22; Ezek. 37:28

MORNING

Praise is due to you, O God, in Zion.

Yet for us there is one God, the Father, from whom are all things and for whom we exist, and one Lord, Jesus Christ, through whom are all things and through whom we exist.—"That all may honor the Son, just as they honor the Father. Whoever does not honor the Son does not honor the Father who sent him."—Through him then let us continually offer up a sacrifice of praise to God, that is, the fruit of lips that acknowledge his name.—The one who offers thanksgiving as his sacrifice glorifies me; to one who orders his way rightly I will show the salvation of God!

After this I looked, and behold, a great multitude that no one could number, from every nation, from all tribes and peoples and languages, standing before the throne and before the Lamb, clothed in white robes, with palm branches in their hands, and crying out with a loud voice, "Salvation belongs to our God who sits on the throne, and to the Lamb! . . . Amen! Blessing and glory and wisdom and thanksgiving and honor and power and might be to our God forever and ever! Amen."

Ps. 65:1; 1 Cor. 8:6; John 5:23; Heb. 13:15; Ps. 50:23; Rev. 7:9–10, 12

EVENING

Who redeems your life from the pit.

"Their Redeemer is strong; the Lord of hosts is his name."—Shall I ransom them from the power of Sheol? Shall I redeem them from Death? O Death, where are your plagues? O Sheol, where is your sting? Compassion is hidden from my eyes.

Since therefore the children share in flesh and blood, he himself likewise partook of the same things, that through death he might destroy the one who has the power of death, that is, the devil, and deliver all those who through fear of death were subject to lifelong slavery.

Whoever believes in the Son has eternal life; whoever does not obey the Son shall not see life, but the wrath of God remains on him.

For you have died, and your life is hidden with Christ in God. When Christ who is your life appears, then you also will appear with him in glory.—When he comes on that day to be glorified in his saints, and to be marveled at among all who have believed.

Ps. 103:4; Jer. 50:34; Hos. 13:14; Heb. 2:14–15;
John 3:36; Col. 3:3–4; 2 Thess. 1:10

MORNING

The only [KJV: wise] God, our Savior.

Christ Jesus, who became to us wisdom from God, righteousness and sancti-fication and redemption.—"Can you find out the deep things of God? Can you find out the limit of the Almighty? It is higher than heaven—what can you do? Deeper than Sheol—what can you know?"

But we impart a secret and hidden wisdom of God, which God decreed before the ages for our glory.—The plan of the mystery hidden for ages in God who created all things, so that through the church the manifold wisdom of God might now be made known to the rulers and authorities in the heavenly places.

If any of you lacks wisdom, let him ask God, who gives generously to all without reproach, and it will be given him.—But the wisdom from above is first pure, then peaceable, gentle, open to reason, full of mercy and good fruits, impartial and sincere.

Jude 25; 1 Cor. 1:30; Job 11:7–8; 1 Cor. 2:7; Eph. 3:9–10;
James 1:5; James 3:17

EVENING

"'When shall I arise?' But the night is long."

"Watchman, what time of the night?" . . . The watchman says: "Morning comes."

Yet a little while, and the coming one will come and will not delay.—"He dawns on them like the morning light, like the sun shining forth on a cloud-less morning."

"In my Father's house are many rooms. If it were not so, would I have told you that I go to prepare a place for you? And if I go and prepare a place for you, I will come again and will take you to myself, that where I am you may be also. . . . Let not your hearts be troubled, neither let them be afraid. You heard me say to you, 'I am going away, and I will come to you.'"

"So may all your enemies perish, O Lord! But your friends be like the sun as he rises in his might."—For you are all children of light, children of the day. We are not of the night or of the darkness.

And there will be no night there.

Job 7:4; Isa. 21:11–12; Heb. 10:37; 2 Sam. 23:4; John 14:2–3, 27–28;
Judg. 5:31; 1 Thess. 5:5; Rev. 21:25

MORNING

"You keep him in perfect peace whose mind is stayed on you."

Cast your burden on the Lord, and he will sustain you; he will never permit the righteous to be moved.—"I will trust, and will not be afraid; for the Lord God is my strength and my song, and he has become my salvation."

"Why are you afraid, O you of little faith?"—Do not be anxious about anything, but in everything by prayer and supplication with thanksgiving let your requests be made known to God. And the peace of God, which surpasses all understanding, will guard your hearts and your minds in Christ Jesus.— "In quietness and in trust shall be your strength."

And the result of righteousness [shall be] quietness and trust forever.— "Peace I leave with you; my peace I give to you. Not as the world gives do I give to you. Let not your hearts be troubled, neither let them be afraid."—Peace from him who is and who was and who is to come.

Isa. 26:3; Ps. 55:22; Isa. 12:2; Matt. 8:26; Phil. 4:6–7;
Isa. 30:15; Isa. 32:17; John 14:27; Rev. 1:4

EVENING

Do not let the sun go down on your anger.

"If your brother sins against you, go and tell him his fault, between you and him alone. If he listens to you, you have gained your brother." Then Peter came up and said to him, "Lord, how often will my brother sin against me, and I forgive him? As many as seven times?" Jesus said to him, "I do not say to you seven times, but seventy-seven times."—"And whenever you stand praying, forgive, if you have anything against anyone, so that your Father also who is in heaven may forgive you your trespasses."

Put on then, as God's chosen ones, holy and beloved, compassionate hearts, kindness, humility, meekness, and patience, bearing with one another and, if one has a complaint against another, forgiving each other; as the Lord has forgiven you, so you also must forgive.—Be kind to one another, tenderhearted, forgiving one another, as God in Christ forgave you.

The apostles said to the Lord, "Increase our faith!"

Eph. 4:26; Matt. 18:15, 21–22; Mark 11:25; Col. 3:12–13; Eph. 4:32; Luke 17:5

MORNING

"For the Father is greater than I."

"When you pray, say: Father, hallowed be your name."—"To my Father and your Father, to my God and your God."

"But I do as the Father has commanded me."—"The words that I say to you I do not speak on my own authority, but the Father who dwells in me does his works."

The Father loves the Son and has given all things into his hand.—"You have given him authority over all flesh, to give eternal life to all whom you have given him."

Philip said to him, "Lord, show us the Father, and it is enough for us." Jesus said to him, "Have I been with you so long, and you still do not know me, Philip? Whoever has seen me has seen the Father. How can you say, 'Show us the Father'? Do you not believe that I am in the Father and the Father is in me?"—"I and the Father are one."—"As the Father has loved me, so have I loved you. Abide in my love. If you keep my commandments, you will abide in my love, just as I have kept my Father's commandments and abide in his love."

John 14:28; Luke 11:2; John 20:17; John 14:31; John 14:10;
John 3:35; John 17:2; John 14:8-10; John 10:30; John 15:9-10

EVENING

"[The woman's seed] shall bruise your head,
and you shall bruise his heel."

His appearance was so marred, beyond human semblance, and his form beyond that of the children of mankind.—But he was pierced for our transgressions; he was crushed for our iniquities; upon him was the chastisement that brought us peace, and with his wounds we are healed.—"But this is your hour, and the power of darkness."—"You would have no authority over me at all unless it had been given you from above."

The reason the Son of God appeared was to destroy the works of the devil.—And he . . . cast out many demons. And he would not permit the demons to speak, because they knew him.

"All authority in heaven and on earth has been given to me."—"In my name they will cast out demons."

The God of peace will soon crush Satan under your feet.

Gen. 3:15; Isa. 52:14; Isa. 53:5; Luke 22:53; John 19:11; 1 John 3:8;
Mark 1:34; Matt. 28:18; Mark 16:17; Rom. 16:20

MORNING

My soul clings to the dust; give me life according to your word!

If then you have been raised with Christ, seek the things that are above, where Christ is, seated at the right hand of God. Set your minds on things that are above, not on things that are on earth. For . . . your life is hidden with Christ in God.—But our citizenship is in heaven, and from it we await a Savior, the Lord Jesus Christ, who will transform our lowly body to be like his glorious body, by the power that enables him even to subject all things to himself.

For the desires of the flesh are against the Spirit, and the desires of the Spirit are against the flesh, for these are opposed to each other, to keep you from doing the things you want to do.—So then, brothers, we are debtors, not to the flesh, to live according to the flesh. For if you live according to the flesh you will die, but if by the Spirit you put to death the deeds of the body, you will live.—Beloved, I urge you as sojourners and exiles to abstain from the passions of the flesh, which wage war against your soul.

Ps. 119:25; Col. 3:1–3; Phil. 3:20–21; Gal. 5:17; Rom. 8:12–13; 1 Pet. 2:11

EVENING

The measure of faith.

As for the one who is weak in faith . . . —But he grew strong in his faith as he gave glory to God.—"O you of little faith, why did you doubt?"—"Great is your faith! Be it done for you as you desire."

"Do you believe that I am able to do this?" They said to him, "Yes, Lord." . . . "According to your faith be it done to you."

"Increase our faith!"—But you, beloved, building yourselves up in your most holy faith.—Rooted and built up in him and established in the faith.— And it is God who establishes us with you in Christ.—And after you have suffered a little while, the God of all grace . . . will himself restore, confirm, strengthen, and establish you.

We who are strong have an obligation to bear with the failings of the weak, and not to please ourselves.—Therefore let us not pass judgment on one another any longer, but rather decide never to put a stumbling block or hindrance in the way of a brother.

Rom. 12:3; Rom. 14:1; Rom. 4:20; Matt. 14:31; Matt. 15:28; Matt. 9:28–29; Luke 17:5; Jude 20; Col. 2:7; 2 Cor. 1:21; 1 Pet. 5:10; Rom. 15:1; Rom. 14:13

MORNING

For in him all the fullness of God was pleased to dwell.

The Father loves the Son and has given all things into his hand.—Therefore God has highly exalted him and bestowed on him the name that is above every name, so that at the name of Jesus every knee should bow, in heaven and on earth and under the earth, and every tongue confess that Jesus Christ is Lord, to the glory of God the Father.—Far above all rule and authority and power and dominion, and above every name that is named, not only in this age but also in the one to come.—For by him all things were created, in heaven and on earth, visible and invisible, whether thrones or dominions or rulers or authorities—all things were created through him and for him.

For to this end Christ died and lived again, that he might be Lord both of the dead and of the living.—And you have been filled in him, who is the head of all rule and authority.—For from his fullness we have all received.

Col. 1:19; John 3:35; Phil. 2:9–11; Eph. 1:21; Col. 1:16;
Rom. 14:9; Col. 2:10; John 1:16

EVENING

"Write therefore the things that you have seen, those that are and those that are to take place after this."

Men spoke from God as they were carried along by the Holy Spirit.—That which we have seen and heard we proclaim also to you, so that you too may have fellowship with us; and indeed our fellowship is with the Father and with his Son Jesus Christ.

"See my hands and my feet, that it is I myself. Touch me, and see. For a spirit does not have flesh and bones as you see that I have." And when he had said this, he showed them his hands and his feet.—He who saw it has borne witness—his testimony is true, and he knows that he is telling the truth—that you also may believe.

For we did not follow cleverly devised myths when we made known to you the power and coming of our Lord Jesus Christ, but we were eyewitnesses of his majesty.—That your faith might not rest in the wisdom of men but in the power of God.

Rev. 1:19; 2 Pet. 1:21; 1 John 1:3; Luke 24:39–40;
John 19:35; 2 Pet. 1:16; 1 Cor. 2:5

MORNING

*But in love you have delivered my
life from the pit of destruction.*

God sent his only Son into the world, so that we might live through him. In this is love, not that we have loved God but that he loved us and sent his Son to be the propitiation for our sins.

Who is a God like you, pardoning iniquity and passing over transgression for the remnant of his inheritance? He does not retain his anger forever, because he delights in steadfast love. He will again have compassion on us; he will tread our iniquities underfoot. You will cast all our sins into the depths of the sea.—O Lord my God, I cried to you for help, and you have healed me. O Lord, you have brought up my soul from Sheol; you restored me to life from among those who go down to the pit.—"When my life was fainting away, I remembered the Lord, and my prayer came to you, into your holy temple."—I waited patiently for the Lord; he inclined to me and heard my cry. He drew me up from the pit of destruction, out of the miry bog, and set my feet upon a rock.

Isa. 38:17; 1 John 4:9-10; Mic. 7:18-19; Ps. 30:2-3; Jonah 2:7; Ps. 40:1-2

EVENING

"Write therefore the things . . . that are."

For now we see in a mirror dimly.—At present, we do not yet see everything in subjection to him.

And we have the prophetic word more fully confirmed, to which you will do well to pay attention as to a lamp shining in a dark place, until the day dawns and the morning star rises in your hearts.—Your word is a lamp to my feet and a light to my path.

But you must remember, beloved, the predictions of the apostles of our Lord Jesus Christ. They said to you, "In the last time there will be scoffers, following their own ungodly passions."—Now the Spirit expressly says that in later times some will depart from the faith by devoting themselves to deceitful spirits and teachings of demons.

Children, it is the last hour.—The night is far gone; the day is at hand. So then let us cast off the works of darkness and put on the armor of light.

Rev. 1:19; 1 Cor. 13:12; Heb. 2:8; 2 Pet. 1:19; Ps. 119:105;
Jude 17-18; 1 Tim. 4:1; 1 John 2:18; Rom. 13:12

MORNING

The one who was to come.

But we see him who for a little while was made lower than the angels, namely Jesus, crowned with glory and honor because of the suffering of death, so that by the grace of God he might taste death for everyone.—One has died for all.—For as by the one man's disobedience the many were made sinners, so by the one man's obedience the many will be made righteous.—Thus it is written, "The first man Adam became a living being"; the last Adam became a life-giving spirit.—Then God said, "Let us make man in our image, after our likeness." So God created man in his own image, in the image of God he created him; male and female he created them.—But in these last days [God] has spoken to us by his Son. . . . He is the radiance of the glory of God and the exact imprint of his nature.—"You have given him authority over all flesh."

    The first man was from the earth, a man of dust; the second man is from heaven. As was the man of dust, so also are those who are of the dust, and as is the man of heaven, so also are those who are of heaven.

Rom. 5:14; Heb. 2:9; 2 Cor. 5:14; Rom. 5:19; 1 Cor. 15:45–46; Gen. 1:26–27; Heb. 1:1–3; John 17:2; 1 Cor. 15:47–48

EVENING

"Write therefore the things . . . that are to take place after this."

But, as it is written, "What no eye has seen, nor ear heard, nor the heart of man imagined, what God has prepared for those who love him"— these things God has revealed to us through the Spirit.—"When the Spirit of truth comes, . . . he will declare to you the things that are to come."—Behold, he is coming with the clouds, and every eye will see him, even those who pierced him, and all tribes of the earth will wail on account of him. Even so. Amen.

    But we do not want you to be uninformed, brothers, about those who are asleep, that you may not grieve as others do who have no hope. For since we believe that Jesus died and rose again, even so, through Jesus, God will bring with him those who have fallen asleep. . . . For the Lord himself will descend from heaven with a cry of command, with the voice of an archangel, and with the sound of the trumpet of God. And the dead in Christ will rise first. Then we who are alive, who are left, will be caught up together with them in the clouds to meet the Lord in the air, and so we will always be with the Lord.

Rev. 1:19; 1 Cor. 2:9–10; John 16:13; Rev. 1:7; 1 Thess. 4:13–14, 16–17

MORNING

"Serving the Lord with all humility."

"But whoever would be great among you must be your servant, and whoever would be first among you must be your slave, even as the Son of Man came not to be served but to serve, and to give his life as a ransom for many."

For if anyone thinks he is something, when he is nothing, he deceives himself.—For by the grace given to me I say to everyone among you not to think of himself more highly than he ought to think, but to think with sober judgment, each according to the measure of faith that God has assigned.—"So you also, when you have done all that you were commanded, say, 'We are unworthy servants; we have only done what was our duty.'"

For our boast is this, . . . that we behaved in the world with simplicity and godly sincerity, not by earthly wisdom but by the grace of God.—But we have this treasure in jars of clay, to show that the surpassing power belongs to God and not to us.

Acts 20:19; Matt. 20:26–28; Gal. 6:3; Rom. 12:3;
Luke 17:10; 2 Cor. 1:12; 2 Cor. 4:7

EVENING

We have turned—every one—to his own way.

Noah . . . planted a vineyard. He drank of the wine and became drunk.— [Abram] said to Sarai his wife, . . . "Say you are my sister, that it may go well with me because of you."—Then Isaac said to Jacob. . . . "Are you really my son Esau?" He answered, "I am."—Moses . . . spoke rashly with his lips.—So the men took some of their provisions, but did not ask counsel from the Lord. And Joshua made peace with them.—David did what was right in the eyes of the Lord and did not turn aside from anything that he commanded him all the days of his life, except in the matter of Uriah the Hittite.

And all these . . . [were] commended through their faith.—And are justified by his grace as a gift, through the redemption that is in Christ Jesus.— And the Lord has laid on him the iniquity of us all.

"It is not for your sake that I will act, declares the Lord God; let that be known to you. Be ashamed and confounded for your ways."

Isa. 53:6; Gen. 9:20–21; Gen. 12:11, 13; Gen. 27:21, 24; Ps. 106:32–33;
Josh. 9:14–15; 1 Kings 15:5; Heb. 11:39; Rom. 3:24; Isa. 53:6; Ezek. 36:32

MORNING

And his name shall be called Wonderful Counselor.

And the Word became flesh and dwelt among us, and we have seen his glory, glory as of the only Son from the Father, full of grace and truth.—For you have exalted above all things your name and your word.

"And they shall call his name Immanuel" (which means, God with us).— "And you shall call his name Jesus, for he will save his people from their sins."

"That all may honor the Son, just as they honor the Father."—Therefore God has highly exalted him and bestowed on him the name that is above every name.—Far above all rule and authority and power and dominion, and above every name that is named, not only in this age but also in the one to come. And he put all things under his feet.—He has a name written that no one knows but himself . . . King of kings and Lord of lords.

The Almighty—we cannot find him.—What is his name, and what is his son's name? Surely you know!

Isa. 9:6; John 1:14; Ps. 138:2; Matt. 1:23; Matt. 1:21; John 5:23;
Phil. 2:9; Eph. 1:21–22; Rev. 19:12, 16; Job. 37:23; Prov. 30:4

EVENING

"But the Lord's portion is his people."

And you are Christ's, and Christ is God's.—I am my beloved's, and his desire is for me.—And I am his.—The Son of God . . . loved me and gave himself for me.

You are not your own, for you were bought with a price. So glorify God in your body.—"But the Lord has taken you and brought you out of the iron furnace, out of Egypt, to be a people of his own inheritance, as you are this day."

You are God's field, God's building.—But Christ is faithful over God's house as a son. And we are his house if indeed we hold fast our confidence and our boasting in our hope.—A spiritual house . . . a holy priesthood.— "They shall be mine, says the Lord of hosts, in the day when I make up my treasured possession."—"All mine are yours, and yours are mine, and I am glorified in them."—The riches of his glorious inheritance in the saints.

Deut. 32:9; 1 Cor. 3:23; Song 7:10; Song 2:16; Gal. 2:20; 1 Cor. 6:19–20;
Deut. 4:20; 1 Cor. 3:9; Heb. 3:6; 1 Pet. 2:5; Mal. 3:17; John 17:10; Eph. 1:18

MORNING

"Every branch in me that does not bear fruit he takes away."

"For he is like a refiner's fire and like fullers' soap. He will sit as a refiner and purifier of silver, and he will purify the sons of Levi and refine them like gold and silver, and they will bring offerings in righteousness to the Lord."

Not only that, but we rejoice in our sufferings, knowing that suffering produces endurance, and endurance produces character, and character produces hope, and hope does not put us to shame, because God's love has been poured into our hearts through the Holy Spirit who has been given to us.—It is for discipline that you have to endure. God is treating you as sons. For what son is there whom his father does not discipline? If you are left without discipline, in which all have participated, then you are illegitimate children and not sons. . . . For the moment all discipline seems painful rather than pleasant, but later it yields the peaceful fruit of righteousness to those who have been trained by it. Therefore lift your drooping hands and strengthen your weak knees.

John 15:2; Mal. 3:2–3; Rom. 5:3–5; Heb. 12:7–8, 11–12

EVENING

"And now we call the arrogant blessed."

For thus says the One who is high and lifted up, who inhabits eternity, whose name is Holy: "I dwell in the high and holy place, and also with him who is of a contrite and lowly spirit, to revive the spirit of the lowly, and to revive the heart of the contrite."

It is better to be of a lowly spirit with the poor than to divide the spoil with the proud.—"Blessed are the poor in spirit, for theirs is the kingdom of heaven."

There are six things that the Lord hates, seven that are an abomination to him: haughty eyes . . . —Everyone who is arrogant in heart is an abomination to the Lord.

Search me, O God, and know my heart! Try me and know my thoughts! And see if there be any grievous way in me, and lead me in the way everlasting!

Grace to you and peace from God our Father and the Lord Jesus Christ. I thank my God in all my remembrance of you.—"Blessed are the meek, for they shall inherit the earth."

Mal. 3:15; Isa. 57:15; Prov. 16:19; Matt. 5:3; Prov. 6:16–17;
Prov. 16:5; Ps. 139:23–24; Phil. 1:2–3; Matt. 5:5

MORNING

This is God, our God forever and ever. He will guide us forever.

O Lord, you are my God; I will exalt you; I will praise your name, for you have done wonderful things, plans formed of old, faithful and sure.—The Lord is my chosen portion and my cup.

He leads me in paths of righteousness for his name's sake. Even though I walk through the valley of the shadow of death, I will fear no evil, for you are with me; your rod and your staff, they comfort me.—You hold my right hand. You guide me with your counsel, and afterward you will receive me to glory. Whom have I in heaven but you? And there is nothing on earth that I desire besides you. My flesh and my heart may fail, but God is the strength of my heart and my portion forever.—For our heart is glad in him, because we trust in his holy name.—The Lord will fulfill his purpose for me; your steadfast love, O Lord, endures forever. Do not forsake the work of your hands.

Ps. 48:14; Isa. 25:1; Ps. 16:5; Ps. 23:3-4; Ps. 73:23-26; Ps. 33:21; Ps. 138:8

EVENING

When the cares of my heart are many,
your consolations cheer my soul.

When my heart is faint . . . lead me to the rock that is higher than I.

O Lord, I am oppressed; be my pledge of safety!—Cast your burden on the Lord, and he will sustain you.

"I am but a little child. I do not know how to go out or come in."—If any of you lacks wisdom, let him ask God . . . and it will be given him.

Who is sufficient for these things?—For I know that nothing good dwells in me, that is, in my flesh.—"My grace is sufficient for you, for my power is made perfect in weakness."

"Take heart, my son; your sins are forgiven. . . . Take heart, daughter; your faith has made you well."

My soul will be satisfied as with fat and rich food . . . when I remember you upon my bed, and meditate on you in the watches of the night.

Ps. 94:19; Ps. 61:2; Isa. 38:14; Ps. 55:22; 1 Kings 3:7; James 1:5;
2 Cor. 2:16; Rom. 7:18; 2 Cor. 12:9; Matt. 9:2, 22; Ps. 63:5-6

MORNING

And hope does not put us to shame.

"I am the Lord; those who wait for me shall not be put to shame."—"Blessed is the man who trusts in the Lord, whose trust is the Lord."—"You keep him in perfect peace whose mind is stayed on you, because he trusts in you. Trust in the Lord forever, for the Lord God is an everlasting rock."—For God alone, O my soul, wait in silence, for my hope is from him. He only is my rock and my salvation.—But I am not ashamed, for I know whom I have believed.

So when God desired to show more convincingly to the heirs of the promise the unchangeable character of his purpose, he guaranteed it with an oath, so that by two unchangeable things, in which it is impossible for God to lie, we who have fled for refuge might have strong encouragement to hold fast to the hope set before us. We have this as a sure and steadfast anchor of the soul, a hope that enters into the inner place behind the curtain, where Jesus has gone as a forerunner on our behalf.

Rom. 5:5; Isa. 49:23; Jer. 17:7; Isa. 26:3–4; Ps. 62:5–6;
2 Tim. 1:12; Heb. 6:17–20

EVENING

The offense of the cross.

"If anyone would come after me, let him deny himself and take up his cross and follow me."—Do you not know that friendship with the world is enmity with God? Therefore whoever wishes to be a friend of the world makes himself an enemy of God.—Through many tribulations we must enter the kingdom of God.—"Whoever believes in him will not be put to shame."—So the honor is for you who believe, but for those who do not believe, "The stone that the builders rejected has become the cornerstone," and "A stone of stumbling, and a rock of offense."

But far be it from me to boast except in the cross of our Lord Jesus Christ, by which the world has been crucified to me, and I to the world.—I have been crucified with Christ.—And those who belong to Christ Jesus have crucified the flesh with its passions and desires.

If we endure, we will also reign with him; if we deny him, he also will deny us.

Gal. 5:11; Matt. 16:24; James 4:4; Acts 14:22; Rom. 9:33;
1 Pet. 2:7–8; Gal. 6:14; Gal. 2:20; Gal. 5:24; 2 Tim. 2:12

MORNING

The Lord is at hand.

For the Lord himself will descend from heaven with a cry of command, with the voice of an archangel, and with the sound of the trumpet of God. And the dead in Christ will rise first. Then we who are alive, who are left, will be caught up together with them in the clouds to meet the Lord in the air, and so we will always be with the Lord. Therefore encourage one another with these words.—He who testifies to these things says, "Surely I am coming soon." Amen. Come, Lord Jesus!

Therefore, beloved, since you are waiting for these, be diligent to be found by him without spot or blemish, and at peace.—Abstain from every form of evil. Now may the God of peace himself sanctify you completely, and may your whole spirit and soul and body be kept blameless at the coming of our Lord Jesus Christ. He who calls you is faithful; he will surely do it.

You also, be patient. Establish your hearts, for the coming of the Lord is at hand.

Phil. 4:5; 1 Thess. 4:16–18; Rev. 22:20; 2 Pet. 3:14; 1 Thess. 5:22–24; James 5:8

EVENING

"The choice vine."

Let me sing for my beloved my love song concerning his vineyard: My beloved had a vineyard on a very fertile hill. He dug it and cleared it of stones, and planted it with choice vines; . . . and he looked for it to yield grapes, but it yielded wild grapes.—"Yet I planted you a choice vine, wholly of pure seed. How then have you turned degenerate and become a wild vine?"

Now the works of the flesh are evident: sexual immorality, impurity, sensuality . . . envy, drunkenness, orgies, and things like these. But the fruit of the Spirit is love, joy, peace, patience, kindness, goodness, faithfulness, gentleness, self-control.

"I am the true vine, and my Father is the vinedresser. Every branch in me that does not bear fruit he takes away, and every branch that does bear fruit he prunes, that it may bear more fruit. . . . Abide in me, and I in you. . . . By this my Father is glorified, that you bear much fruit and so prove to be my disciples."

Gen. 49:11; Isa. 5:1–2; Jer. 2:21; Gal. 5:19, 21–23; John 15:1–2, 4, 8

MORNING

The righteousness of God through faith
in Jesus Christ for all who believe.

For our sake he made him to be sin who knew no sin, so that in him we might become the righteousness of God.—Christ redeemed us from the curse of the law by becoming a curse for us.—Who became to us wisdom from God, righteousness and sanctification and redemption.—Not because of works done by us in righteousness, but according to his own mercy, by the washing of regeneration and renewal of the Holy Spirit, whom he poured out on us richly through Jesus Christ our Savior.

Indeed, I count everything as loss because of the surpassing worth of knowing Christ Jesus my Lord. For his sake I have suffered the loss of all things and count them as rubbish, in order that I may gain Christ and be found in him, not having a righteousness of my own that comes from the law, but that which comes through faith in Christ, the righteousness from God that depends on faith.

Rom. 3:22; 2 Cor. 5:21; Gal. 3:13; 1 Cor. 1:30; Titus 3:5-6; Phil. 3:8-9

EVENING

But you have received the Spirit of adoption as sons,
by whom we cry, "Abba! Father!"

Jesus . . . lifted up his eyes to heaven, and said, "Father, . . . Holy Father, . . . O righteous Father.—And he said, "Abba, Father."—And because you are sons, God has sent the Spirit of his Son into our hearts, crying, "Abba! Father!"—For through him we both have access in one Spirit to the Father. So then you are no longer strangers and aliens, but you are fellow citizens with the saints and members of the household of God.

For you are our Father . . . you, O Lord, are our Father, our Redeemer from of old is your name.

"I will arise and go to my father, and I will say to him, 'Father, I have sinned against heaven and before you. I am no longer worthy to be called your son. Treat me as one of your hired servants.'" And he arose and came to his father.

Therefore be imitators of God, as beloved children.

Rom. 8:15; John 17:1, 11, 25; Mark 14:36; Gal. 4:6;
Eph. 2:18-19; Isa. 63:16; Luke 15:18-20; Eph. 5:1

MORNING

Therefore let us go to him outside the camp and bear the
reproach he endured. For here we have no lasting city,
but we seek the city that is to come.

Beloved, do not be surprised at the fiery trial when it comes upon you to test you, as though something strange were happening to you. But rejoice insofar as you share Christ's sufferings, that you may also rejoice and be glad when his glory is revealed.—For we know that as you share in our sufferings, you will also share in our comfort.—If you are insulted for the name of Christ, you are blessed, because the Spirit of glory and of God rests upon you.—Then they left the presence of the council, rejoicing that they were counted worthy to suffer dishonor for the name.—Choosing rather to be mistreated with the people of God than to enjoy the fleeting pleasures of sin. He considered the reproach of Christ greater wealth than the treasures of Egypt, for he was looking to the reward.

Heb. 13:13–14; 1 Pet. 4:12–13; 2 Cor. 1:7; 1 Pet. 4:14; Acts 5:41; Heb. 11:25–26

EVENING

The Lord Jesus Christ . . . will transform our lowly
body to be like his glorious body.

And above the expanse over their heads there was the likeness of a throne, in appearance like sapphire; and seated above the likeness of a throne was a likeness with a human appearance. And upward from what had the appearance of his waist I saw as it were gleaming metal, like the appearance of fire enclosed all around. And downward from what had the appearance of his waist I saw as it were the appearance of fire, and there was brightness around him. Like the appearance of the bow that is in the cloud on the day of rain, so was the appearance of the brightness all around. Such was the appearance of the likeness of the glory of the Lord.—And we all, with unveiled face, beholding the glory of the Lord, are being transformed into the same image from one degree of glory to another. For this comes from the Lord who is the Spirit.—Beloved, we are God's children now, and what we will be has not yet appeared; but we know that when he appears we shall be like him, because we shall see him as he is.

"They shall hunger no more, neither thirst anymore."—And they sing the song of Moses, the servant of God, and the song of the Lamb.

Phil. 3:20–21; Ezek. 1:26–28; 2 Cor. 3:18; 1 John 3:2; Rev. 7:16; Rev. 15:3

MORNING

***You know that he appeared in order to take away sins,
and in him there is no sin.***

But in these last days [God] has spoken to us by his Son. . . . He is the radiance of the glory of God and the exact imprint of his nature, and he upholds the universe by the word of his power. After making purification for sins, he sat down at the right hand of the Majesty on high.—For our sake he made him to be sin who knew no sin, so that in him we might become the righteousness of God.—Conduct yourselves with fear throughout the time of your exile, knowing that you were ransomed from the futile ways inherited from your forefathers, not with perishable things such as silver or gold, but with the precious blood of Christ, like that of a lamb without blemish or spot. He was foreknown before the foundation of the world but was made manifest in the last times for the sake of you.—For the love of Christ controls us, because we have concluded this: that one has died for all, therefore all have died; and he died for all, that those who live might no longer live for themselves but for him who for their sake died and was raised.

1 John 3:5; Heb. 1:1–3; 2 Cor. 5:21; 1 Pet. 1:17–20; 2 Cor. 5:14–15

EVENING

***"I have set before you life and death, blessing
and curse. Therefore choose life."***

"'For I have no pleasure in the death of anyone,' declares the Lord God; 'so turn, and live'."—"If I had not come and spoken to them, they would not have been guilty of sin, but now they have no excuse for their sin."—"And that servant who knew his master's will but did not get ready or act according to his will, will receive a severe beating."

For the wages of sin is death, but the free gift of God is eternal life in Christ Jesus our Lord.—Whoever believes in the Son has eternal life; whoever does not obey the Son shall not see life, but the wrath of God remains on him.—Do you not know that if you present yourselves to anyone as obedient slaves, you are slaves of the one whom you obey, either of sin, which leads to death, or of obedience, which leads to righteousness?—"If anyone serves me, he must follow me; and where I am, there will my servant be also. If anyone serves me, the Father will honor him."

Deut. 30:19; Ezek. 18:32; John 15:22; Luke 12:47;
Rom. 6:23; John 3:36; Rom. 6:16; John 12:26

MORNING

"As your days, so shall your strength be."

"And when they bring you to trial and deliver you over, do not be anxious beforehand what you are to say, but say whatever is given you in that hour, for it is not you who speak, but the Holy Spirit."—"Therefore do not be anxious about tomorrow, for tomorrow will be anxious for itself. Sufficient for the day is its own trouble."

The God of Israel—he is the one who gives power and strength to his people. Blessed be God!—He gives power to the faint, and to him who has no might he increases strength.

But he said to me, "My grace is sufficient for you, for my power is made perfect in weakness." Therefore I will boast all the more gladly of my weaknesses, so that the power of Christ may rest upon me. For the sake of Christ, then, I am content with weaknesses, insults, hardships, persecutions, and calamities. For when I am weak, then I am strong.—I can do all things through him who strengthens me.—"March on, my soul, with might!"

Deut. 33:25; Mark 13:11; Matt. 6:34; Ps. 68:35; Isa. 40:29;
2 Cor. 12:9–10; Phil. 4:13; Judg. 5:21

EVENING

Awake, O north wind. . . . Blow upon my garden, let its spices flow.

For the moment all discipline seems painful rather than pleasant, but later it yields the peaceful fruit of righteousness to those who have been trained by it.—The fruit of the Spirit.

He removed them with his fierce breath in the day of the east wind.

As a father shows compassion to his children, so the Lord shows compassion to those who fear him.

Though our outer self is wasting away, our inner self is being renewed day by day. For this light momentary affliction is preparing for us an eternal weight of glory beyond all comparison, as we look not to the things that are seen but to the things that are unseen.

Although he was a son, he learned obedience through what he suffered.—But one who in every respect has been tempted as we are, yet without sin.

Song 4:16; Heb. 12:11; Gal. 5:22; Isa. 27:8; Ps. 103:13;
2 Cor. 4:16–18; Heb. 5:8; Heb. 4:15

MORNING

"You are a God of seeing."

O Lord, you have searched me and known me! You know when I sit down and when I rise up; you discern my thoughts from afar. You search out my path and my lying down and are acquainted with all my ways. Even before a word is on my tongue, behold, O Lord, you know it altogether. . . . Such knowledge is too wonderful for me; it is high; I cannot attain it.

The eyes of the Lord are in every place, keeping watch on the evil and the good.—For a man's ways are before the eyes of the Lord, and he ponders all his paths.—"But God knows your hearts. For what is exalted among men is an abomination in the sight of God."—"For the eyes of the Lord run to and fro throughout the whole earth, to give strong support to those whose heart is blameless toward him."

But Jesus . . . knew all people and needed no one to bear witness about man, for he himself knew what was in man.—"Lord, you know everything; you know that I love you."

Gen. 16:13; Ps. 139:1–4, 6; Prov. 15:3; Prov. 5:21; Luke 16:15;
2 Chron. 16:9; John 2:24–25; John 21:17

EVENING

I give thanks to you, O Lord my God, with my whole heart, and I will glorify your name forever.

The one who offers thanksgiving as his sacrifice glorifies me.—It is good to give thanks to the Lord, to sing praises to your name, O Most High; to declare your steadfast love in the morning, and your faithfulness by night.

Let everything that has breath praise the Lord!

I appeal to you therefore, brothers, by the mercies of God, to present your bodies as a living sacrifice, holy and acceptable to God, which is your spiritual worship.—So Jesus also suffered outside the gate in order to sanctify the people through his own blood. . . . Through him then let us continually offer up a sacrifice of praise to God, that is, the fruit of lips that acknowledge his name.—Giving thanks always and for everything to God the Father in the name of our Lord Jesus Christ.

"Worthy is the Lamb who was slain, to receive power and wealth and wisdom and might and honor and glory and blessing!"

Ps. 86:12; Ps. 50:23; Ps. 92:1–2; Ps. 150:6; Rom. 12:1;
Heb. 13:12, 15; Eph. 5:20; Rev. 5:12

MORNING

Let us run with endurance the race that is set before us,
looking to Jesus, the founder and perfecter of our faith.

"If anyone would come after me, let him deny himself and take up his cross daily and follow me."—"So therefore, any one of you who does not renounce all that he has cannot be my disciple."—So then let us cast off the works of darkness and put on the armor of light.

Every athlete exercises self-control in all things. They do it to receive a perishable wreath, but we an imperishable. But I discipline my body and keep it under control, lest after preaching to others I myself should be disqualified.—Brothers, I do not consider that I have made it my own. But one thing I do: forgetting what lies behind and straining forward to what lies ahead, I press on toward the goal for the prize of the upward call of God in Christ Jesus.—"Let us know; let us press on to know the Lord."

Heb. 12:1–2; Luke 9:23; Luke 14:33; Rom. 13:12;
1 Cor. 9:25, 27; Phil. 3:13–14; Hos. 6:3

EVENING

It is good for a man that he bear the yoke in his youth.

Train up a child in the way he should go; even when he is old he will not depart from it.

We have had earthly fathers who disciplined us and we respected them. Shall we not much more be subject to the Father of spirits and live? For they disciplined us for a short time as it seemed best to them, but he disciplines us for our good, that we may share his holiness.

Before I was afflicted I went astray, but now I keep your word. . . . It is good for me that I was afflicted, that I might learn your statutes.

"For I know the plans I have for you, declares the Lord, plans for welfare and not for evil, to give you a future and a hope."—Humble yourselves, therefore, under the mighty hand of God so that at the proper time he may exalt you.

Lam. 3:27; Prov. 22:6; Heb. 12:9–10; Ps. 119:67, 71; Jer. 29:11; 1 Pet. 5:6

MORNING

"But if you do not drive out the inhabitants of the land from before you, then those of them whom you let remain shall be as barbs in your eyes and thorns in your sides, and they shall trouble you in the land where you dwell."

Fight the good fight of the faith.—For the weapons of our warfare are not of the flesh but have divine power to destroy strongholds. We destroy arguments . . . and take every thought captive to obey Christ.

So then, brothers, we are debtors, not to the flesh, to live according to the flesh. For if you live according to the flesh you will die, but if by the Spirit you put to death the deeds of the body, you will live.

For the desires of the flesh are against the Spirit, and the desires of the Spirit are against the flesh, for these are opposed to each other, to keep you from doing the things you want to do.—But I see in my members another law waging war against the law of my mind and making me captive to the law of sin that dwells in my members.—We are more than conquerors through him who loved us.

Num. 33:55; 1 Tim. 6:12; 2 Cor. 10:4–5; Rom. 8:12–13;
Gal. 5:17; Rom. 7:23; Rom. 8:37

EVENING

*"If someone sins against the Lord,
who can intercede for him?"*

But if anyone does sin, we have an advocate with the Father, Jesus Christ the righteous. He is the propitiation for our sins, and not for ours only but also for the sins of the whole world.—Whom God put forward as a propitiation by his blood, to be received by faith. This was to show God's righteousness, because in his divine forbearance he had passed over former sins. It was to show his righteousness at the present time, so that he might be just and the justifier of the one who has faith in Jesus.—"And he is merciful to him, and says, 'Deliver him from going down into the pit; I have found a ransom.'"

What then shall we say to these things? If God is for us, who can be against us? . . . Who shall bring any charge against God's elect? It is God who justifies. Who is to condemn? Christ Jesus is the one who died—more than that, who was raised—who is at the right hand of God, who indeed is interceding for us.

1 Sam. 2:25; 1 John 2:1–2; Rom. 3:25–26; Job 33:24; Rom. 8:31, 33–34

MORNING

Though you have not seen him, you love him.

For we walk by faith, not by sight.—We love because he first loved us.—So we have come to know and to believe the love that God has for us. God is love, and whoever abides in love abides in God, and God abides in him.—In him you also, when you heard the word of truth, the gospel of your salvation, and believed in him, were sealed with the promised Holy Spirit.—To them God chose to make known how great among the Gentiles are the riches of the glory of this mystery, which is Christ in you, the hope of glory.

If anyone says, "I love God," and hates his brother, he is a liar; for he who does not love his brother whom he has seen cannot love God whom he has not seen.

Jesus said to him, "Have you believed because you have seen me? Blessed are those who have not seen and yet have believed."—Blessed are all who take refuge in him.

1 Pet. 1:8; 2 Cor. 5:7; 1 John 4:19; 1 John 4:16; Eph. 1:13;
Col. 1:27; 1 John 4:20; John 20:29; Ps. 2:12

EVENING

"The Lord is our righteousness."

We have all become like one who is unclean, and all our righteous deeds are like a polluted garment.

With the mighty deeds of the Lord God I will come; I will remind them of your righteousness, yours alone.—I will greatly rejoice in the Lord; my soul shall exult in my God, for he has clothed me with the garments of salvation; he has covered me with the robe of righteousness, as a bridegroom decks himself like a priest with a beautiful headdress, and as a bride adorns herself with her jewels.

"Bring quickly the best robe, and put it on him."—"It was granted her to clothe herself with fine linen, bright and pure"—for the fine linen is the righteous deeds of the saints.

Indeed, I count everything as loss because of the surpassing worth of knowing Christ Jesus my Lord . . . in order that I may gain Christ and be found in him, not having a righteousness of my own that comes from the law, but that which comes through faith in Christ, the righteousness from God that depends on faith.

Jer. 23:6; Isa. 64:6; Ps. 71:16; Isa. 61:10; Luke 15:22; Rev. 19:8; Phil. 3:8–9

MORNING

"Oh . . . that you would keep me from harm."

"Why are you sleeping? Rise and pray that you may not enter into temptation."—"The spirit indeed is willing, but the flesh is weak."

Two things I ask of you; deny them not to me before I die: Remove far from me falsehood and lying; give me neither poverty nor riches; feed me with the food that is needful for me, lest I be full and deny you and say, "Who is the Lord?" or lest I be poor and steal and profane the name of my God.

The Lord will keep you from all evil; he will keep your life.—"I will deliver you out of the hand of the wicked, and redeem you from the grasp of the ruthless."—We know that everyone who has been born of God does not keep on sinning, but he who was born of God protects him, and the evil one does not touch him.—"Because you have kept my word about patient endurance, I will keep you from the hour of trial that is coming on the whole world, to try those who dwell on the earth."—The Lord knows how to rescue the godly from trials.

1 Chron. 4:10; Luke 22:46; Matt. 26:41; Prov. 30:7-9; Ps. 121:7; Jer. 15:21; 1 John 5:18; Rev. 3:10; 2 Pet. 2:9

EVENING

Star differs from star in glory.

On the way they had argued with one another about who was the greatest. And he sat down and called the twelve. And he said to them, "If anyone would be first, he must be last of all and servant of all."—Clothe yourselves, all of you, with humility toward one another, for "God opposes the proud but gives grace to the humble." Humble yourselves, therefore, under the mighty hand of God so that at the proper time he may exalt you.

Have this mind among yourselves, which is yours in Christ Jesus, who . . . emptied himself, by taking the form of a servant, being born in the likeness of men. Therefore God has highly exalted him and bestowed on him the name that is above every name, so that at the name of Jesus every knee should bow.

And those who are wise shall shine like the brightness of the sky above; and those who turn many to righteousness, like the stars forever and ever.

1 Cor. 15:41; Mark 9:34-35; 1 Pet. 5:5-6; Phil. 2:5-7, 9, 10; Dan. 12:3

MORNING

"Be strong . . . work, for I am with you, declares the Lord of hosts."

"I am the vine; you are the branches. Whoever abides in me and I in him, he it is that bears much fruit, for apart from me you can do nothing."—I can do all things through him who strengthens me.—Finally, be strong in the Lord and in the strength of his might.—"The joy of the Lord is your strength."

Thus says the Lord of hosts: "Let your hands be strong, you who in these days have been hearing these words from the mouth of the prophets."—Strengthen the weak hands, and make firm the feeble knees. Say to those who have an anxious heart, "Be strong; fear not!"—And the Lord turned to him and said, "Go in this might of yours."

If God is for us, who can be against us?—Therefore, having this ministry by the mercy of God, we do not lose heart.

And let us not grow weary of doing good, for in due season we will reap, if we do not give up.—But thanks be to God, who gives us the victory through our Lord Jesus Christ.

Hag. 2:4; John 15:5; Phil. 4:13; Eph. 6:10; Neh. 8:10; Zech. 8:9;
Isa. 35:3–4; Judg. 6:14; Rom. 8:31; 2 Cor. 4:1; Gal. 6:9; 1 Cor. 15:57

EVENING

Even the darkness is not dark to you.

"For his eyes are on the ways of a man, and he sees all his steps. There is no gloom or deep darkness where evildoers may hide themselves."—"Can a man hide himself in secret places so that I cannot see him? . . . Do I not fill heaven and earth? declares the Lord."

You will not fear the terror of the night . . . nor the pestilence that stalks in darkness. . . . [b]ecause you have made the Lord your dwelling place—the Most High, who is my refuge—no evil shall be allowed to befall you, no plague come near your tent.

He who keeps you will not slumber. The Lord is your keeper; the Lord is your shade on your right hand. The sun shall not strike you by day, nor the moon by night. The Lord will keep you from all evil.

Even though I walk through the valley of the shadow of death, I will fear no evil, for you are with me.

Ps. 139:12; Job 34:21–22; Jer. 23:24; Ps. 91:5–6, 9–10; Ps. 121:3, 5–7; Ps. 23:4

MORNING

"The Lord has said to you,
'You shall never return that way again.'"

If they had been thinking of that land from which they had gone out, they would have had opportunity to return. But as it is, they desire a better country, that is, a heavenly one . . . choosing rather to be mistreated with the people of God than to enjoy the fleeting pleasures of sin. He considered the reproach of Christ greater wealth than the treasures of Egypt.—"But my righteous one shall live by faith, and if he shrinks back, my soul has no pleasure in him." But we are not of those who shrink back and are destroyed, but of those who have faith and preserve their souls.—"No one who puts his hand to the plow and looks back is fit for the kingdom of God."

But far be it from me to boast except in the cross of our Lord Jesus Christ, by which the world has been crucified to me, and I to the world.—"Therefore go out from their midst, and be separate from them, says the Lord, and touch no unclean thing; then I will welcome you."

He who began a good work in you will bring it to completion at the day of Jesus Christ.

Deut. 17:16; Heb. 11:15–16, 25–26; Heb. 10:38–39;
Luke 9:62; Gal. 6:14; 2 Cor. 6:17; Phil. 1:6

EVENING

They recount the pain of those you have wounded.

"While I was angry but a little, they furthered the disaster."

Brothers, if anyone is caught in any transgression, you who are spiritual should restore him in a spirit of gentleness. Keep watch on yourself, lest you too be tempted.

Let him know that whoever brings back a sinner from his wandering will save his soul from death and will cover a multitude of sins.—Encourage the fainthearted, help the weak, be patient with them all.

Therefore let us not pass judgment on one another any longer, but rather decide never to put a stumbling block or hindrance in the way of a brother.—We who are strong have an obligation to bear with the failings of the weak, and not to please ourselves.

Love . . . does not rejoice at wrongdoing.—Therefore let anyone who thinks that he stands take heed lest he fall.

Ps. 69:26; Zech. 1:15; Gal. 6:1; James 5:20; 1 Thess. 5:14;
Rom. 14:13; Rom. 15:1; 1 Cor. 13:4, 6; 1 Cor. 10:12

MORNING

"I came that they may have life and have it abundantly."

"In the day that you eat of it you shall surely die."—She took of its fruit and ate, and she also gave some to her husband who was with her, and he ate.

For the wages of sin is death, but the free gift of God is eternal life in Christ Jesus our Lord.—For if, because of one man's trespass, death reigned through that one man, much more will those who receive the abundance of grace and the free gift of righteousness reign in life through the one man Jesus Christ.—For as by a man came death, by a man has come also the resurrection of the dead. For as in Adam all die, so also in Christ shall all be made alive.—Our Savior Christ Jesus . . . abolished death and brought life and immortality to light through the gospel.

God gave us eternal life, and this life is in his Son. Whoever has the Son has life; whoever does not have the Son of God does not have life.—"For God did not send his Son into the world to condemn the world, but in order that the world might be saved through him."

John 10:10; Gen. 2:17; Gen. 3:6; Rom. 6:23; Rom. 5:17;
1 Cor. 15:21–22; 2 Tim. 1:10; 1 John 5:11–12; John 3:17

EVENING

The judgment seat.

We know that the judgment of God rightly falls on those who practice such things.—"When the Son of Man comes in his glory, and all the angels with him, then he will sit on his glorious throne. Before him will be gathered all the nations, and he will separate people one from another as a shepherd separates the sheep from the goats."

"Then the righteous will shine like the sun in the kingdom of their Father."—Who shall bring any charge against God's elect? It is God who justifies. Who is to condemn? Christ Jesus is the one who died—more than that, who was raised—who is at the right hand of God, who indeed is interceding for us.—There is therefore now no condemnation for those who are in Christ Jesus.

But when we are judged by the Lord, we are disciplined so that we may not be condemned along with the world.

2 Cor. 5:10; Rom. 2:2; Matt. 25:31–32; Matt. 13:43;
Rom. 8:33–34; Rom. 8:1; 1 Cor. 11:32

MORNING

The grace of our Lord overflowed for me with the faith and love that are in Christ Jesus.

For you know the grace of our Lord Jesus Christ, that though he was rich, yet for your sake he became poor, so that you by his poverty might become rich.—But where sin increased, grace abounded all the more.

So that in the coming ages he might show the immeasurable riches of his grace in kindness toward us in Christ Jesus. For by grace you have been saved through faith. And this is not your own doing; it is the gift of God, not a result of works, so that no one may boast.—Yet we know that a person is not justified by works of the law but through faith in Jesus Christ, so we also have believed in Christ Jesus, in order to be justified by faith in Christ and not by works of the law, because by works of the law no one will be justified.—He saved us, not because of works done by us in righteousness, but according to his own mercy, by the washing of regeneration and renewal of the Holy Spirit, whom he poured out on us richly through Jesus Christ our Savior.

1 Tim. 1:14; 2 Cor. 8:9; Rom. 5:20; Eph. 2:7–9; Gal. 2:16; Titus 3:5–6

EVENING

"I am . . . the bright morning star."

"A star shall come out of Jacob."

The night is far gone; the day is at hand. So then let us cast off the works of darkness and put on the armor of light.—Until the day breathes and the shadows flee, turn, my beloved, be like a gazelle or a young stag on cleft mountains.

"Watchman, what time of the night?" The watchman says: "Morning comes, and also the night. If you will inquire, inquire; come back again."

"I am the light of the world."—"And I will give him the morning star."

"Be on guard, keep awake. For you do not know when the time will come. It is like a man going on a journey, when he leaves home and puts his servants in charge, each with his work, and commands the doorkeeper to stay awake. Therefore stay awake . . . lest he come suddenly and find you asleep. And what I say to you I say to all: Stay awake."

Rev. 22:16; Num. 24:17; Rom. 13:12; Song 2:17; Isa. 21:11–12;
John 8:12; Rev. 2:28; Mark 13:33–37

MORNING

"And you shall eat and be full, and you shall bless the Lord your God for the good land he has given you."

"Take care lest you forget the Lord your God."—Then one of them, when he saw that he was healed, turned back, praising God with a loud voice; and he fell on his face at Jesus' feet, giving him thanks. Now he was a Samaritan. Then Jesus answered, "Were not ten cleansed? Where are the nine? Was no one found to return and give praise to God except this foreigner?"

For everything created by God is good, and nothing is to be rejected if it is received with thanksgiving, for it is made holy by the word of God and prayer.—The one who eats, eats in honor of the Lord, since he gives thanks to God.—The blessing of the Lord makes rich, and he adds no sorrow with it.—Bless the Lord, O my soul, and all that is within me, bless his holy name! Bless the Lord, O my soul . . . who forgives all your iniquity . . . who crowns you with steadfast love and mercy.

Deut. 8:10; Deut. 8:11; Luke 17:15–18; 1 Tim. 4:4–5; Rom. 14:6; Prov. 10:22; Ps. 103:1–4

EVENING

[Jesus] had compassion on them.

Jesus Christ is the same yesterday and today and forever.—For we do not have a high priest who is unable to sympathize with our weaknesses, but one who in every respect has been tempted as we are, yet without sin.—He can deal gently with the ignorant and wayward.—And he came and found them sleeping, and he said to Peter, "Simon, are you asleep? Could you not watch one hour? Watch and pray that you may not enter into temptation. The spirit indeed is willing, but the flesh is weak."

As a father shows compassion to his children, so the Lord shows compassion to those who fear him. For he knows our frame; he remembers that we are dust.

But you, O Lord, are a God merciful and gracious, slow to anger and abounding in steadfast love and faithfulness. Turn to me and be gracious to me; give your strength to your servant, and save the son of your maidservant.

Matt. 14:14; Heb. 13:8; Heb. 4:15; Heb. 5:2; Mark 14:37–38; Ps. 103:13–14; Ps. 86:15–16

MORNING

"No longer do I call you servants, for the servant does not know what his master is doing; but I have called you friends."

The Lord said, "Shall I hide from Abraham what I am about to do?"—"To you it has been given to know the secrets of the kingdom of heaven."—These things God has revealed to us through the Spirit. For the Spirit searches everything, even the depths of God.—Hidden wisdom of God, which God decreed before the ages for our glory.

Blessed is the one you choose and bring near, to dwell in your courts! We shall be satisfied with the goodness of your house, the holiness of your temple!—The friendship of the Lord is for those who fear him, and he makes known to them his covenant.—"For I have given them the words that you gave me, and they have received them and have come to know in truth that I came from you; and they have believed that you sent me."

"You are my friends if you do what I command you."

John 15:15; Gen. 18:17; Matt. 13:11; 1 Cor. 2:10; 1 Cor. 2:7;
Ps. 65:4; Ps. 25:14; John 17:8; John 15:14

EVENING

You shall call your walls Salvation, and your gates Praise.

And the wall of the city had twelve foundations, and on them were the twelve names of the twelve apostles of the Lamb.

So then you are no longer strangers and aliens, but you are fellow citizens with the saints and members of the household of God, built on the foundation of the apostles and prophets, Christ Jesus himself being the cornerstone, in whom the whole structure, being joined together, grows into a holy temple in the Lord. In him you also are being built together into a dwelling place for God by the Spirit.—If indeed you have tasted that the Lord is good. As you come to him, a living stone rejected by men but in the sight of God chosen and precious, you yourselves like living stones are being built up as a spiritual house, to be a holy priesthood, to offer spiritual sacrifices acceptable to God through Jesus Christ.

Praise is due to you, O God, in Zion.

Isa. 60:18; Rev. 21:14; Eph. 2:19–22; 1 Pet. 2:3–5; Ps. 65:1

MORNING

"But now he is comforted here."

Your sun shall no more go down, nor your moon withdraw itself; for the Lord will be your everlasting light, and your days of mourning shall be ended.—He will swallow up death forever; and the Lord God will wipe away tears from all faces, and the reproach of his people he will take away from all the earth.—"These are the ones coming out of the great tribulation. They have washed their robes and made them white in the blood of the Lamb. Therefore they are before the throne of God, and serve him day and night in his temple; and he who sits on the throne will shelter them with his presence. They shall hunger no more, neither thirst anymore; the sun shall not strike them, nor any scorching heat. For the Lamb in the midst of the throne will be their shepherd, and he will guide them to springs of living water."—"He will wipe away every tear from their eyes, and death shall be no more, neither shall there be mourning, nor crying, nor pain anymore, for the former things have passed away."

Luke 16:25; Isa. 60:20; Isa. 25:8; Rev. 7:14–17; Rev. 21:4

EVENING

"Night is coming, when no one can work."

"Blessed are the dead who die in the Lord . . . that they may rest from their labors, for their deeds follow them!"—"There the wicked cease from troubling, and there the weary are at rest."— Then Samuel said to Saul, "Why have you disturbed me by bringing me up?"

"Whatever your hand finds to do, do it with your might, for there is no work or thought or knowledge or wisdom in Sheol, to which you are going."—The dead do not praise the Lord, nor do any who go down into silence.

For I am already being poured out as a drink offering, and the time of my departure has come. I have fought the good fight, I have finished the race, I have kept the faith. Henceforth there is laid up for me the crown of righteousness, which the Lord, the righteous judge, will award to me on that Day.

So then, there remains a Sabbath rest for the people of God, for whoever has entered God's rest has also rested from his works as God did from his.

John 9:4; Rev. 14:13; Job 3:17; 1 Sam. 28:15; Eccles. 9:10;
Ps. 115:17; 2 Tim. 4:6–8; Heb. 4:9–10

MORNING

"Your eye is the lamp of your body. When your eye is healthy, your whole body is full of light."

The natural person does not accept the things of the Spirit of God, for they are folly to him, and he is not able to understand them because they are spiritually discerned.—Open my eyes, that I may behold wondrous things out of your law.

"I am the light of the world. Whoever follows me will not walk in darkness, but will have the light of life."—And we all, with unveiled face, beholding the glory of the Lord, are being transformed into the same image. . . . For this comes from the Lord who is the Spirit.—For God, who said, "Let light shine out of darkness," has shone in our hearts to give the light of the knowledge of the glory of God in the face of Jesus Christ.

The God of our Lord Jesus Christ, the Father of glory . . . give you the Spirit of wisdom and of revelation in the knowledge of him . . . that you may know what is the hope to which he has called you, what are the riches of his glorious inheritance in the saints.

Luke 11:34; 1 Cor. 2:14; Ps. 119:18; John 8:12; 2 Cor. 3:18; 2 Cor. 4:6; Eph. 1:17–18

EVENING

"He struck the rock so that water gushed out and streams overflowed."

Our fathers were all under the cloud, and all passed through the sea, and all were baptized into Moses in the cloud and in the sea, and all ate the same spiritual food, and all drank the same spiritual drink. For they drank from the spiritual Rock that followed them, and the Rock was Christ.—But one of the soldiers pierced his side with a spear, and at once there came out blood and water.—But he was pierced for our transgressions; he was crushed for our iniquities; upon him was the chastisement that brought us peace, and with his wounds we are healed.

"Yet you refuse to come to me that you may have life."—"For my people have committed two evils: they have forsaken me, the fountain of living waters, and hewed out cisterns for themselves, broken cisterns that can hold no water."—"If anyone thirsts, let him come to me and drink."—Let the one who desires take the water of life without price.

Ps. 78:20; 1 Cor. 10:1–4; John 19:34; Isa. 53:5;
John 5:40; Jer. 2:13; John 7:37; Rev. 22:17

MORNING

Then those who feared the Lord spoke with one another. The Lord paid attention and heard them, and a book of remembrance was written before him of those who feared the Lord and esteemed his name.

While they were talking and discussing together, Jesus himself drew near and went with them.—"For where two or three are gathered in my name, there am I among them."—My fellow workers, whose names are in the book of life.

Let the word of Christ dwell in you richly, teaching and admonishing one another in all wisdom, singing psalms and hymns and spiritual songs, with thankfulness in your hearts to God.—But exhort one another every day, as long as it is called "today," that none of you may be hardened by the deceitfulness of sin.

"I tell you, on the day of judgment people will give account for every careless word they speak, for by your words you will be justified, and by your words you will be condemned."—Behold, it is written before me.

Mal. 3:16; Luke 24:15; Matt. 18:20; Phil. 4:3; Col. 3:16;
Heb. 3:13; Matt. 12:36–37; Isa. 65:6

EVENING

The trees of the Lord are watered abundantly.

I will be like the dew to Israel; he shall blossom like the lily; he shall take root like the trees of Lebanon.—"Blessed is the man who trusts in the Lord, whose trust is the Lord. He is like a tree planted by water, that sends out its roots by the stream, and does not fear when heat comes, for its leaves remain green, and is not anxious in the year of drought, for it does not cease to bear fruit."

"I bring low the high tree, and make high the low tree, dry up the green tree, and make the dry tree flourish."

The righteous flourish like the palm tree and grow like a cedar in Lebanon. They are planted in the house of the Lord; they flourish in the courts of our God. They still bear fruit in old age; they are ever full of sap and green.

Ps. 104:16; Hos. 14:5–6; Jer. 17:7–8; Ezek. 17:24; Ps. 92:12–14

MORNING

"They shall be mine, says the Lord of hosts, in the day when I make up my treasured possession."

"I have manifested your name to the people whom you gave me out of the world. Yours they were, and you gave them to me, and they have kept your word. . . . I am praying for them. I am not praying for the world but for those whom you have given me, for they are yours. All mine are yours, and yours are mine, and I am glorified in them. . . . Father, I desire that they also, whom you have given me, may be with me where I am, to see my glory that you have given me because you loved me before the foundation of the world."

"I will come again and will take you to myself."—When he comes on that day to be glorified in his saints, and to be marveled at among all who have believed.—Then we who are alive, who are left, will be caught up together with them in the clouds to meet the Lord in the air, and so we will always be with the Lord.—You shall be a crown of beauty in the hand of the Lord, and a royal diadem in the hand of your God.

Mal. 3:17; John 17:6, 9–10, 24; John 14:3; 2 Thess. 1:10; 1 Thess. 4:17; Isa. 62:3

EVENING

"Please show me your glory."

For God, who said, "Let light shine out of darkness," has shone in our hearts to give the light of the knowledge of the glory of God in the face of Jesus Christ.—And the Word became flesh and dwelt among us, and we have seen his glory, glory as of the only Son from the Father, full of grace and truth. . . . No one has ever seen God; the only God, who is at the Father's side, he has made him known.

My soul thirsts for God, for the living God. When shall I come and appear before God?—You have said, "Seek my face." My heart says to you, "Your face, Lord, do I seek."

And we all, with unveiled face, beholding the glory of the Lord, are being transformed into the same image from one degree of glory to another. For this comes from the Lord who is the Spirit.—"Father, I desire that they also, whom you have given me, may be with me where I am, to see my glory that you have given me because you loved me before the foundation of the world."

Ex. 33:18; 2 Cor. 4:6; John 1:14, 18; Ps. 42:2; Ps. 27:8; 2 Cor. 3:18; John 17:24

MORNING

Seated above the likeness of a throne was a likeness with a human appearance.

The man Christ Jesus.—Being born in the likeness of men. And being found in human form.—Since therefore the children share in flesh and blood, he himself likewise partook of the same things, that through death he might destroy the one who has the power of death.

"[I am] the living one. I died, and behold I am alive forevermore."—We know that Christ, being raised from the dead, will never die again; death no longer has dominion over him. For the death he died he died to sin, once for all, but the life he lives he lives to God.—"Then what if you were to see the Son of Man ascending to where he was before?"—He raised him from the dead and seated him at his right hand in the heavenly places.—For in him the whole fullness of deity dwells bodily.—For he was crucified in weakness, but lives by the power of God. For we also are weak in him, but in dealing with you we will live with him by the power of God.

Ezek. 1:26; 1 Tim. 2:5; Phil. 2:7–8; Heb. 2:14; Rev. 1:18;
Rom. 6:9–10; John 6:62; Eph. 1:20; Col. 2:9; 2 Cor. 13:4

EVENING

Your promise gives me life.

Thus it is written, "The first man Adam became a living being"; the last Adam became a life-giving spirit.

"For as the Father has life in himself, so he has granted the Son also to have life in himself."—"I am the resurrection and the life. Whoever believes in me, though he die, yet shall he live, and everyone who lives and believes in me shall never die."

In him was life, and the life was the light of men. . . . But to all who did receive him, who believed in his name, he gave the right to become children of God, who were born, not of blood nor of the will of the flesh nor of the will of man, but of God.

"It is the Spirit who gives life; the flesh is no help at all. The words that I have spoken to you are spirit and life."—For the word of God is living and active, sharper than any two-edged sword, piercing to the division of soul and of spirit, of joints and of marrow, and discerning the thoughts and intentions of the heart.

Ps. 119:50; 1 Cor. 15:45; John 5:26; John 11:25–26;
John 1:4, 12–13; John 6:63; Heb. 4:12

MORNING

"Let it be so now, for thus it is fitting for us to fulfill all righteousness."

"I delight to do your will, O my God; your law is within my heart."

"Do not think that I have come to abolish the Law or the Prophets; I have not come to abolish them but to fulfill them. For truly, I say to you, until heaven and earth pass away, not an iota, not a dot, will pass from the Law until all is accomplished."—The Lord was pleased, for his righteousness' sake, to magnify his law and make it glorious.—"For I tell you, unless your righteousness exceeds that of the scribes and Pharisees, you will never enter the kingdom of heaven."

For God has done what the law, weakened by the flesh, could not do. By sending his own Son in the likeness of sinful flesh and for sin, he condemned sin in the flesh, in order that the righteous requirement of the law might be fulfilled in us, who walk not according to the flesh but according to the Spirit.—For Christ is the end of the law for righteousness to everyone who believes.

Matt. 3:15; Ps. 40:8; Matt. 5:17–18; Isa. 42:21; Matt. 5:20;
Rom. 8:3–4; Rom. 10:4

EVENING

"I am your portion and your inheritance."

Whom have I in heaven but you? And there is nothing on earth that I desire besides you. My flesh and my heart may fail, but God is the strength of my heart and my portion forever.—The Lord is my chosen portion and my cup; you hold my lot. The lines have fallen for me in pleasant places; indeed, I have a beautiful inheritance.

"The Lord is my portion," says my soul, "therefore I will hope in him."—Your testimonies are my heritage forever, for they are the joy of my heart.

O God, you are my God; earnestly I seek you; my soul thirsts for you; my flesh faints for you, as in a dry and weary land where there is no water . . . for you have been my help, and in the shadow of your wings I will sing for joy.—My beloved is mine, and I am his.

Num. 18:20; Ps. 73:25–26; Ps. 16:5–6; Lam. 3:24;
Ps. 119:111; Ps. 63:1, 7; Song 2:16

MORNING

Who can say, "I have made my heart pure"?

The Lord looks down from heaven on the children of man, to see if there are any who understand, who seek after God. They have all turned aside; together they have become corrupt; there is none who does good, not even one.—Those who are in the flesh cannot please God.

For I have the desire to do what is right, but not the ability to carry it out. For I do not do the good I want, but the evil I do not want is what I keep on doing.—We have all become like one who is unclean, and all our righteous deeds are like a polluted garment. We all fade like a leaf, and our iniquities, like the wind, take us away.

But the Scripture imprisoned everything under sin, so that the promise by faith in Jesus Christ might be given to those who believe.—In Christ God was reconciling the world to himself, not counting their trespasses against them.—If we say we have no sin, we deceive ourselves, and the truth is not in us. If we confess our sins, he is faithful and just to forgive us our sins and to cleanse us from all unrighteousness.

Prov. 20:9; Ps. 14:2–3; Rom. 8:8; Rom. 7:18–19;
Isa. 64:6; Gal. 3:22; 2 Cor. 5:19; 1 John 1:8–9

EVENING

The floods lift up their roaring.

Mightier than the thunders of many waters, mightier than the waves of the sea, the Lord on high is mighty!—O Lord God of hosts, who is mighty as you are, O Lord, with your faithfulness all around you? You rule the raging of the sea; when its waves rise, you still them.

"Do you not fear me? declares the Lord. Do you not tremble before me? I placed the sand as the boundary for the sea, a perpetual barrier that it cannot pass."—"When you pass through the waters, I will be with you; and through the rivers, they shall not overwhelm you; when you walk through fire you shall not be burned, and the flame shall not consume you."

He said, "Come." So Peter got out of the boat and walked on the water and came to Jesus. But when he saw the wind, he was afraid, and beginning to sink he cried out, "Lord, save me." Jesus immediately reached out his hand and took hold of him, saying to him, "O you of little faith, why did you doubt?"—When I am afraid, I put my trust in you.

Ps. 93:3; Ps. 93:4; Ps. 89:8–9; Jer. 5:22; Isa. 43:2; Matt. 14:29–31; Ps. 56:3

MORNING

Your name is oil poured out.

Christ loved us and gave himself up for us, a fragrant offering and sacrifice to God.—So the honor is for you who believe.—Therefore God has highly exalted him and bestowed on him the name that is above every name, so that at the name of Jesus every knee should bow.—For in him the whole fullness of deity dwells bodily.

"If you love me, you will keep my commandments."—God's love has been poured into our hearts through the Holy Spirit who has been given to us.—The house was filled with the fragrance of the perfume.—And they recognized that they had been with Jesus.

O Lord, our Lord, how majestic is your name in all the earth! You have set your glory above the heavens.—"Immanuel" (which means, God with us).—His name shall be called Wonderful Counselor, Mighty God, Everlasting Father, Prince of Peace.—The name of the Lord is a strong tower; the righteous man runs into it and is safe.

Song 1:3; Eph. 5:2; 1 Pet. 2:7; Phil. 2:9–10; Col. 2:9; John 14:15; Rom. 5:5;
John 12:3; Acts 4:13; Ps. 8:1; Matt. 1:23; Isa. 9:6; Prov. 18:10

EVENING

For while we are still in this tent, we groan, being burdened.

O Lord, all my longing is before you; my sighing is not hidden from you. . . . For my iniquities have gone over my head; like a heavy burden, they are too heavy for me.—Wretched man that I am! Who will deliver me from this body of death?

The whole creation has been groaning together in the pains of childbirth until now. And not only the creation, but we ourselves, who have the firstfruits of the Spirit, groan inwardly as we wait eagerly for adoption as sons, the redemption of our bodies.—Now for a little while, if necessary, you have been grieved by various trials.

The putting off of my body will be soon, as our Lord Jesus Christ made clear to me.—For this perishable body must put on the imperishable, and this mortal body must put on immortality. When the perishable puts on the imperishable, and the mortal puts on immortality, then shall come to pass the saying that is written: "Death is swallowed up in victory."

2 Cor. 5:4; Ps. 38:9, 4; Rom. 7:24; Rom. 8:22–23;
1 Pet. 1:6; 2 Pet. 1:14; 1 Cor. 15:53–54

MORNING

"All the rest of the bull—he shall carry outside the camp to a clean place, to the ash heap, and shall burn it up on a fire of wood."

So they took Jesus, and he went out, bearing his own cross, to the place called The Place of a Skull, which in Aramaic is called Golgotha. There they crucified him.—For the bodies of those animals whose blood is brought into the holy places by the high priest as a sacrifice for sin are burned outside the camp. So Jesus also suffered outside the gate in order to sanctify the people through his own blood. Therefore let us go to him outside the camp and bear the reproach he endured.—Share his sufferings.

But rejoice insofar as you share Christ's sufferings, that you may also rejoice and be glad when his glory is revealed.—For this light momentary affliction is preparing for us an eternal weight of glory beyond all comparison.

Lev. 4:12; John 19:16–18; Heb. 13:11–13; Phil. 3:10;
1 Pet. 4:13; 2 Cor. 4:17

EVENING

So God created man in his own image.

"Being then God's offspring, we ought not to think that the divine being is like gold or silver or stone, an image formed by the art and imagination of man."

But God, being rich in mercy, because of the great love with which he loved us, even when we were dead in our trespasses, made us alive together with Christ. . . . For we are his workmanship, created in Christ Jesus for good works, which God prepared beforehand, that we should walk in them.—For those whom he foreknew he also predestined to be conformed to the image of his Son, in order that he might be the firstborn among many brothers.

But we know that when he appears we shall be like him, because we shall see him as he is.—When I awake, I shall be satisfied with your likeness.

"The one who conquers will have this heritage, and I will be his God and he will be my son."—And if children, then heirs—heirs of God and fellow heirs with Christ

Gen. 1:27; Acts 17:29; Eph. 2:4–5, 10; Rom. 8:29;
1 John 3:2; Ps. 17:15; Rev. 21:7; Rom. 8:17

MORNING

You are my refuge in the day of disaster.

There are many who say, "Who will show us some good? Lift up the light of your face upon us, O Lord!"—But I will sing of your strength; I will sing aloud of your steadfast love in the morning. For you have been to me a fortress and a refuge in the day of my distress.

As for me, I said in my prosperity, "I shall never be moved." You hid your face; I was dismayed. To you, O Lord, I cry, and to the Lord I plead for mercy: "What profit is there in my death, if I go down to the pit? Will the dust praise you? Will it tell of your faithfulness? Hear, O Lord, and be merciful to me! O Lord, be my helper!"

"For a brief moment I deserted you, but with great compassion I will gather you. In overflowing anger for a moment I hid my face from you, but with everlasting love I will have compassion on you," says the Lord, your Redeemer.—"Your sorrow will turn into joy."—Weeping may tarry for the night, but joy comes with the morning.

Jer. 17:17; Ps. 4:6; Ps. 59:16; Ps. 30:6–10; Isa. 54:7–8;
John 16:20; Ps. 30:5

EVENING

Adam . . . fathered a son in his own likeness.

"Who can bring a clean thing out of an unclean?"—Behold, I was brought forth in iniquity, and in sin did my mother conceive me.

And you were dead in the trespasses and sins . . . and were by nature children of wrath, like the rest of mankind.—I am of the flesh, sold under sin. . . . For I do not do what I want, but I do the very thing I hate. . . . For I know that nothing good dwells in me, that is, in my flesh.

Sin came into the world through one man . . . by the one man's disobedience the many were made sinners.—If many died through one man's trespass, much more have the grace of God and the free gift by the grace of that one man Jesus Christ abounded for many.

For the law of the Spirit of life has set you free in Christ Jesus from the law of sin and death.

But thanks be to God, who gives us the victory through our Lord Jesus Christ.

Gen. 5:3; Job 14:4; Ps. 51:5; Eph. 2:1, 3; Rom. 7:14–15, 18;
Rom. 5:12, 19; Rom. 5:15; Rom. 8:2; 1 Cor. 15:57

MORNING

For the Lord gives wisdom; from his mouth come knowledge and understanding.

Trust in the Lord with all your heart, and do not lean on your own under-standing.—If any of you lacks wisdom, let him ask God, who gives generously to all without reproach, and it will be given him.—For the foolishness of God is wiser than men, and the weakness of God is stronger than men.—But God chose what is foolish in the world to shame the wise . . . so that no human being might boast in the presence of God.

The unfolding of your words gives light; it imparts understanding to the simple.—I have stored up your word in my heart, that I might not sin against you.

And all spoke well of him and marveled at the gracious words that were coming from his mouth.—"No one ever spoke like this man!"—And because of him you are in Christ Jesus, who became to us wisdom from God, righteousness and sanctification and redemption.

Prov. 2:6; Prov. 3:5; James 1:5; 1 Cor. 1:25; 1 Cor. 1:27, 29;
Ps. 119:130; Ps. 119:11; Luke 4:22; John 7:46; 1 Cor. 1:30

EVENING

"My year of redemption had come."

"And you shall consecrate the fiftieth year, and proclaim liberty throughout the land to all its inhabitants. It shall be a jubilee for you, when each of you shall return to his property and each of you shall return to his clan."

Your dead shall live; their bodies shall rise. You who dwell in the dust, awake and sing for joy! For your dew is a dew of light, and the earth will give birth to the dead.

For the Lord himself will descend from heaven with a cry of command, with the voice of an archangel, and with the sound of the trumpet of God. And the dead in Christ will rise first. Then we who are alive, who are left, will be caught up together with them in the clouds to meet the Lord in the air, and so we will always be with the Lord.

Shall I ransom them from the power of Sheol? Shall I redeem them from Death? O Death, where are your plagues? O Sheol, where is your sting?—"Their Redeemer is strong; the Lord of hosts is his name."

Isa. 63:4; Lev. 25:10; Isa. 26:19; 1 Thess. 4:16–17; Hos. 13:14; Jer. 50:34

MORNING

Out of the anguish of his soul he shall see and be satisfied.

Jesus . . . said, "It is finished," and he bowed his head and gave up his spirit.—For our sake he made him to be sin who knew no sin, so that in him we might become the righteousness of God.

"The people whom I formed for myself that they might declare my praise."—So that through the church the manifold wisdom of God might now be made known to the rulers and authorities in the heavenly places. This was according to the eternal purpose that he has realized in Christ Jesus our Lord.—So that in the coming ages he might show the immeasurable riches of his grace in kindness toward us in Christ Jesus.

In him you also, when you heard the word of truth, the gospel of your salvation, and believed in him, were sealed with the promised Holy Spirit, who is the guarantee of our inheritance until we acquire possession of it, to the praise of his glory.—But you are a chosen race, a royal priesthood, a holy nation, a people for his own possession, that you may proclaim the excellencies of him who called you out of darkness into his marvelous light.

Isa. 53:11; John 19:30; 2 Cor. 5:21; Isa. 43:21;
Eph. 3:10–11; Eph. 2:7; Eph. 1:13–14; 1 Pet. 2:9

EVENING

"The day of testing in the wilderness."

Let no one say when he is tempted, "I am being tempted by God," for God cannot be tempted with evil, and he himself tempts no one. But each person is tempted when he is lured and enticed by his own desire. Then desire when it has conceived gives birth to sin.

But they had a wanton craving in the wilderness, and put God to the test in the desert.—And Jesus, full of the Holy Spirit . . . was led by the Spirit in the wilderness for forty days, being tempted by the devil. And he ate nothing during those days. And when they were ended, he was hungry. The devil said to him, "If you are the Son of God, command this stone to become bread."

For because he himself has suffered when tempted, he is able to help those who are being tempted.—"Simon, Simon, . . . Satan demanded to have you, that he might sift you like wheat, but I have prayed for you that your faith may not fail."

Heb. 3:8; James 1:13–15; Ps. 106:14; Luke 4:1–3; Heb. 2:18; Luke 22:31–32

MORNING

"I am the Lord who sanctifies you."

"I am the Lord your God, who has separated you from the peoples. . . . You shall be holy to me, for I the Lord am holy and have separated you from the peoples, that you should be mine."

Beloved in God the Father.—"Sanctify them in the truth; your word is truth."— Now may the God of peace himself sanctify you completely, and may your whole spirit and soul and body be kept blameless at the coming of our Lord Jesus Christ.

So Jesus also suffered outside the gate in order to sanctify the people through his own blood.—Our . . . Savior Jesus Christ . . . gave himself for us to redeem us from all lawlessness and to purify for himself a people for his own possession who are zealous for good works.—For he who sanctifies and those who are sanctified all have one source. That is why he is not ashamed to call them brothers.—"And for their sake I consecrate myself, that they also may be sanctified in truth."—In the sanctification of the Spirit, for obedience to Jesus Christ and for sprinkling with his blood.

Lev. 20:8; Lev. 20:24, 26; Jude 1; John 17:17; 1 Thess. 5:23;
Heb. 13:12; Titus 2:13–14; Heb. 2:11; John 17:19; 1 Pet. 1:2

EVENING

Light is sown for the righteous, and joy for the upright in heart.

Those who sow in tears shall reap with shouts of joy! He who goes out weeping, bearing the seed for sowing, shall come home with shouts of joy, bringing his sheaves with him.

And what you sow is not the body that is to be.

Blessed be the God and Father of our Lord Jesus Christ! According to his great mercy, he has caused us to be born again to a living hope through the resurrection of Jesus Christ from the dead. . . . In this you rejoice, though now for a little while, if necessary, you have been grieved by various trials, so that the tested genuineness of your faith—more precious than gold that perishes though it is tested by fire—may be found to result in praise and glory and honor at the revelation of Jesus Christ.

Ps. 97:11; Ps. 126:5–6; 1 Cor. 15:37; 1 Pet. 1:3, 6–7

MORNING

Who is the man who fears the Lord? Him will he
instruct in the way that he should choose.

"The eye is the lamp of the body. So, if your eye is healthy, your whole body will be full of light."

Your word is a lamp to my feet and a light to my path.—And your ears shall hear a word behind you, saying, "This is the way, walk in it," when you turn to the right or when you turn to the left.—I will instruct you and teach you in the way you should go; I will counsel you with my eye upon you. Be not like a horse or a mule, without understanding, which must be curbed with bit and bridle, or it will not stay near you. Many are the sorrows of the wicked, but steadfast love surrounds the one who trusts in the Lord. Be glad in the Lord, and rejoice, O righteous, and shout for joy, all you upright in heart!

I know, O Lord, that the way of man is not in himself, that it is not in man who walks to direct his steps.

Ps. 25:12; Matt. 6:22; Ps. 119:105; Is. 30:21; Ps. 32:8–11; Jer. 10:23

EVENING

If you lie down, you will not be afraid;
when you lie down, your sleep will be sweet.

And a great windstorm arose, and the waves were breaking into the boat, so that the boat was already filling. But he was in the stern, asleep on the cushion.

Do not be anxious about anything, but in everything by prayer and supplication with thanksgiving let your requests be made known to God. And the peace of God, which surpasses all understanding, will guard your hearts and your minds in Christ Jesus.

In peace I will both lie down and sleep; for you alone, O Lord, make me dwell in safety.—He gives to his beloved sleep.

And as they were stoning Stephen, he called out, "Lord Jesus, receive my spirit." And falling to his knees he cried out with a loud voice, "Lord, do not hold this sin against them." And when he had said this, he fell asleep.—Away from the body and at home with the Lord.

Prov. 3:24; Mark 4:37–38; Phil. 4:6–7; Ps. 4:8;
Ps. 127:2; Acts 7:59–60; 2 Cor. 5:8

MORNING

The sprinkled blood that speaks a
better word than the blood of Abel.

"Behold, the Lamb of God, who takes away the sin of the world!"—The Lamb who was slain.— For it is impossible for the blood of bulls and goats to take away sins. Consequently, when Christ came into the world, he said, "Sacrifices and offerings you have not desired, but a body have you prepared for me. . . . And by that will we have been sanctified through the offering of the body of Jesus Christ once for all.

And Abel . . . brought of the firstborn of his flock and of their fat portions. And the Lord had regard for Abel and his offering.—Christ loved us and gave himself up for us, a fragrant offering and sacrifice to God.

Let us draw near with a true heart in full assurance of faith, with our hearts sprinkled clean from an evil conscience and our bodies washed with pure water.—Therefore, brothers . . . we have confidence to enter the holy places by the blood of Jesus.

Heb. 12:24; John 1:29; Rev. 13:8; Heb. 10:4–5, 10;
Gen. 4:4; Eph. 5:2; Heb. 10:22; Heb. 10:19

EVENING

Who considers the power of your anger?

Now from the sixth hour there was darkness over all the land until the ninth hour. And about the ninth hour Jesus cried out with a loud voice, saying, "Eli, Eli, lema sabachthani?" that is, "My God, my God, why have you forsaken me?"—The Lord has laid on him the iniquity of us all.

There is therefore now no condemnation for those who are in Christ Jesus.—Therefore, since we have been justified by faith, we have peace with God through our Lord Jesus Christ.—Christ redeemed us from the curse of the law by becoming a curse for us.

God sent his only Son into the world, so that we might live through him. In this is love, not that we have loved God but that he loved us and sent his Son to be the propitiation for our sins.—So that he might be just and the justifier of the one who has faith in Jesus.

Ps. 90:11; Matt. 27:45–46; Isa. 53:6; Rom. 8:1; Rom. 5:1;
Gal. 3:13; 1 John 4:9–10; Rom. 3:26

MORNING

"Thus says the Lord God: This also I will let the house of Israel ask me to do for them."

You do not have, because you do not ask.—"Ask, and it will be given to you; seek, and you will find; knock, and it will be opened to you. For everyone who asks receives, and the one who seeks finds, and to the one who knocks it will be opened."—And this is the confidence that we have toward him, that if we ask anything according to his will he hears us. And if we know that he hears us in whatever we ask, we know that we have the requests that we have asked of him.—If any of you lacks wisdom, let him ask God, who gives generously to all without reproach, and it will be given him.—Open your mouth wide, and I will fill it.—And he told them a parable to the effect that they ought always to pray and not lose heart.—The eyes of the Lord are toward the righteous and his ears toward their cry. . . . The Lord hears and delivers them out of all their troubles.—"In that day you will ask in my name, and I do not say to you that I will ask the Father on your behalf; for the Father himself loves you, because you have loved me. . . . Ask, and you will receive, that your joy may be full."

Ezek. 36:37; James 4:2; Matt. 7:7–8; 1 John 5:14–15; James 1:5;
Ps. 81:10; Luke 18:1; Ps. 34:15, 17; John 16:26–27, 24

EVENING

"Shall we receive good from God, and shall we not receive evil?"

I know, O Lord, that your rules are righteous, and that in faithfulness you have afflicted me.—But now, O Lord, you are our Father; we are the clay, and you are our potter; we are all the work of your hand.—"It is the Lord. Let him do what seems good to him."

Righteous are you, O Lord, when I complain to you; yet I would plead my case before you.—He will sit as a refiner and purifier of silver.—"For the Lord disciplines the one he loves, and chastises every son whom he receives."—"It is enough for the disciple to be like his teacher, and the servant like his master."—Although he was a son, he learned obedience through what he suffered.—But rejoice insofar as you share Christ's sufferings, that you may also rejoice and be glad when his glory is revealed.—"These are the ones coming out of the great tribulation. They have washed their robes and made them white in the blood of the Lamb."

Job 2:10; Ps. 119:75; Isa. 64:8; 1 Sam. 3:18; Jer. 12:1; Mal. 3:3;
Heb. 12:6; Matt. 10:25; Heb. 5:8; 1 Pet. 4:13; Rev. 7:14

MORNING

Resist the devil, and he will flee from you.

For he will come like a rushing stream, which the wind of the Lord drives.—
"Be gone, Satan! For it is written, 'You shall worship the Lord your God and
him only shall you serve.'" Then the devil left him, and behold, angels came
and were ministering to him.

Finally, be strong in the Lord and in the strength of his might. Put on the
whole armor of God, that you may be able to stand against the schemes of the
devil.—Take no part in the unfruitful works of darkness, but instead expose
them.—So that we would not be outwitted by Satan; for we are not ignorant of
his designs.—Be sober-minded; be watchful. Your adversary the devil prowls
around like a roaring lion, seeking someone to devour. Resist him, firm in
your faith, knowing that the same kinds of suffering are being experienced
by your brotherhood throughout the world.—And this is the victory that has
overcome the world—our faith.

Who shall bring any charge against God's elect? It is God who justifies.

James 4:7; Isa. 59:19; Matt. 4:10–11; Eph. 6:10–11; Eph. 5:11;
2 Cor. 2:11; 1 Pet. 5:8–9; 1 John 5:4; Rom. 8:33

EVENING

"Oh, that I knew where I might find him."

"Who among you fears the Lord and obeys the voice of his servant? Let him
who walks in darkness and has no light trust in the name of the Lord and rely
on his God."

"You will seek me and find me, when you seek me with all your heart."—
"Seek, and you will find; knock, and it will be opened to you. For everyone
who asks receives, and the one who seeks finds, and to the one who knocks it
will be opened."—Indeed our fellowship is with the Father and with his Son
Jesus Christ."—But now in Christ Jesus you who once were far off have been
brought near by the blood of Christ. . . . For through him we both have access
in one Spirit to the Father.

If we say we have fellowship with him while we walk in darkness, we
lie and do not practice the truth.—"And behold, I am with you always, to the
end of the age."—"I will never leave you nor forsake you."—"[The] Helper . . .
dwells with you and will be in you."

Job 23:3; Isa. 50:10; Jer. 29:13; Luke 11:9–10; 1 John 1:3; Eph. 2:13, 18;
1 John 1:6; Matt. 28:20; Heb. 13:5; John 14:16–17

MORNING

Let us test and examine our ways, and return to the Lord!

Prove me, O Lord, and try me; test my heart and my mind.—Behold, you delight in truth in the inward being, and you teach me wisdom in the secret heart.—When I think on my ways, I turn my feet to your testimonies; I hasten and do not delay to keep your commandments.—Let a person examine himself, then, and so eat of the bread and drink of the cup.

If we confess our sins, he is faithful and just to forgive us our sins and to cleanse us from all unrighteousness.—We have an advocate with the Father, Jesus Christ the righteous. He is the propitiation for our sins.—Therefore, brothers, since we have confidence to enter the holy places by the blood of Jesus, by the new and living way that he opened for us through the curtain, that is, through his flesh, and since we have a great priest over the house of God, let us draw near with a true heart in full assurance of faith, with our hearts sprinkled clean from an evil conscience and our bodies washed with pure water.

Lam. 3:40; Ps. 26:2; Ps. 51:6; Ps. 119:59–60; 1 Cor. 11:28;
1 John 1:9; 1 John 2:1–2; Heb. 10:19–22

EVENING

Around the throne was a rainbow that had the appearance of an emerald.

"This is the sign of the covenant that I make between me and you and every living creature that is with you, for all future generations: I have set my bow in the cloud. . . . I will see it and remember the everlasting covenant between God and every living creature of all flesh that is on the earth."—An everlasting covenant, ordered in all things and secure.—So that by two unchangeable things, in which it is impossible for God to lie, we who have fled for refuge might have strong encouragement to hold fast to the hope set before us.

"And we bring you the good news that what God promised to the fathers, this he has fulfilled to us their children by raising Jesus."

Jesus Christ is the same yesterday and today and forever.

Rev. 4:3; Gen. 9:12–13, 16; 2 Sam. 23:5; Heb. 6:18; Acts 13:32–33; Heb. 13:8

MORNING

So you also must consider yourselves dead to
sin and alive to God in Christ Jesus.

"Truly, truly, I say to you, whoever hears my word and believes him who sent me has eternal life. He does not come into judgment, but has passed from death to life."—For through the law I died to the law, so that I might live to God. I have been crucified with Christ. It is no longer I who live, but Christ who lives in me. And the life I now live in the flesh I live by faith in the Son of God, who loved me and gave himself for me.

"Because I live, you also will live."—"I give them eternal life, and they will never perish, and no one will snatch them out of my hand. My Father, who has given them to me, is greater than all, and no one is able to snatch them out of the Father's hand. I and the Father are one."

If then you have been raised with Christ, seek the things that are above, where Christ is, seated at the right hand of God. . . . For you have died, and your life is hidden with Christ in God.

Rom. 6:11; John 5:24; Gal. 2:19–20; John 14:19; John 10:28–30; Col. 3:1, 3

EVENING

God . . . gives generously to all without reproach.

"Woman, where are they? Has no one condemned you?" She said, "No one, Lord." And Jesus said, "Neither do I condemn you; go, and from now on sin no more."

The grace of God and the free gift by the grace of that one man Jesus Christ abounded for many . . . the free gift following many trespasses brought justification.

But God, being rich in mercy, because of the great love with which he loved us, even when we were dead in our trespasses, made us alive together with Christ—by grace you have been saved—and raised us up with him and seated us with him in the heavenly places in Christ Jesus, so that in the coming ages he might show the immeasurable riches of his grace in kindness toward us in Christ Jesus.

He who did not spare his own Son but gave him up for us all, how will he not also with him graciously give us all things?

James 1:5; John 8:10–11; Rom. 5:15–16; Eph. 2:4–7; Rom. 8:32

MORNING

"For God so loved the world, that he gave his only Son, that whoever believes in him should not perish but have eternal life."

All this is from God, who through Christ reconciled us to himself and gave us the ministry of reconciliation; that is, in Christ God was reconciling the world to himself, not counting their trespasses against them, and entrusting to us the message of reconciliation. Therefore, we are ambassadors for Christ, God making his appeal through us. We implore you on behalf of Christ, be reconciled to God. For our sake he made him to be sin who knew no sin, so that in him we might become the righteousness of God.—God is love. In this the love of God was made manifest among us, that God sent his only Son into the world, so that we might live through him. In this is love, not that we have loved God but that he loved us and sent his Son to be the propitiation for our sins. Beloved, if God so loved us, we also ought to love one another.

John 3:16; 2 Cor. 5:18–21; 1 John 4:8–11

EVENING

The spirit of man is the lamp of the Lord.

"Let him who is without sin among you be the first to throw a stone at her." . . . But when they heard it, they went away one by one, beginning with the older ones, and Jesus was left alone with the woman standing before him.

"Who told you that you were naked? Have you eaten of the tree of which I commanded you not to eat?"

So whoever knows the right thing to do and fails to do it, for him it is sin.—For whenever our heart condemns us, God is greater than our heart, and he knows everything. Beloved, if our heart does not condemn us, we have confidence before God.

Everything is indeed clean, but it is wrong for anyone to make another stumble by what he eats. . . . Blessed is the one who has no reason to pass judgment on himself for what he approves.

Search me, O God, and know my heart! Try me and know my thoughts! And see if there be any grievous way in me, and lead me in the way everlasting!

Prov. 20:27; John 8:7, 9; Gen. 3:11; James 4:17;
1 John 3:20–21; Rom. 14:20, 22; Ps. 139:23–24

MORNING

Do not boast about tomorrow, for you do not know what a day may bring.

Behold, now is the favorable time; behold, now is the day of salvation.—"The light is among you for a little while longer. Walk while you have the light, lest darkness overtake you. The one who walks in the darkness does not know where he is going. While you have the light, believe in the light, that you may become sons of light."—Whatever your hand finds to do, do it with your might, for there is no work or thought or knowledge or wisdom in Sheol, to which you are going.

"'Soul, you have ample goods laid up for many years; relax, eat, drink, be merry.' . . . 'Fool! This night your soul is required of you, and the things you have prepared, whose will they be?' So is the one who lays up treasure for himself and is not rich toward God."

What is your life? For you are a mist that appears for a little time and then vanishes.—And the world is passing away along with its desires, but whoever does the will of God abides forever.

Prov. 27:1; 2 Cor. 6:2; John 12:35–36; Eccles. 9:10;
Luke 12:19–21; James 4:14; 1 John 2:17

EVENING

But you are the same, and your years have no end.

Before the mountains were brought forth, or ever you had formed the earth and the world, from everlasting to everlasting you are God.

"For I the Lord do not change; therefore you, O children of Jacob, are not consumed."—Jesus Christ is the same yesterday and today and forever.

Every good gift and every perfect gift is from above, coming down from the Father of lights with whom there is no variation or shadow due to change.—For the gifts and the calling of God are irrevocable.

God is not man, that he should lie, or a son of man, that he should change his mind.—The steadfast love of the Lord never ceases; his mercies never come to an end.

But he holds his priesthood permanently, because he continues forever. Consequently, he is able to save to the uttermost those who draw near to God through him, since he always lives to make intercession for them.—"Fear not, I am the first and the last."

Ps. 102:27; Ps. 90:2; Mal. 3:6; Heb. 13:8; James 1:17; Rom. 11:29;
Num. 23:19; Lam. 3:22; Heb. 7:24–25; Rev. 1:17

MORNING

But the fruit of the Spirit is love.

God is love, and whoever abides in love abides in God, and God abides in him.—God's love has been poured into our hearts through the Holy Spirit who has been given to us.—So the honor is for you who believe.—We love because he first loved us.—For the love of Christ controls us, because we have concluded this: that one has died for all, therefore all have died; and he died for all, that those who live might no longer live for themselves but for him who for their sake died and was raised.

You yourselves have been taught by God to love one another.—"This is my commandment, that you love one another as I have loved you."—Above all, keep loving one another earnestly, since love covers a multitude of sins.—And walk in love, as Christ loved us and gave himself up for us, a fragrant offering and sacrifice to God.

Gal. 5:22; 1 John 4:16; Rom. 5:5; 1 Pet. 2:7; 1 John 4:19;
2 Cor. 5:14–15; 1 Thess. 4:9; John 15:12; 1 Pet. 4:8; Eph. 5:2

EVENING

The Lord Is My Banner.

If God is for us, who can be against us?—The Lord is on my side; I will not fear. What can man do to me?

You have set up a banner for those who fear you.

The Lord is my light and my salvation; whom shall I fear? The Lord is the stronghold of my life; of whom shall I be afraid? . . . Though an army encamp against me, my heart shall not fear; though war arise against me, yet I will be confident.

"Behold, God is with us at our head."—The Lord of hosts is with us; the God of Jacob is our fortress.

"They will make war on the Lamb, and the Lamb will conquer them."

Why do the nations rage and the peoples plot in vain? . . . He who sits in the heavens laughs; the Lord holds them in derision.—Take counsel together, but it will come to nothing; speak a word, but it will not stand, for God is with us.

Ex. 17:15; Rom. 8:31; Ps. 118:6; Ps. 60:4; Ps. 27:1, 3;
2 Chron. 13:12; Ps. 46:7; Rev. 17:14; Ps. 2:1, 4; Isa. 8:10

MORNING

"For God has made me fruitful in the land of my affliction."

Blessed be the God and Father of our Lord Jesus Christ, the Father of mercies and God of all comfort, who comforts us in all our affliction, so that we may be able to comfort those who are in any affliction, with the comfort with which we ourselves are comforted by God. For as we share abundantly in Christ's sufferings, so through Christ we share abundantly in comfort too.

Now for a little while, if necessary, you have been grieved by various trials, so that the tested genuineness of your faith—more precious than gold that perishes though it is tested by fire—may be found to result in praise and glory and honor at the revelation of Jesus Christ.—But the Lord stood by me and strengthened me.

Therefore let those who suffer according to God's will entrust their souls to a faithful Creator while doing good.

Gen. 41:52; 2 Cor. 1:3–5; 1 Pet. 1:6–7;
2 Tim. 4:17; 1 Pet. 4:19

EVENING

So then, there remains a Sabbath rest for the people of God.

"There the wicked cease from troubling, and there the weary are at rest. There the prisoners are at ease together; they hear not the voice of the taskmaster."

"Blessed are the dead who die in the Lord from now on. . . . They . . . rest from their labors, for their deeds follow them!"

"Our friend Lazarus has fallen asleep . . ." Now Jesus had spoken of his death, but they thought that he meant taking rest in sleep.

For while we are still in this tent, we groan, being burdened.—We ourselves, who have the firstfruits of the Spirit, groan inwardly as we wait eagerly for adoption as sons, the redemption of our bodies. For in this hope we were saved. Now hope that is seen is not hope. For who hopes for what he sees? But if we hope for what we do not see, we wait for it with patience.

Heb. 4:9; Job 3:17–18; Rev. 14:13; John 11:11, 13;
2 Cor. 5:4; Rom. 8:23–25

MORNING

Trust in the Lord with all your heart, and do not lean on
your own understanding. In all your ways acknowledge
him, and he will make straight your paths.

Trust in him at all times, O people; pour out your heart before him; God is a refuge for us.

I will instruct you and teach you in the way you should go; I will counsel you with my eye upon you. Be not like a horse or a mule, without understanding, which must be curbed with bit and bridle, or it will not stay near you. Many are the sorrows of the wicked, but steadfast love surrounds the one who trusts in the Lord.—And your ears shall hear a word behind you, saying, "This is the way, walk in it," when you turn to the right or when you turn to the left.

"If your presence will not go with me, do not bring us up from here. For how shall it be known that I have found favor in your sight, I and your people? Is it not in your going with us, so that we are distinct, I and your people, from every other people on the face of the earth?"

Prov. 3:5–6; Ps. 62:8; Ps. 32:8–10; Isa. 30:21; Ex. 33:15–16

EVENING

The prize of the upward call of God in Christ Jesus.

"You will have treasure in heaven; . . . come, follow me."—"Fear not, Abram, I am your shield; your reward shall be very great."

"Well done, good and faithful servant. You have been faithful over a little; I will set you over much. Enter into the joy of your master."—And they will reign forever and ever.

You will receive the unfading crown of glory.—The crown of life.—The crown of righteousness.—They do it to receive a perishable wreath, but we an imperishable.

"Father, I desire that they also, whom you have given me, may be with me where I am, to see my glory that you have given me."—So we will always be with the Lord.

For I consider that the sufferings of this present time are not worth comparing with the glory that is to be revealed to us.

Phil. 3:14; Matt. 19:21; Gen. 15:1; Matt. 25:21; Rev. 22:5; 1 Pet. 5:4;
James 1:12; 2 Tim. 4:8; 1 Cor. 9:25; John 17:24; 1 Thess. 4:17; Rom. 8:18

MORNING

Set your minds on things that are above,
not on things that are on earth.

Do not love the world or the things in the world. If anyone loves the world, the love of the Father is not in him.— "Do not lay up for yourselves treasures on earth, where moth and rust destroy and where thieves break in and steal, but lay up for yourselves treasures in heaven, where neither moth nor rust destroys and where thieves do not break in and steal. For where your treasure is, there your heart will be also."

For we walk by faith, not by sight.—So we do not lose heart. Though our outer self is wasting away, our inner self is being renewed day by day. For this light momentary affliction is preparing for us an eternal weight of glory beyond all comparison, as we look not to the things that are seen but to the things that are unseen. For the things that are seen are transient, but the things that are unseen are eternal.—An inheritance that is imperishable, undefiled, and unfading, kept in heaven for you.

Col. 3:2; 1 John 2:15; Matt. 6:19–21; 2 Cor. 5:7; 2 Cor. 4:16–18; 1 Pet. 1:4

EVENING

"He bowed his shoulder to bear."

As an example of suffering and patience, brothers, take the prophets who spoke in the name of the Lord.—Now these things happened to them as an example, but they were written down for our instruction, on whom the end of the ages has come.

"Shall we receive good from God, and shall we not receive evil?" In all this Job did not sin with his lips.—And Aaron held his peace.—"It is the Lord. Let him do what seems good to him."

Cast your burden on the Lord, and he will sustain you.—Surely he has borne our griefs and carried our sorrows.

"Come to me, all who labor and are heavy laden, and I will give you rest. Take my yoke upon you, and learn from me, for I am gentle and lowly in heart, and you will find rest for your souls. For my yoke is easy, and my burden is light."

Gen. 49:15; James 5:10; 1 Cor. 10:11; Job 2:10; Lev. 10:3;
1 Sam. 3:18; Ps. 55:22; Isa. 53:4; Matt. 11:28–30

MORNING

O Lord, I am oppressed; be my pledge of safety!

To you I lift up my eyes, O you who are enthroned in the heavens! Behold, as the eyes of servants look to the hand of their master, as the eyes of a maidservant to the hand of her mistress, so our eyes look to the Lord our God.—Hear my cry, O God, listen to my prayer; from the end of the earth I call to you when my heart is faint. Lead me to the rock that is higher than I, for you have been my refuge, a strong tower against the enemy. Let me dwell in your tent forever! Let me take refuge under the shelter of your wings!—For you have been a stronghold to the poor, a stronghold to the needy in his distress, a shelter from the storm.

Christ also suffered for you, leaving you an example, so that you might follow in his steps. He committed no sin, neither was deceit found in his mouth. When he was reviled, he did not revile in return; when he suffered, he did not threaten, but continued entrusting himself to him who judges justly.

Isa. 38:14; Ps. 123:1–2; Ps. 61:1–4; Isa. 25:4; 1 Pet. 2:21–23

EVENING

Fight the good fight of the faith.

We were afflicted at every turn—fighting without and fear within.—"Do not be afraid, for those who are with us are more than those who are with them."—Strong in the Lord and in the strength of his might.

"You come to me with a sword and with a spear and with a javelin, but I come to you in the name of the Lord of hosts, the God of the armies of Israel, whom you have defied."—"This God is my strong refuge and has made my way blameless. . . . He trains my hands for war, so that my arms can bend a bow of bronze."—Our sufficiency is from God.

The angel of the Lord encamps around those who fear him, and delivers them.—Behold, the mountain was full of horses and chariots of fire all around Elisha.

For time would fail me to tell of [those] who through faith conquered kingdoms. . . . were made strong out of weakness, became mighty in war, put foreign armies to flight.

1 Tim. 6:12; 2 Cor. 7:5; 2 Kings 6:16; Eph. 6:10; 1 Sam. 17:45;
2 Sam. 22:33, 35; 2 Cor. 3:5; Ps. 34:7; 2 Kings 6:17; Heb. 11:32–34

MORNING

Watching over the way of his saints.

The Lord your God . . . went before you in the way to seek you out a place to pitch your tents, in fire by night and in the cloud by day, to show you by what way you should go.—Like an eagle that stirs up its nest, that flutters over its young, spreading out its wings, catching them, bearing them on its pinions, the Lord alone guided him.—The steps of a man are established by the Lord, when he delights in his way; though he fall, he shall not be cast headlong, for the Lord upholds his hand.—Many are the afflictions of the righteous, but the Lord delivers him out of them all.—For the Lord knows the way of the righteous, but the way of the wicked will perish.—And we know that for those who love God all things work together for good, for those who are called according to his purpose.—"With us is the Lord our God, to help us and to fight our battles."

The Lord your God is in your midst, a mighty one who will save; he will rejoice over you with gladness.

Prov. 2:8; Deut. 1:32–33; Deut. 32:11–12; Ps. 37:23–24;
Ps. 34:19; Ps. 1:6; Rom. 8:28; 2 Chron. 32:8; Zeph. 3:17

EVENING

"My God, my God, why have you forsaken me?"

But he was pierced for our transgressions; he was crushed for our iniquities; upon him was the chastisement that brought us peace . . . and the Lord has laid on him the iniquity of us all. . . . stricken for the transgression of my people. . . . Yet it was the will of the Lord to crush him; he has put him to grief.

Jesus our Lord . . . was delivered up for our trespasses.—For Christ also suffered once for sins, the righteous for the unrighteous, that he might bring us to God.—He himself bore our sins in his body on the tree, that we might die to sin and live to righteousness. By his wounds you have been healed.

For our sake he made him to be sin who knew no sin, so that in him we might become the righteousness of God.—Christ redeemed us from the curse of the law by becoming a curse for us.

Matt. 27:46; Isa. 53:5–6, 8, 10; Rom. 4:24–25;
1 Pet. 3:18; 1 Pet. 2:24; 2 Cor. 5:21; Gal. 3:13

MORNING

"For your Maker is your husband,
the Lord of hosts is his name."

This mystery is profound, and I am saying that it refers to Christ and the church.—You shall no more be termed Forsaken . . . but you shall be called My Delight Is in Her . . . for the Lord delights in you . . . and as the bridegroom rejoices over the bride, so shall your God rejoice over you.—He has sent me . . . to comfort all who mourn; to grant to those who mourn in Zion—to give them a beautiful headdress instead of ashes, the oil of gladness instead of mourning, the garment of praise instead of a faint spirit.

I will greatly rejoice in the Lord; my soul shall exult in my God, for he has clothed me with the garments of salvation; . . . as a bridegroom decks himself like a priest with a beautiful headdress, and as a bride adorns herself with her jewels.

"And I will betroth you to me forever. I will betroth you to me in righteousness and in justice, in steadfast love and in mercy."

Who shall separate us from the love of Christ?

Isa. 54:5; Eph. 5:32; Isa. 62:4–5; Isa. 61:1–3; Isa. 61:10; Hos. 2:19; Rom. 8:35

EVENING

My times are in your hand.

"All his holy ones were in his hand."—And the word of the Lord came to [Elijah]: "Depart from here and turn eastward and hide yourself by the brook Cherith, which is east of the Jordan. You shall drink from the brook, and I have commanded the ravens to feed you there." . . . Then the word of the Lord came to him, "Arise, go to Zarephath, which belongs to Sidon, and dwell there. Behold, I have commanded a widow there to feed you."

"Therefore I tell you, do not be anxious about your life, what you will eat or what you will drink, nor about your body, what you will put on. . . . Your heavenly Father knows that you need them all."

Trust in the Lord with all your heart, and do not lean on your own understanding. In all your ways acknowledge him, and he will make straight your paths.—Casting all your anxieties on him, because he cares for you.

Ps. 31:15; Deut. 33:3; 1 Kings 17:2–4, 8–9; Matt. 6:25, 32; Prov. 3:5–6; 1 Pet. 5:7

MORNING

You have cast all my sins behind your back.

Who is a God like you, pardoning iniquity and passing over transgression for the remnant of his inheritance? He does not retain his anger forever, because he delights in steadfast love. He will again have compassion on us; he will tread our iniquities underfoot. You will cast all our sins into the depths of the sea.

"For a brief moment I deserted you, but with great compassion I will gather you. In overflowing anger for a moment I hid my face from you, but with everlasting love I will have compassion on you," says the Lord, your Redeemer.—"I will forgive their iniquity, and I will remember their sin no more."

Blessed is the one whose transgression is forgiven, whose sin is covered. Blessed is the man against whom the Lord counts no iniquity, and in whose spirit there is no deceit.—The blood of Jesus his Son cleanses us from all sin.

Isa. 38:17; Mic. 7:18-19; Isa. 54:7-8; Jer. 31:34; Ps. 32:1-2; 1 John 1:7

EVENING

I know whom I have believed, and I am convinced that he is able.

Able to do far more abundantly than all that we ask or think.

Able to make all grace abound to you, so that having all sufficiency in all things at all times, you may abound in every good work.

Able to help those who are being tempted.

Able to save to the uttermost those who draw near to God through him, since he always lives to make intercession for them.

Able to keep you from stumbling and to present you blameless before the presence of his glory with great joy.

Able to guard until that Day what has been entrusted to me.

Who will transform our lowly body to be like his glorious body, by the power that enables him even to subject all things to himself.

"Do you believe that I am able to do this?" . . . "Yes, Lord." "According to your faith be it done to you."

2 Tim. 1:12; Eph. 3:20; 2 Cor. 9:8; Heb. 2:18; Heb. 7:25;
Jude 24; 2 Tim. 1:12; Phil. 3:21; Matt. 9:28-29

MORNING

God . . . richly provides us with everything to enjoy.

"Take care lest you forget the Lord your God by not keeping his commandments and his rules and his statutes, which I command you today, lest, when you have eaten and are full and have built good houses and live in them . . . then your heart be lifted up, and you forget the Lord your God . . . for it is he who gives you power to get wealth."

Unless the Lord builds the house, those who build it labor in vain. Unless the Lord watches over the city, the watchman stays awake in vain. It is in vain that you rise up early and go late to rest, eating the bread of anxious toil; for he gives to his beloved sleep.—For not by their own sword did they win the land, nor did their own arm save them, but your right hand and your arm, and the light of your face, for you delighted in them.—There are many who say, "Who will show us some good? Lift up the light of your face upon us, O Lord!"

1 Tim. 6:17; Deut. 8:11–12, 14, 18; Ps. 127:1–2; Ps. 44:3; Ps. 4:6

EVENING

They were singing a new song.

The new and living way that he opened for us.—Not because of works done by us in righteousness, but according to his own mercy, by the washing of regeneration and renewal of the Holy Spirit, whom he poured out on us richly through Jesus Christ our Savior.—For by grace you have been saved through faith. And this is not your own doing; it is the gift of God, not a result of works, so that no one may boast.

Not to us, O Lord, not to us, but to your name give glory.—To him who loves us and has freed us from our sins by his blood and made us a kingdom, priests to his God and Father, to him be glory and dominion forever and ever. Amen.—"You were slain, and by your blood you ransomed people for God from every tribe and language and people and nation."— After this I looked, and behold, a great multitude that no one could number . . . crying out with a loud voice, "Salvation belongs to our God who sits on the throne, and to the Lamb!"

Rev. 14:3; Heb. 10:20; Titus 3:5–6; Eph. 2:8–9;
Ps. 115:1; Rev. 1:5–6; Rev. 5:9; Rev. 7:9–10

MORNING

"The Lord will provide."

"God will provide for himself the lamb for a burnt offering, my son."

Behold, the Lord's hand is not shortened, that it cannot save, or his ear dull, that it cannot hear.—"The Deliverer will come from Zion, he will banish ungodliness from Jacob."

Blessed is he whose help is the God of Jacob, whose hope is in the Lord his God.—Behold, the eye of the Lord is on those who fear him, on those who hope in his steadfast love, that he may deliver their soul from death.

And my God will supply every need of yours according to his riches in glory in Christ Jesus.—He has said, "I will never leave you nor forsake you." So we can confidently say, "The Lord is my helper; I will not fear; what can man do to me?"—The Lord is my strength and my shield; in him my heart trusts, and I am helped; my heart exults, and with my song I give thanks to him.

Gen. 22:14; Gen. 22:8; Isa. 59:1; Rom. 11:26; Ps. 146:5;
Ps. 33:18–19; Phil. 4:19; Heb. 13:5–6; Ps. 28:7

EVENING

He grazes among the lilies.

"For where two or three are gathered in my name, there am I among them."—"If anyone loves me, he will keep my word, and my Father will love him, and we will come to him and make our home with him."

"If you keep my commandments, you will abide in my love, just as I have kept my Father's commandments and abide in his love."

Let my beloved come to his garden, and eat its choicest fruits.—I came to my garden, my sister, my bride, I gathered my myrrh with my spice, I ate my honeycomb with my honey.—But the fruit of the Spirit is love, joy, peace, patience, kindness, goodness, faithfulness, gentleness, self-control.

"By this my Father is glorified, that you bear much fruit and so prove to be my disciples."—"Every branch in me that does not bear fruit he takes away, and every branch that does bear fruit he prunes, that it may bear more fruit."—[Being] filled with the fruit of righteousness that comes through Jesus Christ, to the glory and praise of God.

Song 2:16; Matt. 18:20; John 14:23; John 15:10; Song 4:16;
Song 5:1; Gal. 5:22–23; John 15:8; John 15:2; Phil. 1:11

MORNING

"The Lord bless you and keep you."

The blessing of the Lord makes rich, and he adds no sorrow with it.—For you bless the righteous, O Lord; you cover him with favor as with a shield.

He will not let your foot be moved; he who keeps you will not slumber. Behold, he who keeps Israel will neither slumber nor sleep. The Lord is your keeper; the Lord is your shade on your right hand. . . . The Lord will keep you from all evil; he will keep your life. The Lord will keep your going out and your coming in from this time forth and forevermore.—I, the Lord, am its [the vineyard's] keeper; every moment I water it. Lest anyone punish it, I keep it night and day.

"Holy Father, keep them in your name, which you have given me. While I was with them, I kept them in your name, which you have given me."

The Lord will rescue me from every evil deed and bring me safely into his heavenly kingdom. To him be the glory forever and ever. Amen.

Num. 6:24; Prov. 10:22; Ps. 5:12; Ps. 121:3–5, 7–8;
Isa. 27:3; John 17:11–12; 2 Tim. 4:18

EVENING

Jesus wept.

A man of sorrows, and acquainted with grief.—For we do not have a high priest who is unable to sympathize with our weaknesses.—For it was fitting that he, for whom and by whom all things exist, in bringing many sons to glory, should make the founder of their salvation perfect through suffering.—Although he was a son, he learned obedience through what he suffered.

I was not rebellious; I turned not backward. I gave my back to those who strike, and my cheeks to those who pull out the beard; I hid not my face from disgrace and spitting.

"See how he loved him!"—For surely it is not angels that he helps, but he helps the offspring of Abraham. Therefore he had to be made like his brothers in every respect, so that he might become a merciful and faithful high priest in the service of God, to make propitiation for the sins of the people.

John 11:35; Isa. 53:3; Heb. 4:15; Heb. 2:10; Heb. 5:8;
Isa. 50:5–6; John 11:36; Heb. 2:16–17

MORNING

"The Lord make his face to shine upon you and be gracious to you;
the Lord lift up his countenance upon you and give you peace."

No one has ever seen God; the only God, who is at the Father's side, he has made him known.—He is the radiance of the glory of God and the exact imprint of his nature.—The god of this world has blinded the minds of the unbelievers, to keep them from seeing the light of the gospel of the glory of Christ, who is the image of God.

Make your face shine on your servant; save me in your steadfast love! O Lord, let me not be put to shame, for I call upon you.—By your favor, O Lord, you made my mountain stand strong; you hid your face; I was dismayed.—Blessed are the people who know the festal shout, who walk, O Lord, in the light of your face.

May the Lord give strength to his people! May the Lord bless his people with peace!

"Take heart; it is I. Do not be afraid."

Num. 6:25–26; John 1:18; Heb. 1:3; 2 Cor. 4:4; Ps. 31:16–17;
Ps. 30:7; Ps. 89:15; Ps. 29:11; Matt. 14:27

EVENING

What pleases him.

And without faith it is impossible to please him.—Those who are in the flesh cannot please God.—The Lord takes pleasure in his people.

For this is a gracious thing, when, mindful of God, one endures sorrows while suffering unjustly. But if when you do good and suffer for it you endure, this is a gracious thing in the sight of God.—Your adorning . . . with the imperishable beauty of a gentle and quiet spirit . . . in God's sight is very precious.

"The one who offers thanksgiving as his sacrifice glorifies me; to one who orders his way rightly I will show the salvation of God!"—I will praise the name of God with a song; I will magnify him with thanksgiving. This will please the Lord more than an ox or a bull with horns and hoofs.

I appeal to you therefore, brothers, by the mercies of God, to pre-sent your bodies as a living sacrifice, holy and acceptable to God, which is your spiritual worship.

1 John 3:22; Heb. 11:6; Rom. 8:8; Ps. 149:4; 1 Pet. 2:19–20;
1 Pet. 3:4; Ps. 50:23; Ps. 69:30–31; Rom. 12:1

MORNING

For there is one God, and there is one mediator between God and men, the man Christ Jesus.

Since therefore the children share in flesh and blood, he himself likewise partook of the same things.

"Turn to me and be saved, all the ends of the earth! For I am God, and there is no other."

We have an advocate with the Father, Jesus Christ the righteous.—But now in Christ Jesus you who once were far off have been brought near by the blood of Christ. For he himself is our peace.—He entered once for all into the holy places, not by means of the blood of goats and calves but by means of his own blood, thus securing an eternal redemption. . . . Therefore he is the mediator of a new covenant, so that those who are called may receive the promised eternal inheritance, since a death has occurred that redeems them from the transgressions committed under the first covenant.—Consequently, he is able to save to the uttermost those who draw near to God through him, since he always lives to make intercession for them.

1 Tim. 2:5; Heb. 2:14; Isa. 45:22; 1 John 2:1; Eph. 2:13–14;
Heb. 9:12, 15; Heb. 7:25

EVENING

And my God. My soul is cast down within me.

You keep him in perfect peace whose mind is stayed on you, because he trusts in you. Trust in the Lord forever, for the Lord God is an everlasting rock.

Cast your burden on the Lord, and he will sustain you.—For he has not despised or abhorred the affliction of the afflicted, and he has not hidden his face from him, but has heard, when he cried to him.—Is anyone among you suffering? Let him pray.

"Let not your hearts be troubled, neither let them be afraid."— "Therefore I tell you, do not be anxious about your life, what you will eat or what you will drink, nor about your body, what you will put on. . . . Look at the birds of the air: they neither sow nor reap nor gather into barns, and yet your heavenly Father feeds them. Are you not of more value than they?"—"Do not disbelieve, but believe."—"And behold, I am with you always."

Ps. 42:6; Isa. 26:3–4; Ps. 55:22; Ps. 22:24; James 5:13;
John 14:27; Matt. 6:25–26; John 20:27; Matt. 28:20

MORNING

In everything . . . may adorn the doctrine of God our Savior.

Only let your manner of life be worthy of the gospel of Christ.—Abstain from every form of evil.—If you are insulted for the name of Christ, you are blessed, because the Spirit of glory and of God rests upon you. But let none of you suffer as a murderer or a thief or an evildoer or as a meddler.—Be blameless and innocent, children of God without blemish in the midst of a crooked and twisted generation, among whom you shine as lights in the world.—"In the same way, let your light shine before others, so that they may see your good works and give glory to your Father who is in heaven."

Let not steadfast love and faithfulness forsake you; bind them around your neck; write them on the tablet of your heart. So you will find favor and good success in the sight of God and man.—Finally, brothers, whatever is true, whatever is honorable, whatever is just, whatever is pure, whatever is lovely, whatever is commendable, if there is any excellence, if there is anything worthy of praise, think about these things.

Titus 2:10; Phil. 1:27; 1 Thess. 5:22; 1 Pet. 4:14–15; Phil. 2:15;
Matt. 5:16; Prov. 3:3–4; Phil. 4:8

EVENING

"The words that I have spoken to you are spirit and life."

Of his own will he brought us forth by the word of truth.—The letter kills, but the Spirit gives life.

Christ loved the church and gave himself up for her, that he might sanctify her, having cleansed her by the washing of water with the word, so that he might present the church to himself in splendor, without spot or wrinkle or any such thing, that she might be holy and without blemish.

How can a young man keep his way pure? By guarding it according to your word. . . . Your promise gives me life. . . . I have stored up your word in my heart, that I might not sin against you. I will not forget your word. . . . I trust in your word. . . . The law of your mouth is better to me than thousands of gold and silver pieces. . . . I will never forget your precepts, for by them you have given me life. . . . How sweet are your words to my taste, sweeter than honey to my mouth! Through your precepts I get understanding; therefore I hate every false way.

John 6:63; James 1:18; 2 Cor. 3:6; Eph. 5:25–27;
Ps. 119:9, 50, 11, 16, 42, 72, 93, 103–104

MORNING

Perfect through suffering.

"My soul is very sorrowful, even to death; remain here, and watch with me." And going a little farther he fell on his face and prayed, saying, "My Father, if it be possible, let this cup pass from me; nevertheless, not as I will, but as you will."—And being in an agony he prayed more earnestly; and his sweat became like great drops of blood falling down to the ground.

The snares of death encompassed me; the pangs of Sheol laid hold on me; I suffered distress and anguish.—Reproaches have broken my heart, so that I am in despair. I looked for pity, but there was none, and for comforters, but I found none.—Look to the right and see: there is none who takes notice of me; no refuge remains to me; no one cares for my soul.

He was despised and rejected by men; a man of sorrows, and acquainted with grief; and as one from whom men hide their faces he was despised, and we esteemed him not.

Heb. 2:10 Matt. 26:38–39; Luke 22:44; Ps. 116:3; Ps. 69:20;
Ps. 142:4; Isa. 53:3

EVENING

The Lord made heaven and earth,
the sea, and all that is in them.

The heavens declare the glory of God, and the sky above proclaims his handiwork.—By the word of the Lord the heavens were made, and by the breath of his mouth all their host. For he spoke, and it came to be; he commanded, and it stood firm.—Behold, the nations are like a drop from a bucket, and are accounted as the dust on the scales; behold, he takes up the coastlands like fine dust.

By faith we understand that the universe was created by the word of God, so that what is seen was not made out of things that are visible.

When I look at your heavens, the work of your fingers, the moon and the stars, which you have set in place, what is man that you are mindful of him, and the son of man that you care for him?

Ex. 20:11; Ps. 19:1; Ps. 33:6, 9; Isa. 40:15; Heb. 11:3; Ps. 8:3–4

MORNING

What is your life? For you are a mist that appears
for a little time and then vanishes.

"My days are swifter than a runner; they flee away; they see no good. They go by like skiffs of reed, like an eagle swooping on the prey."—You sweep them away as with a flood; they are like a dream, like grass that is renewed in the morning: in the morning it flourishes and is renewed; in the evening it fades and withers.—"Man who is born of a woman is few of days and full of trouble. He comes out like a flower and withers."

And the world is passing away along with its desires, but whoever does the will of God abides forever.—They will perish, but you will remain; they will all wear out like a garment. You will change them like a robe, and they will pass away, but you are the same, and your years have no end.—Jesus Christ is the same yesterday and today and forever.

James 4:14; Job 9:25-26; Ps. 90:5-6; Job 14:1-2;
1 John 2:17; Ps. 102:26-27; Heb. 13:8

EVENING

I will sing praise with my spirit, but
I will sing with my mind also.

Be filled with the Spirit, addressing one another in psalms and hymns and spiritual songs, singing and making melody to the Lord with your heart.— Let the word of Christ dwell in you richly, teaching and admonishing one another in all wisdom, singing psalms and hymns and spiritual songs, with thankfulness in your hearts to God.

My mouth will speak the praise of the Lord, and let all flesh bless his holy name forever and ever.

Praise the Lord! For it is good to sing praises to our God; for it is pleasant, and a song of praise is fitting. . . . Sing to the Lord with thanksgiving; make melody to our God on the lyre!

And I heard a voice from heaven like the roar of many waters and like the sound of loud thunder. The voice I heard was like the sound of harpists playing on their harps.

1 Cor. 14:15; Eph. 5:18-19; Col. 3:16; Ps. 145:21; Ps. 147:1, 7; Rev. 14:2

MORNING

He shall lay his hand on the head of the burnt offering, and it shall be accepted for him to make atonement for him.

Knowing that you were ransomed from the futile ways inherited from your forefathers, not with perishable things such as silver or gold, but with the precious blood of Christ, like that of a lamb without blemish or spot.—He himself bore our sins in his body on the tree.

He has blessed us in the Beloved.

You yourselves like living stones are being built up as a spiritual house, to be a holy priesthood, to offer spiritual sacrifices acceptable to God through Jesus Christ.— I appeal to you therefore, brothers, by the mercies of God, to present your bodies as a living sacrifice, holy and acceptable to God, which is your spiritual worship.

Now to him who is able to keep you from stumbling and to present you blameless before the presence of his glory with great joy, to the only God, our Savior, through Jesus Christ our Lord, be glory, majesty, dominion, and authority, before all time and now and forever. Amen.

Lev. 1:4; 1 Pet. 1:18-19; 1 Pet. 2:24; Eph. 1:6; 1 Pet. 2:5;
Rom. 12:1; Jude 24-25

EVENING

One who in every respect has been tempted as we are, yet without sin.

So when the woman saw that the tree was good for food, and that it was a delight to the eyes, and that the tree was to be desired to make one wise, she took of its fruit and ate, and she also gave some to her husband who was with her, and he ate.

And the tempter came and said to him, "If you are the Son of God, command these stones to become loaves of bread." But he answered, "It is written, 'Man shall not live by bread alone, but by every word that comes from the mouth of God.'" . . . Again, the devil . . . showed him all the kingdoms of the world and their glory. And he said to him, "All these I will give you, if you will fall down and worship me." Then Jesus said to him, "Be gone, Satan!"

For because he himself has suffered when tempted, he is able to help those who are being tempted.

Blessed is the man who remains steadfast under trial.

Heb. 4:15; Gen. 3:6; Matt. 4:3-4, 8-10; Heb. 2:18; James 1:12

MORNING

My eyes are weary with looking upward.

Be gracious to me, O Lord, for I am languishing; heal me, O Lord, for my bones are troubled. My soul also is greatly troubled. But you, O Lord—how long? Turn, O Lord, deliver my life; save me for the sake of your steadfast love.—My heart is in anguish within me; the terrors of death have fallen upon me. Fear and trembling come upon me, and horror overwhelms me. And I say, "Oh, that I had wings like a dove! I would fly away and be at rest."—For you have need of endurance.

And while they were gazing into heaven as he went, behold, two men stood by them in white robes, and said, "Men of Galilee, why do you stand looking into heaven? This Jesus, who was taken up from you into heaven, will come in the same way as you saw him go into heaven."—But our citizenship is in heaven, and from it we await a Savior, the Lord Jesus Christ.—Our blessed hope, the appearing of the glory of our great God and Savior Jesus Christ.

Isa. 38:14; Ps. 6:2–4; Ps. 55:4–6; Heb. 10:36; Acts 1:10–11;
Phil. 3:20; Titus 2:13

EVENING

His name will be on their foreheads.

"I am the good shepherd. I know my own."—But God's firm foundation stands, bearing this seal: "The Lord knows those who are his," and, "Let everyone who names the name of the Lord depart from iniquity."—The Lord is good, a stronghold in the day of trouble; he knows those who take refuge in him.— "Do not harm the earth or the sea or the trees, until we have sealed the servants of our God on their foreheads."—In him you also, when you heard the word of truth, the gospel of your salvation, and believed in him, were sealed with the promised Holy Spirit, who is the guarantee of our inheritance.—And it is God who establishes us with you in Christ, and has anointed us, and who has also put his seal on us and given us his Spirit in our hearts as a guarantee.

"I will write on him the name of my God, and the name of the city of my God, the new Jerusalem, which comes down from my God out of heaven, and my own new name."—"And this is the name by which it will be called: 'The Lord is our righteousness.'"

Rev. 22:4; John 10:14; 2 Tim. 2:19; Nah. 1:7; Rev. 7:3;
Eph. 1:13–14; 2 Cor. 1:21–22; Rev. 3:12; Jer. 33:16

MORNING

"God, having raised up his servant, sent him to you first, to bless you by turning every one of you from your wickedness."

Blessed be the God and Father of our Lord Jesus Christ! According to his great mercy, he has caused us to be born again to a living hope through the resurrection of Jesus Christ from the dead.—Saved by his life.

Our . . . Savior Jesus Christ, who gave himself for us to redeem us from all lawlessness and to purify for himself a people for his own possession who are zealous for good works.—But as he who called you is holy, you also be holy in all your conduct, since it is written, "You shall be holy, for I am holy."

The God and Father of our Lord Jesus Christ . . . has blessed us in Christ with every spiritual blessing in the heavenly places.—For in him the whole fullness of deity dwells bodily, and you have been filled in him.—For from his fullness we have all received, grace upon grace.

He who did not spare his own Son but gave him up for us all, how will he not also with him graciously give us all things?

Acts 3:26; 1 Pet. 1:3; Rom. 5:10; Titus 2:13–14; 1 Pet. 1:15–16;
Eph. 1:3; Col. 2:9–10; John 1:16; Rom. 8:32

EVENING

Strengthen me according to your word!

Remember your word to your servant, in which you have made me hope.—O Lord, I am oppressed; be my pledge of safety!

"Heaven and earth will pass away, but my words will not pass away."— "You know in your hearts and souls, all of you, that not one word has failed of all the good things that the Lord your God promised concerning you. All have come to pass for you; not one of them has failed."

"Fear not, peace be with you; be strong and of good courage." And as he spoke to me, I was strengthened and said, "Let my lord speak, for you have strengthened me."—"Be strong, all you people of the land, declares the Lord. Work, for I am with you, declares the Lord of hosts."—"Not by might, nor by power, but by my Spirit, says the Lord of hosts."

Be strong in the Lord and in the strength of his might.

Ps. 119:28; Ps. 119:49; Isa. 38:14; Luke 21:33; Josh. 23:14;
Dan. 10:19; Hag. 2:4; Zech. 4:6; Eph. 6:10

MORNING

The unfolding of your words gives light.

This is the message we have heard from him and proclaim to you, that God is light, and in him is no darkness at all.—For God, who said, "Let light shine out of darkness," has shone in our hearts to give the light of the knowledge of the glory of God in the face of Jesus Christ.—The Word was God. . . . In him was life, and the life was the light of men.—But if we walk in the light, as he is in the light, we have fellowship with one another, and the blood of Jesus his Son cleanses us from all sin.—I have stored up your word in my heart, that I might not sin against you.—"Already you are clean because of the word that I have spoken to you."

For at one time you were darkness, but now you are light in the Lord. Walk as children of light.—But you are a chosen race, a royal priesthood, a holy nation, a people for his own possession, that you may proclaim the excellencies of him who called you out of darkness into his marvelous light.

Ps. 119:130; 1 John 1:5; 2 Cor. 4:6; John 1:1, 4; 1 John 1:7;
Ps. 119:11; John 15:3; Eph. 5:8; 1 Pet. 2:9

EVENING

Noah was a righteous man.

"The righteous shall live by faith."—Then Noah built an altar to the Lord and took some of every clean animal and some of every clean bird and offered burnt offerings on the altar. And . . . the Lord smelled the pleasing aroma.—The Lamb who was slain.

Therefore, since we have been justified by faith, we have peace with God through our Lord Jesus Christ.

For by works of the law no human being will be justified in his sight, since through the law comes knowledge of sin. But now the righteousness of God has been manifested apart from the law, although the Law and the Prophets bear witness to it—the righteousness of God through faith in Jesus Christ for all who believe. For there is no distinction.

More than that, we also rejoice in God through our Lord Jesus Christ, through whom we have now received reconciliation.—Who shall bring any charge against God's elect? It is God who justifies. . . . And those whom he predestined he also called, and those whom he called he also justified.

Gen. 6:9; Gal. 3:11; Gen. 8:20–21; Rev. 13:8; Rom. 5:1;
Rom. 3:20–22; Rom. 5:11; Rom. 8:33, 30

MORNING

"Wake up, and strengthen what remains and is about to die."

The end of all things is at hand; therefore be self-controlled and sober-minded for the sake of your prayers.—Be sober-minded; be watchful. Your adversary the devil prowls around like a roaring lion, seeking someone to devour.—"Only take care, and keep your soul diligently, lest you forget the things that your eyes have seen, and lest they depart from your heart all the days of your life."—"But my righteous one shall live by faith, and if he shrinks back, my soul has no pleasure in him." But we are not of those who shrink back and are destroyed, but of those who have faith and preserve their souls.—"And what I say to you I say to all: Stay awake."

Fear not, for I am with you; be not dismayed, for I am your God; I will strengthen you, I will help you, I will uphold you with my righteous right hand. . . . For I, the Lord your God, hold your right hand.

Rev. 3:2; 1 Pet. 4:7; 1 Pet. 5:8; Deut. 4:9; Heb. 10:38–39;
Mark 13:37; Isa. 41:10, 13

EVENING

Has his steadfast love forever ceased?

His steadfast love endures forever.—"The Lord is slow to anger and abounding in steadfast love."—Who is a God like you, pardoning iniquity. . . . He does not retain his anger forever, because he delights in steadfast love. He will again have compassion on us; he will tread our iniquities underfoot. You will cast all our sins into the depths of the sea.—He saved us, not because of works done by us in righteousness, but according to his own mercy.

Blessed be the God and Father of our Lord Jesus Christ, the Father of mercies and God of all comfort, who comforts us in all our affliction, so that we may be able to comfort those who are in any affliction, with the comfort with which we ourselves are comforted by God.

A merciful and faithful high priest in the service of God, to make propitiation for the sins of the people. For because he himself has suffered when tempted, he is able to help those who are being tempted.

Ps. 77:8; Ps. 136:23; Num. 14:18; Mic. 7:18–19;
Titus 3:5; 2 Cor. 1:3–4; Heb. 2:17–18

MORNING

And Lot lifted up his eyes and saw that the Jordan Valley was well
watered everywhere like the garden of the Lord, like the land of Egypt,
in the direction of Zoar. (This was before the Lord destroyed Sodom
and Gomorrah.) So Lot chose for himself all the Jordan Valley.

Lot . . . that righteous man.

Do not be deceived: God is not mocked, for whatever one sows, that will
he also reap.—"Remember Lot's wife."

Do not be unequally yoked with unbelievers. For what partnership has
righteousness with lawlessness? Or what fellowship has light with darkness?
. . . "Therefore go out from their midst, and be separate from them, says the
Lord, and touch no unclean thing."—Therefore do not become partners with
them; for at one time you were darkness, but now you are light in the Lord.
Walk as children of light . . . and try to discern what is pleasing to the Lord.
Take no part in the unfruitful works of darkness, but instead expose them.

Gen. 13:10–11.; 2 Pet. 2:7–8; Gal. 6:7; Luke 17:32;
2 Cor. 6:14, 17; Eph. 5:7–8, 10–11

EVENING

"It may be that the Lord will be with me, and
I shall drive them out just as the Lord said."

He has said, "I will never leave you nor forsake you." So we can confidently
say, "The Lord is my helper; I will not fear; what can man do to me?"—With
the mighty deeds of the Lord God I will come; I will remind them of your
righteousness, yours alone.

And the effect of righteousness will be peace, and the result of righteousness, quietness and trust forever.

Stand therefore, having fastened on the belt of truth, and having put on
the breastplate of righteousness. . . . For we do not wrestle against flesh and
blood, but against the rulers, against the authorities, against the cosmic powers over this present darkness, against the spiritual forces of evil in the heavenly places. Therefore take up the whole armor of God, that you may be able
to withstand in the evil day, and having done all, to stand firm.—"The Lord is
with you. . . . Go in this might of yours."

Josh. 14:12; Heb. 13:5–6; Ps. 71:16; Isa. 32:17;
Eph. 6:14, 12–13; Judg. 6:12, 14

MORNING

"Holy, holy, holy, is the Lord God Almighty, who was and is and is to come!"

Yet you are holy, enthroned on the praises of Israel.—"Do not come near; take your sandals off your feet, for the place on which you are standing is holy ground. . . . I am the God of your father, the God of Abraham, the God of Isaac, and the God of Jacob." And Moses hid his face, for he was afraid to look at God.—To whom then will you compare me, that I should be like him? says the Holy One.—For I am the Lord your God, the Holy One of Israel, your Savior. . . . I, I am the Lord, and besides me there is no savior.

But as he who called you is holy, you also be holy in all your conduct, since it is written, "You shall be holy, for I am holy."—Or do you not know that your body is a temple of the Holy Spirit within you, whom you have from God? You are not your own.—For we are the temple of the living God; as God said, "I will make my dwelling among them and walk among them, and I will be their God, and they shall be my people."—"Do two walk together, unless they have agreed to meet?"

Rev. 4:8; Ps. 22:3; Ex. 3:5–6; Isa. 40:25; Isa. 43:3, 11;
1 Pet. 1:15–16; 1 Cor. 6:19; 2 Cor. 6:16; Amos 3:3

EVENING

But they urged him strongly, saying, "Stay with us."

"Behold, I stand at the door and knock. If anyone hears my voice and opens the door, I will come in to him and eat with him, and he with me."—Tell me, you whom my soul loves, where you pasture your flock, where you make it lie down at noon; for why should I be like one who veils herself beside the flocks of your companions?—I found him whom my soul loves. I held him, and would not let him go.

Let my beloved come to his garden, and eat its choicest fruits.—I came to my garden.—"I did not say to the offspring of Jacob, 'Seek me in vain.'"

"And behold, I am with you always, to the end of the age."—"I will never leave you nor forsake you."—"For where two or three are gathered in my name, there am I among them."—"The world will see me no more, but you will see me."

Luke 24:29; Rev. 3:20; Song 1:7; Song 3:4; Song 4:16; Song 5:1;
Isa. 45:19; Matt. 28:20; Heb. 13:5; Matt. 18:20; John 14:19

MORNING

And [Abraham] believed the Lord, and
he counted it to him as righteousness.

No unbelief made him waver concerning the promise of God, but he grew strong in his faith as he gave glory to God, fully convinced that God was able to do what he had promised. That is why his faith was "counted to him as righteousness." But the words "it was counted to him" were not written for his sake alone, but for ours also. It will be counted to us who believe in him who raised from the dead Jesus our Lord.

For the promise to Abraham and his offspring that he would be heir of the world did not come through the law but through the righteousness of faith.—"The righteous shall live by faith."— Let us hold fast the confession of our hope without wavering, for he who promised is faithful.—Our God is in the heavens; he does all that he pleases.—"For nothing will be impossible with God." . . . "And blessed is she who believed that there would be a fulfillment of what was spoken to her from the Lord."

Gen. 15:6; Rom. 4:20-24; Rom. 4:13; Rom. 1:17;
Heb. 10:23; Ps. 115:3; Luke 1:37, 45

EVENING

God . . . calls you into his own kingdom and glory.

"My kingdom is not of this world. If my kingdom were of this world, my servants would have been fighting. . . . But my kingdom is not from the world."—Waiting from that time until his enemies should be made a footstool for his feet.—"The kingdom of the world has become the kingdom of our Lord and of his Christ, and he shall reign forever and ever."—"And you have made them a kingdom and priests to our God, and they shall reign on the earth."—Then I saw thrones, and seated on them were those to whom the authority to judge was committed. . . . They came to life and reigned with Christ for a thousand years.—"Then the righteous will shine like the sun in the kingdom of their Father."—"Fear not, little flock, for it is your Father's good pleasure to give you the kingdom."

"And I assign to you, as my Father assigned to me, a kingdom, that you may eat and drink at my table in my kingdom and sit on thrones judging the twelve tribes of Israel."—"Your kingdom come."

1 Thess. 2:12; John 18:36; Heb. 10:13; Rev. 11:15; Rev. 5:10; Rev. 20:4;
Matt. 13:43; Luke 12:32; Luke 22:29-30; Matt. 6:10

MORNING

"I will never leave you nor forsake you."

So we can confidently say, "The Lord is my helper; I will not fear; what can man do to me?"

"Behold, I am with you and will keep you wherever you go, and will bring you back to this land. For I will not leave you until I have done what I have promised you."—"Be strong and courageous. Do not fear or be in dread of them, for it is the Lord your God who goes with you. He will not leave you or forsake you."

For Demas, in love with this present world has deserted me. . . . At my first defense no one came to stand by me, but all deserted me. May it not be charged against them! But the Lord stood by me and strengthened me.—For my father and my mother have forsaken me, but the Lord will take me in.

"And behold, I am with you always, to the end of the age."—"[I am] the living one. I died, and behold I am alive forevermore."— "I will not leave you as orphans; I will come to you."—"My peace I give to you. "

Heb. 13:5; Heb. 13:6; Gen. 28:15; Deut. 31:6; 2 Tim. 4:10, 16–17;
Ps. 27:10; Matt. 28:20; Rev. 1:18; John 14:18; John 14:27

EVENING

"Master, we toiled all night and took nothing!
But at your word I will let down the nets."

"All authority in heaven and on earth has been given to me. Go therefore and make disciples of all nations, baptizing them in the name of the Father and of the Son and of the Holy Spirit. . . . And behold, I am with you always, to the end of the age."

"The kingdom of heaven is like a net that was thrown into the sea."

For if I preach the gospel, that gives me no ground for boasting. For necessity is laid upon me. Woe to me if I do not preach the gospel! . . . I have become all things to all people, that by all means I might save some.

And let us not grow weary of doing good, for in due season we will reap, if we do not give up.—"So shall my word be that goes out from my mouth; it shall not return to me empty, but it shall accomplish that which I purpose."—So neither he who plants nor he who waters is anything, but only God who gives the growth.

Luke 5:5; Matt. 28:18–20; Matt. 13:47; 1 Cor. 9:16, 22;
Gal. 6:9; Isa. 55:11; 1 Cor. 3:7

MORNING

"[The kingdom of heaven] will be like a man going on a journey, who called his servants and entrusted to them his property . . . to each according to his ability."

Do you not know that if you present yourselves to anyone as obedient slaves, you are slaves of the one whom you obey?

All these are empowered by one and the same Spirit, who apportions to each one individually as he wills. . . . To each is given the manifestation of the Spirit for the common good.—As each has received a gift, use it to serve one another, as good stewards of God's varied grace.—Moreover, it is required of stewards that they be found faithful.—"Everyone to whom much was given, of him much will be required, and from him to whom they entrusted much, they will demand the more."

Who is sufficient for these things?—I can do all things through him who strengthens me.

Matt. 25:14–15; Rom. 6:16; 1 Cor. 12:11, 7; 1 Pet. 4:10;
1 Cor. 4:2; Luke 12:48; 2 Cor. 2:16; Phil. 4:13

EVENING

Contribute to the needs of the saints.

And David said, "Is there still anyone left of the house of Saul, that I may show him kindness for Jonathan's sake?"

"Come, you who are blessed by my Father, inherit the kingdom prepared for you from the foundation of the world. For I was hungry and you gave me food, I was thirsty and you gave me drink, I was a stranger and you welcomed me, I was naked and you clothed me, I was sick and you visited me, I was in prison and you came to me. . . . Truly, I say to you, as you did it to one of the least of these my brothers, you did it to me."—"And whoever gives one of these little ones even a cup of cold water because he is a disciple, truly, I say to you, he will by no means lose his reward."

Do not neglect to do good and to share what you have, for such sacrifices are pleasing to God.—For God is not unjust so as to overlook your work and the love that you have shown for his name in serving the saints, as you still do.

Rom. 12:13; 2 Sam. 9:1; Matt. 25:34–36, 40; Matt. 10:42; Heb. 13:16; Heb. 6:10

MORNING

One who sows righteousness gets a sure reward.

"Now after a long time the master of those servants came and settled accounts with them. And he who had received the five talents came forward, bringing five talents more, saying, 'Master, you delivered to me five talents; here I have made five talents more.' His master said to him, 'Well done, good and faithful servant. You have been faithful over a little; I will set you over much. Enter into the joy of your master.'"

For we must all appear before the judgment seat of Christ, so that each one may receive what is due for what he has done in the body, whether good or evil.

I have fought the good fight, I have finished the race, I have kept the faith. Henceforth there is laid up for me the crown of righteousness, which the Lord, the righteous judge, will award to me on that Day, and not only to me but also to all who have loved his appearing.

"I am coming soon. Hold fast what you have, so that no one may seize your crown."

Prov. 11:18; Matt. 25:19–21; 2 Cor. 5:10; 2 Tim. 4:7–8; Rev. 3:11

EVENING

God is faithful.

"God is not man, that he should lie, or a son of man, that he should change his mind. Has he said, and will he not do it? Or has he spoken, and will he not fulfill it?"—"The Lord has sworn and will not change his mind."

So when God desired to show more convincingly to the heirs of the promise the unchangeable character of his purpose, he guaranteed it with an oath, so that by two unchangeable things, in which it is impossible for God to lie, we who have fled for refuge might have strong encouragement to hold fast to the hope set before us.—Therefore let those who suffer according to God's will entrust their souls to a faithful Creator while doing good.

I know whom I have believed, and I am convinced that he is able to guard until that Day what has been entrusted to me.—He who calls you is faithful; he will surely do it.—For all the promises of God find their Yes in him. That is why it is through him that we utter our Amen to God for his glory.

1 Cor. 10:13; Num. 23:19; Heb. 7:21; Heb. 6:17–18;
1 Pet. 4:19; 2 Tim. 1:12; 1 Thess. 5:24; 2 Cor. 1:20

MORNING

"Be strong and courageous."

The Lord is my light and my salvation; whom shall I fear? The Lord is the stronghold of my life; of whom shall I be afraid?—He gives power to the faint, and to him who has no might he increases strength. Even youths shall faint and be weary, and young men shall fall exhausted; but they who wait for the Lord shall renew their strength; they shall mount up with wings like eagles; they shall run and not be weary; they shall walk and not faint.—My flesh and my heart may fail, but God is the strength of my heart and my portion forever.

If God is for us, who can be against us?—The Lord is on my side; I will not fear. What can man do to me?—Through you we push down our foes; through your name we tread down those who rise up against us.—We are more than conquerors through him who loved us.

"Arise and work! The Lord be with you!"

Josh. 1:18; Ps. 27:1; Isa. 40:29–31; Ps. 73:26; Rom. 8:31;
Ps. 118:6; Ps. 44:5; Rom. 8:37; 1 Chron. 22:16

EVENING

"Our friend Lazarus has fallen asleep."

But we do not want you to be uninformed, brothers, about those who are asleep, that you may not grieve as others do who have no hope. For since we believe that Jesus died and rose again, even so, through Jesus, God will bring with him those who have fallen asleep.

For if the dead are not raised, not even Christ has been raised. And if Christ has not been raised, your faith is futile and you are still in your sins. Then those also who have fallen asleep in Christ have perished. . . . But in fact Christ has been raised from the dead, the firstfruits of those who have fallen asleep.

When all the nation had finished passing over the Jordan, the Lord said to Joshua . . . "Take twelve stones from here out of the midst of the Jordan, from the very place where the priests' feet stood firmly. . . . So these stones shall be to the people of Israel a memorial forever."—"This Jesus God raised up, and of that we all are witnesses."—Chosen by God as witnesses, who ate and drank with him after he rose from the dead.

John 11:11; 1 Thess. 4:13–14; 1 Cor. 15:16–18, 20;
Josh. 4:1, 3, 7; Acts 2:32; Acts 10:41

MORNING

"Come, you who are blessed by my Father, inherit the kingdom prepared for you from the foundation of the world."

"Fear not, little flock, for it is your Father's good pleasure to give you the kingdom."—Has not God chosen those who are poor in the world to be rich in faith and heirs of the kingdom, which he has promised to those who love him?—Heirs of God and fellow heirs with Christ, provided we suffer with him in order that we may also be glorified with him.—"For the Father himself loves you, because you have loved me."—Therefore God is not ashamed to be called their God, for he has prepared for them a city.

"The one who conquers will have this heritage, and I will be his God and he will be my son."—Henceforth there is laid up for me the crown of righteousness, which the Lord, the righteous judge, will award to me on that Day, and not only to me but also to all who have loved his appearing.—He who began a good work in you will bring it to completion at the day of Jesus Christ.

Matt. 25:34; Luke 12:32; James 2:5; Rom. 8:17; John 16:27;
Heb. 11:16; Rev. 21:7; 2 Tim. 4:8; Phil. 1:6

EVENING

For riches do not last forever; and does a crown endure to all generations?

Surely a man goes about as a shadow! Surely for nothing they are in turmoil; man heaps up wealth and does not know who will gather!—Set your minds on things that are above, not on things that are on earth.—"Do not lay up for yourselves treasures on earth, where moth and rust destroy and where thieves break in and steal, but lay up for yourselves treasures in heaven. . . . For where your treasure is, there your heart will be also."

They do it to receive a perishable wreath, but we an imperishable.—We look not to the things that are seen but to the things that are unseen.—One who sows righteousness gets a sure reward.—Henceforth there is laid up for me the crown of righteousness, which the Lord, the righteous judge, will award to me on that Day, and not only to me but also to all who have loved his appearing.—The unfading crown of glory.

Prov. 27:24; Ps. 39:6; Col. 3:2; Matt. 6:19–21; 1 Cor. 9:25;
2 Cor. 4:18; Prov. 11:18; 2 Tim. 4:8; 1 Pet. 5:4

MORNING

And Isaac went out to meditate in the field toward evening.

Let the words of my mouth and the meditation of my heart be acceptable in your sight, O Lord, my rock and my redeemer.

When I look at your heavens, the work of your fingers, the moon and the stars, which you have set in place, what is man that you are mindful of him, and the son of man that you care for him?—Great are the works of the Lord, studied by all who delight in them.

Blessed is the man who walks not in the counsel of the wicked, nor stands in the way of sinners, nor sits in the seat of scoffers; but his delight is in the law of the Lord, and on his law he meditates day and night.—"This Book of the Law shall not depart from your mouth, but you shall meditate on it day and night."—My soul will be satisfied as with fat and rich food, and my mouth will praise you with joyful lips, when I remember you upon my bed, and meditate on you in the watches of the night.

Gen. 24:63; Ps. 19:14; Ps. 8:3–4; Ps. 111:2; Ps. 1:1–2; Josh. 1:8; Ps. 63:5–6

EVENING

How long, O Lord? Will you forget me forever?
How long will you hide your face from me?

Every good gift and every perfect gift is from above, coming down from the Father of lights with whom there is no variation or shadow due to change.—But Zion said, "The Lord has forsaken me; my Lord has forgotten me." "Can a woman forget her nursing child, that she should have no compassion on the son of her womb? Even these may forget, yet I will not forget you."

O Israel, you will not be forgotten by me. I have blotted out your transgressions like a cloud and your sins like mist.

Now Jesus loved Martha and her sister and Lazarus. So, when he heard that Lazarus was ill, he stayed two days longer in the place where he was.—A . . . woman . . . was crying, "Have mercy on me, O Lord, Son of David . . ." But he did not answer her a word.

The tested genuineness of your faith—more precious than gold that perishes.

Ps. 13:1; James 1:17; Isa. 49:14–15; Isa. 44:21–22;
John 11:5–6; Matt. 15:22–23; 1 Pet. 1:7

MORNING

And my God will supply every need of yours according to his riches in glory in Christ Jesus.

"But seek first the kingdom of God and his righteousness, and all these things will be added to you."—He who did not spare his own Son but gave him up for us all, how will he not also with him graciously give us all things?—For all things are yours, whether Paul or Apollos or Cephas or the world or life or death or the present or the future—all are yours, and you are Christ's, and Christ is God's.—As having nothing, yet possessing everything.

The Lord is my shepherd; I shall not want.—For the Lord God is a sun and shield; the Lord bestows favor and honor. No good thing does he withhold from those who walk uprightly.—God . . . richly provides us with everything to enjoy.—And God is able to make all grace abound to you, so that having all sufficiency in all things at all times, you may abound in every good work.

Phil. 4:19; Matt. 6:33; Rom. 8:32; 1 Cor. 3:21-23; 2 Cor. 6:10;
Ps. 23:1; Ps. 84:11; 1 Tim. 6:17; 2 Cor. 9:8

EVENING

What fellowship has light with darkness?

"And this is the judgment: the light has come into the world, and people loved the darkness rather than the light because their works were evil."—For you are all children of light, children of the day. We are not of the night or of the darkness.

The darkness has blinded his eyes.—Your word is a lamp to my feet and a light to my path.

The dark places of the land are full of the habitations of violence.—Love is from God, and whoever loves has been born of God and knows God. Anyone who does not love does not know God, because God is love.

The way of the wicked is like deep darkness; they do not know over what they stumble. But the path of the righteous is like the light of dawn, which shines brighter and brighter until full day.

"I have come into the world as light, so that whoever believes in me may not remain in darkness."—At one time you were darkness, but now you are light in the Lord. Walk as children of light.

2 Cor. 6:14; John 3:19; 1 Thess. 5:5; 1 John 2:11; Ps. 119:105;
Ps. 74:20; 1 John 4:7-8; Prov. 4:19, 18; John 12:46; Eph. 5:8

MORNING

But the fruit of the Spirit is . . . joy.

Joy in the Holy Spirit.—Joy that is inexpressible and filled with glory.

As sorrowful, yet always rejoicing.—In all our affliction, I am overflowing with joy.—We rejoice in our sufferings.

Jesus, the founder and perfecter of our faith . . . for the joy that was set before him endured the cross, despising the shame.—"These things I have spoken to you, that my joy may be in you, and that your joy may be full."—For as we share abundantly in Christ's sufferings, so through Christ we share abundantly in comfort too.—Rejoice in the Lord always; again I will say, rejoice.—"The joy of the Lord is your strength."

In your presence there is fullness of joy; at your right hand are pleasures forevermore.—"For the Lamb in the midst of the throne will be their shepherd, and he will guide them to springs of living water, and God will wipe away every tear from their eyes."

Gal. 5:22; Rom. 14:17; 1 Pet. 1:8; 2 Cor. 6:10; 2 Cor. 7:4; Rom. 5:3;
Heb. 12:2; John 15:11; 2 Cor. 1:5; Phil. 4:4; Neh. 8:10; Ps. 16:11; Rev. 7:17

EVENING

The Lord Is Peace.

"Behold, a son shall be born to you who shall be a man of rest. I will give him rest from all his surrounding enemies. For his name shall be Solomon, and I will give peace and quiet to Israel in his days."

"Behold, something greater than Solomon is here."—For to us a child is born, to us a son is given; and the government shall be upon his shoulder, and his name shall be called Wonderful Counselor, Mighty God, Everlasting Father, Prince of Peace.—My people will abide in a peaceful habitation, in secure dwellings, and in quiet resting places. And it will hail when the forest falls down, and the city will be utterly laid low.

He himself is our peace.—And he shall be their peace. When the Assyrian comes into our land.

"They will make war on the Lamb, and the Lamb will conquer them, for he is Lord of lords and King of kings."

"Peace I leave with you; my peace I give to you."

Judg. 6:24; 1 Chron. 22:9; Matt. 12:42; Isa. 9:6; Isa. 32:18–19;
Eph. 2:14; Mic. 5:5; Rev. 17:14; John 14:27

MORNING

"If you are returning to the Lord with all your heart, then put away the foreign gods and the Ashtaroth from among you and direct your heart to the Lord and serve him only."

Little children, keep yourselves from idols.—"Therefore go out from their midst, and be separate from them, says the Lord, and touch no unclean thing; then I will welcome you, and I will be a father to you, and you shall be sons and daughters to me, says the Lord Almighty."—"You cannot serve God and money."

"You shall worship no other god, for the Lord, whose name is Jealous, is a jealous God."—"Serve him with a whole heart and with a willing mind, for the Lord searches all hearts and understands every plan and thought."

Behold, you delight in truth in the inward being, and you teach me wisdom in the secret heart.—"Man looks on the outward appearance, but the Lord looks on the heart."—Beloved, if our heart does not condemn us, we have confidence before God.

1 Sam. 7:3; 1 John 5:21; 2 Cor. 6:17–18; Matt. 6:24; Ex. 34:14;
1 Chron. 28:9; Ps. 51:6; 1 Sam. 16:7; 1 John 3:21

EVENING

"When the Son of Man comes, will he find faith on earth?"

He came to his own, and his own people did not receive him.—Now the Spirit expressly says that in later times some will depart from the faith.—Preach the word; be ready in season and out of season; reprove, rebuke, and exhort, with complete patience and teaching. For the time is coming when people will not endure sound teaching, but having itching ears they will accumulate for themselves teachers to suit their own passions, and will turn away from listening to the truth and wander off into myths.

"But concerning that day or that hour, no one knows, not even the angels in heaven, nor the Son, but only the Father. Be on guard, keep awake. For you do not know when the time will come."—"Blessed are those servants whom the master finds awake when he comes."—Waiting for our blessed hope, the appearing of the glory of our great God and Savior Jesus Christ.

Luke 18:8; John 1:11; 1 Tim. 4:1; 2 Tim. 4:2–4;
Mark 13:32–33; Luke 12:37; Titus 2:13

MORNING

But do not overlook this one fact, beloved, that with the Lord one day is as a thousand years, and a thousand years as one day. The Lord is not slow to fulfill his promise as some count slowness.

For my thoughts are not your thoughts, neither are your ways my ways, declares the Lord. For as the heavens are higher than the earth, so are my ways higher than your ways and my thoughts than your thoughts. "For as the rain and the snow come down from heaven and do not return there but water the earth . . . so shall my word be that goes out from my mouth; it shall not return to me empty, but it shall accomplish that which I purpose, and shall succeed in the thing for which I sent it."

For God has consigned all to disobedience, that he may have mercy on all. Oh, the depth of the riches and wisdom and knowledge of God! How unsearchable are his judgments and how inscrutable his ways!

2 Pet. 3:8–9; Isa. 55:8–11; Rom. 11:32–33

EVENING

"You were as a brand plucked out of the burning."

The sinners in Zion are afraid; trembling has seized the godless: "Who among us can dwell with the consuming fire? Who among us can dwell with everlasting burnings?"—Indeed, we felt that we had received the sentence of death. But that was to make us rely not on ourselves but on God who raises the dead. He delivered us from such a deadly peril, and he will deliver us. On him we have set our hope that he will deliver us again.—For the wages of sin is death, but the free gift of God is eternal life in Christ Jesus our Lord.

It is a fearful thing to fall into the hands of the living God.—Therefore, knowing the fear of the Lord, we persuade others.

Be ready in season and out of season.—Save others by snatching them out of the fire; to others show mercy with fear.

"Not by might, nor by power, but by my Spirit, says the Lord of hosts."—Who desires all people to be saved and to come to the knowledge of the truth.

Amos 4:11; Isa. 33:14; 2 Cor. 1:9–10; Rom. 6:23; Heb. 10:31; 2 Cor. 5:11; 2 Tim. 4:2; Jude 23; Zech. 4:6; 1 Tim. 2:4

MORNING

"Fear not, I am the first and the last."

For you have not come to what may be touched, a blazing fire and darkness and gloom and a tempest. . . . But you have come to Mount Zion . . . and to God, the judge of all, and to the spirits of the righteous made perfect, and to Jesus, the mediator of a new covenant.—Jesus, the founder and perfecter of our faith.—For we do not have a high priest who is unable to sympathize with our weaknesses, but one who in every respect has been tempted as we are, yet without sin. Let us then with confidence draw near to the throne of grace, that we may receive mercy and find grace to help in time of need.

Thus says the Lord, the King of Israel and his Redeemer, the Lord of hosts: "I am the first and I am the last; besides me there is no god."—Mighty God, Everlasting Father, Prince of Peace.

Are you not from everlasting, O Lord my God, my Holy One?—"For who is God, but the Lord? And who is a rock, except our God?"

Rev. 1:17; Heb. 12:18, 22–24; Heb. 12:2; Heb. 4:15–16;
Isa. 44:6; Isa. 9:6; Hab. 1:12; 2 Sam. 22:32

EVENING

Lead me to the rock that is higher than I.

Do not be anxious about anything, but in everything by prayer and supplication with thanksgiving let your requests be made known to God. And the peace of God, which surpasses all understanding, will guard your hearts and your minds in Christ Jesus.

When my spirit faints within me, you know my way!—"But he knows the way that I take; when he has tried me, I shall come out as gold."—Lord, you have been our dwelling place in all generations.—For you have been a stronghold to the poor, a stronghold to the needy in his distress, a shelter from the storm and a shade from the heat.

And who is a rock, except our God?—"They will never perish, and no one will snatch them out of my hand."—Uphold me according to your promise, that I may live, and let me not be put to shame in my hope!—We have this as a sure and steadfast anchor of the soul, a hope that enters into the inner place behind the curtain.

Ps. 61:2; Phil. 4:6–7; Ps. 142:3; Job 23:10; Ps. 90:1; Isa. 25:4;
Ps. 18:31; John 10:28; Ps. 119:116; Heb. 6:19

MORNING

"I will not let you go unless you bless me."

"Let them lay hold of my protection, let them make peace with me, let them make peace with me."

"O woman, great is your faith! Be it done for you as you desire."—"According to your faith be it done to you."—But let him ask in faith, with no doubting, for the one who doubts is like a wave of the sea that is driven and tossed by the wind. For that person must not suppose that he will receive anything from the Lord.

So they drew near to the village to which they were going. He acted as if he were going farther, but they urged him strongly, saying, "Stay with us . . ." . . . And he vanished from their sight. They said to each other, "Did not our hearts burn within us while he talked to us on the road, while he opened to us the Scriptures?"—"Now therefore, if I have found favor in your sight, please show me now your ways, that I may know you in order to find favor in your sight." "My presence will go with you, and I will give you rest."

Gen. 32:26; Isa. 27:5; Matt. 15:28; Matt. 9:29; James 1:6-7;
Luke 24:28-29, 31-32; Ex. 33:13-14

EVENING

Jesus, the founder and perfecter of our faith.

"I am the Alpha and the Omega," says the Lord God, "who is and who was and who is to come, the Almighty."—Who has performed and done this, calling the generations from the beginning? I, the Lord, the first, and with the last; I am he.

Now may the God of peace himself sanctify you completely, and may your whole spirit and soul and body be kept blameless at the coming of our Lord Jesus Christ. He who calls you is faithful; he will surely do it.—He who began a good work in you will bring it to completion at the day of Jesus Christ.—Are you so foolish? Having begun by the Spirit, are you now being perfected by the flesh?—The Lord will fulfill his purpose for me.

For it is God who works in you, both to will and to work for his good pleasure.

Heb. 12:2; Rev. 1:8; Isa. 41:4; 1 Thess. 5:23-24;
Phil. 1:6; Gal. 3:3; Ps. 138:8; Phil. 2:13

MORNING

He always lives to make intercession for them.

Who is to condemn? Christ Jesus is the one who died . . . , who indeed is interceding for us.—For Christ has entered, not into holy places made with hands, which are copies of the true things, but into heaven itself, now to appear in the presence of God on our behalf.—But if anyone does sin, we have an advocate with the Father, Jesus Christ the righteous.—There is one mediator between God and men, the man Christ Jesus.

Since then we have a great high priest who has passed through the heavens, Jesus, the Son of God, let us hold fast our confession. For we do not have a high priest who is unable to sympathize with our weaknesses, but one who in every respect has been tempted as we are, yet without sin. Let us then with confidence draw near to the throne of grace, that we may receive mercy and find grace to help in time of need.—For through him we both have access in one Spirit to the Father.

Heb. 7:25; Rom. 8:34; Heb. 9:24; 1 John 2:1; 1 Tim. 2:5; Heb. 4:14–16; Eph. 2:18

EVENING

And those who know your name put their trust in you.

"And this is the name by which he will be called: 'The Lord is our righteousness.'"—With the mighty deeds of the Lord God I will come; I will remind them of your righteousness, yours alone.

His name shall be called Wonderful Counselor.—I know, O Lord, that the way of man is not in himself, that it is not in man who walks to direct his steps.—Mighty God, Everlasting Father.—I know whom I have believed, and I am convinced that he is able to guard until that Day what has been entrusted to me.—Prince of Peace.—For he himself is our peace.—Therefore, since we have been justified by faith, we have peace with God through our Lord Jesus Christ.

The name of the Lord is a strong tower; the righteous man runs into it and is safe.—Woe to those who go down to Egypt for help.—"Like birds hovering, so the Lord of hosts will protect Jerusalem; he will protect and deliver it; he will spare and rescue it."

Ps. 9:10; Jer. 23:6; Ps. 71:16; Isa. 9:6; Jer. 10:23; Isa. 9:6; 2 Tim. 1:12;
Isa. 9:6; Eph. 2:14; Rom. 5:1; Prov. 18:10; Isa. 31:1; Isa. 31:5

MORNING

As sorrowful, yet always rejoicing; as poor, yet making many
rich; as having nothing, yet possessing everything.

We rejoice in hope of the glory of God. Not only that, but we rejoice in our sufferings.—I am filled with comfort. In all our affliction, I am overflowing with joy.—You believe in him and rejoice with joy that is inexpressible and filled with glory.

In a severe test of affliction, their abundance of joy and their extreme poverty have overflowed in a wealth of generosity on their part.—To me, though I am the very least of all the saints, this grace was given, to preach to the Gentiles the unsearchable riches of Christ, and to bring to light for everyone what is the plan of the mystery hidden for ages in God who created all things.—Has not God chosen those who are poor in the world to be rich in faith and heirs of the kingdom, which he has promised to those who love him?—And God is able to make all grace abound to you, so that having all sufficiency in all things at all times, you may abound in every good work.

2 Cor. 6:10; Rom. 5:2-3; 2 Cor. 7:4; 1 Pet. 1:8;
2 Cor. 8:2; Eph. 3:8-9; James 2:5; 2 Cor. 9:8

EVENING

The Lord sustains him on his sickbed; in his
illness you restore him to full health.

In all their affliction he was afflicted, and the angel of his presence saved them; in his love and in his pity he redeemed them; he lifted them up and carried them.—"Lord, he whom you love is ill."—"My grace is sufficient for you, for my power is made perfect in weakness." Therefore I will boast all the more gladly of my weaknesses, so that the power of Christ may rest upon me.—I can do all things through him who strengthens me.

So we do not lose heart. Though our outer self is wasting away, our inner self is being renewed day by day.—"In him we live and move and have our being."—He gives power to the faint, and to him who has no might he increases strength. Even youths shall faint and be weary, and young men shall fall exhausted; but they who wait for the Lord shall renew their strength.—"The eternal God is your dwelling place, and underneath are the everlasting arms."

Ps. 41:3; Isa. 63:9; John 11:3; 2 Cor. 12:9; Phil. 4:13;
2 Cor. 4:16; Acts 17:28; Isa. 40:29-31; Deut. 33:27

MORNING

In every way you were enriched in him.

For while we were still weak, at the right time Christ died for the ungodly.—He who did not spare his own Son but gave him up for us all, how will he not also with him graciously give us all things?

For in him the whole fullness of deity dwells bodily, and you have been filled in him, who is the head of all rule and authority.

"Abide in me, and I in you. As the branch cannot bear fruit by itself, unless it abides in the vine, neither can you, unless you abide in me. I am the vine; you are the branches. Whoever abides in me and I in him, he it is that bears much fruit, for apart from me you can do nothing."—For I have the desire to do what is right, but not the ability to carry it out.—But grace was given to each one of us according to the measure of Christ's gift.

"If you abide in me, and my words abide in you, ask whatever you wish, and it will be done for you."—Let the word of Christ dwell in you richly . . . in all wisdom.

1 Cor. 1:5; Rom. 5:6; Rom. 8:32; Col. 2:9–10; John 15:4–5;
Rom. 7:18; Eph. 4:7; John 15:7; Col. 3:16

EVENING

They will see his face.

"Please show me your glory." . . . "But," he said, "you cannot see my face, for man shall not see me and live."—No one has ever seen God; the only God, who is at the Father's side, he has made him known.

Every eye will see him, even those who pierced him, and all tribes of the earth will wail on account of him.—"I see him, but not now; I behold him, but not near."

"For I know that my Redeemer lives, and at the last he will stand upon the earth. And after my skin has been thus destroyed, yet in my flesh I shall see God."—I shall behold your face in righteousness; when I awake, I shall be satisfied with your likeness.—We shall be like him, because we shall see him as he is.—For the Lord himself will descend from heaven. . . . And the dead in Christ will rise first. Then we who are alive, who are left, will be caught up together with them in the clouds to meet the Lord in the air, and so we will always be with the Lord.

Rev. 22:4; Ex. 33:18, 20; John 1:18; Rev. 1:7; Num. 24:17;
Job 19:25—26; Ps. 17:15; 1 John 3:2; 1 Thess. 4:16—17

MORNING

"Fear not, for I have redeemed you."

"Fear not, for you will not be ashamed; be not confounded, for you will not be disgraced; for you will forget the shame of your youth, and the reproach of your widowhood you will remember no more. For your Maker is your husband, the Lord of hosts is his name; and the Holy One of Israel is your Redeemer."—I have blotted out your transgressions like a cloud and your sins like mist; return to me, for I have redeemed you.—But with the precious blood of Christ, like that of a lamb without blemish or spot.

"Their Redeemer is strong; the Lord of hosts is his name. He will surely plead their cause."—"My Father, who has given them to me, is greater than all, and no one is able to snatch them out of the Father's hand."

Grace to you and peace from God our Father and the Lord Jesus Christ, who gave himself for our sins to deliver us from the present evil age, according to the will of our God and Father, to whom be the glory forever and ever. Amen.

Isa. 43:1; Isa. 54:4–5; Isa. 44:22; 1 Pet. 1:19; Jer. 50:34;
John 10:29; Gal. 1:3–5

EVENING

I will recount the steadfast love of the Lord, the praises of the Lord, according to all that the Lord has granted us.

He drew me up from the pit of destruction, out of the miry bog, and set my feet upon a rock, making my steps secure.—The Son of God . . . loved me and gave himself for me.—He who did not spare his own Son but gave him up for us all, how will he not also with him graciously give us all things?—But God shows his love for us in that while we were still sinners, Christ died for us.

Who has also put his seal on us and given us his Spirit in our hearts as a guarantee.—Who is the guarantee of our inheritance until we acquire possession of it, to the praise of his glory.

But God, being rich in mercy, because of the great love with which he loved us, even when we were dead in our trespasses, made us alive together with Christ—by grace you have been saved—and raised us up with him and seated us with him in the heavenly places in Christ Jesus.

Isa. 63:7; Ps. 40:2; Gal. 2:20; Rom. 8:32; Rom. 5:8;
2 Cor. 1:22; Eph. 1:14; Eph. 2:4–6

MORNING

I am very dark, but lovely.

Behold, I was brought forth in iniquity, and in sin did my mother conceive me.—"And your renown went forth among the nations because of your beauty, for it was perfect through the splendor that I had bestowed on you, declares the Lord God."—"I am a sinful man, O Lord."—Behold, you are beautiful, my love, behold, you are beautiful!—"I despise myself, and repent in dust and ashes."—You are altogether beautiful, my love; there is no flaw in you."—When I want to do right, evil lies close at hand.—"Take heart, my son; your sins are forgiven."—For I know that nothing good dwells in me, that is, in my flesh.—And you have been filled in him.—Mature in Christ.

You were washed, you were sanctified, you were justified in the name of the Lord Jesus Christ and by the Spirit of our God.—That you may proclaim the excellencies of him who called you out of darkness into his marvelous light.

Song 1:5; Ps. 51:5; Ezek. 16:14; Luke 5:8; Song 4:1; Job 42:6; Song 4:7;
Rom. 7:21; Matt. 9:2; Rom. 7:18; Col. 2:10; Col. 1:28; 1 Cor. 6:11; 1 Pet. 2:9

EVENING

Indeed, all who desire to live a godly life in Christ Jesus will be persecuted.

"For I have come to set a man against his father, and a daughter against her mother, and a daughter-in-law against her mother-in-law. And a person's enemies will be those of his own household."—Whoever wishes to be a friend of the world makes himself an enemy of God.—Do not love the world or the things in the world. If anyone loves the world, the love of the Father is not in him. For all that is in the world—the desires of the flesh and the desires of the eyes and pride of life—is not from the Father but is from the world.—"If the world hates you, know that it has hated me before it hated you. If you were of the world, the world would love you as its own; but because you are not of the world, but I chose you out of the world, therefore the world hates you. . . . 'A servant is not greater than his master.'"—"I have given them your word, and the world has hated them because they are not of the world, just as I am not of the world."

2 Tim. 3:12; Matt. 10:35–36; James 4:4;
1 John 2:15–16; John 15:18–20; John 17:14

MORNING

When words are many, transgression is not lacking,
but whoever restrains his lips is prudent.

Know this, my beloved brothers: let every person be quick to hear, slow to speak, slow to anger.—Whoever is slow to anger is better than the mighty, and he who rules his spirit than he who takes a city.—If anyone does not stumble in what he says, he is a perfect man, able also to bridle his whole body.—"By your words you will be justified, and by your words you will be condemned."—Set a guard, O Lord, over my mouth; keep watch over the door of my lips!—Christ also suffered for you, leaving you an example, so that you might follow in his steps. He committed no sin, neither was deceit found in his mouth. When he was reviled, he did not revile in return; when he suffered, he did not threaten, but continued entrusting himself to him who judges justly.—Consider him who endured from sinners such hostility against himself, so that you may not grow weary or fainthearted.

And in their mouth no lie was found, for they are blameless.

Prov. 10:19; James 1:19; Prov. 16:32; James 3:2; Matt. 12:37;
Ps. 141:3; 1 Pet. 2:21–23; Heb. 12:3; Rev. 14:5

EVENING

Teach me your way, O Lord.

I will instruct you and teach you in the way you should go; I will counsel you with my eye upon you.—Good and upright is the Lord; therefore he instructs sinners in the way. He leads the humble in what is right, and teaches the humble his way.

"I am the door. If anyone enters by me, he will be saved and will go in and out and find pasture."

Jesus said to him, "I am the way, and the truth, and the life. No one comes to the Father except through me."— Therefore, brothers, since we have confidence to enter the holy places by the blood of Jesus, by the new and living way that he opened for us through the curtain, that is, through his flesh, and since we have a great priest over the house of God, let us draw near with a true heart in full assurance of faith.

"Let us know; let us press on to know the Lord."—All the paths of the Lord are steadfast love and faithfulness, for those who keep his covenant and his testimonies.

Ps. 27:11; Ps. 32:8; Ps. 25:8–9; John 10:9; John 14:6;
Heb. 10:19–22; Hos. 6:3; Ps. 25:10

MORNING

For God has done what the law, weakened by the flesh,
could not do. By sending his own Son in the likeness of sinful
flesh and for sin, he condemned sin in the flesh.

For since the law has but a shadow of the good things to come instead of the true form of these realities, it can never, by the same sacrifices that are continually offered every year, make perfect those who draw near. Otherwise, would they not have ceased to be offered?—"By him everyone who believes is freed from everything from which you could not be freed by the law of Moses."

Since therefore the children share in flesh and blood, he himself likewise partook of the same things, that through death he might destroy the one who has the power of death, that is, the devil, and deliver all those who through fear of death were subject to lifelong slavery. For surely it is not angels that he helps, but he helps the offspring of Abraham. Therefore he had to be made like his brothers in every respect.

Rom. 8:3; Heb. 10:1–2; Acts 13:39; Heb. 2:14–17

EVENING

All have sinned and fall short of the glory of God.

"None is righteous, no, not one; . . . no one does good, not even one."—Surely there is not a righteous man on earth who does good and never sins.—"How can he who is born of woman be pure?"

Therefore, while the promise of entering his rest still stands, let us fear lest any of you should seem to have failed to reach it.

For I know my transgressions, and my sin is ever before me. . . . Behold, I was brought forth in iniquity, and in sin did my mother conceive me.

"The Lord also has put away your sin; you shall not die."—Those whom he justified he also glorified.—And we all, with unveiled face, beholding the glory of the Lord, are being transformed into the same image from one degree of glory to another. For this comes from the Lord who is the Spirit.—If indeed you continue in the faith, stable and steadfast, not shifting from the hope of the gospel.

Walk in a manner worthy of God, who calls you into his own kingdom and glory.

Rom. 3:23; Rom. 3:10, 12; Eccles. 7:20; Job 25:4; Heb. 4:1; Ps. 51:3,
5; 2 Sam. 12:13; Rom. 8:30; 2 Cor. 3:18; Col. 1:23; 1 Thess. 2:12

MORNING

Honor the Lord with your wealth and with the firstfruits of all your produce.

Whoever sows sparingly will also reap sparingly, and whoever sows bountifully will also reap bountifully.—On the first day of every week, each of you is to put something aside and store it up, as he may prosper.

For God is not unjust so as to overlook your work and the love that you have shown for his name in serving the saints, as you still do.

I appeal to you therefore, brothers, by the mercies of God, to present your bodies as a living sacrifice, holy and acceptable to God, which is your spiritual worship.—For the love of Christ controls us, because we have concluded this: that one has died for all, therefore all have died; and he died for all, that those who live might no longer live for themselves but for him who for their sake died and was raised.—So, whether you eat or drink, or whatever you do, do all to the glory of God.

Prov. 3:9; 2 Cor. 9:6; 1 Cor. 16:2; Heb. 6:10; Rom. 12:1; 2 Cor. 5:14–15; 1 Cor. 10:31

EVENING

There will be no night there.

But the Lord will be your everlasting light, and your God will be your glory.

And the city has no need of sun or moon to shine on it, for the glory of God gives it light, and its lamp is the Lamb.—They will need no light of lamp or sun, for the Lord God will be their light.

But you are a chosen race, a royal priesthood, a holy nation, a people for his own possession, that you may proclaim the excellencies of him who called you out of darkness into his marvelous light.—Giving thanks to the Father, who has qualified you to share in the inheritance of the saints in light. He has delivered us from the domain of darkness and transferred us to the kingdom of his beloved Son.—At one time you were darkness, but now you are light in the Lord. Walk as children of light.

We are not of the night or of the darkness.

But the path of the righteous is like the light of dawn, which shines brighter and brighter until full day.

Rev. 21:25; Isa. 60:19; Rev. 21:23; Rev. 22:5; 1 Pet. 2:9;
Col. 1:12–13; Eph. 5:8; 1 Thess. 5:5; Prov. 4:18

MORNING

My soul will be satisfied as with fat and rich food, and my mouth will praise you with joyful lips, when I remember you upon my bed, and meditate on you in the watches of the night.

How precious to me are your thoughts, O God! How vast is the sum of them! If I would count them, they are more than the sand. I awake, and I am still with you.—How sweet are your words to my taste, sweeter than honey to my mouth!—Your love is better than wine.

Whom have I in heaven but you? And there is nothing on earth that I desire besides you.—You are the most handsome of the sons of men; grace is poured upon your lips; therefore God has blessed you forever.

As an apple tree among the trees of the forest, so is my beloved among the young men. With great delight I sat in his shadow, and his fruit was sweet to my taste. He brought me to the banqueting house, and his banner over me was love.—His appearance is like Lebanon, choice as the cedars. His mouth is most sweet, and he is altogether desirable. This is my beloved and this is my friend.

Ps. 63:5–6; Ps. 139:17–18; Ps. 119:103; Song 1:2; Ps. 73:25;
Ps. 45:2; Song 2:3–4; Song 5:15–16

EVENING

Restore to me the joy of your salvation.

I have seen his ways, but I will heal him; I will lead him and restore comfort to him and his mourners.—"Come now, let us reason together, says the Lord: though your sins are like scarlet, they shall be as white as snow; though they are red like crimson, they shall become like wool."—"Return, O faithless sons; I will heal your faithlessness." "Behold, we come to you, for you are the Lord our God."—Let me hear what God the Lord will speak, for he will speak peace to his people, to his saints; but let them not turn back to folly.

Bless the Lord, O my soul, and forget not all his benefits, who forgives all your iniquity, who heals all your diseases.—He restores my soul.—"I will give thanks to you, O Lord, for though you were angry with me, your anger turned away, that you might comfort me."

Hold me up, that I may be safe.—"I, I am he who blots out your transgressions for my own sake, and I will not remember your sins."

Ps. 51:12; Isa. 57:18; Isa. 1:18; Jer. 3:22; Ps. 85:8; Ps. 103:2–3;
Ps. 23:3; Isa. 12:1; Ps. 119:117; Isa. 43:25

MORNING

"Their Redeemer is strong."

For I know how many are your transgressions and how great are your sins.—"I have granted help to one who is mighty."—"Lord your Savior, and your Redeemer, the Mighty One of Jacob."—"Mighty to save."—Able to keep you from stumbling.—Where sin increased, grace abounded all the more.

"Whoever believes in him is not condemned, but whoever does not believe is condemned already, because he has not believed in the name of the only Son of God."—He is able to save to the uttermost those who draw near to God through him.

"Is my hand shortened, that it cannot redeem?"—Who shall separate us from the love of Christ? . . . For I am sure that neither death nor life, nor angels nor rulers, nor things present nor things to come, nor powers, nor height nor depth, nor anything else in all creation, will be able to separate us from the love of God in Christ Jesus our Lord.

Jer. 50:34; Amos 5:12; Ps. 89:19; Isa. 49:26; Isa. 63:1; Jude 24;
Rom. 5:20; John 3:18; Heb. 7:25; Isa. 50:2; Rom. 8:35, 38–39

EVENING

"And do you seek great things for yourself? Seek them not."

"Take my yoke upon you, and learn from me, for I am gentle and lowly in heart, and you will find rest for your souls."—Have this mind among yourselves, which is yours in Christ Jesus, who, though he was in the form of God, did not count equality with God a thing to be grasped, but emptied himself, by taking the form of a servant, being born in the likeness of men. And being found in human form, he humbled himself by becoming obedient to the point of death, even death on a cross.

"And whoever does not take his cross and follow me is not worthy of me."—Christ . . . suffered for you, leaving you an example, so that you might follow in his steps.

But godliness with contentment is great gain, for we brought nothing into the world, and we cannot take anything out of the world. But if we have food and clothing, with these we will be content.—I have learned in whatever situation I am to be content.

Jer. 45:5; Matt. 11:29; Phil. 2:5–8; Matt. 11:38; 1 Pet. 2:21; 1 Tim. 6:6–8; Phil. 4:11

MORNING

I had said in my alarm, "I am cut off from your sight." But you heard the voice of my pleas for mercy when I cried to you for help.

I sink in deep mire, where there is no foothold; I have come into deep waters, and the flood sweeps over me.—"Water closed over my head; I said, 'I am lost.' I called on your name, O Lord, from the depths of the pit; you heard my plea, 'Do not close your ear to my cry for help!' You came near when I called on you; you said, 'Do not fear!'"

"Will the Lord spurn forever, and never again be favorable? Has his steadfast love forever ceased? Are his promises at an end for all time? Has God forgotten to be gracious? Has he in anger shut up his compassion?" Then I said, "I will appeal to this, to the years of the right hand of the Most High." I will remember the deeds of the Lord; yes, I will remember your wonders of old.—I believe that I shall look upon the goodness of the Lord in the land of the living!

Ps. 31:22; Ps. 69:2; Lam. 3:54–57; Ps. 77:7–11; Ps. 27:13

EVENING

"When he calls to me, I will answer him; I will be with him in trouble; I will rescue him."

Jabez called upon the God of Israel, saying, "Oh that you would bless me and enlarge my border, and that your hand might be with me, and that you would keep me from harm so that it might not bring me pain!" And God granted what he asked.—"Ask what I shall give you." And Solomon said to God, . . . "Give me now wisdom and knowledge to go out and come in before this people."—And God gave Solomon wisdom and understanding beyond measure, and breadth of mind like the sand on the seashore.

And Asa cried to the Lord his God, "O Lord, there is none like you to help, between the mighty and the weak. . . . O Lord, you are our God; let not man prevail against you." So the Lord defeated the Ethiopians before Asa.

O you who hear prayer, to you shall all flesh come.

Ps. 91:15; 1 Chron. 4:10; 2 Chron. 1:7–8, 10;
1 Kings 4:29; 2 Chron. 14:11–12; Ps. 65:2

MORNING

"The one who offers thanksgiving as his sacrifice glorifies me."

Let the word of Christ dwell in you richly, teaching and admonishing one another in all wisdom, singing psalms and hymns and spiritual songs, with thankfulness in your hearts to God. And whatever you do, in word or deed, do everything in the name of the Lord Jesus, giving thanks to God the Father through him.— Glorify God in your body.

But you are a . . . a royal priesthood . . . that you may proclaim the excellencies of him who called you out of darkness into his marvelous light.—You yourselves like living stones are being built up as a spiritual house, to be a holy priesthood, to offer spiritual sacrifices acceptable to God through Jesus Christ.—Through him then let us continually offer up a sacrifice of praise to God, that is, the fruit of lips that acknowledge his name.

My soul makes its boast in the Lord; let the humble hear and be glad. Oh, magnify the Lord with me, and let us exalt his name together!

Ps. 50:23; Col. 3:16–17; 1 Cor. 6:20; 1 Pet. 2:9; 1 Pet. 2:5; Heb. 13:15; Ps. 34:2–3

EVENING

Draw me after you; let us run.

"I have loved you with an everlasting love; therefore I have continued my faithfulness to you."—I led them with cords of kindness, with the bands of love.—"And I, when I am lifted up from the earth, will draw all people to myself."—"Behold, the Lamb of God!"—"And as Moses lifted up the serpent in the wilderness, so must the Son of Man be lifted up, that whoever believes in him may have eternal life."

Whom have I in heaven but you? And there is nothing on earth that I desire besides you.—We love because he first loved us.

My beloved speaks and says to me: "Arise, my love, my beautiful one, and come away, for behold, the winter is past; the rain is over and gone. The flowers appear on the earth, the time of singing has come, and the voice of the turtledove is heard in our land. The fig tree ripens its figs, and the vines are in blossom; they give forth fragrance. Arise, my love, my beautiful one, and come away."

Song 1:4; Jer. 31:3; Hos. 11:4; John 12:32; John 1:36;
John 3:14–15; Ps. 73:25; 1 John 4:19; Song 2:10–13

MORNING

"I will raise up for them a prophet like you from among their brothers."

"[Moses] stood between the Lord and you at that time, to declare to you the word of the Lord. For you were afraid."—There is one God, and there is one mediator between God and men, the man Christ Jesus.

Now the man Moses was very meek, more than all people who were on the face of the earth.—"Take my yoke upon you, and learn from me, for I am gentle and lowly in heart, and you will find rest for your souls."—Have this mind among yourselves, which is yours in Christ Jesus, who, though he was in the form of God, did not count equality with God a thing to be grasped, but emptied himself, by taking the form of a servant, being born in the likeness of men.

Now Moses was faithful in all God's house as a servant, to testify to the things that were to be spoken later, but Christ is faithful over God's house as a son. And we are his house if indeed we hold fast our confidence and our boasting in our hope.

Deut. 18:18; Deut. 5:5; 1 Tim. 2:5; Num. 12:3; Matt. 11:29; Phil. 2:5-7; Heb. 3:5-6

EVENING

Eternal comfort.

"I will remember my covenant with you in the days of your youth, and I will establish for you an everlasting covenant."

By a single offering he has perfected for all time those who are being sanctified.— Consequently, he is able to save to the uttermost those who draw near to God through him, since he always lives to make intercession for them.—I know whom I have believed, and I am convinced that he is able to guard until that Day what has been entrusted to me.—The gifts and the calling of God are irrevocable.—Who shall separate us from the love of Christ?—"For the Lamb in the midst of the throne will be their shepherd, and he will guide them to springs of living water, and God will wipe away every tear from their eyes."—So we will always be with the Lord. Therefore encourage one another with these words.—This is no place to rest.—For here we have no lasting city, but we seek the city that is to come.

2 Thess. 2:16; Ezek. 16:60; Heb. 10:14; Heb. 7:25; 2 Tim. 1:12; Rom. 11:29; Rom. 8:35; Rev. 7:17; 1 Thess. 4:17-18; Mic. 2:10; Heb. 13:14

MORNING

"Truly, truly, I say to you, I am the door of the sheep."

And behold, the curtain of the temple was torn in two, from top to bottom. And the earth shook, and the rocks were split.—For Christ also suffered once for sins, the righteous for the unrighteous, that he might bring us to God.—By this the Holy Spirit indicates that the way into the holy places is not yet opened as long as the first section is still standing.

"I am the door. If anyone enters by me, he will be saved and will go in and out and find pasture."

"No one comes to the Father except through me."—For through him we . . . have access in one Spirit to the Father. So then you are no longer strangers and aliens, but you are fellow citizens with the saints and members of the household of God.—Therefore, brothers, since we have confidence to enter the holy places by the blood of Jesus, by the new and living way that he opened for us through the curtain, that is, through his flesh . . . —We have peace with God through our Lord Jesus Christ. Through him we have also obtained access by faith into this grace in which we stand, and we rejoice in hope of the glory of God.

John 10:7; Matt. 27:51; 1 Pet. 3:18; Heb. 9:8; John 10:9;
John 14:6; Eph. 2:18–19; Heb. 10:19–20; Rom. 5:1–2

EVENING

There is in my heart as it were a burning fire shut up in my bones, and I am weary with holding it in, and I cannot.

Necessity is laid upon me. Woe to me if I do not preach the gospel! . . . What then is my reward? That in my preaching I may present the gospel free of charge, so as not to make full use of my right in the gospel.—So they called them and charged them not to speak or teach at all in the name of Jesus. But Peter and John answered them, . . . "We cannot but speak of what we have seen and heard."—For the love of Christ controls us.—"I was afraid, and I went and hid your talent in the ground. . . ." "You wicked and slothful servant! . . . You ought to have invested my money with the bankers, and at my coming I should have received what was my own with interest."

"Go home to your friends and tell them how much the Lord has done for you."

Jer. 20:9; 1 Cor. 9:16, 18; Acts 4:18–20; 2 Cor. 5:14; Matt. 25:25–27; Mark 5:19

MORNING

"None of the devoted things shall stick to your hand."

"Therefore go out from their midst, and be separate from them, says the Lord, and touch no unclean thing."—Beloved, I urge you as sojourners and exiles to abstain from the passions of the flesh, which wage war against your soul.—Hating even the garment stained by the flesh.

Beloved, we are God's children now, and what we will be has not yet appeared; but we know that when he appears we shall be like him, because we shall see him as he is. And everyone who thus hopes in him purifies himself as he is pure.—For the grace of God has appeared, bringing salvation for all people, training us to renounce ungodliness and worldly passions, and to live self-controlled, upright, and godly lives in the present age, waiting for our blessed hope, the appearing of the glory of our great God and Savior Jesus Christ, who gave himself for us to redeem us from all lawlessness and to purify for himself a people for his own possession who are zealous for good works.

Deut. 13:17; 2 Cor. 6:17; 1 Pet. 2:11; Jude 23; 1 John 3:2–3; Titus 2:11–14

EVENING

"Who are you, Lord?" . . . "I am Jesus."

"It is I. Do not be afraid."—"When you pass through the waters, I will be with you; and through the rivers, they shall not overwhelm you; when you walk through fire you shall not be burned, and the flame shall not consume you. For I am the Lord your God . . . your Savior."

Even though I walk through the valley of the shadow of death, I will fear no evil, for you are with me; your rod and your staff, they comfort me.—"Immanuel" (which means, God with us).

"You shall call his name Jesus, for he will save his people from their sins."—If anyone does sin, we have an advocate with the Father, Jesus Christ the righteous.—Who is to condemn? Christ Jesus is the one who died—more than that, who was raised—who is at the right hand of God, who indeed is interceding for us. Who shall separate us from the love of Christ? Shall tribulation, or distress, or persecution, or famine, or nakedness, or danger, or sword?

Acts 26:15; Matt. 14:27; Isa. 43:2–3; Ps. 23:4; Matt. 1:23;
Matt. 1:21; 1 John 2:1; Rom. 8:34–35

MORNING

Stand firm thus in the Lord.

"My foot has held fast to his steps; I have kept his way and have not turned aside."

For the Lord loves justice; he will not forsake his saints. They are preserved forever.—The Lord will keep you from all evil; he will keep your life.

"My righteous one shall live by faith, and if he shrinks back, my soul has no pleasure in him." But we are not of those who shrink back and are destroyed, but of those who have faith and preserve their souls.—If they had been of us, they would have continued with us. But they went out, that it might become plain that they all are not of us.

"If you abide in my word, you are truly my disciples."—"The one who endures to the end will be saved."—Be watchful, stand firm in the faith, act like men, be strong.—"Hold fast what you have, so that no one may seize your crown."—"The one who conquers will be clothed thus in white garments, and I will never blot his name out of the book of life."

Phil. 4:1; Job 23:11; Ps. 37:28; Ps. 121:7; Heb. 10:38-39; 1 John 2:19;
John 8:31; Matt. 24:13; 1 Cor. 16:13; Rev. 3:11; Rev. 3:5

EVENING

Enoch walked with God.

"Do two walk together, unless they have agreed to meet?"

Making peace by the blood of his cross. . . . And you, who once were alienated and hostile in mind, doing evil deeds, he has now reconciled in his body of flesh by his death, in order to present you holy and blameless and above reproach before him.—But now in Christ Jesus you who once were far off have been brought near by the blood of Christ.

For if while we were enemies we were reconciled to God by the death of his Son, much more, now that we are reconciled, shall we be saved by his life. More than that, we also rejoice in God through our Lord Jesus Christ.

Our fellowship is with the Father and with his Son Jesus Christ.

The grace of the Lord Jesus Christ and the love of God and the fellowship of the Holy Spirit be with you all.

Gen. 5:22; Amos 3:3; Col. 1:20-22; Eph. 2:13;
Rom. 5:10-11; 1 John 1:3; 2 Cor. 13:14

MORNING

"If his offering is a burnt offering from the herd, he shall offer a male without blemish. He shall bring it to the entrance of the tent of meeting, that he may be accepted before the Lord. He shall lay his hand on the head of the burnt offering, and it shall be accepted for him to make atonement for him."

"God will provide for himself the lamb for a burnt offering."—"Behold, the Lamb of God, who takes away the sin of the world!"—And by that will we have been sanctified through the offering of the body of Jesus Christ once for all.—"A ransom for many."

"No one takes it from me, but I lay it down of my own accord. I have authority to lay it down, and I have authority to take it up again."—I will love them freely.—The Son of God . . . loved me and gave himself for me.

For our sake he made him to be sin who knew no sin, so that in him we might become the righteousness of God.—He has blessed us in the Beloved.

Lev. 1:3–4; Gen. 22:8; John 1:29; Heb. 10:10; Matt. 20:28;
John 10:18; Hos. 14:4; Gal. 2:20; 2 Cor. 5:21; Eph. 1:6

EVENING

*For great is your steadfast love toward me;
you have delivered my soul from the depths of Sheol.
"Fear him who can destroy both soul and body in hell."*

"Fear not, for I have redeemed you; I have called you by name, you are mine. . . . I, I am the Lord, and besides me there is no savior. . . . I, I am he who blots out your transgressions for my own sake, and I will not remember your sins."— . . . those who trust in their wealth and boast of the abundance of their riches? Truly no man can ransom another, or give to God the price of his life, for the ransom of their life is costly.—"I have found a ransom."—But God, being rich in mercy, because of the great love with which he loved us, even when we were dead in our trespasses, made us alive together with Christ.

"And there is salvation in no one else, for there is no other name under heaven given among men by which we must be saved."

Ps. 86:13; Matt. 10:28; Isa. 43:1, 11, 25; Ps. 49:6–8;
Job 33:24; Eph. 2:4–5; Acts 4:12

MORNING

The Lord was my support.

"Truly the hills are a delusion, the orgies on the mountains. Truly in the Lord our God is the salvation of Israel."—The Lord is my rock and my fortress and my deliverer, my God, my rock, in whom I take refuge, my shield, and the horn of my salvation, my stronghold.—"Shout, and sing for joy, O inhabitant of Zion, for great in your midst is the Holy One of Israel."

The angel of the Lord encamps around those who fear him, and delivers them. . . . When the righteous cry for help, the Lord hears and delivers them out of all their troubles.—"The eternal God is your dwelling place, and underneath are the everlasting arms."—So we can confidently say, "The Lord is my helper; I will not fear; what can man do to me?"—For who is God, but the Lord? And who is a rock, except our God?—the God who equipped me with strength and made my way blameless.

But by the grace of God I am what I am.

Ps. 18:18; Jer. 3:23; Ps. 18:2; Isa. 12:6; Ps. 34:7, 17;
Deut. 33:27; Heb. 13:6; Ps. 18:31–32; 1 Cor. 15:10

EVENING

All we like sheep have gone astray.

If we say we have no sin, we deceive ourselves, and the truth is not in us.— "None is righteous, no, not one; no one understands; . . . All have turned aside; together they have become worthless."

For you were straying like sheep, but have now returned to the Shepherd and Overseer of your souls.—I have gone astray like a lost sheep; seek your servant, for I do not forget your commandments.

He restores my soul. He leads me in paths of righteousness for his name's sake.

"My sheep hear my voice, and I know them, and they follow me. I give them eternal life, and they will never perish, and no one will snatch them out of my hand."

"What man of you, having a hundred sheep, if he has lost one of them, does not leave the ninety-nine in the open country, and go after the one that is lost, until he finds it?"

Isa. 53:6; 1 John 1:8; Rom. 3:10–12; 1 Pet. 2:25;
Ps. 119:176; Ps. 23:3; John 10:27–28; Luke 15:4

MORNING

*The Lord visited Sarah as he had said, and
the Lord did to Sarah as he had promised.*

Trust in him at all times, O people; pour out your heart before him; God is a refuge for us.—David strengthened himself in the Lord his God.—"God will visit you and bring you up out of this land to the land that he swore to Abraham, to Isaac, and to Jacob."—"'I have surely seen the affliction of my people who are in Egypt, and have heard their groaning, and I have come down to deliver them.' This man led them out, performing wonders and signs in Egypt and at the Red Sea and in the wilderness for forty years."—Not one word of all the good promises that the Lord had made to the house of Israel had failed; all came to pass.

He who promised is faithful.—Has he said, and will he not do it? Or has he spoken, and will he not fulfill it?—"Heaven and earth will pass away, but my words will not pass away."—The grass withers, the flower fades, but the word of our God will stand forever.

Gen. 21:1; Ps. 62:8; 1 Sam. 30:6; Gen. 50:24; Acts 7:34, 36;
Josh. 21:45; Heb. 10:23; Num. 23:19; Matt. 24:35; Isa. 40:8

EVENING

The eyes of all look to you.

"He himself gives to all mankind life and breath and everything."—The Lord is good to all, and his mercy is over all that he has made.—"Look at the birds of the air: they neither sow nor reap nor gather into barns, and yet your heavenly Father feeds them."

For the same Lord is Lord of all, bestowing his riches on all who call on him.—I lift up my eyes to the hills. From where does my help come?—Behold, as the eyes of servants look to the hand of their master, as the eyes of a maidservant to the hand of her mistress, so our eyes look to the Lord our God.

For the Lord is a God of justice; blessed are all those who wait for him.—It will be said on that day, "Behold, this is our God; we have waited for him, that he might save us. This is the Lord; we have waited for him; let us be glad and rejoice in his salvation."—But if we hope for what we do not see, we wait for it with patience.

Ps. 145:15; Acts 17:25; Ps. 145:9; Matt. 6:26; Rom. 10:12;
Ps. 121:1; Ps. 123:2; Isa. 30:18; Isa. 25:9; Rom. 8:25

MORNING

"You shall call his name Jesus, for he will save his people from their sins."

You know that he appeared in order to take away sins.—That we might die to sin and live to righteousness.—Consequently, he is able to save to the uttermost those who draw near to God through him.

But he was pierced for our transgressions; he was crushed for our iniquities; upon him was the chastisement that brought us peace, and with his wounds we are healed. . . . The Lord has laid on him the iniquity of us all.— "Thus it is written, that the Christ should suffer . . . and that repentance and forgiveness of sins should be proclaimed in his name to all nations."—He has appeared . . . to put away sin by the sacrifice of himself.

"God exalted him at his right hand as Leader and Savior, to give repentance."—"Through this man forgiveness of sins is proclaimed to you, and by him everyone who believes is freed from everything from which you could not be freed by the law of Moses."—Your sins are forgiven for his name's sake.

Matt. 1:21; 1 John 3:5; 1 Pet. 2:24; Heb. 7:25; Isa. 53:5-6;
Luke 24:46-47; Heb. 9:26; Acts 5:31; Acts 13:38-39; 1 John 2:12

EVENING

Our Lord Jesus Christ . . . though he was rich, yet for your sake he became poor, so that you by his poverty might become rich.

For in him all the fullness of God was pleased to dwell.—He is the radiance of the glory of God and the exact imprint of his nature, and he upholds the universe by the word of his power. After making purification for sins, he sat down at the right hand of the Majesty on high, having become as much superior to angels as the name he has inherited is more excellent than theirs.— Who, though he was in the form of God, did not count equality with God a thing to be grasped, but emptied himself.

"Foxes have holes, and birds of the air have nests, but the Son of Man has nowhere to lay his head."

All things are yours, whether Paul or Apollos or Cephas or the world or life or death or the present or the future—all are yours, and you are Christ's, and Christ is God's.

2 Cor. 8:9; Col. 1:19; Heb. 1:3-4; Phil. 2:6-7; Matt. 8:20; 1 Cor. 3:21-23

MORNING

His left hand is under my head, and his right hand embraces me!

"Underneath are the everlasting arms."—But when he saw the wind, he was afraid, and beginning to sink he cried out, "Lord, save me." Jesus immediately reached out his hand and took hold of him, saying to him, "O you of little faith, why did you doubt?"—The steps of a man are established by the Lord, when he delights in his way; though he fall, he shall not be cast headlong, for the Lord upholds his hand.

"The beloved of the Lord dwells in safety. The High God surrounds him all day long, and dwells between his shoulders."—Casting all your anxieties on him, because he cares for you.—He who touches you touches the apple of his eye.

"They will never perish, and no one will snatch them out of my hand. My Father, who has given them to me, is greater than all."

Song 2:6; Deut. 33:27; Matt. 14:30–31; Ps. 37:23–24;
Deut. 33:12; 1 Pet. 5:7; Zech. 2:8; John 10:28–29

EVENING

"Who is this who looks down like the dawn, beautiful as the moon, bright as the sun, awesome as an army with banners?"

"The church of God, which he obtained with his own blood."

Christ loved the church and gave himself up for her, that he might sanctify her, having cleansed her by the washing of water with the word, so that he might present the church to himself in splendor, without spot or wrinkle or any such thing, that she might be holy and without blemish.

And a great sign appeared in heaven: a woman clothed with the sun.— "The marriage of the Lamb has come, and his Bride has made herself ready; it was granted her to clothe herself with fine linen, bright and pure"—for the fine linen is the righteous deeds of the saints.—The righteousness of God through faith in Jesus Christ for all who believe.

"The glory that you have given me I have given to them."

Song 6:10; Acts 20:28; Eph. 5:25–27; Rev. 12:1;
Rev. 19:7–8; Rom. 3:22; John 17:22

MORNING

This is what I mean, brothers: the appointed time has grown very short.

"Man who is born of a woman is few of days and full of trouble. He comes out like a flower and withers; he flees like a shadow and continues not."—And the world is passing away along with its desires, but whoever does the will of God abides forever.—For as in Adam all die, so also in Christ shall all be made alive. . . . "Death is swallowed up in victory."—For if we live, we live to the Lord, and if we die, we die to the Lord. So then, whether we live or whether we die, we are the Lord's.—For to me to live is Christ, and to die is gain.

Therefore do not throw away your confidence, which has a great reward. For you have need of endurance, so that when you have done the will of God you may receive what is promised. For, "Yet a little while, and the coming one will come and will not delay."—The night is far gone; the day is at hand. So then let us cast off the works of darkness and put on the armor of light.—The end of all things is at hand; therefore be self-controlled and sober-minded for the sake of your prayers.

1 Cor. 7:29; Job 14:1-2; 1 John 2:17; 1 Cor. 15:22, 54; Rom. 14:8;
Phil. 1:21; Heb. 10:35-37; Rom. 13:12; 1 Pet. 4:7

EVENING

"A new name."

And in Antioch the disciples were first called Christians.—"Let everyone who names the name of the Lord depart from iniquity."—And those who belong to Christ Jesus have crucified the flesh with its passions and desires.—You were bought with a price. So glorify God in your body.

But far be it from me to boast except in the cross of our Lord Jesus Christ, by which the world has been crucified to me, and I to the world. For neither circumcision counts for anything, nor uncircumcision, but a new creation.—Therefore be imitators of God, as beloved children. And walk in love, as Christ loved us and gave himself up for us, a fragrant offering and sacrifice to God. But sexual immorality and all impurity or covetousness must not even be named among you, as is proper among saints. . . . Now you are light in the Lord. Walk as children of light.

Rev. 2:17; Acts 11:26; 2 Tim. 2:19; Gal. 5:24;
1 Cor. 6:20; Gal. 6:14-15; Eph. 5:1-3, 8

MORNING

"Behold, the Lamb of God."

For it is impossible for the blood of bulls and goats to take away sins. Consequently, when Christ came into the world, he said, "Sacrifices and offerings you have not desired, but a body have you prepared for me; in burnt offerings and sin offerings you have taken no pleasure. Then I said, 'Behold, I have come to do your will, O God.'"—He was oppressed, and he was afflicted, yet he opened not his mouth; like a lamb that is led to the slaughter, and like a sheep that before its shearers is silent, so he opened not his mouth.

You were ransomed . . . not with perishable things such as silver or gold, but with the precious blood of Christ, like that of a lamb without blemish or spot. He was . . . made manifest in the last times for the sake of you, . . . so that your faith and hope are in God.

"Worthy is the Lamb who was slain, to receive power and wealth and wisdom and might and honor and glory and blessing!"

John 1:29; Heb. 10:4–7; Isa. 53:7; 1 Pet. 1:18–21; Rev. 5:12

EVENING

But I will hope continually and will
praise you yet more and more.

Not that I have already obtained this or am already perfect.—Therefore let us leave the elementary doctrine of Christ and go on to maturity, not laying again a foundation of repentance from dead works and of faith toward God.— But the path of the righteous is like the light of dawn, which shines brighter and brighter until full day.

I love the Lord, because he has heard my voice and my pleas for mercy. Because he inclined his ear to me, therefore I will call on him as long as I live.—I will bless the Lord at all times; his praise shall continually be in my mouth.

Praise is due to you, O God, in Zion.—Day and night they never cease to say, "Holy, holy, holy, is the Lord God Almighty."—"The one who offers thanksgiving as his sacrifice glorifies me."—Rejoice always, pray without ceasing, give thanks in all circumstances; for this is the will of God in Christ Jesus for you.—Rejoice in the Lord always; again I will say, rejoice.

Ps. 71:14; Phil. 3:12; Heb. 6:1; Prov. 4:18; Ps. 116:1–2; Ps. 34:1;
Ps. 65:1; Rev. 4:8; Ps. 50:23; 1 Thess. 5:16–18; Phil. 4:4

MORNING

"Consider what great things he has done for you."

"And you shall remember the whole way that the Lord your God has led you these forty years in the wilderness, that he might humble you, testing you to know what was in your heart, whether you would keep his commandments or not. Know then in your heart that, as a man disciplines his son, the Lord your God disciplines you."

I know, O Lord, that your rules are righteous, and that in faithfulness you have afflicted me. . . . It is good for me that I was afflicted, that I might learn your statutes. . . . Before I was afflicted I went astray, but now I keep your word.—The Lord has disciplined me severely, but he has not given me over to death.—He does not deal with us according to our sins, nor repay us according to our iniquities. For as high as the heavens are above the earth, so great is his steadfast love toward those who fear him. For he knows our frame; he remembers that we are dust.

1 Sam. 12:24; Deut. 8:2, 5; Ps. 119:75, 71, 67; Ps. 118:18; Ps. 103:10, 11, 14

EVENING

Our blessed hope, the appearing of the glory of our great God and Savior Jesus Christ.

We have this as a sure and steadfast anchor of the soul, a hope that enters into the inner place behind the curtain, where Jesus has gone as a forerunner on our behalf.—Whom heaven must receive until the time for restoring all the things about which God spoke.—When he comes on that day to be glorified in his saints, and to be marveled at among all who have believed.

The whole creation has been groaning together in the pains of childbirth until now. And not only the creation, but we ourselves . . . groan inwardly as we wait eagerly for adoption as sons, the redemption of our bodies.—Beloved, we are God's children now, and what we will be has not yet appeared; but we know that when he appears we shall be like him, because we shall see him as he is.—When Christ who is your life appears, then you also will appear with him in glory.

"Surely I am coming soon." Amen. Come, Lord Jesus!

Titus 2:13; Heb. 6:19–20; Acts 3:21; 2 Thess. 1:10;
Rom. 8:22–23; 1 John 3:2; Col. 3:4; Rev. 22:20

MORNING

Whoever keeps his word, in him truly the love of God is perfected.

Now may the God of peace who brought again from the dead our Lord Jesus, the great shepherd of the sheep, by the blood of the eternal covenant, equip you with everything good that you may do his will, working in us that which is pleasing in his sight, through Jesus Christ, to whom be glory forever and ever. Amen.

And by this we know that we have come to know him, if we keep his commandments.—"If anyone loves me, he will keep my word, and my Father will love him, and we will come to him and make our home with him."— No one who abides in him keeps on sinning; no one who keeps on sinning has either seen him or known him. Little children, let no one deceive you. Whoever practices righteousness is righteous, as he is righteous.—By this is love perfected with us, so that we may have confidence for the day of judgment, because as he is so also are we in this world.

1 John 2:5; Heb. 13:20–21; 1 John 2:3; John 14:23; 1 John 3:6–7; 1 John 4:17

EVENING

Whoever is slow to anger has great understanding.

The Lord passed before him and proclaimed, "The Lord, the Lord, a God merciful and gracious, slow to anger."—The Lord is not slow to fulfill his promise as some count slowness, but is patient toward you, not wishing that any should perish, but that all should reach repentance.

Therefore be imitators of God, as beloved children. And walk in love.— But the fruit of the Spirit is love, joy, peace, patience, kindness, goodness, faithfulness, gentleness, self-control; against such things there is no law.— For this is a gracious thing, when, mindful of God, one endures sorrows while suffering unjustly. . . . If when you do good and suffer for it you endure, this is a gracious thing in the sight of God. . . . Christ also suffered for you, leaving you an example, so that you might follow in his steps. . . . When he was reviled, he did not revile in return; when he suffered, he did not threaten, but continued entrusting himself to him who judges justly.—Be angry and do not sin.

Prov. 14:29; Ex. 34:6; 2 Pet. 3:9; Eph. 5:1–2;
Gal. 5:22–23; 1 Pet. 2:19–21, 23; Eph. 4:26

MORNING

But the fruit of the Spirit is . . . peace.

To set the mind on the Spirit is life and peace.

God has called you to peace.—"Peace I leave with you; my peace I give to you. Not as the world gives do I give to you."—May the God of hope fill you with all joy and peace in believing, so that by the power of the Holy Spirit you may abound in hope.

I know whom I have believed, and I am convinced that he is able to guard until that Day what has been entrusted to me.—You keep him in perfect peace whose mind is stayed on you, because he trusts in you.

And the effect of righteousness will be peace, and the result of righteousness, quietness and trust forever. My people will abide in a peaceful habitation, in secure dwellings, and in quiet resting places.—"Whoever listens to me will dwell secure and will be at ease, without dread of disaster."

Great peace have those who love your law.

Gal. 5:22; Rom. 8:6; 1 Cor. 7:15; John 14:27; Rom. 15:13; 2 Tim. 1:12;
Isa. 26:3; Isa. 32:17–18; Prov. 1:33; Ps. 119:165

EVENING

"The Lord Is There."

"Behold, the dwelling place of God is with man. He will dwell with them, and they will be his people, and God himself will be with them as their God."

And I saw no temple . . . for its temple is the Lord God the Almighty and the Lamb. And the city has no need of sun or moon to shine on it, for the glory of God gives it light, and its lamp is the Lamb.

When I awake, I shall be satisfied with your likeness.—Whom have I in heaven but you? And there is nothing on earth that I desire besides you.

"But Judah shall be inhabited forever, and Jerusalem to all generations. I will avenge their blood, blood I have not avenged, for the Lord dwells in Zion."—"Sing and rejoice, O daughter of Zion, for behold, I come and I will dwell in your midst, declares the Lord."— No longer will there be anything accursed, but the throne of God and of the Lamb will be in it, and his servants will worship him.

Ezek. 48:35; Rev. 21:3; Rev. 21:22–23; Ps. 17:15; Ps. 73:25;
Joel 3:20–21; Zech. 2:10; Rev. 22:3

MORNING

"Surely the Lord is in this place, and I did not know it."

"For where two or three are gathered in my name, there am I among them."—"And behold, I am with you always, to the end of the age."—"My presence will go with you, and I will give you rest."

Where shall I go from your Spirit? Or where shall I flee from your presence? If I ascend to heaven, you are there! If I make my bed in Sheol, you are there!—"Am I a God at hand, declares the Lord, and not a God far away? Can a man hide himself in secret places so that I cannot see him? declares the Lord. Do I not fill heaven and earth? declares the Lord."

"Behold, heaven and the highest heaven cannot contain you; how much less this house that I have built!"—For thus says the One who is high and lifted up, who inhabits eternity, whose name is Holy: "I dwell in the high and holy place, and also with him who is of a contrite and lowly spirit, to revive the spirit of the lowly, and to revive the heart of the contrite."—We are the temple of the living God.

Gen. 28:16; Matt. 18:20; Matt. 28:20; Ex. 33:14; Ps. 139:7–8;
Jer. 23:23–24; 1 Kings 8:27; Isa. 57:15; 2 Cor. 6:16

EVENING

Keep yourselves from idols.

My son, give me your heart.—Set your minds on things that are above, not on things that are on earth.—"Son of man, these men have taken their idols into their hearts, and set the stumbling block of their iniquity before their faces. Should I indeed let myself be consulted by them?"—Put to death therefore what is earthly in you: sexual immorality, impurity, passion, evil desire, and covetousness, which is idolatry.—But those who desire to be rich fall into temptation, into a snare, into many senseless and harmful desires that plunge people into ruin and destruction. For the love of money is a root of all kinds of evils. It is through this craving that some have wandered away from the faith and pierced themselves with many pangs. But as for you, O man of God, flee these things.—If riches increase, set not your heart on them.—My fruit is better than gold, even fine gold, and my yield than choice silver.—"Where your treasure is, there your heart will be also."—"The Lord looks on the heart."

1 John 5:21; Prov. 23:26; Col. 3:2; Ezek. 14:3; Col. 3:5;
1 Tim. 6:9–11; Ps. 62:10; Prov. 8:19; Matt. 6:21; 1 Sam. 16:7

MORNING

"You therefore must be perfect,
as your heavenly Father is perfect."

"I am God Almighty; walk before me, and be blameless."—"You shall be holy to me, for I the Lord am holy and have separated you from the peoples, that you should be mine."

You were bought with a price. So glorify God in your body.

You have been filled in him, who is the head of all rule and authority.—Who gave himself for us to redeem us from all lawlessness.—Be diligent to be found by him without spot or blemish, and at peace.

Blessed are those whose way is blameless, who walk in the law of the Lord!—But the one who looks into the perfect law, the law of liberty, and perseveres, being no hearer who forgets but a doer who acts, he will be blessed in his doing.—Search me, O God, and know my heart! Try me and know my thoughts! And see if there be any grievous way in me, and lead me in the way everlasting!

Matt. 5:48; Gen. 17:1; Lev. 20:26; 1 Cor. 6:20; Col. 2:10; Titus 2:14;
2 Pet. 3:14; Ps. 119:1; James 1:25; Ps. 139:23–24

EVENING

Bringing holiness to completion in the fear of God.

Beloved, let us cleanse ourselves from every defilement of body and spirit.

Behold, you delight in truth in the inward being, and you teach me wisdom in the secret heart.—Training us to renounce ungodliness and worldly passions, and to live self-controlled, upright, and godly lives in the present age.—"Let your light shine before others, so that they may see your good works and give glory to your Father who is in heaven."—Not that I have already obtained this or am already perfect.

And everyone who thus hopes in him purifies himself as he is pure.

He who has prepared us for this very thing is God, who has given us the Spirit as a guarantee.—To equip the saints for the work of ministry, for building up the body of Christ, until we all attain to the unity of the faith and of the knowledge of the Son of God, to mature manhood, to the measure of the stature of the fullness of Christ.

2 Cor. 7:1; 2 Cor. 7:1; Ps. 51:6; Titus 2:12; Matt. 5:16;
Phil. 3:12; 1 John 3:3; 2 Cor. 5:5; Eph. 4:12—13

MORNING

Behold, the Lord's hand is not shortened, that it cannot save, or his ear dull, that it cannot hear.

On the day I called, you answered me; my strength of soul you increased.— While I was speaking in prayer, the man Gabriel, whom I had seen in the vision at the first, came to me in swift flight at the time of the evening sacrifice.—Hide not your face from me. Turn not your servant away in anger, O you who have been my help. Cast me not off; forsake me not, O God of my salvation!—But you, O Lord, do not be far off! O you my help, come quickly to my aid!

"Ah, Lord God! It is you who have made the heavens and the earth by your great power and by your outstretched arm! Nothing is too hard for you."—He delivered us from such a deadly peril, and he will deliver us. On him we have set our hope that he will deliver us again.—"And will not God give justice to his elect, who cry to him day and night? Will he delay long over them? I tell you, he will give justice to them speedily."

Isa. 59:1; Ps. 138:2; Dan. 9:21; Ps. 27:9; Ps. 22:19;
Jer. 32:17; 2 Cor. 1:10; Luke 18:7-8

EVENING

"I glorified you on earth."

"My food is to do the will of him who sent me and to accomplish his work."— "We must work the works of him who sent me while it is day; night is coming, when no one can work."

"Did you not know that I must be in my Father's house?" And they did not understand the saying that he spoke to them.—"This illness does not lead to death. It is for the glory of God, so that the Son of God may be glorified through it. . . . Did I not tell you that if you believed you would see the glory of God?"—And Jesus increased in wisdom and in stature and in favor with God and man.—"You are my beloved Son; with you I am well pleased."—And all spoke well of him and marveled at the gracious words that were coming from his mouth.—"Worthy are you . . . for you were slain, and by your blood you ransomed people for God from every tribe and language and people and nation, and you have made them a kingdom and priests to our God, and they shall reign on the earth."

John 17:4; John 4:34; John 9:4; Luke 2:49-50; John 11:4,
40; Luke 2:52; Luke 3:22; Luke 4:22; Rev. 5:9-10

MORNING

"Therefore do not be anxious, saying, 'What shall we eat?'
or 'What shall we drink?' or 'What shall we wear?' For . . .
your heavenly Father knows that you need them all."

Oh, fear the Lord, you his saints, for those who fear him have no lack! The young lions suffer want and hunger; but those who seek the Lord lack no good thing.—No good thing does he withhold from those who walk uprightly. O Lord of hosts, blessed is the one who trusts in you!

I want you to be free from anxieties.—Do not be anxious about anything, but in everything by prayer and supplication with thanksgiving let your requests be made known to God.

"Are not two sparrows sold for a penny? And not one of them will fall to the ground apart from your Father. But even the hairs of your head are all numbered. Fear not, therefore; you are of more value than many sparrows."—"Why are you so afraid? Have you still no faith?"—"Have faith in God."

Matt. 6:31–32; Ps. 34:9–10; Ps. 84:11–12; 1 Cor. 7:32;
Phil. 4:6; Matt. 10:29–31; Mark 4:40; Mark 11:22

EVENING

He spread a cloud for a covering, and fire to give light by night.

As a father shows compassion to his children, so the Lord shows compassion to those who fear him. For he knows our frame; he remembers that we are dust.

The sun shall not strike you by day, nor the moon by night.—There will be a booth for shade by day from the heat, and for a refuge and a shelter from the storm and rain.

The Lord is your keeper; the Lord is your shade on your right hand. The Lord will keep your going out and your coming in from this time forth and forevermore.—And the Lord went before them by day in a pillar of cloud to lead them along the way, and by night in a pillar of fire to give them light, that they might travel by day and by night. The pillar of cloud by day and the pillar of fire by night did not depart from before the people.

Jesus Christ is the same yesterday and today and forever.

Ps. 105:39; Ps. 103:13–14; Ps. 121:6; Isa. 4:6; Ps. 121:5, 8;
Ex. 13:21–22; Heb. 13:8

MORNING

*Steadfast love and faithfulness meet;
righteousness and peace kiss each other.*

"A righteous God and a Savior."—The Lord was pleased, for his righteousness' sake, to magnify his law and make it glorious.

In Christ God was reconciling the world to himself, not counting their trespasses against them.—Whom God put forward as a propitiation by his blood, to be received by faith. This was to show God's righteousness, because in his divine forbearance he had passed over former sins. It was to show his righteousness at the present time, so that he might be just and the justifier of the one who has faith in Jesus.—But he was pierced for our transgressions; he was crushed for our iniquities; upon him was the chastisement that brought us peace, and with his wounds we are healed.—Who shall bring any charge against God's elect? It is God who justifies.—And to the one who does not work but believes in him who justifies the ungodly, his faith is counted as righteousness.

Ps. 85:10; Isa. 45:21; Isa. 42:21; 2 Cor. 5:19;
Rom. 3:25-26; Isa. 53:5; Rom. 8:33; Rom. 4:5

EVENING

*"How are the dead raised? With what
kind of body do they come?"*

Beloved, we are God's children now, and what we will be has not yet appeared; but we know that when he appears we shall be like him, because we shall see him as he is.—Just as we have borne the image of the man of dust, we shall also bear the image of the man of heaven.

A Savior, the Lord Jesus Christ . . . will transform our lowly body to be like his glorious body, by the power that enables him even to subject all things to himself.

Jesus himself stood among them, and said to them, "Peace to you!" But they were startled and frightened and thought they saw a spirit.—He appeared to Cephas, then to the twelve. Then he appeared to more than five hundred brothers at one time.

If the Spirit of him who raised Jesus from the dead dwells in you, he who raised Christ Jesus from the dead will also give life to your mortal bodies through his Spirit who dwells in you.

1 Cor. 15:35; 1 John 3:2; 1 Cor. 15:49; Phil. 3:20-21;
Luke 24:36-37; 1 Cor. 15:5-6; Rom. 8:11

MORNING

"And you will hear of wars and rumors of wars.
See that you are not alarmed."

God is our refuge and strength, a very present help in trouble. Therefore we will not fear though the earth gives way, though the mountains be moved into the heart of the sea, though its waters roar and foam, though the mountains tremble at its swelling.—Come, my people, enter your chambers, and shut your doors behind you; hide yourselves for a little while until the fury has passed by. For behold, the Lord is coming out from his place to punish the inhabitants of the earth for their iniquity.—In the shadow of your wings I will take refuge, till the storms of destruction pass by.—Your life is hidden with Christ in God.

He is not afraid of bad news; his heart is firm, trusting in the Lord.

"I have said these things to you, that in me you may have peace. In the world you will have tribulation. But take heart; I have overcome the world."

Matt. 24:6; Ps. 46:1–3; Isa. 26:20–21; Ps. 57:1; Col. 3:3; Ps. 112:7; John 16:33

EVENING

For they persecute him whom you have struck down.

"Temptations to sin are sure to come, but woe to the one through whom they come!"—"This Jesus, delivered up according to the definite plan and fore-knowledge of God, you crucified and killed by the hands of lawless men."—Then they spit in his face and struck him. And some slapped him, saying, "Prophesy to us, you Christ! Who is it that struck you?"—So also the chief priests, with the scribes and elders, mocked him, saying, "He saved others; he cannot save himself. He is the King of Israel; let him come down now from the cross."—"For truly in this city there were gathered together against your holy servant Jesus, whom you anointed, both Herod and Pontius Pilate, along with the Gentiles and the peoples of Israel, to do whatever your hand and your plan had predestined to take place."

Surely he has borne our griefs and carried our sorrows; yet we esteemed him stricken, smitten by God, and afflicted.

Ps. 69:26; Luke 17:1; Acts 2:23; Matt. 26:67–68;
Matt. 27:41–42; Acts 4:27–28; Isa. 53:4

MORNING

Yet it was the will of the Lord to crush him; he has put him to grief.

"Now is my soul troubled. And what shall I say? 'Father, save me from this hour'? But for this purpose I have come to this hour. Father, glorify your name." Then a voice came from heaven: "I have glorified it, and I will glorify it again."—"Father, if you are willing, remove this cup from me. Nevertheless, not my will, but yours, be done." And there appeared to him an angel from heaven, strengthening him.

And being found in human form, he humbled himself by becoming obedient to the point of death, even death on a cross.—"For this reason the Father loves me, because I lay down my life that I may take it up again."—"For I have come down from heaven, not to do my own will but the will of him who sent me."—"Shall I not drink the cup that the Father has given me?"—"He has not left me alone, for I always do the things that are pleasing to him."—"My beloved Son, with whom I am well pleased."—My chosen, in whom my soul delights.

Isa. 53:10; John 12:27-28; Luke 22:42-43; Phil. 2:8; John 10:17;
John 6:38; John 18:11; John 8:29; Matt. 3:17; Isa. 42:1

EVENING

You who put the Lord in remembrance, take no rest.

"You have made them a kingdom and priests to our God."—"And the sons of Aaron, the priests, shall blow the trumpets. The trumpets shall be to you for a perpetual statute throughout your generations. And when you go to war in your land against the adversary who oppresses you, then you shall sound an alarm with the trumpets, that you may be remembered before the Lord your God, and you shall be saved from your enemies."

"I did not say to the offspring of Jacob, 'Seek me in vain.'"—Their voice was heard, and their prayer came to his holy habitation in heaven.—The eyes of the Lord are toward the righteous and his ears toward their cry.—Pray for one another. . . . The prayer of a righteous person has great power as it is working.

Come, Lord Jesus!—Do not delay, O my God!—Waiting for and hastening the coming of the day of God.

Isa. 62:6; Rev. 5:10; Num. 10:8-9; Isa. 45:19; 2 Chron. 30:27;
Ps. 34:15; James 5:16; Rev. 22:20; Ps. 40:17; 2 Pet. 3:12

MORNING

Now faith is the assurance of things hoped for, the conviction of things not seen.

If in Christ we have hope in this life only, we are of all people most to be pitied.

"What no eye has seen, nor ear heard, nor the heart of man imagined, what God has prepared for those who love him"—these things God has revealed to us through the Spirit.—When you . . . believed in him, [you] were sealed with the promised Holy Spirit, who is the guarantee of our inheritance until we acquire possession of it.

Jesus said to him, "Have you believed because you have seen me? Blessed are those who have not seen and yet have believed."—Though you have not seen him, you love him. Though you do not now see him, you believe in him and rejoice with joy that is inexpressible and filled with glory, obtaining the outcome of your faith, the salvation of your souls.

We walk by faith, not by sight.—Therefore do not throw away your confidence, which has a great reward.

Heb. 11:1; 1 Cor. 15:19; 1 Cor. 2:9–10; Eph. 1:13–14;
John 20:29; 1 Pet. 1:8–9; 2 Cor. 5:7; Heb. 10:35

EVENING

"It is I; do not be afraid."

When I saw him, I fell at his feet as though dead. But he laid his right hand on me, saying, "Fear not, I am the first and the last, and the living one. I died, and behold I am alive forevermore, and I have the keys of Death and Hades."—"I, I am he who blots out your transgressions for my own sake, and I will not remember your sins."

"Woe is me! For I am lost; . . . for my eyes have seen the King, the Lord of hosts!" Then one of the seraphim flew to me, having in his hand a burning coal that he had taken with tongs from the altar. And he touched my mouth and said: "Behold, this has touched your lips; your guilt is taken away, and your sin atoned for."—I have blotted out your transgressions like a cloud and your sins like mist; return to me, for I have redeemed you.

If anyone does sin, we have an advocate with the Father, Jesus Christ the righteous.

John 6:20; Rev. 1:17–18; Isa. 43:25; Isa. 6:5–7; Isa. 44:22; 1 John 2:1

MORNING

The reason the Son of God appeared was to destroy the works of the devil.

For we do not wrestle against flesh and blood, but against the rulers, against the authorities, against the cosmic powers over this present darkness, against the spiritual forces of evil in the heavenly places.—Since therefore the children share in flesh and blood, he himself likewise partook of the same things, that through death he might destroy the one who has the power of death, that is, the devil.—He disarmed the rulers and authorities and put them to open shame, by triumphing over them in him.—And I heard a loud voice in heaven, saying, "Now the salvation and the power and the kingdom of our God and the authority of his Christ have come, for the accuser of our brothers has been thrown down, who accuses them day and night before our God. And they have conquered him by the blood of the Lamb and by the word of their testimony, for they loved not their lives even unto death.—But thanks be to God, who gives us the victory through our Lord Jesus Christ.

1 John 3:8; Eph. 6:12; Heb. 2:14; Col. 2:15; Rev. 12:10–11; 1 Cor. 15:57

EVENING

Vanity of vanities! All is vanity.

For all our days pass away under your wrath; we bring our years to an end like a sigh. The years of our life are seventy, or even by reason of strength eighty; yet their span is but toil and trouble; they are soon gone, and we fly away.

If in Christ we have hope in this life only, we are of all people most to be pitied.—For here we have no lasting city, but we seek the city that is to come.—"I the Lord do not change."—But our citizenship is in heaven, and from it we await a Savior, the Lord Jesus Christ, who will transform our lowly body to be like his glorious body, by the power that enables him even to subject all things to himself.—For the creation was subjected to futility, not willingly, but because of him who subjected it, in hope.

Jesus Christ is the same yesterday and today and forever.—"Holy, holy, holy, is the Lord God Almighty, who was and is and is to come!"

Eccles. 1:2; Ps. 90:9—10; 1 Cor. 15:19; Heb. 13:14; Mal. 3:6; Phil. 3:20–21; Rom. 8:20; Heb. 13:8; Rev. 4:8

MORNING

Wake up from your drunken stupor,
as is right, and do not go on sinning.

For you are all children of light, children of the day. We are not of the night or of the darkness. So then let us not sleep, as others do, but let us keep awake and be sober.

Besides this you know the time, that the hour has come for you to wake from sleep. For salvation is nearer to us now than when we first believed. The night is far gone; the day is at hand. So then let us cast off the works of darkness and put on the armor of light.—Therefore take up the whole armor of God, that you may be able to withstand in the evil day, and having done all, to stand firm.—Cast away from you all the transgressions that you have committed, and make yourselves a new heart and a new spirit!—Therefore put away all filthiness and rampant wickedness and receive with meekness the implanted word, which is able to save your souls.—And now, little children, abide in him, so that when he appears we may have confidence and not shrink from him in shame at his coming. If you know that he is righteous, you may be sure that everyone who practices righteousness has been born of him.

1 Cor. 15:34; 1 Thess. 5:5–6; Rom. 13:11–12; Eph. 6:13;
Ezek. 18:31; James 1:21; 1 John 2:28–29

EVENING

"My sheep hear my voice."

"Behold, I stand at the door and knock. If anyone hears my voice and opens the door, I will come in to him and eat with him, and he with me."—I slept, but my heart was awake. A sound! My beloved is knocking. "Open to me, my sister, my love, my dove, my perfect one." . . . I opened to my beloved, but my beloved had turned and gone. My soul failed me when he spoke. I sought him, but found him not; I called him, but he gave no answer.

"Speak, for your servant hears."—And when Jesus came to the place, he looked up and said to him, "Zacchaeus, hurry and come down, for I must stay at your house today." So he hurried and came down and received him joyfully.—Let me hear what God the Lord will speak, for he will speak peace to his people, to his saints; but let them not turn back to folly.

John 10:27; Rev. 3:20; Song 5:2, 6; 1 Sam. 3:10; Luke 19:5–6; Ps. 85:8

MORNING

Beloved, let us love one another, for love is from God, and whoever loves has been born of God and knows God.

God's love has been poured into our hearts through the Holy Spirit who has been given to us.—For you did not receive the spirit of slavery to fall back into fear, but you have received the Spirit of adoption as sons, by whom we cry, "Abba! Father!" The Spirit himself bears witness with our spirit that we are children of God.—Whoever believes in the Son of God has the testimony in himself.

In this the love of God was made manifest among us, that God sent his only Son into the world, so that we might live through him.—In him we have redemption through his blood, the forgiveness of our trespasses, according to the riches of his grace.—So that in the coming ages he might show the immeasurable riches of his grace in kindness toward us in Christ Jesus.

Beloved, if God so loved us, we also ought to love one another.

1 John 4:7; Rom. 5:5; Rom. 8:15-16; 1 John 5:10;
1 John 4:9; Eph. 1:7; Eph. 2:7; 1 John 4:11

EVENING

Reproaches have broken my heart.

"Is not this the carpenter's son?"—"Can anything good come out of Nazareth?"—"Are we not right in saying that you are a Samaritan and have a demon?"—"He casts out demons by the prince of demons."—"We know that this man is a sinner."—"He is leading the people astray."—"This man is blaspheming."— "Look at him! A glutton and a drunkard, a friend of tax collectors and sinners!"

"It is enough for the disciple to be like his teacher, and the servant like his master."—For this is a gracious thing, when, mindful of God, one endures sorrows while suffering unjustly. For to this you have been called, because Christ also suffered for you, leaving you an example, so that you might follow in his steps. He committed no sin, neither was deceit found in his mouth. When he was reviled, he did not revile in return; when he suffered, he did not threaten, but continued entrusting himself to him who judges justly.—If you are insulted for the name of Christ, you are blessed.

Ps. 69:20; Matt. 13:55; John 1:46; John 8:48; Matt. 9:34; John 9:24;
John 7:12; Matt. 9:3; Matt. 11:19; Matt. 10:25; 1 Pet. 2:19-23; 1 Pet. 4:14

MORNING

I desire then that in every place the men should pray,
lifting holy hands without anger or quarreling.

"The true worshipers will worship the Father in spirit and truth, for the Father is seeking such people to worship him. God is spirit, and those who worship him must worship in spirit and truth."—"Then you shall call, and the Lord will answer; you shall cry, and he will say, 'Here I am.'"—"And whenever you stand praying, forgive, if you have anything against anyone."—And without faith it is impossible to please him, for whoever would draw near to God must believe that he exists and that he rewards those who seek him.—But let him ask in faith, with no doubting, for the one who doubts is like a wave of the sea that is driven and tossed by the wind. For that person must not suppose that he will receive anything from the Lord.

If I had cherished iniquity in my heart, the Lord would not have listened.—My little children, I am writing these things to you so that you may not sin. But if anyone does sin, we have an advocate with the Father, Jesus Christ the righteous. He is the propitiation for our sins.

1 Tim. 2:8; John 4:23–24; Isa. 58:9; Mark 11:25;
Heb. 11:6; James 1:6–7; Ps. 66:18; 1 John 2:1–2

EVENING

My heart throbs; my strength fails me.

Hear my cry, O God, listen to my prayer; from the end of the earth I call to you when my heart is faint. Lead me to the rock that is higher than I.—But he said to me, "My grace is sufficient for you, for my power is made perfect in weakness." Therefore I will boast all the more gladly of my weaknesses, so that the power of Christ may rest upon me. . . . For when I am weak, then I am strong.

But when he saw the wind, he was afraid, and beginning to sink he cried out, "Lord, save me." Jesus immediately reached out his hand and took hold of him, saying to him, "O you of little faith, why did you doubt?"—If you faint in the day of adversity, your strength is small.—He gives power to the faint, and to him who has no might he increases strength.—"The eternal God is your dwelling place, and underneath are the everlasting arms."—May you be strengthened with all power, according to his glorious might.

Ps. 38:10; Ps. 61:1–2; 2 Cor. 12:9–10; Matt. 14:30–31;
Prov. 24:10; Isa. 40:29; Deut. 33:27; Col. 1:11

MORNING

Share his sufferings.

"It is enough for the disciple to be like his teacher, and the servant like his master."

He was despised and rejected by men; a man of sorrows, and acquainted with grief; and as one from whom men hide their faces he was despised, and we esteemed him not.—"In the world you will have tribulation."—"Because you are not of the world, but I chose you out of the world, therefore the world hates you."

I looked for pity, but there was none.—At my first defense no one came to stand by me, but all deserted me.

"Foxes have holes, and birds of the air have nests, but the Son of Man has nowhere to lay his head."—For here we have no lasting city, but we seek the city that is to come.

Let us run with endurance the race that is set before us, looking to Jesus, the founder and perfecter of our faith, who for the joy that was set before him endured the cross, despising the shame, and is seated at the right hand of the throne of God.

Phil. 3:10; Matt. 10:25; Isa. 53:3; John 16:33; John 15:19;
Ps. 69:20; 2 Tim. 4:16; Matt. 8:20; Heb. 13:14; Heb. 12:1-2

EVENING

"And they have conquered him by the blood of the Lamb."

Who shall bring any charge against God's elect? It is God who justifies. Who is to condemn? Christ Jesus is the one who died.—It is the blood that makes atonement by the life.—"I am the Lord. The blood shall be a sign for you, on the houses where you are. And when I see the blood, I will pass over you."—There is therefore now no condemnation for those who are in Christ Jesus.

"Who are these, clothed in white robes, and from where have they come? These are the ones coming out of the great tribulation. They have washed their robes and made them white in the blood of the Lamb."

To him who loves us and has freed us from our sins by his blood and made us a kingdom, priests to his God and Father, to him be glory and dominion forever and ever. Amen.

Rev. 12:11; Rom. 8:33-34; Lev. 17:11; Ex. 12:12-13;
Rom. 8:1; Rev. 7:13-14; Rev. 1:5-6

MORNING

"He will wipe away every tear . . . and death shall be no more, neither . . . mourning . . . , for the former things have passed away."

He will swallow up death forever; and the Lord God will wipe away tears from all faces, and the reproach of his people he will take away from all the earth, for the Lord has spoken.—Your sun shall no more go down, nor your moon withdraw itself; for the Lord will be your everlasting light, and your days of mourning shall be ended.—And no inhabitant will say, "I am sick"; the people who dwell there will be forgiven their iniquity.—"No more shall be heard in it the sound of weeping and the cry of distress."—And sorrow and sighing shall flee away.

Shall I ransom them from the power of Sheol? Shall I redeem them from Death? O Death, where are your plagues? O Sheol, where is your sting?—The last enemy to be destroyed is death. . . . Then shall come to pass the saying that is written: "Death is swallowed up in victory."

The things that are unseen are eternal.

Rev. 21:4; Isa. 25:8; Isa. 60:20; Isa. 33:24; Isa. 65:19;
Isa. 35:10; Hos. 13:14; 1 Cor. 15:26, 54; 2 Cor. 4:18

EVENING

Raised us up with him . . . in Christ Jesus.

"Fear not, I am . . . the living one."—"Father, I desire that they also, whom you have given me, may be with me where I am."

We are members of his body.—And he is the head of the body, the church. He is the beginning, the firstborn from the dead.—You have been filled in him, who is the head.

Since therefore the children share in flesh and blood, he himself likewise partook of the same things, that through death he might destroy the one who has the power of death, that is, the devil, and deliver all those who through fear of death were subject to lifelong slavery.

For this perishable body must put on the imperishable, and this mortal body must put on immortality. When the perishable puts on the imperishable, and the mortal puts on immortality, then shall come to pass the saying that is written: "Death is swallowed up in victory."

Eph. 2:6; Rev. 1:17—18; John 17:24; Eph. 5:30; Col. 1:18;
Col. 2:10; Heb. 2:14—15; 1 Cor. 1:53—54

MORNING

A servant of Christ Jesus.

"You call me Teacher and Lord, and you are right, for so I am."—"If anyone serves me, he must follow me; and where I am, there will my servant be also. If anyone serves me, the Father will honor him."—"Take my yoke upon you, and learn from me, for I am gentle and lowly in heart, and you will find rest for your souls. For my yoke is easy, and my burden is light."

But whatever gain I had, I counted as loss for the sake of Christ.—But now that you have been set free from sin and have become slaves of God, the fruit you get leads to sanctification and its end, eternal life.

"No longer do I call you servants, for the servant does not know what his master is doing; but I have called you friends, for all that I have heard from my Father I have made known to you."—So you are no longer a slave, but a son.—Stand firm therefore, and do not submit again to a yoke of slavery. . . . For you were called to freedom, brothers. Only do not use your freedom as an opportunity for the flesh.

Rom. 1:1; John 13:13; John 12:26; Matt. 11:29–30; Phil. 3:7;
Rom. 6:22; John 15:15; Gal. 4:7; Gal. 5:1, 13

EVENING

I bless the Lord who gives me counsel.

His name shall be called Wonderful Counselor.—I have counsel and sound wisdom; I have insight; I have strength.—Your word is a lamp to my feet and a light to my path.—Trust in the Lord with all your heart, and do not lean on your own understanding. In all your ways acknowledge him, and he will make straight your paths.

I know, O Lord, that the way of man is not in himself, that it is not in man who walks to direct his steps.—And your ears shall hear a word behind you, saying, "This is the way, walk in it," when you turn to the right or when you turn to the left.—Commit your work to the Lord, and your plans will be established.—"But he knows the way that I take."—A man's steps are from the Lord; how then can man understand his way?—You guide me with your counsel, and afterward you will receive me to glory.—This is God, our God forever and ever. He will guide us forever.

Ps. 16:7; Isa. 9:6; Prov. 8:14; Ps. 119:105; Prov. 3:5–6; Jer. 10:23;
Isa. 30:21; Prov. 16:3; Job. 23:10; Prov. 20:24; Ps. 73:24; Ps. 48:14

MORNING

"I am the Lord your God; walk in my statutes, and be careful to obey my rules."

But as he who called you is holy, you also be holy in all your conduct.—Whoever says he abides in him ought to walk in the same way in which he walked. . . . If you know that he is righteous, you may be sure that everyone who practices righteousness has been born of him.—For neither circumcision counts for anything nor uncircumcision, but keeping the commandments of God.—For whoever keeps the whole law but fails in one point has become accountable for all of it.

Not that we are sufficient in ourselves to claim anything as coming from us, but our sufficiency is from God.—Teach me, O Lord, the way of your statutes.

Work out your own salvation with fear and trembling, for it is God who works in you, both to will and to work for his good pleasure.—Now may the God of peace . . . equip you with everything good that you may do his will, working in us that which is pleasing in his sight, through Jesus Christ.

Ezek. 20:19; 1 Pet. 1:15; 1 John 2:6, 29; 1 Cor. 7:19; James 2:10;
2 Cor. 3:5; Ps. 119:33; Phil. 2:12–13; Heb. 13:20–21

EVENING

"I have exalted one chosen from the people."

For surely it is not angels that he helps, but he helps the offspring of Abraham. Therefore he had to be made like his brothers in every respect.—Seated above the likeness of a throne was a likeness with a human appearance.—"He who descended from heaven, the Son of Man."—"See my hands and my feet, that it is I myself. Touch me, and see. For a spirit does not have flesh and bones as you see that I have."

[He] emptied himself, by taking the form of a servant, being born in the likeness of men. And being found in human form, he humbled himself by becoming obedient to the point of death, even death on a cross. Therefore God has highly exalted him and bestowed on him the name that is above every name, so that at the name of Jesus every knee should bow.—"Wake up, and strengthen what remains and is about to die, for I have not found your works complete in the sight of my God."

Ps. 89:19; Heb. 2:16–17; Ezek. 1:26; John 3:13; Luke 24:39;
Phil. 2:7–10; Rev. 3:2

MORNING

"For as the Father has life in himself, so he has granted the Son also to have life in himself."

Our Savior Christ Jesus . . . abolished death and brought life and immortality to light through the gospel.—"I am the resurrection and the life."—"Because I live, you also will live."—We have come to share in Christ.—Those who . . . have shared in the Holy Spirit.—Partakers of the divine nature.—"The first man Adam became a living being"; the last Adam became a life-giving spirit. . . . Behold! I tell you a mystery. We shall not all sleep, but we shall all be changed, in a moment, in the twinkling of an eye, at the last trumpet. For the trumpet will sound, and the dead will be raised imperishable, and we shall be changed.

"Holy, holy, holy, is the Lord God Almighty, who was and is and is to come!" . . . who lives forever and ever.—He who is the blessed and only Sovereign, the King of kings and Lord of lords, who alone has immortality.—To the King of the ages, immortal, be honor and glory forever and ever. Amen.

John 5:26; 2 Tim. 1:10; John 11:25; John 14:19; Heb. 3:14; Heb. 6:4;
2 Pet. 1:4; 1 Cor. 15:45, 51–52; Rev. 4:8–9; 1 Tim. 6:15–16; 1 Tim. 1:17

EVENING

Let us not become conceited.

And Gideon said to them, "Let me make a request of you: every one of you give me the earrings from his spoil." (For they had golden earrings, because they were Ishmaelites.) And they answered, "We will willingly give them." And they spread a cloak, and every man threw in it the earrings of his spoil. . . . And Gideon made an ephod of it and put it in his city, in Ophrah. And all Israel whored after it there, and it became a snare to Gideon and to his family.

"And do you seek great things for yourself? Seek them not."—So to keep me from becoming conceited because of the surpassing greatness of the revelations, a thorn was given me in the flesh.

Do nothing from selfish ambition or conceit, but in humility count others more significant than yourselves.—Love does not envy or boast; it is not arrogant or rude. It does not insist on its own way.

"Take my yoke upon you, and learn from me."

Gal. 5:26; Judg. 8:24–25, 27; Jer. 45:5; 2 Cor. 12:7;
Phil. 2:3; 1 Cor. 13:4–5; Matt. 11:29

MORNING

Wash me thoroughly from my iniquity.

"I will cleanse them from all the guilt of their sin against me, and I will forgive all the guilt of their sin and rebellion against me."—"I will sprinkle clean water on you, and you shall be clean from all your uncleannesses, and from all your idols I will cleanse you."

"Unless one is born of water and the Spirit, he cannot enter the kingdom of God."—If the blood of goats and bulls, and the sprinkling of defiled persons with the ashes of a heifer, sanctify for the purification of the flesh, how much more will the blood of Christ, who through the eternal Spirit offered himself without blemish to God, purify our conscience from dead works to serve the living God.

Yet he saved them for his name's sake, that he might make known his mighty power.—Not to us, O Lord, not to us, but to your name give glory, for the sake of your steadfast love and your faithfulness!

Ps. 51:2; Jer. 33:8; Ezek. 36:25; John 3:5; Heb. 9:13–14; Ps. 106:8; Ps. 115:1

EVENING

Partnership in the gospel.

For just as the body is one and has many members, and all the members of the body, though many, are one body, so it is with Christ. For in one Spirit we were all baptized into one body—Jews or Greeks, slaves or free—and all were made to drink of one Spirit.

God is faithful, by whom you were called into the fellowship of his Son, Jesus Christ our Lord.—That which we have seen and heard we proclaim also to you, so that you too may have fellowship with us; and indeed our fellowship is with the Father and with his Son Jesus Christ.

But if we walk in the light, as he is in the light, we have fellowship with one another, and the blood of Jesus his Son cleanses us from all sin.—When Jesus had spoken these words, he lifted up his eyes to heaven, and said, . . . "I do not ask for these only, but also for those who will believe in me through their word, that they may all be one, just as you, Father, are in me, and I in you, that they also may be in us."

Phil. 1:5; 1 Cor. 12:12–13; 1 Cor. 1:9; 1 John 1:3; 1 John 1:7; John 17:1, 20–21

MORNING

Keep a close watch on yourself.

Every athlete exercises self-control in all things. They do it to receive a perishable wreath, but we an imperishable. So I do not run aimlessly; I do not box as one beating the air. But I discipline my body and keep it under control, lest after preaching to others I myself should be disqualified.—Put on the whole armor of God, that you may be able to stand against the schemes of the devil. For we do not wrestle against flesh and blood, but against the rulers, against the authorities, against the cosmic powers over this present darkness, against the spiritual forces of evil in the heavenly places.

And those who belong to Christ Jesus have crucified the flesh with its passions and desires. If we live by the Spirit, let us also keep in step with the Spirit.—For all who are led by the Spirit of God are sons of God.—Practice these things, immerse yourself in them, so that all may see your progress.

1 Tim. 4:16; 1 Cor. 9:25–27; Eph. 6:11–12; Gal. 5:24–25; Rom. 8:14; 1 Tim. 4:15

EVENING

Jesus said to her, "Mary."

"Fear not, for I have redeemed you; I have called you by name, you are mine."—"To him the gatekeeper opens. The sheep hear his voice, and he calls his own sheep by name and leads them out. When he has brought out all his own, he goes before them, and the sheep follow him, for they know his voice."

"Behold, I have engraved you on the palms of my hands; your walls are continually before me."

But God's firm foundation stands, bearing this seal: "The Lord knows those who are his."—We have a great high priest who has passed through the heavens, Jesus, the Son of God.

"You shall take two onyx stones, and engrave on them the names of the sons of Israel. . . . And Aaron shall bear their names before the Lord on his two shoulders for remembrance. . . . You shall make a breastpiece of judgment. . . . You shall set in it four rows of stones. . . . There shall be twelve stones with their names according to the names of the sons of Israel. . . . They shall be on Aaron's heart, when he goes in before the Lord.

John 20:16; Isa. 43:1; John 10:3–4; Isa. 49:16; 2 Tim. 2:19;
Heb. 4:14; Ex. 28:9, 12, 15, 17, 21, 30

MORNING

Finally, be strong in the Lord and in the strength of his might.

"My grace is sufficient for you, for my power is made perfect in weakness." Therefore I will boast all the more gladly of my weaknesses, so that the power of Christ may rest upon me. For the sake of Christ, then, I am content with weaknesses, insults, hardships, persecutions, and calamities. For when I am weak, then I am strong.—With the mighty deeds of the Lord God I will come; I will remind them of your righteousness, yours alone.—The gospel . . . is the power of God for salvation.

I can do all things through him who strengthens me.—I toil, struggling with all his energy that he powerfully works within me.—But we have this treasure in jars of clay, to show that the surpassing power belongs to God and not to us.

"The joy of the Lord is your strength."—May you be strengthened with all power, according to his glorious might, for all endurance and patience with joy.

Eph. 6:10; 2 Cor. 12:9–10; Ps. 71:16; Rom. 1:16; Phil. 4:13;
Col. 1:29; 2 Cor. 4:7; Neh. 8:10; Col. 1:11

EVENING

Jesus Christ our Lord.

"Jesus, for he will save his people from their sins."—He humbled himself by becoming obedient to the point of death, even death on a cross. Therefore God has highly exalted him and bestowed on him the name that is above every name, so that at the name of Jesus every knee should bow, in heaven and on earth and under the earth.

"Messiah . . . (he who is called Christ)."—"The Lord has anointed me to bring good news to the poor; he has sent me to bind up the brokenhearted, to proclaim liberty to the captives."

The last Adam became a life-giving spirit. . . . The second man is from heaven.—"My Lord and my God!"—"You call me Teacher and Lord, and you are right, for so I am. If I then, your Lord and Teacher, have washed your feet, you also ought to wash one another's feet. For I have given you an example, that you also should do just as I have done to you."

1 Cor. 1:9; Matt. 1:21; Phil. 2:8–10; John 4:25; Isa. 61:1;
1 Cor. 15:45, 47; John 20:28; John 13:13–15

MORNING

"Peace I leave with you; my peace I give to you.
Not as the world gives do I give to you."

And the world is passing away along with its desires.—Surely a man goes about as a shadow! Surely for nothing they are in turmoil; man heaps up wealth and does not know who will gather!—But what fruit were you getting at that time from the things of which you are now ashamed? For the end of those things is death.

"Martha, Martha, you are anxious and troubled about many things, but one thing is necessary. Mary has chosen the good portion, which will not be taken away from her."—I want you to be free from anxieties.

"I have said these things to you, that in me you may have peace. In the world you will have tribulation. But take heart; I have overcome the world."—Now may the Lord of peace himself give you peace at all times in every way.—The Lord bless you and keep you; the Lord make his face to shine upon you and be gracious to you; the Lord lift up his countenance upon you and give you peace.

John 14:27; 1 John 2:17; Ps. 39:6; Rom. 6:21; Luke 10:41–42;
1 Cor. 7:32; John 16:33; 2 Thess. 3:16; Num. 6:24–26

EVENING

The Spirit helps us in our weakness.

"The Helper, the Holy Spirit."—Do you not know that your body is a temple of the Holy Spirit within you, whom you have from God?—For it is God who works in you.

For we do not know what to pray for as we ought, but the Spirit himself intercedes for us with groanings too deep for words. And he who searches hearts knows what is the mind of the Spirit, because the Spirit intercedes for the saints according to the will of God.

For he knows our frame; he remembers that we are dust.—A bruised reed he will not break, and a faintly burning wick he will not quench.

"The spirit indeed is willing, but the flesh is weak."

The Lord is my shepherd; I shall not want. He makes me lie down in green pastures. He leads me beside still waters.

Rom. 8:26; John 14:26; 1 Cor. 6:19; Phil. 2:13; Rom. 8:26–27;
Ps. 103:14; Isa. 42:3; Matt. 26:41; Ps. 23:1–2

MORNING

"And you shall set the two stones on the shoulder pieces of the ephod, as stones of remembrance for the sons of Israel. And Aaron shall bear their names before the Lord."

[Jesus] holds his priesthood permanently, because he continues forever. Consequently, he is able to save to the uttermost those who draw near to God through him, since he always lives to make intercession for them.—Him who is able to keep you from stumbling and to present you blameless before the presence of his glory.

Since then we have a great high priest who has passed through the heavens, Jesus, the Son of God, let us hold fast our confession. For we do not have a high priest who is unable to sympathize with our weaknesses, but one who in every respect has been tempted as we are, yet without sin. Let us then with confidence draw near to the throne of grace.

"The beloved of the Lord dwells in safety. The High God surrounds him all day long, and dwells between his shoulders."

Ex. 28:12; Heb. 7:24–25; Jude 24; Heb. 4:14–16; Deut. 33:12

EVENING

"On that night the king could not sleep."

You hold my eyelids open.—Who is like the Lord our God, who looks far down on the heavens and the earth?

He does according to his will among the host of heaven and among the inhabitants of the earth.—Your way was through the sea, your path through the great waters; yet your footprints were unseen.—Surely the wrath of man shall praise you; the remnant of wrath you will put on like a belt.

"For the eyes of the Lord run to and fro throughout the whole earth, to give strong support to those whose heart is blameless toward him."—And we know that for those who love God all things work together for good.

"Are not two sparrows sold for a penny? And not one of them will fall to the ground apart from your Father. But even the hairs of your head are all numbered."

Est. 6:1; Ps. 77:4; Ps. 113:5–6; Dan. 4:35; Ps. 77:19; Ps. 76:10;
2 Chron. 16:9; Rom. 8:28; Matt. 10:29–30

MORNING

And do not grieve the Holy Spirit of God, by whom you were sealed for the day of redemption.

The love of the Spirit.—"The Helper, the Holy Spirit."—In all their affliction he was afflicted, and the angel of his presence saved them; in his love and in his pity he redeemed them; he lifted them up and carried them all the days of old. But they rebelled and grieved his Holy Spirit; therefore he turned to be their enemy, and himself fought against them.

By this we know that we abide in him and he in us, because he has given us of his Spirit.—When you . . . believed in him, [you] were sealed with the promised Holy Spirit, who is the guarantee of our inheritance until we acquire possession of it.—But I say, walk by the Spirit, and you will not gratify the desires of the flesh. For the desires of the flesh are against the Spirit, and the desires of the Spirit are against the flesh, for these are opposed to each other, to keep you from doing the things you want to do.

The Spirit helps us in our weakness.

Eph. 4:30; Rom. 15:30; John 14:26; Isa. 63:9–10;
1 John 4:13; Eph. 1:13–14; Gal. 5:16–17; Rom. 8:26

EVENING

I will return again to my place, until they acknowledge their guilt and seek my face, and in their distress earnestly seek me.

Your iniquities have made a separation between you and your God, and your sins have hidden his face from you.—My beloved had turned and gone. . . . I sought him, but found him not; I called him, but he gave no answer.—"I hid my face and was angry, but he went on backsliding in the way of his own heart. I have seen his ways, but I will heal him."—"Have you not brought this upon yourself by forsaking the Lord your God, when he led you in the way?"

"And he arose and came to his father. But while he was still a long way off, his father saw him and felt compassion, and ran and embraced him and kissed him."—I will heal their apostasy; I will love them freely, for my anger has turned from them.

If we confess our sins, he is faithful and just to forgive us our sins and to cleanse us from all unrighteousness.

Hos. 5:15; Isa. 59:2; Song 5:6; Isa. 57:17–18; Jer. 2:17;
Luke 15:20; Hos. 14:4; 1 John 1:9

MORNING

Oh, how abundant is your goodness, which you have stored up for those who fear you.

From of old no one has heard or perceived by the ear, no eye has seen a God besides you, who acts for those who wait for him.—"What no eye has seen, nor ear heard, nor the heart of man imagined, what God has prepared for those who love him"—these things God has revealed to us through the Spirit.—You make known to me the path of life; in your presence there is fullness of joy; at your right hand are pleasures forevermore.

How precious is your steadfast love, O God! The children of mankind take refuge in the shadow of your wings. They feast on the abundance of your house, and you give them drink from the river of your delights. For with you is the fountain of life; in your light do we see light.

Godliness is of value in every way, as it holds promise for the present life and also for the life to come.

Ps. 31:19; Isa. 64:4; 1 Cor. 2:9–10; Ps. 16:11; Ps. 36:7–9; 1 Tim. 4:8

EVENING

"The Son of God . . . has eyes like a flame of fire."

The heart is deceitful above all things, and desperately sick; who can understand it? "I the Lord search the heart and test the mind, to give every man according to his ways, according to the fruit of his deeds."—You have set our iniquities before you, our secret sins in the light of your presence.—And the Lord turned and looked at Peter. . . . And he went out and wept bitterly.

But Jesus on his part did not entrust himself to them, because he knew all people and needed no one to bear witness about man, for he himself knew what was in man.—For he knows our frame; he remembers that we are dust.—A bruised reed he will not break, and a faintly burning wick he will not quench.—"The Lord knows those who are his."—"I am the good shepherd. I know my own. . . . My sheep hear my voice, and I know them, and they follow me. I give them eternal life, and they will never perish, and no one will snatch them out of my hand."

Rev. 2:18; Jer. 17:9–10; Ps. 90:8; Luke 22:61–62; John 2:24–25;
Ps. 103:14; Isa. 42:3; 2 Tim. 2:19; John 10:14, 27–28

MORNING

Our Lord Jesus, the great shepherd of the sheep.

The chief Shepherd.—"I am the good shepherd. I know my own and my own know me. . . . My sheep hear my voice, and I know them, and they follow me. I give them eternal life, and they will never perish, and no one will snatch them out of my hand."

The Lord is my shepherd; I shall not want. He makes me lie down in green pastures. He leads me beside still waters. He restores my soul. He leads me in paths of righteousness for his name's sake.

All we like sheep have gone astray; we have turned—every one—to his own way; and the Lord has laid on him the iniquity of us all.—"I am the good shepherd. The good shepherd lays down his life for the sheep."—"I will seek the lost, and I will bring back the strayed, and I will bind up the injured, and I will strengthen the weak."—For you were straying like sheep, but have now returned to the Shepherd and Overseer of your souls.

Heb. 13:20; 1 Pet. 5:4; John 10:14, 27–28; Ps. 23:1–3;
Isa. 53:6; John 10:11; Ezek. 34:16; 1 Pet. 2:25

EVENING

And the city has no need of sun or moon to shine on it,
for the glory of God gives it light, and its lamp is the Lamb.

"At midday, O king, I saw on the way a light from heaven, brighter than the sun, that shone around me. . . . And I said, 'Who are you, Lord?' And the Lord said, 'I am Jesus whom you are persecuting.'"—Jesus took with him Peter and James, and John his brother, and led them up a high mountain by themselves. And he was transfigured before them, and his face shone like the sun, and his clothes became white as light.—The sun shall be no more your light by day, nor for brightness shall the moon give you light; but the Lord will be your everlasting light, and your God will be your glory. Your sun shall no more go down, nor your moon withdraw itself; for the Lord will be your everlasting light, and your days of mourning shall be ended.

The God of all grace . . . has called you to his eternal glory in Christ.

Rev. 21:23; Acts 26:13, 15; Matt. 17:1–2; Isa. 60:19–20; 1 Pet. 5:10

MORNING

The Lord is good, a stronghold in the day of trouble;
he knows those who take refuge in him.

"Give thanks to the Lord of hosts, for the Lord is good, for his steadfast love endures forever!"—God is our refuge and strength, a very present help in trouble.—I will say to the Lord, "My refuge and my fortress, my God, in whom I trust."—"Who is like you, a people saved by the Lord, the shield of your help, and the sword of your triumph!"—This God—his way is perfect; the word of the Lord proves true; he is a shield for all those who take refuge in him. "For who is God, but the Lord? And who is a rock, except our God?"

But if anyone loves God, he is known by God.—But God's firm foundation stands, bearing this seal: "The Lord knows those who are his," and, "Let everyone who names the name of the Lord depart from iniquity."—The Lord knows the way of the righteous, but the way of the wicked will perish.—"You have found favor in my sight, and I know you by name."

Nah. 1:7; Jer. 33:11; Ps. 46:1; Ps. 91:2; Deut. 33:29;
2 Sam. 22:31-32; 1 Cor. 8:3; 2 Tim. 2:19; Ps. 1:6; Ex. 33:17

EVENING

I want you to be free from anxieties.

He cares for you.—"The eyes of the Lord run to and fro throughout the whole earth, to give strong support to those whose heart is blameless toward him."—Oh, taste and see that the Lord is good! Blessed is the man who takes refuge in him! . . . The young lions suffer want and hunger; but those who seek the Lord lack no good thing.— "Therefore I tell you, do not be anxious about your life, what you will eat or what you will drink, nor about your body, what you will put on. Is not life more than food, and the body more than clothing? Look at the birds of the air: they neither sow nor reap nor gather into barns, and yet your heavenly Father feeds them. Are you not of more value than they?"

Do not be anxious about anything, but in everything by prayer and supplication with thanksgiving let your requests be made known to God. And the peace of God, which surpasses all understanding, will guard your hearts and your minds in Christ Jesus.

1 Cor. 7:32; 1 Pet. 5:7; 2 Chron. 16:9; Ps. 34:8, 10; Matt. 6:25-26; Phil. 4:6-7

MORNING

We await a Savior.

For the grace of God has appeared, bringing salvation for all people, training us to renounce ungodliness and worldly passions, and to live self-controlled, upright, and godly lives in the present age, waiting for our blessed hope, the appearing of the glory of our great God and Savior Jesus Christ, who gave himself for us to redeem us from all lawlessness and to purify for himself a people for his own possession who are zealous for good works.—But according to his promise we are waiting for new heavens and a new earth in which righteousness dwells. Therefore, beloved, since you are waiting for these, be diligent to be found by him without spot or blemish, and at peace.

Christ, having been offered once to bear the sins of many, will appear a second time, not to deal with sin but to save those who are eagerly waiting for him.—It will be said on that day, "Behold, this is our God; we have waited for him, that he might save us. This is the Lord; we have waited for him; let us be glad and rejoice in his salvation."

Phil. 3:20; Titus 2:11-14; 2 Pet. 3:13-14; Heb. 9:28; Isa. 25:9

EVENING

So run that you may obtain it.

The sluggard says, "There is a lion outside!"—Let us also lay aside every weight, and sin which clings so closely, and let us run with endurance the race that is set before us, looking to Jesus, the founder and perfecter of our faith.

Let us cleanse ourselves from every defilement of body and spirit, bringing holiness to completion in the fear of God.

I press on toward the goal.—So I do not run aimlessly. . . . But I discipline my body and keep it under control, lest . . . I myself should be disqualified.—For the present form of this world is passing away.

But according to his promise we are waiting for new heavens and a new earth in which righteousness dwells. Therefore, beloved, since you are waiting for these, be diligent.—Therefore, preparing your minds for action, and being sober-minded, set your hope fully on the grace that will be brought to you at the revelation of Jesus Christ.

1 Cor. 9:24; Prov. 22:13; Heb. 12:1-2; 2 Cor. 7:1; Phil. 3:14;
1 Cor. 9:26-27; 1 Cor. 7:31; 2 Pet. 3:13-14; 1 Pet. 1:13

MORNING

"For the life of the flesh is in the blood, and I have given it
for you on the altar to make atonement for your souls, for
it is the blood that makes atonement by the life."

"Behold, the Lamb of God, who takes away the sin of the world!"—The blood of the Lamb.—The precious blood of Christ, like that of a lamb without blemish or spot.—Without the shedding of blood there is no forgiveness of sins.—The blood of Jesus his Son cleanses us from all sin.

He entered once for all into the holy places, not by means of the blood of goats and calves but by means of his own blood, thus securing an eternal redemption.—Therefore, brothers, since we have confidence to enter the holy places by the blood of Jesus, by the new and living way that he opened for us through the curtain, that is, through his flesh . . . let us draw near with a true heart in full assurance of faith.

You were bought with a price. So glorify God in your body.

Lev. 17:11; John 1:29; Rev. 7:14; 1 Pet. 1:19; Heb. 9:22; 1 John 1:7;
Heb. 9:12; Heb. 10:19–20, 22; 1 Cor. 6:20

EVENING

"Oh, that I had wings like a dove!
I would fly away and be at rest."

When the sun rose, God appointed a scorching east wind, and the sun beat down on the head of Jonah so that he was faint. And he asked that he might die and said, "It is better for me to die than to live."

And Job said: . . . "Why is light given to him who is in misery, and life to the bitter in soul, who long for death, but it comes not, and dig for it more than for hidden treasures?"—Many are the afflictions of the righteous, but the Lord delivers him out of them all.

"Now is my soul troubled. And what shall I say? 'Father, save me from this hour'?"—Therefore he had to be made like his brothers in every respect, so that he might become a merciful and faithful high priest in the service of God, to make propitiation for the sins of the people. For because he himself has suffered when tempted, he is able to help those who are being tempted.

Ps. 55:6; Jonah 4:8; Job 3:2, 20–21; Ps. 34:19;
John 12:27; Heb. 2:17–18

MORNING

Let us therefore strive to enter that rest.

"Enter by the narrow gate. For the gate is wide and the way is easy that leads to destruction. . . . For the gate is narrow and the way is hard that leads to life, and those who find it are few."—"The kingdom of heaven has suffered violence, and the violent take it by force."—"Do not work for the food that perishes, but for the food that endures to eternal life, which the Son of Man will give to you."—Therefore, brothers, be all the more diligent to confirm your calling and election. . . . For in this way there will be richly provided for you an entrance into the eternal kingdom of our Lord and Savior Jesus Christ.—So run that you may obtain it. Every athlete exercises self-control in all things. They do it to receive a perishable wreath, but we an imperishable.

Whoever has entered God's rest has also rested from his works as God did from his.—The Lord will be your everlasting light, and your God will be your glory.

Heb. 4:11; Matt. 7:13–14; Matt. 11:12; John 6:27; 2 Pet. 1:10–11;
1 Cor. 9:24–25; Heb. 4:10; Isa. 60:19

EVENING

"You always hear me."

And Jesus lifted up his eyes and said, "Father, I thank you that you have heard me."—"Father, glorify your name." Then a voice came from heaven: "I have glorified it, and I will glorify it again."—"Behold, I have come to do your will, O God."—"Not my will, but yours, be done."

As he is so also are we in this world.—And this is the confidence that we have toward him, that if we ask anything according to his will he hears us.

Whatever we ask we receive from him, because we keep his commandments and do what pleases him.

And without faith it is impossible to please him, for whoever would draw near to God must believe that he exists and that he rewards those who seek him.

He always lives to make intercession for them.—We have an advocate with the Father, Jesus Christ the righteous.

John 11:42; John 11:41; John 12:28; Heb. 10:7; Luke 22:42; 1 John 4:17;
1 John 5:14; 1 John 3:22; Heb. 11:6; Heb. 7:25; 1 John 2:1

MORNING

"Your name shall . . . be called . . . Israel, for you have striven with God and with men, and have prevailed."

In his manhood he strove with God. He strove with the angel and prevailed; he wept and sought his favor.—No unbelief made [Abraham] waver concerning the promise of God, but he grew strong in his faith as he gave glory to God.

"Have faith in God. Truly, I say to you, whoever says to this mountain, 'Be taken up and thrown into the sea,' and does not doubt in his heart, but believes that what he says will come to pass, it will be done for him. Therefore I tell you, whatever you ask in prayer, believe that you have received it, and it will be yours."—"'If you can'! All things are possible for one who believes."—"And blessed is she who believed that there would be a fulfillment of what was spoken to her from the Lord."

"Increase our faith!"

Gen. 32:28; Hos. 12:3–4; Rom. 4:20; Mark 11:22–24;
Mark 9:23; Luke 1:45; Luke 17:5

EVENING

Little children, abide in him.

The one who doubts is like a wave of the sea that is driven and tossed by the wind. For that person must not suppose that he will receive anything from the Lord; he is a double-minded man, unstable in all his ways.

I am astonished that you are so quickly deserting him who called you in the grace of Christ and are turning to a different gospel—not that there is another one. . . . But even if we or an angel from heaven should preach to you a gospel contrary to the one we preached to you, let him be accursed.

You are severed from Christ, you who would be justified by the law; you have fallen away from grace. . . . You were running well. Who hindered you from obeying the truth?

"As the branch cannot bear fruit by itself, unless it abides in the vine, neither can you, unless you abide in me. If you abide in me, and my words abide in you, ask whatever you wish, and it will be done for you."—For all the promises of God find their Yes in him. That is why it is through him that we utter our Amen to God for his glory.

1 John 2:28; James 1:6–8; Gal. 1:6–8; Gal. 5:4, 7; John 15:4, 7; 2 Cor. 1:20

MORNING

But the fruit of the Spirit is . . . patience . . . gentleness.

"The Lord, the Lord, a God merciful and gracious, slow to anger, and abounding in steadfast love and faithfulness."

Walk in a manner worthy of the calling to which you have been called, with all humility and gentleness, with patience, bearing with one another in love.—Be kind to one another, tenderhearted, forgiving one another, as God in Christ forgave you.—But the wisdom from above is first pure, then peaceable, gentle, open to reason, full of mercy and good fruits, impartial and sincere.—Love is patient and kind.

In due season we will reap, if we do not give up.—Be patient, therefore, brothers, until the coming of the Lord. See how the farmer waits for the precious fruit of the earth, being patient about it, until it receives the early and the late rains. You also, be patient. Establish your hearts, for the coming of the Lord is at hand.

Gal. 5:22—23; Ex. 34:6; Eph. 4:1—2; Eph. 4:32;
James 3:17; 1 Cor. 13:4; Gal. 6:9; James 5:7—8

EVENING

"Immanuel" (which means, God with us).

"But will God indeed dwell with man on the earth? Behold, heaven and the highest heaven cannot contain you."—And the Word became flesh and dwelt among us, and we have seen his glory, glory as of the only Son from the Father, full of grace and truth.—Great indeed, we confess, is the mystery of godliness: He was manifested in the flesh.

But in these last days he has spoken to us by his Son, whom he appointed the heir of all things, through whom also he created the world.

On the evening of that day, the first day of the week, the doors being locked where the disciples were . . . Jesus came and stood among them. . . . Then the disciples were glad when they saw the Lord. Eight days later, his disciples were inside again, and Thomas was with them. . . . Then [Jesus] said to Thomas, "Put your finger here, and see my hands; and put out your hand, and place it in my side. Do not disbelieve, but believe." Thomas answered him, "My Lord and my God!"—To us a son is given; . . . Mighty God.

Matt. 1:23; 2 Chron. 6:18; John 1:14; 1 Tim. 3:16;
Heb. 1:2; John 20:19—20, 26—28; Isa. 9:6

MORNING

"In this manner you shall eat it: with your belt fastened. . . .
And you shall eat it in haste. It is the Lord's Passover."

Arise and go, for this is no place to rest.—For here we have no lasting city, but we seek the city that is to come.—So then, there remains a Sabbath rest for the people of God.

"Stay dressed for action and keep your lamps burning, and be like men who are waiting for their master to come home from the wedding feast, so that they may open the door to him at once when he comes and knocks. Blessed are those servants whom the master finds awake when he comes."— Therefore, preparing your minds for action, and being sober-minded, set your hope fully on the grace that will be brought to you at the revelation of Jesus Christ.—But one thing I do: forgetting what lies behind, . . . I press on toward the goal for the prize of the upward call of God in Christ Jesus. Let those of us who are mature think this way.

Ex. 12:11; Mic. 2:10; Heb. 13:14; Heb. 4:9; Luke 12:35–37; 1 Pet. 1:13; Phil. 3:13–15

EVENING

The Lord is my chosen portion and my cup.

Heirs of God and fellow heirs with Christ.—All things are yours.—My beloved is mine.—The Son of God . . . loved me and gave himself for me.

And the Lord said to Aaron, "You shall have no inheritance in their land, neither shall you have any portion among them. I am your portion and your inheritance among the people of Israel."

Whom have I in heaven but you? And there is nothing on earth that I desire besides you. My flesh and my heart may fail, but God is the strength of my heart and my portion forever.

Even though I walk through the valley of the shadow of death, I will fear no evil, for you are with me; your rod and your staff, they comfort me.—I know whom I have believed, and I am convinced that he is able to guard until that Day what has been entrusted to me.

O God, you are my God; earnestly I seek you; my soul thirsts for you; my flesh faints for you, as in a dry and weary land.

Ps. 16:5; Rom. 8:17; 1 Cor. 3:21; Song 2:16; Gal. 2:20;
Num 18:20; Ps. 73:25–26; Ps. 23:4; 2 Tim. 1:12; Ps. 63:1

MORNING

"Watch therefore, for you know neither the day nor the hour."

"But watch yourselves lest your hearts be weighed down with dissipation and drunkenness and cares of this life, and that day come upon you suddenly like a trap. For it will come upon all who dwell on the face of the whole earth. But stay awake at all times, praying that you may have strength to escape all these things that are going to take place, and to stand before the Son of Man."

The Lord will come like a thief in the night. While people are saying, "There is peace and security," then sudden destruction will come upon them as labor pains come upon a pregnant woman, and they will not escape. But you are not in darkness, brothers, for that day to surprise you like a thief. For you are all children of light, children of the day. We are not of the night or of the darkness. So then let us not sleep, as others do, but let us keep awake and be sober.

Matt. 25:13; Luke 21:34–36; 1 Thess. 5:2–6

EVENING

"I am God Almighty; walk before me, and be blameless."

Not that I have already obtained this or am already perfect. . . . Brothers, I do not consider that I have made it my own. But one thing I do: forgetting what lies behind and straining forward to what lies ahead, I press on toward the goal for the prize of the upward call of God in Christ Jesus.

Enoch walked with God, and he was not, for God took him.

But grow in the grace and knowledge of our Lord and Savior Jesus Christ.—And we all, with unveiled face, beholding the glory of the Lord, are being transformed into the same image from one degree of glory to another. For this comes from the Lord who is the Spirit.

When Jesus had spoken these words, he lifted up his eyes to heaven, and said, . . . "I do not ask that you take them out of the world, but that you keep them from the evil one. I in them and you in me, that they may become perfectly one."

Gen. 17:1; Phil. 3:12–14; Gen. 5:24; 2 Pet. 3:18; 2 Cor. 3:18; John 17:1, 15, 23

MORNING

"The latter glory of this house shall be greater than the former. . . . And in this place I will give peace."

"The house that is to be built for the Lord must be exceedingly magnificent, of fame and glory throughout all lands."—The glory of the Lord filled the Lord's house.

"Destroy this temple, and in three days I will raise it up." . . . But he was speaking about the temple of his body.—Indeed, in this case, what once had glory has come to have no glory at all, because of the glory that surpasses it.—And the Word became flesh and dwelt among us, and we have seen his glory, glory as of the only Son from the Father, full of grace and truth.—In these last days [God] has spoken to us by his Son, whom he appointed the heir of all things, through whom also he created the world.

"Glory to God in the highest, and on earth peace among those with whom he is pleased!"—Prince of Peace.—For he himself is our peace.—And the peace of God, which surpasses all understanding, will guard your hearts and your minds in Christ Jesus.

Hag. 2:9; 1 Chron. 22:5; 2 Chron. 7:2; John 2:19, 21; 2 Cor. 3:10;
John 1:14; Heb. 1:2; Luke 2:14; Isa. 9:6; Eph. 2:14; Phi. 4:7

EVENING

Let us . . . put on the armor of light.

But put on the Lord Jesus Christ.—That I may gain Christ and be found in him, not having a righteousness of my own that comes from the law, but that which comes through faith in Christ, the righteousness from God that depends on faith.—The righteousness of God through faith in Jesus Christ for all who believe.

He has covered me with the robe of righteousness.—With the mighty deeds of the Lord God I will come; I will remind them of your righteousness, yours alone.—At one time you were darkness, but now you are light in the Lord. Walk as children of light. . . . Take no part in the unfruitful works of darkness, but instead expose them. . . . But when anything is exposed by the light, it becomes visible, for anything that becomes visible is light. Therefore it says, "Awake, O sleeper, and arise from the dead, and Christ will shine on you." Look carefully then how you walk.

Rom. 13:12; Rom. 13:14; Phil. 3:8-9; Rom. 3:22;
Isa. 61:10; Ps. 71:16; Eph. 5:8, 11, 13-15

MORNING

"So you also, when you have done all that you were commanded, say, 'We are unworthy servants.'"

Then what becomes of our boasting? It is excluded. By what kind of law? By a law of works? No, but by the law of faith.—What do you have that you did not receive? If then you received it, why do you boast as if you did not receive it?—For by grace you have been saved through faith. And this is not your own doing; it is the gift of God, not a result of works, so that no one may boast. For we are his workmanship, created in Christ Jesus for good works, which God prepared beforehand, that we should walk in them.

But by the grace of God I am what I am, and his grace toward me was not in vain. On the contrary, I worked harder than any of them, though it was not I, but the grace of God that is with me.—For from him and through him and to him are all things.— "For all things come from you, and of your own have we given you."—Enter not into judgment with your servant, for no one living is righteous before you.

Luke 17:10; Rom. 3:27; 1 Cor. 4:7; Eph. 2:8–10; 1 Cor. 15:10;
Rom. 11:36; 1 Chron. 29:14; Ps. 143:2

EVENING

For he knows our frame; he remembers that we are dust.

The Lord God formed the man of dust from the ground and breathed into his nostrils the breath of life, and the man became a living creature.

I praise you, for I am fearfully and wonderfully made. Wonderful are your works; my soul knows it very well. My frame was not hidden from you, when I was being made in secret. . . . Your eyes saw my unformed substance; in your book were written, every one of them, the days that were formed for me, when as yet there was none of them.

Have we not all one Father? Has not one God created us?—"In him we live and move and have our being."—As a father shows compassion to his children, so the Lord shows compassion to those who fear him.—Yet he, being compassionate, atoned for their iniquity and did not destroy them; he restrained his anger often and did not stir up all his wrath. He remembered that they were but flesh, a wind that passes and comes not again.

Ps. 103:14; Gen. 2:7; Ps. 139:14–16; Mal. 2:10;
Acts 17:28; Ps. 103:13; Ps. 78:38–39

MORNING

He will quiet you by his love.

"It was not because you were more in number than any other people that the Lord set his love on you and chose you, for you were the fewest of all peoples, but it is because the Lord loves you."—We love because he first loved us.—And you . . . he has now reconciled in his body of flesh by his death, in order to present you holy and blameless and above reproach before him.

In this is love, not that we have loved God but that he loved us and sent his Son to be the propitiation for our sins.—But God shows his love for us in that while we were still sinners, Christ died for us.—And behold, a voice from heaven said, "This is my beloved Son, with whom I am well pleased."—"For this reason the Father loves me, because I lay down my life that I may take it up again."—His Son . . . He is the radiance of the glory of God and the exact imprint of his nature, and he upholds the universe by the word of his power. After making purification for sins, he sat down at the right hand of the Majesty on high.

Zeph. 3:17; Deut. 7:7–8; 1 John 4:19; Col. 1:21–22; 1 John 4:10;
Rom. 5:8; Matt. 3:17; John 10:17; Heb. 1:2–3

EVENING

The new and living way.

Then Cain went away from the presence of the Lord.—But your iniquities have made a separation between you and your God, and your sins have hidden his face from you.—The holiness without which no one will see the Lord.—"I am the way, and the truth, and the life. No one comes to the Father except through me."—Our Savior Christ Jesus . . . abolished death and brought life and immortality to light through the gospel.—The way into the holy places is not yet opened as long as the first section is still standing.—For he himself is our peace, who has made us both one and has broken down in his flesh the dividing wall of hostility.—And behold, the curtain of the temple was torn in two, from top to bottom.

"For the gate is narrow and the way is hard that leads to life, and those who find it are few."—You make known to me the path of life; in your presence there is fullness of joy; at your right hand are pleasures forevermore.

Heb. 10:20; Gen. 4:16; Isa. 59:2; Heb. 12:14; John 14:6; 2 Tim. 1:10;
Heb. 9:8; Eph. 2:14; Matt. 27:51; Matt. 7:14; Ps. 16:11

MORNING

They ought always to pray and not lose heart.

And he said to them, "Which of you who has a friend will go to him at midnight and say to him, 'Friend, lend me three loaves, for a friend of mine has arrived on a journey, and I have nothing to set before him'; and he will answer from within, 'Do not bother me; the door is now shut, and my children are with me in bed. I cannot get up and give you anything'? I tell you, though he will not get up and give him anything because he is his friend, yet because of his impudence he will rise and give him whatever he needs."—Praying at all times in the Spirit, with all prayer and supplication. To that end keep alert with all perseverance, making supplication for all the saints.

"I will not let you go unless you bless me." . . . "You have striven with God and with men."—Continue steadfastly in prayer, being watchful in it with thanksgiving.

[Jesus] went out to the mountain to pray, and all night he continued in prayer to God.

Luke 18:1; Luke 11:5–8; Eph. 6:18; Gen. 32:26, 28; Col. 4:2; Luke 6:12

EVENING

Forgive all my sins.

"Come now, let us reason together, says the Lord: though your sins are like scarlet, they shall be as white as snow; though they are red like crimson, they shall become like wool."—"Take heart, my son; your sins are forgiven."—"I, I am he who blots out your transgressions for my own sake, and I will not remember your sins."

"The Son of Man has authority on earth to forgive sins."—In him we have redemption through his blood, the forgiveness of our trespasses, according to the riches of his grace.—He saved us, not because of works done by us in righteousness, but according to his own mercy, by the washing of regeneration and renewal of the Holy Spirit, whom he poured out on us richly through Jesus Christ our Savior.—Having forgiven us all our trespasses, by canceling the record of debt that stood against us with its legal demands. This he set aside, nailing it to the cross.

Bless the Lord, O my soul, . . . who forgives all your iniquity.

Ps. 25:18; Isa. 1:18; Matt. 9:2; Isa. 43:25; Matt. 9:6;
Eph. 1:7; Titus 3:5–6; Col. 2:13–14; Ps. 103:2–3

MORNING

The Lord caused all that he did to succeed in his hands.

Blessed is everyone who fears the Lord, who walks in his ways! You shall eat the fruit of the labor of your hands; you shall be blessed, and it shall be well with you.—Trust in the Lord, and do good; dwell in the land and befriend faithfulness. Delight yourself in the Lord, and he will give you the desires of your heart.—"Do not be frightened, and do not be dismayed, for the Lord your God is with you wherever you go."—"But seek first the kingdom of God and his righteousness, and all these things will be added to you."

As long as he sought the Lord, God made him prosper.—"Take care lest you forget the Lord your God by not keeping his commandments and his rules and his statutes, which I command you today. . . . Lest you say in your heart, 'My power and the might of my hand have gotten me this wealth.'"—"Is not the Lord your God with you? And has he not given you peace on every side?"

Gen. 39:3; Ps. 128:1–2; Ps. 37:3–4; Josh. 1:9; Matt. 6:33;
2 Chron. 26:5; Deut. 8:11, 17; 1 Chron. 22:18

EVENING

"Why do you question these things in your hearts?"

He did not weaken in faith when he considered his own body, which was as good as dead (since he was about a hundred years old), or when he considered the barrenness of Sarah's womb. No unbelief made him waver concerning the promise of God, but he grew strong in his faith as he gave glory to God.—"Which is easier, to say to the paralytic, 'Your sins are forgiven,' or to say, 'Rise, take up your bed and walk?'"—"All things are possible for one who believes."

"All authority in heaven and on earth has been given to me."—"Why are you so afraid? Have you still no faith?"—"Look at the birds of the air: . . . your heavenly Father feeds them. Are you not of more value than they?"—"Why are you discussing among yourselves the fact that you have no bread? Do you not remember the five loaves for the five thousand?"

And my God will supply every need of yours according to his riches in glory in Christ Jesus.

Mark 2:8; Rom. 4:19–20; Mark 2:9; Mark 9:23; Matt. 28:18;
Mark 4:40; Matt. 6:26; Matt. 16:8–9; Phil. 4:19

MORNING

"No one ever spoke like this man!"

You are the most handsome of the sons of men; grace is poured upon your lips; therefore God has blessed you forever.—The Lord God has given me the tongue of those who are taught, that I may know how to sustain with a word him who is weary.—His mouth is most sweet, and he is altogether desirable. This is my beloved and this is my friend.

And all spoke well of him and marveled at the gracious words that were coming from his mouth.—He was teaching them as one who had authority, and not as their scribes.

Let the word of Christ dwell in you richly . . . in all wisdom.—The sword of the Spirit . . . is the word of God.—For the word of God is living and active, sharper than any two-edged sword.—For the weapons of our warfare are not of the flesh but have divine power to destroy strongholds. We destroy arguments and every lofty opinion raised against the knowledge of God, and take every thought captive to obey Christ.

John 7:46; Ps. 45:2; Isa. 50:4; Song 5:16; Luke 4:22;
Matt. 7:29; Col. 3:16; Eph. 6:17; Heb. 4:12; 2 Cor. 10:4–5

EVENING

"The exulting of the wicked is short."

"You shall bruise his heel."—"This is your hour, and the power of darkness."—Since therefore the children share in flesh and blood, he himself likewise partook of the same things, that through death he might destroy the one who has the power of death, that is, the devil.—He disarmed the rulers and authorities and put them to open shame, by triumphing over them in him.

Be sober-minded; be watchful. Your adversary the devil prowls around like a roaring lion, seeking someone to devour. Resist him, firm in your faith.—Resist the devil, and he will flee from you.

The wicked plots against the righteous and gnashes his teeth at him, but the Lord laughs at the wicked, for he sees that his day is coming.—The God of peace will soon crush Satan under your feet.—The devil . . . was thrown into the lake of fire and sulfur, . . . and they will be tormented day and night forever and ever.

Job 20:5; Gen. 3:15; Luke 22:53; Heb. 2:14; Col. 2:15; 1 Pet. 5:8–9;
James 4:7; Ps. 37:12–13; Rom. 16:20; Rev. 20:10

MORNING

"The younger son gathered all he had and took a journey into a far country, and there he squandered his property in reckless living."

And such were some of you. But you were washed, you were sanctified, you were justified in the name of the Lord Jesus Christ and by the Spirit of our God.—We . . . were by nature children of wrath, like the rest of mankind. But God, being rich in mercy, because of the great love with which he loved us, even when we were dead in our trespasses, made us alive together with Christ—by grace you have been saved—and raised us up with him and seated us with him in the heavenly places in Christ Jesus.—In this is love, not that we have loved God but that he loved us and sent his Son to be the propitiation for our sins.

God shows his love for us in that while we were still sinners, Christ died for us. . . . For if while we were enemies we were reconciled to God by the death of his Son, much more, now that we are reconciled, shall we be saved by his life.

Luke 15:13; 1 Cor. 6:11; Eph. 2:3–6; 1 John 4:10; Rom. 5:8, 10

EVENING

As the Lord has forgiven you, so you also must forgive.

"A certain moneylender had two debtors. One owed five hundred denarii, and the other fifty. When they could not pay, he cancelled the debt of both."—"I forgave you all that debt because you pleaded with me. And should not you have had mercy on your fellow servant, as I had mercy on you?"

"And whenever you stand praying, forgive, if you have anything against anyone, so that your Father also who is in heaven may forgive you your trespasses."—Put on then, as God's chosen ones, holy and beloved, compassionate hearts, kindness, humility, meekness, and patience, bearing with one another and, if one has a complaint against another, forgiving each other.

"Lord, how often will my brother sin against me, and I forgive him? As many as seven times?" Jesus said to him, "I do not say to you seven times, but seventy-seven times."

Love . . . binds everything together in perfect harmony.

Col. 3:13; Luke 7:41–42; Matt. 18:32–33; Mark 11:25–26;
Col. 3:12–13; Matt. 18:21–22; Col. 3:14

MORNING

And he arose and came to his father. But while he was still
a long way off, his father saw him and felt compassion,
and ran and embraced him and kissed him.

The Lord is merciful and gracious, slow to anger and abounding in steadfast love. He will not always chide, nor will he keep his anger forever. He does not deal with us according to our sins, nor repay us according to our iniquities. For as high as the heavens are above the earth, so great is his steadfast love toward those who fear him; as far as the east is from the west, so far does he remove our transgressions from us. As a father shows compassion to his children, so the Lord shows compassion to those who fear him.

You have received the Spirit of adoption as sons, by whom we cry, "Abba! Father!" The Spirit himself bears witness with our spirit that we are children of God.—But now in Christ Jesus you who once were far off have been brought near by the blood of Christ. . . . So then you are no longer strangers and aliens, but you are fellow citizens with the saints and members of the household of God.

Luke 15:20; Ps. 103:8–13; Rom. 8:15–16; Eph. 2:13, 19

EVENING

"Behold, I am making all things new."

"Unless one is born again he cannot see the kingdom of God."—If anyone is in Christ, he is a new creation. The old has passed away; behold, the new has come.

"And I will give you a new heart, and a new spirit I will put within you. And I will remove the heart of stone from your flesh and give you a heart of flesh."—Cleanse out the old leaven that you may be a new lump.—The new self, created after the likeness of God in true righteousness and holiness.—You shall be called by a new name that the mouth of the Lord will give.

"For behold, I create new heavens and a new earth, and the former things shall not be remembered or come into mind."—Since all these things are thus to be dissolved, what sort of people ought you to be in lives of holiness and godliness.

Rev. 21:5; John 3:3; 2 Cor. 5:17; Ezek. 36:26; 1 Cor. 5:7;
Eph. 4:24; Isa. 62:2; Isa. 65:17; 2 Pet. 3:11

MORNING

"Everything that can stand the fire, you shall pass through the fire, and it shall be clean."

"The Lord your God is testing you, to know whether you love the Lord your God with all your heart and with all your soul."—"He will sit as a refiner and purifier of silver, and he will purify the sons of Levi and refine them like gold and silver, and they will bring offerings in righteousness to the Lord."—Each one's work will become manifest, for the Day will disclose it, because it will be revealed by fire, and the fire will test what sort of work each one has done.

"I will turn my hand against you and will smelt away your dross as with lye and remove all your alloy."—"I will refine them and test them."

You, O God, have tested us; you have tried us as silver is tried. . . . We went through fire and through water; yet you have brought us out to a place of abundance.

"When you walk through fire you shall not be burned, and the flame shall not consume you."

Num. 31:23; Deut. 13:3; Mal. 3:3; 1 Cor. 3:13;
Isa. 1:25; Jer. 9:7; Ps. 66:10, 12; Isa. 43:2

EVENING

. . . that we might die to sin and live to righteousness.

Put off your old self, which belongs to your former manner of life and is corrupt through deceitful desires, and . . . be renewed in the spirit of your minds, and . . . put on the new self, created after the likeness of God in true righteousness and holiness.

For you have died, and your life is hidden with Christ in God.—Just as Christ was raised from the dead by the glory of the Father, we too might walk in newness of life. . . . We know that our old self was crucified with him in order that the body of sin might be brought to nothing, so that we would no longer be enslaved to sin. For one who has died has been set free from sin. . . . So you also must consider yourselves dead to sin and alive to God in Christ Jesus. Let not sin therefore reign in your mortal body, to make you obey its passions. Do not present your members to sin as instruments for unrighteousness, but present yourselves to God as those who have been brought from death to life, and your members to God as instruments for righteousness.

1 Pet. 2:24; Eph. 4:22–24; Col. 3:3; Rom. 6:4, 6–7, 11–13

MORNING

"Abide in me, and I in you."

I have been crucified with Christ. It is no longer I who live, but Christ who lives in me. And the life I now live in the flesh I live by faith in the Son of God, who loved me and gave himself for me.

I know that nothing good dwells in me, that is, in my flesh. For I have the desire to do what is right, but not the ability to carry it out. . . . Wretched man that I am! Who will deliver me from this body of death? Thanks be to God through Jesus Christ our Lord!—But if Christ is in you, although the body is dead because of sin, the Spirit is life because of righteousness.—If indeed you continue in the faith, stable and steadfast, not shifting from the hope of the gospel that you heard.

And now, little children, abide in him, so that when he appears we may have confidence and not shrink from him in shame at his coming.—Whoever says he abides in him ought to walk in the same way in which he walked.

John 15:4; Gal. 2:20; Rom. 7:18, 24–25; Rom. 8:10;
Col. 1:23; 1 John 2:28; 1 John 2:6

EVENING

"Do you believe in the Son of Man?"

"And who is he, sir, that I may believe in him?"

He is the radiance of the glory of God and the exact imprint of his nature.—He who is the blessed and only Sovereign, the King of kings and Lord of lords, who alone has immortality, who dwells in unapproachable light, whom no one has ever seen or can see. To him be honor and eternal dominion. Amen.— "I am the Alpha and the Omega," says the Lord God, "who is and who was and who is to come, the Almighty."

"Lord, I believe."—I know whom I have believed, and I am convinced that he is able to guard until that Day what has been entrusted to me.

"Behold, I am laying in Zion a stone, a cornerstone chosen and precious, and whoever believes in him will not be put to shame." So the honor is for you who believe.

John 9:35; John 9:36; Heb. 1:3; 1 Tim. 6:15–16;
Rev. 1:8; John 9:38; 2 Tim. 1:12; 1 Pet. 2:6–7

MORNING

As we share abundantly in Christ's sufferings, so through
Christ we share abundantly in comfort too.

Share his sufferings.—But rejoice insofar as you share Christ's sufferings, that you may also rejoice and be glad when his glory is revealed.—If we have died with him, we will also live with him.—If children, then heirs—heirs of God and fellow heirs with Christ, provided we suffer with him in order that we may also be glorified with him.

So when God desired to show more convincingly to the heirs of the promise the unchangeable character of his purpose, he guaranteed it with an oath, so that by two unchangeable things, in which it is impossible for God to lie, we who have fled for refuge might have strong encouragement to hold fast to the hope set before us.—Now may our Lord Jesus Christ himself, and God our Father, who loved us and gave us eternal comfort and good hope through grace, comfort your hearts and establish them in every good work and word.

2 Cor. 1:5; Phil. 3:10; 1 Pet. 4:13; 2 Tim. 2:11; Rom. 8:17;
Heb. 6:17–18; 2 Thess. 2:16–17

EVENING

"Martha, Martha, you are anxious and troubled about many things."

"Consider the ravens: they neither sow nor reap. . . . Consider the lilies, how they grow: they neither toil nor spin. . . . And do not seek what you are to eat and what you are to drink, nor be worried. For all the nations of the world seek after these things, and your Father knows that you need them."

But if we have food and clothing, with these we will be content. But those who desire to be rich fall into temptation, into a snare, into many senseless and harmful desires that plunge people into ruin and destruction. For the love of money is a root of all kinds of evils. It is through this craving that some have wandered away from the faith and pierced themselves with many pangs.—"The cares of the world and the deceitfulness of riches and the desires for other things enter in and choke the word, and it proves unfruitful."—Therefore, since we are surrounded by so great a cloud of witnesses, let us also lay aside every weight, and sin which clings so closely, and let us run with endurance the race that is set before us.

Luke 10:41; Luke 12:24, 27, 29–30; 1 Tim. 6:8–10; Mark 4:19; Heb. 12:1

MORNING

*"The secret things belong to the Lord our God, but
the things that are revealed belong to us."*

O Lord, my heart is not lifted up; my eyes are not raised too high; I do not occupy myself with things too great and too marvelous for me. But I have calmed and quieted my soul, like a weaned child with its mother; like a weaned child is my soul within me.

The friendship of the Lord is for those who fear him, and he makes known to them his covenant.—"There is a God in heaven who reveals mysteries."—"Behold, these are but the outskirts of his ways, and how small a whisper do we hear of him!"

"No longer do I call you servants, for the servant does not know what his master is doing; but I have called you friends, for all that I have heard from my Father I have made known to you."— "If you love me, you will keep my commandments. And I will ask the Father, and he will give you another Helper, to be with you forever, even the Spirit of truth."

Deut. 29:29; Ps. 131:1–2; Ps. 25:14; Dan. 2:28;
Job 26:14; John 15:15; John 14:15–17

EVENING

The Spirit intercedes for the saints according to the will of God.

"Truly, truly, I say to you, whatever you ask of the Father in my name, he will give it to you. Until now you have asked nothing in my name. Ask, and you will receive, that your joy may be full."—Praying at all times in the Spirit, with all prayer and supplication.

And this is the confidence that we have toward him, that if we ask anything according to his will he hears us. And if we know that he hears us in whatever we ask, we know that we have the requests that we have asked of him.—For this is the will of God, your sanctification.

For God has . . . called us . . . in holiness . . . who gives his Holy Spirit to you.

Rejoice always, pray without ceasing, give thanks in all circumstances; for this is the will of God in Christ Jesus for you. Do not quench the Spirit.

Rom. 8:27; John 16:23–24; Eph. 6:18; 1 John 5:14–15;
1 Thess. 4:3; 1 Thess. 4:7–8; 1 Thess. 5:16–19

MORNING

Look carefully then how you walk, not as unwise but as wise,
making the best use of the time, because the days are evil.

"Only be very careful to observe the commandment and the law . . . to love the Lord your God, and to walk in all his ways and to keep his commandments and to cling to him and to serve him with all your heart and with all your soul."—Walk in wisdom toward outsiders, making the best use of the time. Let your speech always be gracious, seasoned with salt, so that you may know how you ought to answer each person.—Abstain from every form of evil.

"As the bridegroom was delayed, they all became drowsy and slept. But at midnight there was a cry, 'Here is the bridegroom! Come out to meet him.' . . . Watch therefore, for you know neither the day nor the hour."

Therefore, brothers, be all the more diligent to confirm your calling and election, for if you practice these qualities you will never fall.—"Blessed are those servants whom the master finds awake when he comes."

Eph. 5:15–16; Josh. 22:5; Col. 4:5–6; 1 Thess. 5:22;
Matt. 25:5–6, 13; 2 Pet. 1:10; Luke 12:37

EVENING

"Hold fast what you have, so that
no one may seize your crown."

"If I only touch his garment, I will be made well."—"Lord, if you will, you can make me clean." "I will; be clean."—"Faith like a grain of mustard seed."

Therefore do not throw away your confidence, which has a great reward.—Work out your own salvation with fear and trembling, for it is God who works in you, both to will and to work for his good pleasure.

"First the blade, then the ear, then the full grain in the ear."—"Let us know; let us press on to know the Lord."—"The kingdom of heaven has suffered violence, and the violent take it by force."—So run that you may obtain it.

I have fought the good fight, I have finished the race, I have kept the faith. Henceforth there is laid up for me the crown of righteousness, which the Lord, the righteous judge, will award to me on that Day.

Rev. 3:11; Matt. 9:21; Matt. 8:2–3; Matt. 17:20; Heb. 10:35; Phil. 2:12–13;
Mark 4:28; Hos. 6:3; Matt. 11:12; 1 Cor. 9:24; 2 Tim. 4:7–8

MORNING

In everything by prayer and supplication with thanksgiving let your requests be made known to God.

I love the Lord, because he has heard my voice and my pleas for mercy. Because he inclined his ear to me, therefore I will call on him as long as I live.—"And when you pray, do not heap up empty phrases as the Gentiles do, for they think that they will be heard for their many words."—The Spirit helps us in our weakness. For we do not know what to pray for as we ought, but the Spirit himself intercedes for us with groanings too deep for words.

I desire then that in every place the men should pray, lifting holy hands without anger or quarreling.—Praying at all times in the Spirit, with all prayer and supplication. To that end keep alert with all perseverance, making supplication for all the saints.

"If two of you agree on earth about anything they ask, it will be done for them by my Father in heaven."

Phil. 4:6; Ps. 116:1-2; Matt. 6:7; Rom. 8:26; 1 Tim. 2:8;
Eph. 6:18; Matt. 18:19

EVENING

All your works shall give thanks to you, O Lord, and all your saints shall bless you!

Bless the Lord, O my soul, and all that is within me, bless his holy name! Bless the Lord, O my soul, and forget not all his benefits.—I will bless the Lord at all times; his praise shall continually be in my mouth.—Every day I will bless you and praise your name forever and ever.

Because your steadfast love is better than life, my lips will praise you. So I will bless you as long as I live; in your name I will lift up my hands. My soul will be satisfied as with fat and rich food, and my mouth will praise you with joyful lips.

"My soul magnifies the Lord, and my spirit rejoices in God my Savior."

"Worthy are you, our Lord and God, to receive glory and honor and power, for you created all things, and by your will they existed and were created."

Ps. 145:10; Ps. 103:1-2; Ps. 34:1; Ps. 145:2; Ps. 63:3-5;
Luke 1:46-47; Rev. 4:11

MORNING

"And you shall put the mercy seat on the top of the ark. . . . There I will meet with you."

The way into the holy places is not yet opened.—And Jesus cried out again with a loud voice and yielded up his spirit. And behold, the curtain of the temple was torn in two, from top to bottom.

Therefore, brothers, since we have confidence to enter the holy places by the blood of Jesus, by the new and living way that he opened for us through the curtain, that is, through his flesh, . . . let us draw near with a true heart in full assurance of faith, with our hearts sprinkled clean from an evil conscience and our bodies washed with pure water.—Let us then with confidence draw near to the throne of grace, that we may receive mercy and find grace to help in time of need.

. . . Christ Jesus, whom God put forward as a propitiation by his blood, to be received by faith. This was to show God's righteousness, because in his divine forbearance he had passed over former sins.—Through him we . . . have access in one Spirit to the Father.

Ex. 25:21–22; Heb. 9:8; Matt. 27:50–51; Heb. 10:19–20, 22;
Heb. 4:16; Rom. 3:24–25; Eph. 2:18

EVENING

"Faith like a grain of mustard seed."

Barak said to [Deborah], "If you will go with me, I will go, but if you will not go with me, I will not go." So on that day God subdued Jabin the king of Canaan before the people of Israel.—Gideon . . . was too afraid of his family and the men of the town to do it by day, he did it by night. . . . Then Gideon said to God, "If you will save Israel by my hand, as you have said, . . . Please let me test . . . with the fleece . . . " And God did so.

"I know that you have but little power, and yet you have kept my word and have not denied my name."—Whoever has despised the day of small things shall rejoice.

We ought always to give thanks to God for you, brothers, as is right, because your faith is growing abundantly.—"Increase our faith!"—I will be like the dew to Israel; he shall blossom like the lily; he shall take root like the trees of Lebanon; his shoots shall spread out; his beauty shall be like the olive, and his fragrance like Lebanon.

Matt. 17:20; Judg. 4:8, 23; Judg. 6:27, 36, 39, 40; Rev. 3:8;
Zech. 4:10; 2 Thess. 1:3; Luke 17:5; Hos. 14:5–6

MORNING

The holiness without which no one will see the Lord.

"Unless one is born again he cannot see the kingdom of God."—But nothing unclean will ever enter it.—There is no flaw in you.

"You shall be holy, for I the Lord your God am holy."— As obedient children, do not be conformed to the passions of your former ignorance, but as he who called you is holy, you also be holy in all your conduct, since it is written, "You shall be holy, for I am holy." And if you call on him as Father who judges impartially according to each one's deeds, conduct yourselves with fear throughout the time of your exile.—Put off your old self, which belongs to your former manner of life and is corrupt through deceitful desires, and . . . be renewed in the spirit of your minds, and . . . put on the new self, created after the likeness of God in true righteousness and holiness.—He chose us in him before the foundation of the world, that we should be holy and blameless before him.

Heb. 12:14; John 3:3; Rev. 21:27; Song 4:7; Lev. 19:2;
1 Pet. 1:14–17; Eph. 4:22–24; Eph. 1:4

EVENING

"Gold refined by fire."

"There is no one who has left house or brothers or sisters or mother or father or children or lands, for my sake and for the gospel, who will not receive a hundredfold now in this time, houses and brothers and sisters and mothers and children and lands, with persecutions, and in the age to come eternal life."

Beloved, do not be surprised at the fiery trial when it comes upon you to test you, as though something strange were happening to you.—Now for a little while, if necessary, you have been grieved by various trials, so that the tested genuineness of your faith—more precious than gold that perishes though it is tested by fire—may be found to result in praise and glory and honor at the revelation of Jesus Christ.

And after you have suffered a little while, the God of all grace, who has called you to his eternal glory in Christ, will himself restore, confirm, strengthen, and establish you.—"In the world you will have tribulation. But take heart; I have overcome the world."

Rev. 3:18; Mark 10:29–30; 1 Pet. 4:12; 1 Pet. 1:6–7; 1 Pet. 5:10; John 16:33

MORNING

"Take this child away and nurse him for me, and I will give you your wages."

"You go into the vineyard too, and whatever is right I will give you."—"For truly, I say to you, whoever gives you a cup of water to drink because you belong to Christ will by no means lose his reward."—Whoever brings blessing will be enriched, and one who waters will himself be watered.—God is not unjust so as to overlook your work and the love that you have shown for his name in serving the saints, as you still do.—Each will receive his wages according to his labor.

"Then the righteous will answer him, saying, 'Lord, when did we see you hungry and feed you, or thirsty and give you drink? And when did we see you a stranger and welcome you, or naked and clothe you?' . . . And the King will answer them, . . . 'As you did it to one of the least of these my brothers, you did it to me. . . . Come, you who are blessed by my Father, inherit the kingdom prepared for you from the foundation of the world.'"

Ex. 2:9; Matt. 20:4; Mark 9:41; Prov. 11:25; Heb. 6:10;
1 Cor. 3:8; Matt. 25:37–38, 40, 34

EVENING

You search out my path and my lying down.

Then Jacob awoke from his sleep and said, "Surely the Lord is in this place, and I did not know it." And he was afraid and said, "How awesome is this place! This is none other than the house of God, and this is the gate of heaven."

"The eyes of the Lord run to and fro throughout the whole earth, to give strong support to those whose heart is blameless toward him."

In peace I will both lie down and sleep; for you alone, O Lord, make me dwell in safety.

Because you have made the Lord your dwelling place—the Most High, who is my refuge—no evil shall be allowed to befall you, no plague come near your tent. For he will command his angels concerning you to guard you in all your ways.—If you lie down, you will not be afraid; when you lie down, your sleep will be sweet.—He gives to his beloved sleep.

Ps. 139:3; Gen. 28:16–17; 2 Chron. 16:9; Ps. 4:8; Ps. 91:9–11;
Prov. 3:24; Ps. 127:2

MORNING

Christ also suffered for you, leaving you an example,
so that you might follow in his steps.

"Even the Son of Man came not to be served but to serve."—"Whoever would be first among you must be slave of all."

Jesus of Nazareth . . . went about doing good.—Bear one another's burdens, and so fulfill the law of Christ.

The meekness and gentleness of Christ.—In humility count others more significant than yourselves.

"Father, forgive them, for they know not what they do."—Be kind to one another, tenderhearted, forgiving one another, as God in Christ forgave you.

Whoever says he abides in him ought to walk in the same way in which he walked.—Looking to Jesus, the founder and perfecter of our faith, who for the joy that was set before him endured the cross, despising the shame, and is seated at the right hand of the throne of God.

1 Pet. 2:21; Mark 10:45; Mark 10:44; Acts 10:38; Gal. 6:2; 2 Cor. 10:1;
Phil. 2:3; Luke 23:34; Eph. 4:32; 1 John 2:6; Heb. 12:2

EVENING

I sought him, but found him not;
I called him, but he gave no answer.

"O Lord, what can I say, when Israel has turned their backs before their enemies!" . . . The Lord said to Joshua, "Get up! Why have you fallen on your face? Israel has sinned; . . . they have taken some of the devoted things . . . and put them among their own belongings."

Behold, the Lord's hand is not shortened, that it cannot save, or his ear dull, that it cannot hear; but your iniquities have made a separation between you and your God, and your sins have hidden his face from you so that he does not hear.

If I had cherished iniquity in my heart, the Lord would not have listened.

Beloved, if our heart does not condemn us, we have confidence before God; and whatever we ask we receive from him, because we keep his commandments and do what pleases him.

Song 5:6; Josh. 7:8, 10–11; Isa. 59:1–2; Ps. 66:18; 1 John 3:21–22

MORNING

You have died, and your life is hidden with Christ in God.

How can we who died to sin still live in it?—I have been crucified with Christ. It is no longer I who live, but Christ who lives in me. And the life I now live in the flesh I live by faith in the Son of God, who loved me and gave himself for me.—He died for all, that those who live might no longer live for themselves but for him who for their sake died and was raised.—Therefore, if anyone is in Christ, he is a new creation. The old has passed away; behold, the new has come.

We are in him who is true, in his Son Jesus Christ.—"Just as you, Father, are in me, and I in you, that they also may be in us."—Now you are the body of Christ and individually members of it.—"Because I live, you also will live."

"To the one who conquers I will give some of the hidden manna, and I will give him a white stone, with a new name written on the stone that no one knows except the one who receives it."

Col. 3:3; Rom. 6:2; Gal. 2:20; 2 Cor. 5:15; 2 Cor. 5:17; 1 John 5:20;
John 17:21; 1 Cor. 12:27; John 14:19; Rev. 2:17

EVENING

"See how he loved him!"

He died for all.—"Greater love has no one than this, that someone lay down his life for his friends."

He always lives to make intercession for them.—"I go to prepare a place for you."

"I will come again and will take you to myself, that where I am you may be also."—"Father, I desire that they also, whom you have given me, may be with me where I am."—Having loved his own who were in the world, he loved them to the end.

We love because he first loved us.—The love of Christ controls us, because we have concluded this: that one has died for all, therefore all have died; and he died for all, that those who live might no longer live for themselves but for him who for their sake died and was raised.

"If you keep my commandments, you will abide in my love, just as I have kept my Father's commandments and abide in his love."

John 11:36; 2 Cor. 5:15; John 15:13; Heb. 7:25; John 14:2; John 14:3;
John 17:24; John 13:1; 1 John 4:19; 2 Cor. 5:14–15; John 15:10

MORNING

"I will ask the Father, and he will give you another Helper . . . even the Spirit of truth."

"It is to your advantage that I go away, for if I do not go away, the Helper will not come to you. But if I go, I will send him to you."

The Spirit himself bears witness with our spirit that we are children of God.—You did not receive the spirit of slavery to fall back into fear, but you have received the Spirit of adoption as sons, by whom we cry, "Abba! Father!"—The Spirit helps us in our weakness. For we do not know what to pray for as we ought, but the Spirit himself intercedes for us with groanings too deep for words.

May the God of hope fill you with all joy and peace in believing, so that by the power of the Holy Spirit you may abound in hope.—Hope does not put us to shame, because God's love has been poured into our hearts through the Holy Spirit who has been given to us.

By this we know that we abide in him and he in us, because he has given us of his Spirit.

John 14:16–17; John 16:7; Rom. 8:16; Rom. 8:15;
Rom. 8:26; Rom. 15:13; Rom. 5:5; 1 John 4:13

EVENING

"Should I not seek rest for you, that it may be well with you?"

There remains a Sabbath rest for the people of God.—My people will abide in a peaceful habitation, in secure dwellings, and in quiet resting places.— "There the wicked cease from troubling, and there the weary are at rest."— "They may rest from their labors."

Jesus has gone as a forerunner on our behalf, having become a high priest forever after the order of Melchizedek.

"Come to me, all who labor and are heavy laden, and I will give you rest. Take my yoke upon you, and learn from me, for I am gentle and lowly in heart, and you will find rest for your souls. For my yoke is easy, and my burden is light."—"In returning and rest you shall be saved; in quietness and in trust shall be your strength."

The Lord is my shepherd; I shall not want. He makes me lie down in green pastures. He leads me beside still waters.

Ruth 3:1; Heb. 4:9; Isa. 32:18; Job 3:17; Rev. 14:13;
Heb. 6:20; Matt. 11:28–30; Isa. 30:15; Ps. 23:1–2

MORNING

The ark of the covenant of the Lord went before them three
days' journey, to seek out a resting place for them.

My times are in your hand.—He chose our heritage for us.—Lead me, O Lord, in your righteousness; . . . make your way straight before me.—Commit your way to the Lord; trust in him, and he will act.—In all your ways acknowledge him, and he will make straight your paths.—Your ears shall hear a word behind you, saying, "This is the way, walk in it," when you turn to the right or when you turn to the left.

The Lord is my shepherd; I shall not want. He makes me lie down in green pastures. He leads me beside still waters.—As a father shows compassion to his children, so the Lord shows compassion to those who fear him. For he knows our frame; he remembers that we are dust.—"The Gentiles seek after all these things, and your heavenly Father knows that you need them all."—Casting all your anxieties on him, because he cares for you.

Num. 10:33; Ps. 31:15; Ps. 47:4; Ps. 5:8; Ps. 37:5; Prov. 3:6; Isa. 30:21;
Ps. 23:1-2; Ps. 103:13-14; Matt. 6:32; 1 Pet. 5:7

EVENING

"Rabbi" (which means Teacher), "where are you staying?"
He said to them, "Come and you will see."

"In my Father's house are many rooms. If it were not so, would I have told you that I go to prepare a place for you? And if I go and prepare a place for you, I will come again and will take you to myself, that where I am you may be also."—"The one who conquers, I will grant him to sit with me on my throne."

For thus says the One who is high and lifted up, who inhabits eternity, whose name is Holy: "I dwell in the high and holy place, and also with him who is of a contrite and lowly spirit, to revive the spirit of the lowly, and to revive the heart of the contrite."

"Behold, I stand at the door and knock. If anyone hears my voice and opens the door, I will come in to him and eat with him, and he with me."

"Behold, I am with you always, to the end of the age."—How precious is your steadfast love, O God! The children of mankind take refuge in the shadow of your wings.

John 1:38-39; John 14:2-3; Rev. 3:21; Isa. 57:15; Rev. 3:20;
Matt. 28:20; Ps. 36:7

MORNING

When he appears we shall be like him,
because we shall see him as he is.

To all who did receive him, who believed in his name, he gave the right to become children of God.—By which he has granted to us his precious and very great promises, so that through them you may become partakers of the divine nature, having escaped from the corruption that is in the world because of sinful desire.

From of old no one has heard or perceived by the ear, no eye has seen a God besides you, who acts for those who wait for him.

For now we see in a mirror dimly, but then face to face. Now I know in part; then I shall know fully, even as I have been fully known.—Christ . . . will transform our lowly body to be like his glorious body, by the power that enables him even to subject all things to himself.—As for me, I shall behold your face in righteousness; when I awake, I shall be satisfied with your likeness.

1 John 3:2; John 1:12; 2 Pet. 1:4; Isa. 64:4; 1 Cor. 13:12;
Phil. 3:20–21; Ps. 17:15

EVENING

"The man who stands next to me," declares the Lord of hosts.

In him the whole fullness of deity dwells bodily.—"I have granted help to one who is mighty; I have exalted one chosen from the people."—"I have trodden the winepress alone, and from the peoples no one was with me."

Great indeed, we confess, is the mystery of godliness: He was manifested in the flesh.—To us a child is born, to us a son is given; and the government shall be upon his shoulder, and his name shall be called Wonderful Counselor, Mighty God, Everlasting Father, Prince of Peace.

He is the radiance of the glory of God and the exact imprint of his nature, and he upholds the universe by the word of his power. After making purification for sins, he sat down at the right hand of the Majesty on high. . . . But of the Son he says, "Your throne, O God, is forever and ever." . . . "Let all God's angels worship him."

King of kings and Lord of lords.

Zech. 13:7; Col. 2:9; Ps. 89:19; Isa. 63:3; 1 Tim. 3:16;
Isa. 9:6; Heb. 1:3, 8, 6; Rev. 19:16

MORNING

*"Oh that you would bless me, . . . and that you would keep
me from harm. . . ." And God granted what he asked.*

The blessing of the Lord makes rich, and he adds no sorrow with it.—"When he is quiet, who can condemn? When he hides his face, who can behold him?"

Salvation belongs to the Lord; your blessing be on your people!—Oh, how abundant is your goodness, which you have stored up for those who fear you and worked for those who take refuge in you, in the sight of the children of mankind!—"I do not ask that you take them out of the world, but that you keep them from the evil one."

"Ask, and it will be given to you; seek, and you will find; knock, and it will be opened to you. For everyone who asks receives, and the one who seeks finds, and to the one who knocks it will be opened."—The Lord redeems the life of his servants; none of those who take refuge in him will be condemned.

1 Chron. 4:10; Prov. 10:22; Job 34:29; Ps. 3:8;
Ps. 31:19; John 17:15; Matt. 7:7-8; Ps. 34:22

EVENING

*It was a night of watching by the Lord,
to bring them out of the land of Egypt.*

The Lord Jesus on the night when he was betrayed took bread, and when he had given thanks, he broke it, and said, "This is my body which is for you. Do this in remembrance of me." In the same way also he took the cup, after supper, saying, "This cup is the new covenant in my blood. Do this, as often as you drink it, in remembrance of me."

He . . . knelt down and prayed. . . . And being in an agony he prayed more earnestly; and his sweat became like great drops of blood falling down to the ground.

Now it was the day of Preparation of the Passover. It was about the sixth hour. . . . So he delivered him over to them to be crucified. So they took Jesus, and he went out . . . to the place called . . . Golgotha. There they crucified him.

Christ, our Passover lamb, has been sacrificed. Let us therefore celebrate the festival.

Ex. 12:42; 1 Cor. 11:23-25; Luke 22:41, 44; John 19:14, 16-18; 1 Cor. 5:7-8

MORNING

"Who can stand?"

Who can endure the day of his coming, and who can stand when he appears? For he is like a refiner's fire and like fullers' soap.

I looked, and behold, a great multitude that no one could number, from every nation, from all tribes and peoples and languages, standing before the throne and before the Lamb, clothed in white robes, with palm branches in their hands. . . . "These are the ones coming out of the great tribulation. They have washed their robes and made them white in the blood of the Lamb. They shall hunger no more, neither thirst anymore; the sun shall not strike them, nor any scorching heat. For the Lamb in the midst of the throne will be their shepherd, and he will guide them to springs of living water, and God will wipe away every tear from their eyes."

There is therefore now no condemnation for those who are in Christ Jesus.—For freedom Christ has set us free; stand firm therefore, and do not submit again to a yoke of slavery.

Rev. 6:17; Mal. 3:2; Rev. 7:9, 14-17; Rom. 8:1; Gal. 5:1

EVENING

Enter not into judgment with your servant,
for no one living is righteous before you.

"Come now, let us reason together, says the Lord: though your sins are like scarlet, they shall be as white as snow; though they are red like crimson, they shall become like wool."

"Let them lay hold of my protection, let them make peace with me, let them make peace with me."—"Agree with God, and be at peace; thereby good will come to you."

Since we have been justified by faith, we have peace with God through our Lord Jesus Christ.—A person is not justified by works of the law but through faith in Jesus Christ.—By works of the law no human being will be justified in his sight.

"By him everyone who believes is freed from everything from which you could not be freed by the law of Moses."

But thanks be to God, who gives us the victory through our Lord Jesus Christ.

Ps. 143:2; Isa. 1:18; Isa. 27:5; Job 22:21; Rom. 5:1;
Gal. 2:16; Rom. 3:20; Acts 13:39; 1 Cor. 15:57

MORNING

"I know that my Redeemer lives."

If while we were enemies we were reconciled to God by the death of his Son, much more, now that we are reconciled, shall we be saved by his life.—He holds his priesthood permanently, because he continues forever. Consequently, he is able to save to the uttermost those who draw near to God through him, since he always lives to make intercession for them.

"Because I live, you also will live."—If in Christ we have hope in this life only, we are of all people most to be pitied. But in fact Christ has been raised from the dead, the firstfruits of those who have fallen asleep.

"And a Redeemer will come to Zion, to those in Jacob who turn from transgression," declares the Lord.—We have redemption through his blood, the forgiveness of our trespasses, according to the riches of his grace.—You were ransomed from the futile ways inherited from your forefathers, not with perishable things such as silver or gold, but with the precious blood of Christ, like that of a lamb without blemish or spot.

Job 19:25; Rom. 5:10; Heb. 7:24-25; John 14:19;
1 Cor. 15:19-20; Isa. 59:20; Eph. 1:7; 1 Pet. 1:18-19

EVENING

Now the Spirit expressly says that in later times some will depart from the faith by devoting themselves to deceitful spirits.

"Take care then how you hear."—Let the word of Christ dwell in you richly, teaching and admonishing one another in all wisdom.—In all circumstances take up the shield of faith, with which you can extinguish all the flaming darts of the evil one.

Great peace have those who love your law; nothing can make them stumble. How sweet are your words to my taste, sweeter than honey to my mouth! Through your precepts I get understanding; therefore I hate every false way.

Your word is a lamp to my feet and a light to my path. . . . I have more understanding than all my teachers, for your testimonies are my meditation.

Even Satan disguises himself as an angel of light.—But even if we or an angel from heaven should preach to you a gospel contrary to the one we preached to you, let him be accursed.

1 Tim. 4:1; Luke 8:18; Col. 3:16; Eph. 6:16; Ps. 119:165,
103-104; Ps. 119:105, 99; 2 Cor. 11:14; Gal. 1:8

MORNING

His commandments are not burdensome.

"This is the will of my Father, that everyone who looks on the Son and believes in him should have eternal life."—Whatever we ask we receive from him, because we keep his commandments and do what pleases him.

"My yoke is easy, and my burden is light."—"If you love me, you will keep my commandments. . . . Whoever has my commandments and keeps them, he it is who loves me. And he who loves me will be loved by my Father, and I will love him and manifest myself to him."

Blessed is the one who finds wisdom, and the one who gets understanding. . . . Her ways are ways of pleasantness, and all her paths are peace.—Great peace have those who love your law; nothing can make them stumble.—I delight in the law of God, in my inner being.

This is his commandment, that we believe in the name of his Son Jesus Christ and love one another.—Love does no wrong to a neighbor; therefore love is the fulfilling of the law.

1 John 5:3; John 6:40; 1 John 3:22; Matt. 11:30; John 14:15, 21;
Prov. 3:13, 17; Ps. 119:165; Rom. 7:22; 1 John 3:23; Rom. 13:10

EVENING

Remember not the sins of my youth or my transgressions.

I have blotted out your transgressions like a cloud and your sins like mist.—"I, I am he who blots out your transgressions for my own sake, and I will not remember your sins."—"Come now, let us reason together, says the Lord: though your sins are like scarlet, they shall be as white as snow; though they are red like crimson, they shall become like wool."—"I will forgive their iniquity, and I will remember their sin no more."—You will cast all our sins into the depths of the sea.

In love you have delivered my life from the pit of destruction, for you have cast all my sins behind your back.—Who is a God like you, pardoning iniquity? . . . He does not retain his anger forever, because he delights in steadfast love.—To him who loves us and has freed us from our sins by his blood, . . . to him be glory and dominion forever and ever. Amen.

Ps. 25:7; Isa. 44:22; Isa. 43:25; Isa. 1:18; Jer. 31:34;
Mic. 7:19; Isa. 38:17; Mic. 7:18; Rev. 1:5

MORNING

"Those whom I love, I reprove and discipline."

"My son, do not regard lightly the discipline of the Lord, nor be weary when reproved by him. For the Lord disciplines the one he loves, and chastises every son whom he receives."—As a father the son in whom he delights.—He wounds, but he binds up; he shatters, but his hands heal.—Humble yourselves, therefore, under the mighty hand of God so that at the proper time he may exalt you.—"I have tried you in the furnace of affliction."

He does not afflict from his heart or grieve the children of men.—He does not deal with us according to our sins, nor repay us according to our iniquities. For as high as the heavens are above the earth, so great is his steadfast love toward those who fear him; as far as the east is from the west, so far does he remove our transgressions from us. As a father shows compassion to his children, so the Lord shows compassion to those who fear him. For he knows our frame; he remembers that we are dust.

Rev. 3:19; Heb. 12:5-6; Prov. 3:12; Job 5:18; 1 Pet. 5:6;
Isa. 48:10; Lam. 3:33; Ps. 103:10-14

EVENING

God is in heaven and you are on earth.
Therefore let your words be few.

"And when you pray, do not heap up empty phrases as the Gentiles do, for they think that they will be heard for their many words. Do not be like them, for your Father knows what you need before you ask him."

They . . . called upon the name of Baal from morning until noon, saying, "O Baal, answer us!"

"Two men went up into the temple to pray, one a Pharisee and the other a tax collector. The Pharisee, standing by himself, prayed thus: 'God, I thank you that I am not like other men, extortioners, unjust, adulterers, or even like this tax collector.' . . . But the tax collector, standing far off, would not even lift up his eyes to heaven, but beat his breast, saying, 'God, be merciful to me, a sinner!' I tell you, this man went down to his house justified, rather than the other."

"Lord, teach us to pray."

Eccles. 5:2; Matt. 6:7-8; 1 Kings 18:26; Luke 18:10-11, 13-14; Luke 11:1

MORNING

But the fruit of the Spirit is . . . goodness.

Be imitators of God, as beloved children.—"Love your enemies and pray for those who persecute you, so that you may be sons of your Father who is in heaven. For he makes his sun rise on the evil and on the good, and sends rain on the just and on the unjust."—"Be merciful, even as your Father is merciful."
The fruit of light is found in all that is good and right and true.

But when the goodness and loving kindness of God our Savior appeared, he saved us, not because of works done by us in righteousness, but according to his own mercy, by the washing of regeneration and renewal of the Holy Spirit, whom he poured out on us richly through Jesus Christ our Savior.—The Lord is good to all, and his mercy is over all that he has made.—He who did not spare his own Son but gave him up for us all, how will he not also with him graciously give us all things?

Gal. 5:22; Eph. 5:1; Matt. 5:44–45; Luke 6:36;
Eph. 5:9; Titus 3:4–6; Ps. 145:9; Rom. 8:32

EVENING

Ebenezer; . . . "Till now the Lord has helped us."

When I was brought low, he saved me.—Blessed be the Lord! For he has heard the voice of my pleas for mercy. The Lord is my strength and my shield; in him my heart trusts, and I am helped; my heart exults, and with my song I give thanks to him.

It is better to take refuge in the Lord than to trust in man. It is better to take refuge in the Lord than to trust in princes.—Blessed is he whose help is the God of Jacob, whose hope is in the Lord his God.—He led them by a straight way till they reached a city to dwell in.—Not one word of all the good promises that the Lord had made to the house of Israel had failed; all came to pass.

"When I sent you out with no moneybag or knapsack or sandals, did you lack anything?" They said, "Nothing."—You have been my help, and in the shadow of your wings I will sing for joy.

1 Sam. 7:12; Ps. 116:6; Ps. 28:6–7; Ps. 118:8–9; Ps. 146:5;
Ps. 107:7; Josh. 21:45; Luke 22:35; Ps. 63:7

MORNING

"This is the statute of the Passover: no foreigner shall eat of it."

We have an altar from which those who serve the tent have no right to eat.—"Unless one is born again he cannot see the kingdom of God."—You were at that time separated from Christ, alienated from the commonwealth of Israel and strangers to the covenants of promise. . . . But now in Christ Jesus you who once were far off have been brought near by the blood of Christ.

For he himself is our peace, who has made us both one and has broken down in his flesh the dividing wall of hostility by abolishing the law of commandments expressed in ordinances, that he might create in himself one new man in place of the two, so making peace.

So then you are no longer strangers and aliens, but you are fellow citizens with the saints and members of the household of God.

"Behold, I stand at the door and knock. If anyone hears my voice and opens the door, I will come in to him and eat with him, and he with me."

Ex. 12:43; Heb. 13:10; John 3:3; Eph. 2:12–13; Eph. 2:14–15;
Eph. 2:19; Rev. 3:20

EVENING

[Jesus] prayed for the third time, saying the same words again.

In the days of his flesh, Jesus offered up prayers and supplications, with loud cries and tears, to him who was able to save him from death.

"Let us know; let us press on to know the Lord."—Be constant in prayer.—Praying at all times in the Spirit, with all prayer and supplication. To that end keep alert with all perseverance, making supplication.—By prayer and supplication with thanksgiving let your requests be made known to God. And the peace of God, which surpasses all understanding, will guard your hearts and your minds in Christ Jesus.

"Nevertheless, not as I will, but as you will."—This is the confidence that we have toward him, that if we ask anything according to his will he hears us.—Delight yourself in the Lord, and he will give you the desires of your heart. Commit your way to the Lord; trust in him, and he will act.

Matt. 26:44; Heb. 5:7; Hos. 6:3; Rom. 12:12; Eph. 6:18;
Phil. 4:6–7; Matt. 26:39; 1 John 5:14; Ps. 37:4–5

MORNING

If children, then heirs—heirs of God and fellow heirs with Christ.

If you are Christ's, then you are Abraham's offspring, heirs according to promise.

See what kind of love the Father has given to us, that we should be called children of God.—So you are no longer a slave, but a son, and if a son, then an heir through God.—He predestined us for adoption as sons through Jesus Christ, according to the purpose of his will.

"Father, I desire that they also, whom you have given me, may be with me where I am, to see my glory that you have given me."

"The one who conquers and who keeps my works until the end, to him I will give authority over the nations."—"The one who conquers, I will grant him to sit with me on my throne, as I also conquered and sat down with my Father on his throne."

Rom. 8:17; Gal. 3:29; 1 John 3:1; Gal. 4:7; Eph. 1:5;
John 17:24; Rev. 2:26; Rev. 3:21

EVENING

God chose what is low and despised in the world.

"Are not all these who are speaking Galileans?"

[Jesus] saw two brothers . . . casting a net into the sea, for they were fishermen. And he said to them, "Follow me."—Now when they saw the boldness of Peter and John, and perceived that they were uneducated, common men, they were astonished. And they recognized that they had been with Jesus.

My speech and my message were not in plausible words of wisdom, but in demonstration of the Spirit and of power, so that your faith might not rest in the wisdom of men but in the power of God.

"You did not choose me, but I chose you and appointed you that you should go and bear fruit. . . . Whoever abides in me and I in him, he it is that bears much fruit, for apart from me you can do nothing."—But we have this treasure in jars of clay, to show that the surpassing power belongs to God.

1 Cor. 1:28; Acts 2:7; Matt. 4:18-19; Acts 4:13;
1 Cor. 2:4-5; John 15:16, 5; 2 Cor. 4:7

MORNING

Reclining at table at Jesus' side.

"As one whom his mother comforts, so I will comfort you."—They were bringing children to him that he might touch them. . . . . And he took them in his arms and blessed them, laying his hands on them.—Jesus called his disciples to him and said, "I have compassion on the crowd because they have been with me now three days and have nothing to eat. And I am unwilling to send them away hungry, lest they faint on the way."—For we do not have a high priest who is unable to sympathize with our weaknesses, but one who in every respect has been tempted as we are.—In his love and in his pity he redeemed them.

"I will not leave you as orphans; I will come to you."—"Can a woman forget her nursing child, that she should have no compassion on the son of her womb? Even these may forget, yet I will not forget you."—"The Lamb in the midst of the throne will be their shepherd, and he will guide them to springs of living water, and God will wipe away every tear from their eyes."

John 13:23; Isa. 66:13; Mark 10:13, 16; Matt. 15:32; Heb. 4:15;
Isa. 63:9; John 14:18; Isa. 49:15; Rev. 7:17

EVENING

Jesus Christ the righteous. He is the propitiation for our sins.

Toward the mercy seat shall the faces of the cherubim be. And you shall put the mercy seat on the top of the ark, and in the ark you shall put the testimony that I shall give you. There I will meet with you, and from above the mercy seat.

Surely his salvation is near to those who fear him. . . . Steadfast love and faithfulness meet; righteousness and peace kiss each other.

If you, O Lord, should mark iniquities, O Lord, who could stand? But with you there is forgiveness, that you may be feared. . . . O Israel, hope in the Lord! For with the Lord there is steadfast love, and with him is plentiful redemption. And he will redeem Israel from all his iniquities.—All have sinned and fall short of the glory of God, and are justified by his grace as a gift, through the redemption that is in Christ Jesus, whom God put forward as a propitiation by his blood, to be received by faith. This was to show God's righteousness, because in his divine forbearance he had passed over former sins.

1 John 2:1-2; Ex. 25:20-22; Ps. 85:9-10; Ps. 130:3-4, 7-8; Rom. 3:23-25

MORNING

We have come to know and to believe
the love that God has for us.

But God, being rich in mercy, because of the great love with which he loved us, even when we were dead in our trespasses, made us alive together with Christ—by grace you have been saved—and raised us up with him and seated us with him in the heavenly places in Christ Jesus, so that in the coming ages he might show the immeasurable riches of his grace in kindness toward us in Christ Jesus.

"For God so loved the world, that he gave his only Son, that whoever believes in him should not perish but have eternal life."—He who did not spare his own Son but gave him up for us all, how will he not also with him graciously give us all things?—The Lord is good to all, and his mercy is over all that he has made.

We love because he first loved us.

"Blessed is she who believed that there would be a fulfillment of what was spoken to her from the Lord."

1 John 4:16; Eph. 2:4–7; John 3:16; Rom. 8:32; Ps. 145:9;
1 John 4:19; Luke 1:45

EVENING

Do not be haughty, but associate with the lowly.

My brothers, show no partiality as you hold the faith in our Lord Jesus Christ, the Lord of glory. . . . Has not God chosen those who are poor in the world to be rich in faith and heirs of the kingdom, which he has promised to those who love him?

Let no one seek his own good, but the good of his neighbor.—But if we have food and clothing, with these we will be content. But those who desire to be rich fall into temptation, into a snare, into many senseless and harmful desires that plunge people into ruin and destruction.

But God chose what is foolish in the world to shame the wise; God chose what is weak in the world to shame the strong; God chose what is low and despised in the world, even things that are not, to bring to nothing things that are, so that no human being might boast in the presence of God.

O Lord, my heart is not lifted up; my eyes are not raised too high.

Rom. 12:16; James 2:1, 5; 1 Cor. 10:24; 1 Tim. 6:8–9; 1 Cor. 1:27–29; Ps. 131:1

MORNING

Let your speech always be gracious.

A word fitly spoken is like apples of gold in a setting of silver. Like a gold ring or an ornament of gold is a wise reprover to a listening ear.—Let no corrupting talk come out of your mouths, but only such as is good for building up, as fits the occasion, that it may give grace to those who hear.—"The good person out of his good treasure brings forth good, and the evil person out of his evil treasure brings forth evil. . . . By your words you will be justified."—The tongue of the wise brings healing.

Those who feared the Lord spoke with one another. The Lord paid attention and heard them, and a book of remembrance was written before him of those who feared the Lord and esteemed his name.

"If you utter what is precious, and not what is worthless, you shall be as my mouth."— But as you excel in everything—in faith, in speech, in knowledge, in all earnestness, . . . see that you excel in this act of grace also.

Col. 4:6; Prov. 25:11–12; Eph. 4:29; Matt. 12:35, 37;
Prov. 12:18; Mal. 3:16; Jer. 15:19; 2 Cor. 8:7

EVENING

Your steadfast love is before my eyes.

The Lord is gracious and merciful, slow to anger and abounding in steadfast love.—"Your Father who is in heaven . . . makes his sun rise on the evil and on the good, and sends rain on the just and on the unjust."

Therefore be imitators of God, as beloved children. And walk in love, as Christ loved us and gave himself up for us, a fragrant offering and sacrifice to God.—Be kind to one another, tenderhearted, forgiving one another, as God in Christ forgave you.—Having purified your souls by your obedience to the truth for a sincere brotherly love, love one another earnestly from a pure heart.—The love of Christ controls us.

"Love your enemies, and do good, and lend, expecting nothing in return, and your reward will be great, and you will be sons of the Most High, for he is kind to the ungrateful and the evil. Be merciful, even as your Father is merciful."

Ps. 26:3; Ps. 145:8; Matt. 5:45; Eph. 5:1–2; Eph. 4:32;
1 Pet. 1:22; 2 Cor. 5:14; Luke 6:35–36

MORNING

Then Jesus was led up by the Spirit into the wilderness to be tempted by the devil.

In the days of his flesh, Jesus offered up prayers and supplications, with loud cries and tears, to him who was able to save him from death, and he was heard because of his reverence. Although he was a son, he learned obedience through what he suffered. And being made perfect, he became the source of eternal salvation to all who obey him.—We do not have a high priest who is unable to sympathize with our weaknesses, but one who in every respect has been tempted as we are, yet without sin.

No temptation has overtaken you that is not common to man. God is faithful, and he will not let you be tempted beyond your ability, but with the temptation he will also provide the way of escape, that you may be able to endure it.—"My grace is sufficient for you, for my power is made perfect in weakness."

Matt. 4:1; Heb. 5:7-9; Heb. 4:15; 1 Cor. 10:13; 2 Cor. 12:9

EVENING

"The Son of Man came . . . to give his life as a ransom for many."

If the blood of goats and bulls, and the sprinkling of defiled persons with the ashes of a heifer, sanctify for the purification of the flesh, how much more will the blood of Christ, who through the eternal Spirit offered himself without blemish to God, purify our conscience from dead works to serve the living God.

Like a lamb that is led to the slaughter.—"I lay down my life for the sheep. . . . No one takes it from me, but I lay it down of my own accord. I have authority to lay it down, and I have authority to take it up again."

"For the life of the flesh is in the blood, and I have given it for you on the altar to make atonement for your souls, for it is the blood that makes atonement by the life."—Without the shedding of blood there is no forgiveness of sins.

While we were still sinners, Christ died for us. Since, therefore, we have now been justified by his blood, much more shall we be saved by him from the wrath of God.

Matt. 20:28; Heb. 9:13-14; Isa. 53:7; John 10:15,
18; Lev. 17:11; Heb. 9:22; Rom. 5:8-9

MORNING

If we confess our sins, he is faithful and just to forgive us our sins and to cleanse us from all unrighteousness.

I know my transgressions, and my sin is ever before me. Against you, you only, have I sinned and done what is evil in your sight.

"And he arose and came to his father. But while he was still a long way off, his father saw him and felt compassion, and ran and embraced him and kissed him."—I have blotted out your transgressions like a cloud and your sins like mist; return to me, for I have redeemed you.—Your sins are forgiven for his name's sake.—God in Christ forgave you.—So that he might be just and the justifier of the one who has faith in Jesus.

"I will sprinkle clean water on you, and you shall be clean."—"They will walk with me in white, for they are worthy."

This is he who came by water and blood—Jesus Christ; not by the water only but by the water and the blood.

1 John 1:9; Ps. 51:3–4; Luke 15:20; Isa. 44:22; 1 John 2:12;
Eph. 4:32; Rom. 3:26; Ezek. 36:25; Rev. 3:4; 1 John 5:6

EVENING

Can wicked rulers be allied with you?

Indeed our fellowship is with the Father and with his Son Jesus Christ.— Beloved, we are God's children now, and what we will be has not yet appeared; but we know that when he appears we shall be like him, because we shall see him as he is. And everyone who thus hopes in him purifies himself as he is pure.

"The ruler of this world is coming. He has no claim on me."—A high priest, holy, innocent, unstained.

We do not wrestle against flesh and blood, but against the rulers, against the authorities, against the cosmic powers over this present darkness, against the spiritual forces of evil in the heavenly places.—The prince of the power of the air, the spirit that is now at work in the sons of disobedience.

We know that everyone who has been born of God does not keep on sinning, but he who was born of God protects him, and the evil one does not touch him. We know that we are from God, and the whole world lies in the power of the evil one.

Ps. 94:20; 1 John 1:3; 1 John 3:2–3; John 14:30;
Heb. 7:26; Eph. 6:12; Eph. 2:2; 1 John 5:18–19

MORNING

"I have taken your iniquity away from you, and I will clothe you with pure vestments."

Blessed is the one whose transgression is forgiven, whose sin is covered.—We have all become like one who is unclean.—I know that nothing good dwells in me, that is, in my flesh. For I have the desire to do what is right, but not the ability to carry it out.

For as many of you as were baptized into Christ have put on Christ.—You have put off the old self with its practices and have put on the new self, which is being renewed in knowledge after the image of its creator.—Not having a righteousness of my own that comes from the law, but . . . the righteousness from God that depends on faith.

"Bring quickly the best robe, and put it on him."—The fine linen is the righteous deeds of the saints.—I will greatly rejoice in the Lord; my soul shall exult in my God, for he has clothed me with the garments of salvation; he has covered me with the robe of righteousness.

Zech. 3:4; Ps. 32:1; Isa. 64:6; Rom. 7:18; Gal. 3:27;
Col. 3:9–10; Phil. 3:9; Luke 15:22; Rev. 19:8; Isa. 61:10

EVENING

The Day will disclose it.

Therefore do not pronounce judgment before the time, before the Lord comes, who will bring to light the things now hidden in darkness and will disclose the purposes of the heart. Then each one will receive his commendation from God.

Why do you pass judgment on your brother? Or you, why do you despise your brother? For we will all stand before the judgment seat of God. . . . So then each of us will give an account of himself to God. Therefore let us not pass judgment on one another any longer.

God judges the secrets of men by Christ Jesus.—"The Father judges no one, but has given all judgment to the Son. . . . And he has given him authority to execute judgment, because he is the Son of Man."

"O great and mighty God, whose name is the Lord of hosts, great in counsel and mighty in deed, whose eyes are open to all the ways of the children of man, rewarding each one according to his ways and according to the fruit of his deeds."

1 Cor. 3:13; 1 Cor. 4:5; Rom. 14:10, 12–13; Rom. 2:16; John 5:22, 27; Jer. 32:18–19

MORNING

"A disciple is not above his teacher."

"You call me Teacher and Lord, and you are right, for so I am."

"It is enough for the disciple to be like his teacher, and the servant like his master."—"If they persecuted me, they will also persecute you. If they kept my word, they will also keep yours."—"I have given them your word, and the world has hated them because they are not of the world, just as I am not of the world."

Consider him who endured from sinners such hostility against himself, so that you may not grow weary or fainthearted. In your struggle against sin you have not yet resisted to the point of shedding your blood.

Let us run with endurance the race that is set before us, looking to Jesus, the founder and perfecter of our faith, who for the joy that was set before him endured the cross, despising the shame, and is seated at the right hand of the throne of God.—Since therefore Christ suffered in the flesh, arm yourselves with the same way of thinking.

Matt. 10:24; John 13:13; Matt. 10:25; John 15:20;
John 17:14; Heb. 12:3–4; Heb. 12:1–2; 1 Pet. 4:1

EVENING

My son, give me your heart.

"Oh that they had such a heart as this always, to fear me and to keep all my commandments, that it might go well with them and with their descendants forever!"

"Your heart is not right before God."—For the mind that is set on the flesh is hostile to God, for it does not submit to God's law; indeed, it cannot. Those who are in the flesh cannot please God.

They gave themselves first to the Lord.—And every work that [Hezekiah] undertook, . . . seeking his God, he did with all his heart, and prospered.

Keep your heart with all vigilance, for from it flow the springs of life. . . . Whatever you do, work heartily, as for the Lord.—As bondservants of Christ, doing the will of God from the heart, rendering service with a good will as to the Lord and not to man.

I will run in the way of your commandments when you enlarge my heart!

Prov. 23:26; Deut. 5:29; Acts 8:21; Rom. 8:7–8; 2 Cor. 8:5;
2 Chron. 31:21; Prov. 4:23; Col. 3:23; Eph. 6:6–7; Ps. 119:32

MORNING

"I am with you to save you."

Can the prey be taken from the mighty, or the captives of a tyrant be rescued? For thus says the Lord: "Even the captives of the mighty shall be taken, and the prey of the tyrant be rescued, for I will contend with those who contend with you. . . . Then all flesh shall know that I am the Lord your Savior, and your Redeemer, the Mighty One of Jacob."—Fear not, for I am with you; be not dismayed, for I am your God; I will strengthen you, I will help you, I will uphold you with my righteous right hand.

We do not have a high priest who is unable to sympathize with our weaknesses, but one who in every respect has been tempted as we are, yet without sin.—Because he himself has suffered when tempted, he is able to help those who are being tempted.—The steps of a man are established by the Lord, when he delights in his way; though he fall, he shall not be cast headlong, for the Lord upholds his hand.

Jer. 15:20; Isa. 49:24-26; Isa. 41:10; Heb. 4:15; Heb. 2:18; Ps. 37:23-24

EVENING

He satisfies the longing soul, and
the hungry soul he fills with good things.

You have tasted that the Lord is good.

O God, you are my God; earnestly I seek you; my soul thirsts for you; my flesh faints for you, as in a dry and weary land where there is no water . . . beholding your power and glory.—My soul longs, yes, faints for the courts of the Lord; my heart and flesh sing for joy to the living God.—My desire is to depart and be with Christ, for that is far better.

When I awake, I shall be satisfied with your likeness.—"They shall hunger no more, neither thirst anymore; the sun shall not strike them, nor any scorching heat. For the Lamb in the midst of the throne will be their shepherd, and he will guide them to springs of living water, and God will wipe away every tear from their eyes."—They feast on the abundance of your house, and you give them drink from the river of your delights.—"My people shall be satisfied with my goodness, declares the Lord."

Ps. 107:9; 1 Pet. 2:3; Ps. 63:1-2; Ps. 84:2; Phil. 1:23;
Ps. 17:15; Rev. 7:16-17; Ps. 36:8; Jer. 31:14

MORNING

"My presence will go with you, and I will give you rest."

"Be strong and courageous. Do not fear or be in dread of them, for it is the Lord your God who goes with you. He will not leave you or forsake you. It is the Lord who goes before you. He will be with you; he will not leave you or forsake you. Do not fear or be dismayed."—"Have I not commanded you? Be strong and courageous. Do not be frightened, and do not be dismayed, for the Lord your God is with you wherever you go."—In all your ways acknowledge him, and he will make straight your paths.

He has said, "I will never leave you nor forsake you." So we can confidently say, "The Lord is my helper; I will not fear; what can man do to me?"—Our sufficiency is from God.

"Lead us not into temptation."—I know, O Lord, that the way of man is not in himself, that it is not in man who walks to direct his steps.—My times are in your hand.

Ex. 33:14; Deut. 31:6, 8; Josh. 1:9; Prov. 3:6; Heb. 13:5-6;
2 Cor. 3:5; Matt. 6:13; Jer. 10:23; Ps. 31:15

EVENING

Let us consider how to stir up one another to love and good works.

"How forceful are upright words!"—I am stirring up your sincere mind by way of reminder.

Those who feared the Lord spoke with one another. The Lord paid attention and heard them, and a book of remembrance was written before him of those who feared the Lord and esteemed his name.—"Again I say to you, if two of you agree on earth about anything they ask, it will be done for them by my Father in heaven."

Then the Lord God said, "It is not good that the man should be alone."—Two are better than one, because they have a good reward for their toil. For if they fall, one will lift up his fellow. But woe to him who is alone when he falls and has not another to lift him up!

Let us . . . decide never to put a stumbling block or hindrance in the way of a brother.—Bear one another's burdens, and so fulfill the law of Christ. . . . Keep watch on yourself, lest you too be tempted.

Heb. 10:24; Job 6:25; 2 Pet. 3:1; Mal. 3:16; Matt. 18:19;
Gen. 2:18; Eccles. 4:9-10; Rom. 14:13; Gal. 6:2, 1

MORNING

I am my beloved's, and his desire is for me.

I know whom I have believed, and I am convinced that he is able to guard until that Day what has been entrusted to me.—For I am sure that neither death nor life, nor angels nor rulers, nor things present nor things to come, nor powers, nor height nor depth, nor anything else in all creation, will be able to separate us from the love of God in Christ Jesus our Lord.—"I kept them in your name, which you have given me. I have guarded them, and not one of them has been lost."

For the Lord takes pleasure in his people.—"Delighting in the children of man."—The great love with which he loved us.—"Greater love has no one than this, that someone lay down his life for his friends."

You were bought with a price. So glorify God in your body.—For if we live, we live to the Lord, and if we die, we die to the Lord. So then, whether we live or whether we die, we are the Lord's.

Song 7:10; 2 Tim. 1:12; Rom. 8:38–39; John 17:12; Ps. 149:4;
Prov. 8:31; Eph. 2:4; John 15:13; 1 Cor. 6:20; Rom. 14:8

EVENING

Seek and read from the book of the Lord.

"You shall therefore lay up these words of mine in your heart and in your soul, and you shall bind them as a sign on your hand, and they shall be as frontlets between your eyes."—"This Book of the Law shall not depart from your mouth, but you shall meditate on it day and night, so that you may be careful to do according to all that is written in it. For then you will make your way prosperous, and then you will have good success."

The law of his God is in his heart; his steps do not slip.—By the word of your lips I have avoided the ways of the violent.—I have stored up your word in my heart, that I might not sin against you.

And we have the prophetic word more fully confirmed, to which you will do well to pay attention as to a lamp shining in a dark place, until the day dawns and the morning star rises in your hearts.—That through endurance and through the encouragement of the Scriptures we might have hope.

Isa. 34:16; Deut. 11:18; Josh. 1:8; Ps. 37:31; Ps. 17:4;
Ps. 119:11; 2 Pet. 1:19; Rom. 15:4

MORNING

"Out of the abundance of the heart the mouth speaks."

Let the word of Christ dwell in you richly . . . in all wisdom.

Keep your heart with all vigilance, for from it flow the springs of life.—Death and life are in the power of the tongue.—The mouth of the righteous utters wisdom, and his tongue speaks justice. The law of his God is in his heart; his steps do not slip.—Let no corrupting talk come out of your mouths, but only such as is good for building up, as fits the occasion, that it may give grace to those who hear.

"We cannot but speak of what we have seen and heard."—I believed, even when I spoke.

"So everyone who acknowledges me before men, I also will acknowledge before my Father who is in heaven."—With the heart one believes and is justified, and with the mouth one confesses and is saved.

Matt. 12:34; Col. 3:16; Prov. 4:23; Prov. 18:21; Ps. 37:30–31;
Eph. 4:29; Acts 4:20; Ps. 116:10; Matt. 10:32; Rom. 10:10

EVENING

I hope to see you soon, and we will talk face to face.

Oh that you would rend the heavens and come down.—As a deer pants for flowing streams, so pants my soul for you, O God. My soul thirsts for God, for the living God. When shall I come and appear before God?—Make haste, my beloved, and be like a gazelle or a young stag on the mountains of spices.

But our citizenship is in heaven, and from it we await a Savior, the Lord Jesus Christ.—Waiting for our blessed hope, the appearing of the glory of our great God and Savior Jesus Christ.—God our Savior and . . . Christ Jesus our hope.—Though you have not seen him, you love him.

He who testifies to these things says, "Surely I am coming soon." Amen. Come, Lord Jesus!—It will be said on that day, "Behold, this is our God; we have waited for him, that he might save us. This is the Lord; we have waited for him; let us be glad and rejoice in his salvation."

3 John 14; Isa. 64:1; Ps. 42:1–2; Song 8:14; Phil. 3:20;
Titus 2:13; 1 Tim. 1:1; 1 Pet. 1:8; Rev. 22:20; Isa. 25:9

MORNING

"Your will be done, on earth as it is in heaven."

Bless the Lord, O you his angels, you mighty ones who do his word, obeying the voice of his word! Bless the Lord, all his hosts, his ministers, who do his will!

"I have come down from heaven, not to do my own will but the will of him who sent me."—"I delight to do your will, O my God; your law is within my heart."—"My Father, if this cannot pass unless I drink it, your will be done."—"Not everyone who says to me, 'Lord, Lord,' will enter the kingdom of heaven, but the one who does the will of my Father who is in heaven."—It is not the hearers of the law who are righteous before God, but the doers of the law who will be justified.—"If you know these things, blessed are you if you do them."—So whoever knows the right thing to do and fails to do it, for him it is sin.

Do not be conformed to this world, but be transformed by the renewal of your mind.

Matt. 6:10; Ps. 103:20–21; John 6:38; Ps. 40:8; Matt. 26:42;
Matt. 7:21; Rom. 2:13; John 13:17; James 4:17; Rom. 12:2

EVENING

"The ear tests words as the palate tastes food."

Beloved, do not believe every spirit, but test the spirits to see whether they are from God, for many false prophets have gone out into the world.—"Do not judge by appearances, but judge with right judgment."—I speak as to sensible people; judge for yourselves what I say.—Let the word of Christ dwell in you richly . . . in all wisdom.—"He who has an ear, let him hear what the Spirit says."—The spiritual person judges all things.

"Pay attention to what you hear."—"I know your works . . . and how you . . . have tested those who call themselves apostles and are not, and found them to be false."—Test everything; hold fast what is good.—"He calls his own sheep by name and leads them out. When he has brought out all his own, he goes before them, and the sheep follow him, for they know his voice. A stranger they will not follow, but they will flee from him, for they do not know the voice of strangers."

Job 34:3; 1 John 4:1; John 7:24; 1 Cor. 10:15; Col. 3:16; Rev. 2:29;
1 Cor. 2:15; Mark 4:24; Rev. 2:2; 1 Thess. 5:21; John 10:3–5

MORNING

"You shall be to me a kingdom of priests and a holy nation."

"You were slain, and by your blood you ransomed people for God from every tribe and language and people and nation, and you have made them a kingdom and priests to our God."—But you are a chosen race, a royal priesthood, a holy nation, a people for his own possession, that you may proclaim the excellencies of him who called you out of darkness into his marvelous light.

You shall be called the priests of the Lord; they shall speak of you as the ministers of our God.—Priests of God and of Christ.

Therefore, holy brothers, you who share in a heavenly calling, consider Jesus, the apostle and high priest of our confession.—Through him then let us continually offer up a sacrifice of praise to God, that is, the fruit of lips that acknowledge his name.

For we are his workmanship, created in Christ Jesus for good works, which God prepared beforehand, that we should walk in them.—God's temple is holy, and you are that temple.

Ex. 19:6; Rev. 5:9–10; 1 Pet. 2:9; Isa. 61:6; Rev. 20:6;
Heb. 3:1; Heb. 13:15; Eph. 2:10; 1 Cor. 3:17

EVENING

We prayed to our God and set a guard as a protection against them.

"Watch and pray that you may not enter into temptation."— Continue steadfastly in prayer, being watchful in it with thanksgiving.—Casting all your anxieties on him, because he cares for you. Be sober-minded; be watchful. Your adversary the devil prowls around like a roaring lion, seeking someone to devour. Resist him, firm in your faith.

"Why do you call me 'Lord, Lord,' and not do what I tell you?"—But be doers of the word, and not hearers only, deceiving yourselves.

"Why do you cry to me? Tell the people of Israel to go forward."

Do not be anxious about anything, but in everything by prayer and supplication with thanksgiving let your requests be made known to God. And the peace of God, which surpasses all understanding, will guard your hearts and your minds in Christ Jesus.

Neh. 4:9; Matt. 26:41; Col. 4:2; 1 Pet. 5:7–9; Luke 6:46;
James 1:22; Ex. 14:15; Phil. 4:6–7

MORNING

"You are a gracious God and merciful, slow to anger and abounding in steadfast love, and relenting from disaster."

"Please let the power of the Lord be great as you have promised, saying, 'The Lord is slow to anger and abounding in steadfast love, forgiving iniquity and transgression, but he will by no means clear the guilty, visiting the iniquity of the fathers on the children, to the third and the fourth generation.'"

Do not remember against us our former iniquities; let your compassion come speedily to meet us. . . . Help us, O God of our salvation, for the glory of your name; deliver us, and atone for our sins, for your name's sake!— "Though our iniquities testify against us, act, O Lord, for your name's sake; for our backslidings are many; we have sinned against you." . . . We acknowledge our wickedness, O Lord, and the iniquity of our fathers, for we have sinned against you.

If you, O Lord, should mark iniquities, O Lord, who could stand? But with you there is forgiveness, that you may be feared.

Jonah 4:2; Num. 14:17–18; Ps. 79:8–9; Jer. 14:7, 20; Ps. 130:3–4

EVENING

Sanctification by the Spirit.

Awake, O north wind, and come, O south wind! Blow upon my garden, let its spices flow.

For see what earnestness this godly grief has produced in you, but also what eagerness to clear yourselves, what indignation, what fear, what longing, what zeal, what punishment!—(for the fruit of light is found in all that is good and right and true), and try to discern what is pleasing to the Lord.

"And I will ask the Father, and he will give you another Helper, to be with you forever."—God's love has been poured into our hearts through the Holy Spirit who has been given to us.

The fruit of the Spirit is love, joy, peace.

In a severe test of affliction, their abundance of joy and their extreme poverty have overflowed in a wealth of generosity on their part.

All these are empowered by one and the same Spirit, who apportions to each one individually as he wills.

2 Thess. 2:13; Song 4:16; 2 Cor. 7:11; Eph. 5:9–10; John 14:16;
Rom. 5:5; Gal. 5:22; 2 Cor. 8:2; 1 Cor. 12:11

MORNING

"He calls his own sheep by name and leads them out."

God's firm foundation stands, bearing this seal: "The Lord knows those who are his," and, "Let everyone who names the name of the Lord depart from iniquity."—"Many will say to me, 'Lord, Lord, did we not prophesy in your name, and cast out demons in your name, and do many mighty works in your name?' And then will I declare to them, 'I never knew you; depart from me, you workers of lawlessness.'"—The Lord knows the way of the righteous, but the way of the wicked will perish.

"Behold, I have engraved you on the palms of my hands; your walls are continually before me."—Set me as a seal upon your heart, as a seal upon your arm.—The Lord is good, a stronghold in the day of trouble; he knows those who take refuge in him.

"In my Father's house are many rooms. If it were not so, would I have told you that I go to prepare a place for you? And if I go and prepare a place for you, I will come again and will take you to myself, that where I am you may be also."

John 10:3; 2 Tim. 2:19; Matt. 7:22–23; Ps. 1:6;
Isa. 49:16; Song 8:6; Nah. 1:7; John 14:2–3

EVENING

"She has done what she could."

"This poor widow has put in more than all of them."—"Whoever gives you a cup of water to drink because you belong to Christ will by no means lose his reward."—If the readiness is there, it is acceptable according to what a person has, not according to what he does not have.

Let us not love in word or talk but in deed and in truth.—If a brother or sister is poorly clothed and lacking in daily food, and one of you says to them, "Go in peace, be warmed and filled," without giving them the things needed for the body, what good is that?—Whoever sows bountifully will also reap bountifully. Each one must give as he has decided in his heart, not reluctantly or under compulsion, for God loves a cheerful giver.

"When you have done all that you were commanded, say, 'We are unworthy servants; we have only done what was our duty.'"

Mark 14:8; Luke 21:3; Mark 9:41; 2 Cor. 8:12; 1 John 3:18;
James 2:15–16; 2 Cor. 9:6–7; Luke 17:10

MORNING

"He who is mighty has done great things for me, and holy is his name."

"Who is like you, O Lord, among the gods? Who is like you, majestic in holiness, awesome in glorious deeds, doing wonders?"—There is none like you among the gods, O Lord, nor are there any works like yours.—"Who will not fear, O Lord, and glorify your name? For you alone are holy."—"Hallowed be your name."

"Blessed be the Lord God of Israel, for he has visited and redeemed his people."

Who is this who comes from Edom, in crimsoned garments from Bozrah, he who is splendid in his apparel, marching in the greatness of his strength? "It is I, speaking in righteousness, mighty to save."—"I have granted help to one who is mighty; I have exalted one chosen from the people."

Now to him who is able to do far more abundantly than all that we ask or think, according to the power at work within us, to him be glory.

Luke 1:49; Ex. 15:11; Ps. 86:8; Rev. 15:4; Matt. 6:9;
Luke 1:68; Isa. 63:1; Ps. 89:19; Eph. 3:20–21

EVENING

The dew of Hermon.

Mount Sirion (that is, Hermon).—There the Lord has commanded the blessing, life forevermore.—I will be like the dew to Israel; he shall blossom like the lily; he shall take root like the trees of Lebanon.

"May my teaching drop as the rain, my speech distill as the dew, like gentle rain upon the tender grass, and like showers upon the herb."—"For as the rain and the snow come down from heaven and do not return there but water the earth, making it bring forth and sprout, giving seed to the sower and bread to the eater, so shall my word be that goes out from my mouth; it shall not return to me empty, but it shall accomplish that which I purpose, and shall succeed in the thing for which I sent it."

[God] gives the Spirit without measure.—For from his fullness we have all received, grace upon grace.—It is like the precious oil on the head . . . on the beard of Aaron, running down on the collar of his robes!

Ps. 133:3; Deut. 4:48; Ps. 133:3; Hos. 14:5; Deut. 32:2;
Isa. 55:10–11; John 3:34; John 1:16; Ps. 133:2

MORNING

"They are not of the world, just as I am not of the world."

He was despised and rejected by men; a man of sorrows, and acquainted with grief.—"In the world you will have tribulation. But take heart; I have overcome the world."

It was indeed fitting that we should have such a high priest, holy, innocent, unstained, separated from sinners.—That you may be blameless and innocent, children of God without blemish in the midst of a crooked and twisted generation.

"Jesus of Nazareth . . . went about doing good and healing all who were oppressed by the devil, for God was with him."—So then, as we have opportunity, let us do good to everyone, and especially to those who are of the household of faith.

The true light, which gives light to everyone, was coming into the world.—"You are the light of the world. A city set on a hill cannot be hidden. Let your light shine before others, so that they may see your good works and give glory to your Father who is in heaven."

John 17:16; Isa. 53:3; John 16:33; Heb. 7:26; Phil. 2:15;
Acts 10:38; Gal. 6:10; John 1:9; Matt. 5:14, 16

EVENING

The cheerful of heart has a continual feast.

"The joy of the Lord is your strength."—The kingdom of God is not a matter of eating and drinking but of righteousness and peace and joy in the Holy Spirit.—Be filled with the Spirit, addressing one another in psalms and hymns and spiritual songs, singing and making melody to the Lord with your heart, giving thanks always and for everything to God the Father in the name of our Lord Jesus Christ.

Through him then let us continually offer up a sacrifice of praise to God, that is, the fruit of lips that acknowledge his name.

Though the fig tree should not blossom, nor fruit be on the vines, the produce of the olive fail and the fields yield no food, the flock be cut off from the fold and there be no herd in the stalls, yet I will rejoice in the Lord; I will take joy in the God of my salvation.—As sorrowful, yet always rejoicing.—Not only that, but we rejoice in our sufferings.

Prov. 15:15; Neh. 8:10; Rom. 14:17; Eph. 5:18–20;
Heb. 13:15; Hab. 3:17–18; 2 Cor. 6:10; Rom. 5:3

MORNING

What is the value of circumcision?

Much in every way.—"Circumcise yourselves to the Lord; remove the fore-skin of your hearts."—"If then their uncircumcised heart is humbled and they make amends for their iniquity, then I will remember my covenant with Jacob, and I will remember my covenant with Isaac and my covenant with Abraham."

Christ became a servant to the circumcised to show God's truthfulness, in order to confirm the promises given to the patriarchs.—In him also you were circumcised with a circumcision made without hands, by putting off the body of the flesh, by the circumcision of Christ.—You, who were dead in your trespasses and the uncircumcision of your flesh, God made alive together with him, having forgiven us all our trespasses.

Put off your old self, which belongs to your former manner of life and is corrupt through deceitful desires, and . . . be renewed in the spirit of your minds, and . . . put on the new self, created after the likeness of God in true righteousness and holiness.

Rom. 3:1; Rom. 3:2; Jer. 4:4; Lev. 26:41–42; Rom. 15:8;
Col. 2:11; Col. 2:13; Eph. 4:22–24

EVENING

The curtain of the temple was torn in two, from top to bottom.

The Lord Jesus on the night when he was betrayed took bread, and when he had given thanks, he broke it, and said, "This is my body which is for you. Do this in remembrance of me."—"The bread that I will give for the life of the world is my flesh."

"Unless you eat the flesh of the Son of Man and drink his blood, you have no life in you. Whoever feeds on my flesh and drinks my blood has eter-nal life. . . . Whoever feeds on my flesh and drinks my blood abides in me, and I in him. As the living Father sent me, and I live because of the Father, so whoever feeds on me, he also will live because of me. . . . Do you take offense at this? Then what if you were to see the Son of Man ascending to where he was before? It is the Spirit who gives life; the flesh is no help at all."

The new and living way that he opened for us through the curtain, that is, through his flesh . . . let us draw near.

Matt. 27:51; 1 Cor. 11:23–24; John 6:51; John 6:53–54,
56–57, 61–63; Heb. 10:20, 22

MORNING

The death he died he died to sin, once for all,
but the life he lives he lives to God.

He . . . was numbered with the transgressors.—Christ, having been offered once to bear the sins of many.—He himself bore our sins in his body on the tree, that we might die to sin and live to righteousness. By his wounds you have been healed.—By a single offering he has perfected for all time those who are being sanctified.—He holds his priesthood permanently, because he continues forever. Consequently, he is able to save to the uttermost those who draw near to God through him, since he always lives to make intercession for them.—While we were still sinners, Christ died for us. Since, therefore, we have now been justified by his blood, much more shall we be saved by him from the wrath of God.

Since therefore Christ suffered in the flesh, arm yourselves with the same way of thinking, for whoever has suffered in the flesh has ceased from sin, so as to live for the rest of the time in the flesh no longer for human passions but for the will of God.

Rom. 6:10; Isa. 53:12; Heb. 9:28; 1 Pet. 2:24; Heb. 10:14;
Heb. 7:24–25; Rom. 5:8–9; 1 Pet. 4:1–2

EVENING

Keep yourselves in the love of God.

"Abide in me, and I in you. As the branch cannot bear fruit by itself, unless it abides in the vine, neither can you, unless you abide in me. I am the vine; you are the branches. Whoever abides in me and I in him, he it is that bears much fruit, for apart from me you can do nothing."

The fruit of the Spirit is love.—"By this my Father is glorified, that you bear much fruit and so prove to be my disciples. As the Father has loved me, so have I loved you. Abide in my love. If you keep my commandments, you will abide in my love, just as I have kept my Father's commandments and abide in his love."—Whoever keeps his word, in him truly the love of God is perfected.

"This is my commandment, that you love one another as I have loved you."—God shows his love for us in that while we were still sinners, Christ died for us.—God is love, and whoever abides in love abides in God, and God abides in him.

Jude 21; John 15:4–5; Gal. 5:22; John 15:8–10;
1 John 2:5; John 15:12; Rom. 5:8; 1 John 4:16

MORNING

Then comes the end.

"But concerning that day or that hour, no one knows, not even the angels in heaven, nor the Son, but only the Father. Be on guard, keep awake. For you do not know when the time will come. . . . And what I say to you I say to all: Stay awake."—The Lord is not slow to fulfill his promise as some count slowness, but is patient toward you, not wishing that any should perish, but that all should reach repentance.—The coming of the Lord is at hand. . . . Behold, the Judge is standing at the door.—"Surely I am coming soon."

Since all these things are thus to be dissolved, what sort of people ought you to be in lives of holiness and godliness.

The end of all things is at hand; therefore be self-controlled and sober-minded for the sake of your prayers.—"Stay dressed for action and keep your lamps burning, and be like men who are waiting for their master to come home from the wedding feast, so that they may open the door to him at once when he comes and knocks."

1 Cor. 15:24; Mark 13:32–33, 37; 2 Pet. 3:9; James 5:8–9;
Rev. 22:20; 2 Pet. 3:11; 1 Pet. 4:7; Luke 12:35–36

EVENING

Brothers, pray for us.

Is anyone among you sick? Let him call for the elders of the church, and let them pray over him. . . . And the prayer of faith will save the one who is sick, and the Lord will raise him up. . . . Pray for one another, that you may be healed. The prayer of a righteous person has great power as it is working. Elijah was a man with a nature like ours, and he prayed fervently that it might not rain, and for three years and six months it did not rain on the earth.—Then he prayed again, and heaven gave rain, and the earth bore its fruit.—Praying at all times in the Spirit, with all prayer and supplication. To that end keep alert with all perseverance, making supplication for all the saints.

Without ceasing I mention you always in my prayers.—Always struggling on your behalf in his prayers, that you may stand mature and fully assured in all the will of God.

1 Thess. 5:25; James 5:14–18; Eph. 6:18; Rom. 1:9–10; Col. 4:12

MORNING

Patient in tribulation.

"It is the Lord. Let him do what seems good to him."—"Though I am in the right, I cannot answer him; I must appeal for mercy to my accuser."—"The Lord gave, and the Lord has taken away; blessed be the name of the Lord."—"Shall we receive good from God, and shall we not receive evil?"

Jesus wept.—A man of sorrows, and acquainted with grief. . . . Surely he has borne our griefs and carried our sorrows.

"The Lord disciplines the one he loves, and chastises every son whom he receives." . . . For the moment all discipline seems painful rather than pleasant, but later it yields the peaceful fruit of righteousness to those who have been trained by it.—May you be strengthened with all power, according to his glorious might, for all endurance and patience with joy.—"In the world you will have tribulation. But take heart; I have overcome the world."

Rom. 12:12; 1 Sam. 3:18; Job 9:15; Job 1:21; Job 2:10; John 11:35;
Isa. 53:3–4; Heb. 12:6, 11; Col. 1:11; John 16:33

EVENING

No unbelief made him waver concerning the promise of God.

And Jesus answered them, "Have faith in God. Truly, I say to you, whoever says to this mountain, 'Be taken up and thrown into the sea,' and does not doubt in his heart, but believes that what he says will come to pass, it will be done for him. Therefore I tell you, whatever you ask in prayer, believe that you have received it, and it will be yours."—Without faith it is impossible to please him, for whoever would draw near to God must believe that he exists and that he rewards those who seek him.

He who had received the promises was in the act of offering up his only son, of whom it was said, "Through Isaac shall your offspring be named." He considered that God was able even to raise him from the dead.—Fully convinced that God was able to do what he had promised.

"Is anything too hard for the Lord?"—"With God all things are possible."—"Increase our faith!"

Rom. 4:20; Mark 11:22–24; Heb. 11:6; Heb. 11:17–19;
Rom. 4:21; Gen. 18:14; Matt. 19:26; Luke 17:5

MORNING

We know that we have passed out of death into life.

"Whoever hears my word and believes him who sent me has eternal life. He does not come into judgment, but has passed from death to life."—Whoever has the Son has life; whoever does not have the Son of God does not have life.

It is God who establishes us with you in Christ, and has anointed us, and who has also put his seal on us and given us his Spirit in our hearts as a guarantee.—By this we shall know that we are of the truth and reassure our heart before him. . . . Beloved, if our heart does not condemn us, we have confidence before God.—We know that we are from God, and the whole world lies in the power of the evil one.

You were dead in the trespasses and sins. . . . [God] made us alive together with Christ.—He has delivered us from the domain of darkness and transferred us to the kingdom of his beloved Son.

1 John 3:14; John 5:24; 1 John 5:12; 2 Cor. 1:21–22;
1 John 3:19, 21; 1 John 5:19; Eph. 2:1, 5; Col. 1:13

EVENING

You make known to me the path of life.

"Thus says the Lord: Behold, I set before you the way of life and the way of death."—"I will instruct you in the good and the right way."—"I am the way, and the truth, and the life. No one comes to the Father except through me."—"Follow me."

There is a way that seems right to a man, but its end is the way to death.—"The gate is wide and the way is easy that leads to destruction, and those who enter by it are many. For the gate is narrow and the way is hard that leads to life, and those who find it are few."

And a highway shall be there, and it shall be called the Way of Holiness; the unclean shall not pass over it. It shall belong to those who walk on the way; even if they are fools, they shall not go astray.—"Let us know; let us press on to know the Lord."

"In my Father's house are many rooms. If it were not so, would I have told you that I go to prepare a place for you?"

Ps. 16:11; Jer. 21:8; 1 Sam. 12:23; John 14:6; Matt. 4:19;
Prov. 14:12; Matt. 7:13–14; Isa. 35:8; Hos. 6:3; John 14:2

MORNING

By faith Abraham obeyed when he was called to go out to a place that he was to receive as an inheritance.

He chose our heritage for us.—"He encircled him, he cared for him, he kept him as the apple of his eye. Like an eagle that stirs up its nest, that flutters over its young, spreading out its wings, catching them, bearing them on its pinions, the Lord alone guided him, no foreign god was with him."

"I am the Lord your God, who teaches you to profit, who leads you in the way you should go."—"Who is a teacher like him?"

We walk by faith, not by sight.—Here we have no lasting city, but we seek the city that is to come.—Beloved, I urge you as sojourners and exiles to abstain from the passions of the flesh, which wage war against your soul.— "Arise and go, for this is no place to rest, because of uncleanness that destroys with a grievous destruction."

Heb. 11:8; Ps. 47:4; Deut. 32:10-12; Isa. 48:17; Job 36:22;
2 Cor. 5:7; Heb. 13:14; 1 Pet. 2:11; Mic. 2:10

EVENING

Give thanks to his holy name!

"The heavens are not pure in his sight; how much less one who is abominable and corrupt, a man who drinks injustice like water!"—"And the stars are not pure in his eyes; how much less man, . . . who is a worm!"

"Who is like you, O Lord, among the gods? Who is like you, majestic in holiness?"—"Holy, holy, holy is the Lord of hosts."

As he who called you is holy, you also be holy in all your conduct, since it is written, "You shall be holy, for I am holy."—Share his holiness.

God's temple is holy, and you are that temple.—Since all these things are thus to be dissolved, what sort of people ought you to be in lives of holiness and godliness, . . . without spot or blemish.

Let no corrupting talk come out of your mouths, but only such as is good for building up, as fits the occasion, that it may give grace to those who hear. . . . And do not grieve the Holy Spirit of God, by whom you were sealed for the day of redemption.

Ps. 97:12; Job 15:15-16; Job 25:5-6; Ex. 15:11; Isa. 6:3; 1 Pet. 1:15-16;
Heb. 12:10; 1 Cor. 3:17; 2 Pet. 3:11, 14; Eph. 4:29-30

MORNING

Christ, who is the image of God.

"The glory of the Lord shall be revealed, and all flesh shall see it together."—
No one has ever seen God; the only God, who is at the Father's side, he has
made him known. . . . And the Word became flesh and dwelt among us, and
we have seen his glory, glory as of the only Son from the Father, full of grace
and truth.—"Whoever has seen me has seen the Father."—He is the radiance
of the glory of God and the exact imprint of his nature.—He was manifested
in the flesh.

In whom we have redemption, the forgiveness of sins. He is the image
of the invisible God, the firstborn of all creation.—Those whom he foreknew
he also predestined to be conformed to the image of his Son, in order that he
might be the firstborn among many brothers.

Just as we have borne the image of the man of dust, we shall also bear
the image of the man of heaven.

2 Cor. 4:4; Isa. 40:5; John 1:18, 14; John 14:9; Heb. 1:3;
1 Tim. 3:16; Col. 1:14–15; Rom. 8:29; 1 Cor. 15:49

EVENING

For you equipped me with strength for the battle.

For when I am weak, then I am strong.

And Asa cried to the Lord his God, "O Lord, there is none like you to
help, between the mighty and the weak. Help us, O Lord our God, for we rely
on you, and in your name we have come against this multitude. O Lord, you
are our God; let not man prevail against you."—Jehoshaphat cried out, and
the Lord helped him.

It is better to take refuge in the Lord than to trust in man. It is better to
take refuge in the Lord than to trust in princes.—The king is not saved by his
great army; a warrior is not delivered by his great strength. The war horse is a
false hope for salvation, and by its great might it cannot rescue.

We do not wrestle against flesh and blood, but against the rulers, against
the authorities, against the cosmic powers over this present darkness, against
the spiritual forces of evil in the heavenly places. Therefore take up the whole
armor of God.

Ps. 18:39; 2 Cor. 12:10; 2 Chron. 14:11; 2 Chron. 18:31;
Ps. 118:8–9; Ps. 33:16–17; Eph. 6:12–13

MORNING

Walk in love.

"A new commandment I give to you, that you love one another: just as I have loved you, you also are to love one another."—Above all, keep loving one another earnestly, since love covers a multitude of sins.—Love covers all offenses.

"Whenever you stand praying, forgive, if you have anything against anyone, so that your Father also who is in heaven may forgive you your trespasses."—"Love your enemies, and do good, and lend, expecting nothing in return."—Do not rejoice when your enemy falls, and let not your heart be glad when he stumbles.—Do not repay evil for evil or reviling for reviling, but on the contrary, bless, for to this you were called, that you may obtain a blessing.—If possible, so far as it depends on you, live peaceably with all.—Be kind to one another, tenderhearted, forgiving one another, as God in Christ forgave you.

Little children, let us not love in word or talk but in deed and in truth.

Eph. 5:2; John 13:34; 1 Pet. 4:8; Prov. 10:12; Mark 11:25; Luke 6:35;
Prov. 24:17; 1 Pet. 3:9; Rom. 12:18; Eph. 4:32; 1 John 3:18

EVENING

Let your requests be made known to God.

"Abba, Father, all things are possible for you. Remove this cup from me. Yet not what I will, but what you will."—A thorn was given me in the flesh. . . . Three times I pleaded with the Lord about this, that it should leave me. But he said to me, "My grace is sufficient for you, for my power is made perfect in weakness." Therefore I will boast all the more gladly of my weaknesses.

I pour out my complaint before him; I tell my trouble before him.—Hannah . . . was deeply distressed and prayed to the Lord and wept bitterly. And she vowed a vow and said, "O Lord of hosts, if you will indeed look on the affliction of your servant and . . . will give to your servant a son, then I will give him to the Lord all the days of his life." . . . and the Lord remembered her.—We do not know what to pray for as we ought.—He chose our heritage for us.

Phil. 4:6; Mark 14:36; 2 Cor. 12:7–9; Ps. 142:2;
1 Sam. 1:9–11, 19; Rom. 8:26; Ps. 47:4

MORNING

Oh that you would rend the heavens and come down.

Make haste, my beloved, and be like a gazelle or a young stag on the mountains of spices.—We ourselves . . . groan inwardly as we wait eagerly for adoption as sons, the redemption of our bodies.—Bow your heavens, O Lord, and come down! Touch the mountains so that they smoke!

"This Jesus, who was taken up from you into heaven, will come in the same way as you saw him go into heaven."—Christ . . . will appear a second time, not to deal with sin but to save those who are eagerly waiting for him.— It will be said on that day, "Behold, this is our God; we have waited for him, that he might save us. This is the Lord; we have waited for him; let us be glad and rejoice in his salvation."

He who testifies to these things says, "Surely I am coming soon." Amen. Come, Lord Jesus!—Our blessed hope, the appearing of the glory of our great God and Savior Jesus Christ.—But our citizenship is in heaven.

Isa. 64:1; Song 8:14; Rom. 8:23; Ps. 144:5; Acts 1:11;
Heb. 9:28; Isa. 25:9; Rev. 22:20; Titus 2:13; Phil. 3:20

EVENING

You have given me the heritage of those who fear your name.

"No weapon that is fashioned against you shall succeed, and you shall refute every tongue that rises against you in judgment. This is the heritage of the servants of the Lord and their vindication from me, declares the Lord."—The angel of the Lord encamps around those who fear him, and delivers them. Oh, taste and see that the Lord is good! Blessed is the man who takes refuge in him! Oh, fear the Lord, you his saints, for those who fear him have no lack! The young lions suffer want and hunger; but those who seek the Lord lack no good thing.—The lines have fallen for me in pleasant places; indeed, I have a beautiful inheritance.

But for you who fear my name, the sun of righteousness shall rise with healing in its wings. You shall go out leaping like calves from the stall.—He who did not spare his own Son but gave him up for us all, how will he not also with him graciously give us all things?

Ps. 61:5; Isa. 54:17; Ps. 34:7–10; Ps. 16:6; Mal. 4:2; Rom. 8:32

MORNING

Seek the things that are above, where Christ is, seated at the right hand of God.

Get wisdom; get insight.—The wisdom from above.—"The deep says, 'It is not in me,' and the sea says, 'It is not with me.'"—We were buried therefore with him by baptism into death, in order that, just as Christ was raised from the dead by the glory of the Father, we too might walk in newness of life. For if we have been united with him in a death like his, we shall certainly be united with him in a resurrection like his.

Let us also lay aside every weight, and sin which clings so closely, and let us run with endurance the race that is set before us.—God . . . made us alive together with Christ . . . and raised us up with him and seated us with him in the heavenly places in Christ Jesus.

People who speak thus make it clear that they are seeking a homeland.— Seek the Lord, all you humble of the land, who do his just commands; seek righteousness; seek humility.

Col. 3:1; Prov. 4:5; James 3:17; Job 28:14; Rom. 6:4–5;
Heb. 12:1; Eph. 2:4–6; Heb. 11:14; Zeph. 2:3

EVENING

Nicodemus, who had gone to him before.

Peter was following him at a distance.—Many even of the authorities believed in him, but for fear of the Pharisees they did not confess it, so that they would not be put out of the synagogue; for they loved the glory that comes from man more than the glory that comes from God.—The fear of man lays a snare, but whoever trusts in the Lord is safe.

"Whoever comes to me I will never cast out."—A bruised reed he will not break, and a faintly burning wick he will not quench.—"Faith like a grain of mustard seed."

God gave us a spirit not of fear but of power and love and self-control. Therefore do not be ashamed of the testimony about our Lord.—Little children, abide in him, so that when he appears we may have confidence and not shrink from him in shame at his coming.—"Everyone who acknowledges me before men, I also will acknowledge before my Father who is in heaven."

John 7:50; Matt. 26:58; John 12:42–43; Prov. 29:25; John 6:37;
Isa. 42:3; Matt. 17:20; 2 Tim. 1:7–8; 1 John 2:28; Matt. 10:32

MORNING

Share in suffering as a good soldier of Christ Jesus.

"I made him a witness to the peoples, a leader and commander for the peoples."—It was fitting that he, for whom and by whom all things exist, in bringing many sons to glory, should make the founder of their salvation perfect through suffering.—Through many tribulations we must enter the kingdom of God.

We do not wrestle against flesh and blood, but against the rulers, against the authorities, against the cosmic powers over this present darkness, against the spiritual forces of evil in the heavenly places. Therefore take up the whole armor of God.—We are not waging war according to the flesh. For the weapons of our warfare are not of the flesh but have divine power to destroy strongholds.

After you have suffered a little while, the God of all grace, who has called you to his eternal glory in Christ, will himself restore, confirm, strengthen, and establish you.

2 Tim. 2:3; Isa. 55:4; Heb. 2:10; Acts 14:22;
Eph. 6:12–13; 2 Cor. 10:3–4; 1 Pet. 5:10

EVENING

The unity of the Spirit.

There is one body and one Spirit.—Through him we both have access in one Spirit to the Father. So then you are no longer strangers and aliens, but you are fellow citizens with the saints and members of the household of God, built on the foundation of the apostles and prophets, Christ Jesus himself being the cornerstone, in whom the whole structure, being joined together, grows into a holy temple in the Lord. In him you also are being built together into a dwelling place for God by the Spirit.

Behold, how good and pleasant it is when brothers dwell in unity! It is like the precious oil on the head, running down on the beard, on the beard of Aaron, running down on the collar of his robes!

Having purified your souls by your obedience to the truth for a sincere brotherly love, love one another earnestly from a pure heart.

Eph. 4:3; Eph. 4:4; Eph. 2:18–22; Ps. 133:1–2; 1 Pet. 1:22

MORNING

The fruit of the Spirit is . . . faithfulness.

By grace you have been saved through faith. And this is not your own doing; it is the gift of God.—Without faith it is impossible to please him.—"Whoever believes in him is not condemned, but whoever does not believe is condemned already, because he has not believed in the name of the only Son of God."—"I believe; help my unbelief!"

Whoever keeps his word, in him truly the love of God is perfected. By this we may know that we are in him.—Faith working through love.—Faith apart from works is useless.—We walk by faith, not by sight.—I have been crucified with Christ. It is no longer I who live, but Christ who lives in me. And the life I now live in the flesh I live by faith in the Son of God, who loved me and gave himself for me.—Though you have not seen him, you love him. Though you do not now see him, you believe in him and rejoice with joy that is inexpressible and filled with glory, obtaining the outcome of your faith, the salvation of your souls.

Gal. 5:22; Eph. 2:8; Heb. 11:6; John 3:18; Mark 9:24; 1 John 2:5;
Gal. 5:6; James 2:20; 2 Cor. 5:7; Gal. 2:20; 1 Pet. 1:8-9

EVENING

The Lord is compassionate and merciful.

As a father shows compassion to his children, so the Lord shows compassion to those who fear him.—The Lord is gracious and merciful. . . . He remembers his covenant forever.

He who keeps you will not slumber. Behold, he who keeps Israel will neither slumber nor sleep.—Like an eagle that stirs up its nest, that flutters over its young, spreading out its wings, catching them, bearing them on its pinions, the Lord alone guided him, no foreign god was with him.

His mercies never come to an end; they are new every morning; great is your faithfulness.—[Jesus] went ashore he saw a great crowd, and he had compassion on them and healed their sick.—Jesus Christ is the same yesterday and today and forever.

"Even the hairs of your head are all numbered. . . . Are not two sparrows sold for a penny? And not one of them will fall to the ground apart from your Father. . . . Fear not, therefore."

James 5:11; Ps. 103:13; Ps. 111:4-5; Ps. 121:3-4; Deut. 32:11-12;
Lam. 3:22-23; Matt. 14:14; Heb. 13:8; Matt. 10:30, 29, 31

MORNING

The Lamb who was slain.

"Your lamb shall be without blemish . . . and . . . the whole assembly of the congregation of Israel shall kill their lambs at twilight. Then they shall take some of the blood and put it on the two doorposts and the lintel of the houses in which they eat it. . . . And when I see the blood, I will pass over you.—The sprinkled blood.—Christ, our Passover lamb, has been sacrificed.—"Delivered up according to the definite plan and foreknowledge of God."—Because of his own purpose and grace, which he gave us in Christ Jesus before the ages began.

In him we have redemption through his blood, the forgiveness of our trespasses.—Since therefore Christ suffered in the flesh, arm yourselves with the same way of thinking, for whoever has suffered in the flesh has ceased from sin, so as to live for the rest of the time in the flesh no longer for human passions but for the will of God.

Rev. 13:8; Ex. 12:5–7, 13; Heb. 12:24; 1 Cor. 5:7;
Acts 2:23; 2 Tim. 1:9; Eph. 1:7; 1 Pet. 4:1–2

EVENING

"I have trodden the winepress alone."

"Who is like you, O Lord, among the gods? Who is like you, majestic in holiness, awesome in glorious deeds, doing wonders?"—[The Lord] saw that there was no man, and wondered that there was no one to intercede; then his own arm brought him salvation, and his righteousness upheld him.—He himself bore our sins in his body on the tree.—Becoming a curse for us.

Oh sing to the Lord a new song, for he has done marvelous things! His right hand and his holy arm have worked salvation for him.—He disarmed the rulers and authorities and put them to open shame, by triumphing over them in him.—Out of the anguish of his soul he shall see and be satisfied; by his knowledge shall the righteous one, my servant, make many to be accounted righteous, and he shall bear their iniquities.

"March on, my soul, with might!"—We are more than conquerors through him who loved us.—"They have conquered him by the blood of the Lamb and by the word of their testimony."

Isa. 63:3; Ex. 15:11; Isa. 59:16; 1 Pet. 2:24; Gal. 3:13; Ps. 98:1;
Col. 2:15; Isa. 53:11; Judg. 5:21; Rom. 8:37; Rev. 12:11

MORNING

His mercy is for those who fear him.

Oh, how abundant is your goodness, which you have stored up for those who fear you and worked for those who take refuge in you, in the sight of the children of mankind! In the cover of your presence you hide them from the plots of men; you store them in your shelter from the strife of tongues.

If you call on him as Father who judges impartially according to each one's deeds, conduct yourselves with fear throughout the time of your exile.—The Lord is near to all who call on him . . . in truth. He fulfills the desire of those who fear him; he also hears their cry and saves them.

"Because your heart was penitent, and you humbled yourself before the Lord, . . . and you have torn your clothes and wept before me, I also have heard you, declares the Lord."—"But this is the one to whom I will look: he who is humble and contrite in spirit and trembles at my word."—The Lord is near to the brokenhearted and saves the crushed in spirit.

Luke 1:50; Ps. 31:19–20; 1 Pet. 1:17; Ps. 145:18–19;
2 Kings 22:19; Isa. 66:2; Ps. 34:18

EVENING

"Those who honor me I will honor."

"Everyone who acknowledges me before men, I also will acknowledge before my Father who is in heaven."—"Whoever loves father or mother more than me is not worthy of me, and whoever loves son or daughter more than me is not worthy of me. And whoever does not take his cross and follow me is not worthy of me. Whoever finds his life will lose it, and whoever loses his life for my sake will find it."

Blessed is the man who remains steadfast under trial, for when he has stood the test he will receive the crown of life, which God has promised to those who love him.

"Do not fear what you are about to suffer. . . . Be faithful unto death, and I will give you the crown of life."

This light momentary affliction is preparing for us an eternal weight of glory beyond all comparison.—Praise and glory and honor at the revelation of Jesus Christ.

1 Sam. 2:30; Matt. 10:32; Matt. 10:37–39; James 1:12;
Rev. 2:10; 2 Cor. 4:17; 1 Pet. 1:7

MORNING

"It is finished," and he bowed his head and gave up his spirit.

Jesus, the founder and perfecter of our faith.—"I glorified you on earth, having accomplished the work that you gave me to do."—We have been sanctified through the offering of the body of Jesus Christ once for all. And every priest stands daily at his service, offering repeatedly the same sacrifices, which can never take away sins. But when Christ had offered for all time a single sacrifice for sins, he sat down at the right hand of God, waiting from that time until his enemies should be made a footstool for his feet. For by a single offering he has perfected for all time those who are being sanctified.—Canceling the record of debt that stood against us with its legal demands. This he set aside, nailing it to the cross.

"I lay down my life that I may take it up again. No one takes it from me, but I lay it down of my own accord. I have authority to lay it down, and I have authority to take it up again."—"Greater love has no one than this, that someone lay down his life for his friends."

John 19:30; Heb. 12:2; John 17:4; Heb. 10:10-14;
Col. 2:14; John 10:17-18; John 15:13

EVENING

He sent from on high, he took me;
he drew me out of many waters.

He drew me up from the pit of destruction, out of the miry bog, and set my feet upon a rock, making my steps secure.—You were dead in the trespasses and sins in which you once walked, following the course of this world, following the prince of the power of the air, the spirit that is now at work in the sons of disobedience—among whom we all once lived in the passions of our flesh.

Hear my cry, O God, listen to my prayer; from the end of the earth I call to you when my heart is faint.—"Out of the belly of Sheol I cried, and you heard my voice. For you cast me into the deep, into the heart of the seas, and the flood surrounded me; all your waves and your billows passed over me."—We went through fire and through water; yet you have brought us out to a place of abundance.

"When you pass through the waters, I will be with you; and through the rivers, they shall not overwhelm you."

Ps. 18:16; Ps. 40:2; Eph. 2:1-3; Ps. 61:1-2; Jonah 2:2-3; Ps. 66:12; Isa. 43:2

MORNING

Walk in newness of life.

Just as you once presented your members as slaves to impurity and to lawlessness leading to more lawlessness, so now present your members as slaves to righteousness leading to sanctification.—I appeal to you therefore, brothers, by the mercies of God, to present your bodies as a living sacrifice, holy and acceptable to God, which is your spiritual worship. Do not be conformed to this world, but be transformed by the renewal of your mind.

If anyone is in Christ, he is a new creation. The old has passed away; behold, the new has come.—Neither circumcision counts for anything, nor uncircumcision, but a new creation. And as for all who walk by this rule, peace and mercy be upon them.—Now this I say and testify in the Lord, that you must no longer walk as the Gentiles do, in the futility of their minds. . . . But that is not the way you learned Christ!—assuming that you have heard about him and were taught in him, as the truth is in Jesus. . . . Put on the new self, created after the likeness of God in true righteousness and holiness.

Rom. 6:4; Rom. 6:19; Rom. 12:1–2; 2 Cor. 5:17; Gal. 6:15–16; Eph. 4:17, 20–21, 24

EVENING

"Your will be done."

I know, O Lord, that the way of man is not in himself, that it is not in man who walks to direct his steps.—"Not as I will, but as you will."—But I have calmed and quieted my soul, like a weaned child with its mother; like a weaned child is my soul within me.

We do not know what to pray for as we ought, but the Spirit himself intercedes for us with groanings too deep for words. And he who searches hearts knows what is the mind of the Spirit, because the Spirit intercedes for the saints according to the will of God.

"You do not know what you are asking."—He gave them what they asked, but sent a wasting disease among them.—Now these things took place as examples for us, that we might not desire evil as they did.

I want you to be free from anxieties.—You keep him in perfect peace whose mind is stayed on you, because he trusts in you.

Matt. 26:42; Jer. 10:23; Matt. 26:39; Ps. 131:2; Rom. 8:26–27;
Matt. 20:22; Ps. 106:15; 1 Cor. 10:6; 1 Cor. 7:32; Isa. 26:3

MORNING

The Lord reproves him whom he loves.

"See now that I, even I, am he, and there is no god beside me; I kill and I make alive; I wound and I heal; and there is none that can deliver out of my hand."—"I know the plans I have for you, declares the Lord, plans for welfare and not for evil, to give you a future and a hope."—"My thoughts are not your thoughts, neither are your ways my ways, declares the Lord."

"Therefore, behold, I will allure her, and bring her into the wilderness, and speak tenderly to her."—As a man disciplines his son, the Lord your God disciplines you.—For the moment all discipline seems painful rather than pleasant, but later it yields the peaceful fruit of righteousness to those who have been trained by it.—Humble yourselves, therefore, under the mighty hand of God so that at the proper time he may exalt you.

I know, O Lord, that your rules are righteous, and that in faithfulness you have afflicted me.

Prov. 3:12; Deut. 32:39; Jer. 29:11; Isa. 55:8; Hos. 2:14;
Deut. 8:5; Heb. 12:11; 1 Pet. 5:6; Ps. 119:75

EVENING

The earth is the Lord's and the fullness thereof.

"She did not know that it was I who gave her the grain, the wine, and the oil, and who lavished on her silver and gold. Therefore I will take back my grain in its time, and my wine in its season, and I will take away my wool and my flax."—"All things come from you, and of your own have we given you. For we are strangers before you and sojourners, as all our fathers were. Our days on the earth are like a shadow, and there is no abiding. O Lord our God, all this abundance . . . comes from your hand and is all your own."—From him and through him and to him are all things. To him be glory forever. Amen.

God, who richly provides us with everything to enjoy.—Everything created by God is good, and nothing is to be rejected if it is received with thanksgiving, for it is made holy by the word of God and prayer.

My God will supply every need of yours according to his riches in glory in Christ Jesus.

Ps. 24:1; Hos. 2:8–9; 1 Chron. 29:14–16; Rom. 11:36;
1 Tim. 6:17; 1 Tim. 4:4–5; Phil. 4:19

MORNING

"The Helper, the Holy Spirit, whom the Father will send in my name."

"If you knew the gift of God, and who it is that is saying to you, 'Give me a drink,' you would have asked him, and he would have given you living water."—"If you then, who are evil, know how to give good gifts to your children, how much more will the heavenly Father give the Holy Spirit to those who ask him!"—"Truly, truly, I say to you, whatever you ask of the Father in my name, he will give it to you. Until now you have asked nothing in my name. Ask, and you will receive, that your joy may be full."—You do not have, because you do not ask.

"When the Spirit of truth comes, he will guide you into all the truth, for he will not speak on his own authority, but whatever he hears he will speak, and he will declare to you the things that are to come. He will glorify me, for he will take what is mine and declare it to you."

They rebelled and grieved his Holy Spirit; therefore he turned to be their enemy, and himself fought against them.

John 14:26; John 4:10; Luke 11:13; John 16:23–24;
James 4:2; John 16:13–14; Isa. 63:10

EVENING

"What do you think about the Christ?"

Lift up your heads, O gates! And lift them up, O ancient doors, that the King of glory may come in. Who is this King of glory? The Lord of hosts, he is the King of glory!—On his robe and on his thigh he has a name written, King of kings and Lord of lords.

The honor is for you who believe, but for those who do not believe, "The stone that the builders rejected has become the cornerstone."—Christ crucified, a stumbling block to Jews and folly to Gentiles, but to those who are called, both Jews and Greeks, Christ the power of God and the wisdom of God.

Indeed, I count everything as loss because of the surpassing worth of knowing Christ Jesus my Lord. For his sake I have suffered the loss of all things and count them as rubbish, in order that I may gain Christ.—"Lord, you know everything; you know that I love you."

Matt. 22:42; Ps. 24:9–10; Rev. 19:16; 1 Pet. 2:7;
1 Cor. 1:23–24; Phil. 3:8; John 21:17

MORNING

The path of the righteous is like the light of dawn,
which shines brighter and brighter until full day.

Not that I have already obtained this or am already perfect, but I press on to make it my own, because Christ Jesus has made me his own.—"Let us know; let us press on to know the Lord."

"Then the righteous will shine like the sun in the kingdom of their Father."—We all, with unveiled face, beholding the glory of the Lord, are being transformed into the same image from one degree of glory to another. For this comes from the Lord who is the Spirit.—When the perfect comes, the partial will pass away. . . . For now we see in a mirror dimly, but then face to face. Now I know in part; then I shall know fully, even as I have been fully known.—Beloved, we are God's children now, and what we will be has not yet appeared; but we know that when he appears we shall be like him, because we shall see him as he is. And everyone who thus hopes in him purifies himself as he is pure.

Prov. 4:18; Phil. 3:12; Hos. 6:3; Matt. 13:43;
2 Cor. 3:18; 1 Cor. 13:10, 12; 1 John 3:2-3

EVENING

"Everyone who calls on the name of the Lord will be saved."

"Whoever comes to me I will never cast out."—"Jesus, remember me when you come into your kingdom." And he said to him, "Truly, I say to you, today you will be with me in Paradise."—"What do you want me to do for you?" They said to him, "Lord, let our eyes be opened." And Jesus in pity touched their eyes, and immediately they recovered their sight and followed him.

"If you then, who are evil, know how to give good gifts to your children, how much more will the heavenly Father give the Holy Spirit to those who ask him!"—"I will put my Spirit within you. . . . Thus says the Lord God: This also I will let the house of Israel ask me to do for them: to increase their people like a flock."—And this is the confidence that we have toward him, that if we ask anything according to his will he hears us. And if we know that he hears us in whatever we ask, we know that we have the requests that we have asked of him.

Rom. 10:13; John 6:37; Luke 23:42-43; Matt. 20:32-34;
Luke 11:13; Ezek. 36:27, 37; 1 John 5:14-15

MORNING

You are altogether beautiful, my love; there is no flaw in you.

The whole head is sick, and the whole heart faint. From the sole of the foot even to the head, there is no soundness in it, but bruises and sores and raw wounds; they are not pressed out or bound up or softened with oil.—We have all become like one who is unclean, and all our righteous deeds are like a polluted garment.—I know that nothing good dwells in me, that is, in my flesh.—You were washed, you were sanctified, you were justified in the name of the Lord Jesus Christ and by the Spirit of our God.—All glorious is the princess in her chamber.—"Perfect through the splendor that I had bestowed on you, declares the Lord God."—Let the favor of the Lord our God be upon us.

"They have washed their robes and made them white in the blood of the Lamb."—So that he might present the church to himself in splendor, without spot or wrinkle or any such thing, that she might be holy and without blemish.—You have been filled in him.

Song 4:7; Isa. 1:5–6; Isa. 64:6; Rom. 7:18; 1 Cor. 6:11; Ps. 45:13;
Ezek. 16:14; Ps. 90:17; Rev. 7:14; Eph. 5:27; Col. 2:10

EVENING

"Broken cisterns that can hold no water."

Eve . . . bore Cain, saying, "I have gotten a man with the help of the Lord."—"Come, let us build ourselves a city and a tower with its top in the heavens." . . . So the Lord dispersed them.—So Lot chose for himself all the Jordan Valley. . . . The Jordan Valley was well watered everywhere like the garden of the Lord. . . . Now the men of Sodom were wicked, great sinners against the Lord.—And I applied my heart to know wisdom and to know madness and folly. I perceived that this also is but a striving after wind. For in much wisdom is much vexation, and he who increases knowledge increases sorrow.—I made great works. I built houses and planted vineyards for myself. . . . I also gathered for myself silver and gold. . . . Then I considered all that my hands had done and the toil I had expended in doing it, and behold, all was vanity and a striving after wind.—"If anyone thirsts, let him come to me and drink."—He satisfies the longing soul, and the hungry soul he fills with good things. Set your minds on things that are above, not on things that are on earth.

Jer. 2:13; Gen. 4:1; Gen. 11:4, 8; Gen. 13:11–10, 13; Eccles. 1:17–18;
Eccles. 2:4, 8, 11; John 7:37; Ps. 107:9; Col. 3:2

MORNING

"I do not ask that you take them out of the world, but that you keep them from the evil one."

Blameless and innocent, children of God without blemish in the midst of a crooked and twisted generation, among whom you shine as lights in the world.—"You are the salt of the earth, . . . the light of the world. . . . Let your light shine before others, so that they may see your good works and give glory to your Father who is in heaven."

"It was I who kept you from sinning against me."

But the Lord is faithful. He will establish you and guard you against the evil one.—I did not do so, because of the fear of God.—Who gave himself for our sins to deliver us from the present evil age, according to the will of our God and Father.—Now to him who is able to keep you from stumbling and to present you blameless before the presence of his glory with great joy, to the only God, our Savior, through Jesus Christ our Lord, be glory, majesty, dominion, and authority, before all time and now and forever. Amen.

John 17:15; Phil. 2:15; Matt. 5:13–14, 16; Gen. 20:6;
2 Thess. 3:3; Neh. 5:15; Gal. 1:4; Jude 24–25

EVENING

Whoever trusts in the Lord is safe.

The Lord is exalted, for he dwells on high.—The Lord is high above all nations, and his glory above the heavens! . . . He raises the poor from the dust and lifts the needy from the ash heap, to make them sit with princes.

God, being rich in mercy, because of the great love with which he loved us, even when we were dead in our trespasses, made us alive together with Christ—by grace you have been saved—and raised us up with him and seated us with him in the heavenly places in Christ Jesus.

He who did not spare his own Son but gave him up for us all, how will he not also with him graciously give us all things? . . . For I am sure that neither death nor life, nor angels nor rulers, nor things present nor things to come, nor powers, nor height nor depth, nor anything else in all creation, will be able to separate us from the love of God in Christ Jesus our Lord.

Prov. 29:25; Isa. 33:5; Ps. 113:4, 7–8; Eph. 2:4–6; Rom. 8:32, 38–39

MORNING

That through death he might destroy the
one who has the power of death.

Our Savior Christ Jesus . . . abolished death and brought life and immortality to light through the gospel.—He will swallow up death forever; and the Lord God will wipe away tears from all faces, and the reproach of his people he will take away from all the earth, for the Lord has spoken.—When the perishable puts on the imperishable, and the mortal puts on immortality, then shall come to pass the saying that is written: "Death is swallowed up in victory. O death, where is your victory? O death, where is your sting?" The sting of death is sin, and the power of sin is the law. But thanks be to God, who gives us the victory through our Lord Jesus Christ.

God gave us a spirit not of fear but of power and love and self-control.— Even though I walk through the valley of the shadow of death, I will fear no evil, for you are with me; your rod and your staff, they comfort me.

Heb. 2:14; 2 Tim. 1:10; Isa. 25:8; 1 Cor. 15:54–57; 2 Tim. 1:7; Ps. 23:4

EVENING

"Where is the way to the dwelling of light?"

God is light, and in him is no darkness at all.—"As long as I am in the world, I am the light of the world."

If we say we have fellowship with him while we walk in darkness, we lie and do not practice the truth. But if we walk in the light, as he is in the light, we have fellowship with one another, and the blood of Jesus his Son cleanses us from all sin.—The Father . . . has qualified you to share in the inheritance of the saints in light. He has delivered us from the domain of darkness and transferred us to the kingdom of his beloved Son, in whom we have redemption, the forgiveness of sins.

For you are all children of light, children of the day. We are not of the night or of the darkness.—"You are the light of the world. A city set on a hill cannot be hidden. . . . Let your light shine before others, so that they may see your good works and give glory to your Father who is in heaven."

Job 38:19; 1 John 1:5; John 9:5; 1 John 1:6–7;
Col. 1:12–14; 1 Thess. 5:5; Matt. 5:14, 16

MORNING

For the Lord will not cast off forever, but, though he cause grief, he will have compassion.

"Fear not, . . . declares the Lord, for I am with you. . . . Of you I will not make a full end. I will discipline you in just measure."—"For a brief moment I deserted you, but with great compassion I will gather you. In overflowing anger for a moment I hid my face from you, but with everlasting love I will have compassion on you," says the Lord, your Redeemer. . . . "For the mountains may depart and the hills be removed, but my steadfast love shall not depart from you, and my covenant of peace shall not be removed," says the Lord, who has compassion on you. "O afflicted one, storm-tossed and not comforted, behold, I will set your stones in antimony, and lay your foundations with sapphires."

I will bear the indignation of the Lord because I have sinned against him, until he pleads my cause and executes judgment for me. He will bring me out to the light; I shall look upon his vindication.

Lam. 3:31–32; Jer. 46:28; Isa. 54:7–8, 10–11; Mic. 7:9

EVENING

God chose what is foolish in the world to shame the wise; God chose what is weak in the world to shame the strong.

The people of Israel cried out to the Lord, and the Lord raised up for them a deliverer, Ehud, . . . a left-handed man. . . . After him was Shamgar, . . . who killed 600 of the Philistines with an oxgoad, and he also saved Israel.

And the Lord turned to him and said, "Go in this might of yours; . . . do not I send you?" And he said to him, " Please, Lord, how can I save Israel? Behold, my clan is the weakest in Manasseh, and I am the least in my father's house."

The Lord said to Gideon, "The people with you are too many for me, . . . lest Israel boast over me, saying, 'My own hand has saved me.'"

"Not by might, nor by power, but by my Spirit, says the Lord of hosts."—Finally, be strong in the Lord and in the strength of his might.

1 Cor. 1:27; Judg. 3:15, 31; Judg. 6:14–15; Judg. 7:2; Zech. 4:6; Eph. 6:10

MORNING

He has prepared for them a city.

"And if I go and prepare a place for you, I will come again and will take you to myself, that where I am you may be also."—An inheritance that is imperishable, undefiled, and unfading, kept in heaven for you.—Here we have no lasting city, but we seek the city that is to come.

"This Jesus, who was taken up from you into heaven, will come in the same way as you saw him go into heaven."—Be patient, therefore, brothers, until the coming of the Lord. See how the farmer waits for the precious fruit of the earth, being patient about it, until it receives the early and the late rains. You also, be patient. Establish your hearts, for the coming of the Lord is at hand.—"Yet a little while, and the coming one will come and will not delay."

We who are alive, who are left, will be caught up together with them in the clouds to meet the Lord in the air, and so we will always be with the Lord. Therefore encourage one another with these words.

Heb. 11:16; John 14:3; 1 Pet. 1:4; Heb. 13:14; Acts 1:11;
James 5:7–8; Heb. 10:37; 1 Thess. 4:17–18

EVENING

God chose what is low and despised in the world.

Do not be deceived: neither the sexually immoral, nor idolaters, nor adulterers, nor men who practice homosexuality, nor thieves, nor the greedy, nor drunkards, nor revilers, nor swindlers will inherit the kingdom of God. And such were some of you. But you were washed, you were sanctified, you were justified in the name of the Lord Jesus Christ and by the Spirit of our God.

And you were dead in the trespasses and sins in which you once walked, following the course of this world, . . . among whom we all once lived in the passions of our flesh, carrying out the desires of the body and the mind.

He saved us . . . according to his own mercy, by the washing of regeneration and renewal of the Holy Spirit, whom he poured out on us richly through Jesus Christ our Savior.

"My thoughts are not your thoughts, neither are your ways my ways, declares the Lord."

1 Cor. 1:28; 1 Cor. 6:9–11; Eph. 2:1–3; Titus 3:5–6; Isa. 55:8

MORNING

"The joy of the Lord is your strength."

Sing for joy, O heavens, and exult, O earth; break forth, O mountains, into singing! For the Lord has comforted his people and will have compassion on his afflicted.—"Behold, God is my salvation; I will trust, and will not be afraid; for the Lord God is my strength and my song, and he has become my salvation."—The Lord is my strength and my shield; in him my heart trusts, and I am helped; my heart exults, and with my song I give thanks to him.—My soul shall exult in my God, for he has clothed me with the garments of salvation; he has covered me with the robe of righteousness, as a bridegroom decks himself like a priest with a beautiful headdress, and as a bride adorns herself with her jewels.

In Christ Jesus, then, I have reason to be proud of my work for God.—We also rejoice in God through our Lord Jesus Christ, through whom we have now received reconciliation.—I will take joy in the God of my salvation.

Neh. 8:10; Isa. 49:13; Isa. 12:2; Ps. 28:7; Isa. 61:10;
Rom. 15:17; Rom. 5:11; Hab. 3:18

EVENING

"He has made with me an everlasting covenant, ordered in all things and secure."

I know whom I have believed, and I am convinced that he is able to guard until that Day what has been entrusted to me.

Blessed be the God and Father of our Lord Jesus Christ, who has blessed us in Christ with every spiritual blessing in the heavenly places, even as he chose us in him before the foundation of the world, that we should be holy and blameless before him. In love he predestined us for adoption as sons through Jesus Christ, according to the purpose of his will.

We know that for those who love God all things work together for good, for those who are called according to his purpose. For those whom he foreknew he also predestined to be conformed to the image of his Son. . . . And those whom he predestined he also called, and those whom he called he also justified, and those whom he justified he also glorified.

2 Sam. 23:5; 2 Tim. 1:12; Eph. 1:3–5; Rom. 8:28–30

MORNING

Now may the God of peace . . . equip you with
everything good that you may do his will.

Finally, brothers, rejoice. Aim for restoration, comfort one another, agree with one another, live in peace; and the God of love and peace will be with you.

By grace you have been saved through faith. And this is not your own doing; it is the gift of God, not a result of works, so that no one may boast.—Every good gift and every perfect gift is from above, coming down from the Father of lights with whom there is no variation or shadow due to change.

Work out your own salvation with fear and trembling, for it is God who works in you, both to will and to work for his good pleasure.—Be transformed by the renewal of your mind, that by testing you may discern what is the will of God, what is good and acceptable and perfect.—Filled with the fruit of righteousness that comes through Jesus Christ, to the glory and praise of God.

Not that we are sufficient in ourselves to claim anything as coming from us, but our sufficiency is from God.

Heb. 13:20–21; 2 Cor. 13:11; Eph. 2:8–9; James 1:17;
Phil. 2:12–13; Rom. 12:2; Phil. 1:11; 2 Cor. 3:5

EVENING

"I will allure her, and bring her into the
wilderness, and speak tenderly to her."

"Therefore go out from their midst, and be separate from them, says the Lord, and touch no unclean thing; then I will welcome you, and I will be a father to you, and you shall be sons and daughters to me, says the Lord Almighty."—Since we have these promises, beloved, let us cleanse ourselves from every defilement of body and spirit, bringing holiness to completion in the fear of God.—Jesus also suffered outside the gate in order to sanctify the people through his own blood. Therefore let us go to him outside the camp and bear the reproach he endured.

[Jesus] said to them, "Come away by yourselves to a desolate place and rest a while."—The Lord is my shepherd; I shall not want. He makes me lie down in green pastures. He leads me beside still waters. He restores my soul. He leads me in paths of righteousness for his name's sake.

Hos. 2:14; 2 Cor. 6:17–18; 2 Cor. 7:1; Heb. 13:12–13; Mark 6:31; Ps. 23:1–3

MORNING

"The house that is to be built for the Lord must be exceedingly magnificent."

You yourselves like living stones are being built up as a spiritual house.—Do you not know that you are God's temple and that God's Spirit dwells in you? If anyone destroys God's temple, God will destroy him. For God's temple is holy, and you are that temple.—Do you not know that your body is a temple of the Holy Spirit within you, whom you have from God? You are not your own, for you were bought with a price. So glorify God in your body.—What agreement has the temple of God with idols? For we are the temple of the living God; as God said, "I will make my dwelling among them and walk among them, and I will be their God, and they shall be my people."—You are . . . built on the foundation of the apostles and prophets, Christ Jesus himself being the cornerstone, in whom the whole structure, being joined together, grows into a holy temple in the Lord. In him you also are being built together into a dwelling place for God by the Spirit.

1 Chron. 22:5; 1 Pet. 2:5; 1 Cor. 3:16–17; 1 Cor. 6:19–20;
2 Cor. 6:16; Eph. 2:19–22

EVENING

He is before all things.

"The words of the Amen, . . . the beginning of God's creation."—He is the beginning, the firstborn from the dead, that in everything he might be preeminent.

"The Lord possessed me at the beginning of his work, the first of his acts of old. Ages ago I was set up, at the first, before the beginning of the earth. . . . When he established the heavens, I was there; when he drew a circle on the face of the deep, when he made firm the skies above, when he established the fountains of the deep, when he assigned to the sea its limit, so that the waters might not transgress his command, . . . and I was daily his delight, rejoicing before him always."—"Also henceforth I am he."

The Lamb who was slain.—The founder and perfecter of our faith, who for the joy that was set before him endured the cross, despising the shame, and is seated at the right hand of the throne of God.

Col. 1:17; Rev. 3:14; Col. 1:18; Prov. 8:22–23, 27–30;
Isa. 43:13; Rev. 13:8; Heb. 12:2

MORNING

Pray for one another, that you may be healed.

Abraham answered and said, "Behold, I have undertaken to speak to the Lord, I who am but dust and ashes. Suppose five of the fifty righteous are lacking. Will you destroy the whole city for lack of five?" And he said, "I will not destroy it if I find forty-five there."

"Father, forgive them, for they know not what they do."—"Pray for those who persecute you."

"I am praying for them. I am not praying for the world but for those whom you have given me, for they are yours. . . . I do not ask for these only, but also for those who will believe in me through their word."—Bear one another's burdens, and so fulfill the law of Christ.

The prayer of a righteous person has great power as it is working. Elijah was a man with a nature like ours, and he prayed fervently that it might not rain, and for three years and six months it did not rain on the earth.

James 5:16; Gen. 18:27-28; Luke 23:34; Matt. 5:44;
John 17:9, 20; Gal. 6:2; James 5:16-17

EVENING

As for man, his days are like grass; he flourishes like a flower of the field; for the wind passes over it, and it is gone, and its place knows it no more.

So teach us to number our days that we may get a heart of wisdom.—"What does it profit a man to gain the whole world and forfeit his soul?"

Surely the people are grass. The grass withers, the flower fades, but the word of our God will stand forever.—The world is passing away along with its desires, but whoever does the will of God abides forever.

Behold, now is the favorable time; behold, now is the day of salvation.—Those who deal with the world as though they had no dealings with it. For the present form of this world is passing away.—Let us consider how to stir up one another to love and good works, not neglecting to meet together, as is the habit of some, but encouraging one another, and all the more as you see the Day drawing near.

Ps. 103:15-16; Ps. 90:12; Mark 8:36; Isa. 40:7-8;
1 John 2:17; 2 Cor. 6:2; 1 Cor. 7:31; Heb. 10:24-25

MORNING

"What god is there in heaven or on earth who can do such works and mighty acts as yours?"

Who in the skies can be compared to the Lord? Who among the heavenly beings is like the Lord? . . . O Lord God of hosts, who is mighty as you are, O Lord, with your faithfulness all around you?—There is none like you among the gods, O Lord, nor are there any works like yours.—"Because of your promise, and according to your own heart, you have brought about all this greatness, to make your servant know it. Therefore you are great, O Lord God. For there is none like you, and there is no God besides you, according to all that we have heard with our ears."

"What no eye has seen, nor ear heard, nor the heart of man imagined, what God has prepared for those who love him"—these things God has revealed to us through the Spirit.—"The secret things belong to the Lord our God, but the things that are revealed belong to us and to our children."

Deut. 3:24; Ps. 89:6, 8; Ps. 86:8; 2 Sam. 7:21-22; 1 Cor. 2:9-10; Deut. 29:29

EVENING

"Let the one who boasts, boast in the Lord."

"Let not the wise man boast in his wisdom, let not the mighty man boast in his might, let not the rich man boast in his riches, but let him who boasts boast in this, that he understands and knows me, that I am the Lord."

Indeed, I count everything as loss because of the surpassing worth of knowing Christ Jesus my Lord. For his sake I have suffered the loss of all things and count them as rubbish, in order that I may gain Christ.—I am not ashamed of the gospel, for it is the power of God for salvation to everyone who believes.—In Christ Jesus, then, I have reason to be proud of my work for God.

Whom have I in heaven but you? And there is nothing on earth that I desire besides you.—"My heart exults in the Lord; . . . I rejoice in your salvation."

Not to us, O Lord, not to us, but to your name give glory, for the sake of your steadfast love and your faithfulness!

1 Cor. 1:31; Jer. 9:23-24; Phil. 3:8; Rom. 1:16;
Rom. 15:17; Ps. 73:25; 1 Sam. 2:1; Ps. 115:1

MORNING

*As he who called you is holy, you also
be holy in all your conduct.*

You know how . . . we exhorted each one of you . . . and charged you to walk in a manner worthy of God, who calls you into his own kingdom and glory.—That you may proclaim the excellencies of him who called you out of darkness into his marvelous light.

At one time you were darkness, but now you are light in the Lord. Walk as children of light (for the fruit of light is found in all that is good and right and true), and try to discern what is pleasing to the Lord. Take no part in the unfruitful works of darkness, but instead expose them.—Filled with the fruit of righteousness that comes through Jesus Christ, to the glory and praise of God.

"Let your light shine before others, so that they may see your good works and give glory to your Father who is in heaven."—Whether you eat or drink, or whatever you do, do all to the glory of God.

1 Pet. 1:15; 1 Thess. 2:11–12; 1 Pet. 2:9; Eph. 5:8–11; Phil. 1:11; Matt. 5:16; 1 Cor. 10:31

EVENING

*"Ask me of things to come; will you command me concerning
my children and the work of my hands?"*

"And I will give you a new heart, and a new spirit I will put within you. And I will remove the heart of stone from your flesh and give you a heart of flesh. And I will put my Spirit within you, and cause you to walk in my statutes and be careful to obey my rules. . . . Thus says the Lord God: This also I will let the house of Israel ask me to do for them."

"If two of you agree on earth about anything they ask, it will be done for them by my Father in heaven. For where two or three are gathered in my name, there am I among them."

"Have faith in God. Truly, I say to you, whoever says to this mountain, 'Be taken up and thrown into the sea,' and does not doubt in his heart, but believes that what he says will come to pass, it will be done for him."

Isa. 45:11; Ezek. 36:26–27, 37; Matt. 18:19–20; Mark 11:22–23

MORNING

*"God is not man, that he should lie, or a son of man,
that he should change his mind."*

The Father of lights with whom there is no variation or shadow due to change.—Jesus Christ is the same yesterday and today and forever.

His faithfulness is a shield and buckler.

When God desired to show more convincingly to the heirs of the promise the unchangeable character of his purpose, he guaranteed it with an oath, so that by two unchangeable things, in which it is impossible for God to lie, we who have fled for refuge might have strong encouragement to hold fast to the hope set before us.

"The faithful God who keeps covenant and steadfast love with those who love him and keep his commandments, to a thousand generations."—All the paths of the Lord are steadfast love and faithfulness, for those who keep his covenant and his testimonies.—Blessed is he whose help is the God of Jacob, whose hope is in the Lord his God . . . who keeps faith forever.

Num. 23:19; James 1:17; Heb. 13:8; Ps. 91:4; Heb. 6:17–18;
Deut. 7:9; Ps. 25:10; Ps. 146:5–6

EVENING

If you faint in the day of adversity, your strength is small.

He gives power to the faint, and to him who has no might he increases strength.—"My grace is sufficient for you, for my power is made perfect in weakness."—"When he calls to me, I will answer him; I will be with him in trouble; I will rescue him and honor him."—"The eternal God is your dwelling place, and underneath are the everlasting arms. And he thrust out the enemy before you."

I looked for pity, but there was none, and for comforters, but I found none.—Every high priest chosen from among men is appointed to act on behalf of men in relation to God. . . . He can deal gently with the ignorant and wayward, since he himself is beset with weakness. . . . So also Christ . . . Although he was a son, he learned obedience through what he suffered. And being made perfect, he became the source of eternal salvation to all who obey him.—Surely he has borne our griefs and carried our sorrows.

Prov. 24:10; Isa. 40:29; 2 Cor. 12:9; Ps. 91:15; Deut. 33:27;
Ps. 69:20; Heb. 5:1–2, 5, 8–9; Isa. 53:4

MORNING

The Lord is my portion.

All things are yours, . . . and you are Christ's, and Christ is God's.—Our . . . Savior Jesus Christ . . . gave himself for us.—[God] put all things under his feet and gave him as head over all things to the church.—Christ loved the church and gave himself up for her, . . . so that he might present the church to himself in splendor, without spot or wrinkle or any such thing, that she might be holy and without blemish.

My soul makes its boast in the Lord.—I will greatly rejoice in the Lord; my soul shall exult in my God, for he has clothed me with the garments of salvation; he has covered me with the robe of righteousness.

Whom have I in heaven but you? And there is nothing on earth that I desire besides you. My flesh and my heart may fail, but God is the strength of my heart and my portion forever.—I say to the Lord, "You are my Lord; I have no good apart from you." . . . The Lord is my chosen portion and my cup; you hold my lot. The lines have fallen for me in pleasant places; indeed, I have a beautiful inheritance.

Ps. 119:57; 1 Cor. 3:21, 23; Titus 2:13–14; Eph. 1:22; Eph. 5:25, 27; Ps. 34:2; Isa. 61:10; Ps. 73:25–26; Ps. 16:2, 5–6

EVENING

There is a way that seems right to a man, but its end is the way to death.

Whoever trusts in his own mind is a fool.

Your word is a lamp to my feet and a light to my path.—With regard to the works of man, by the word of your lips I have avoided the ways of the violent.

"If a prophet or a dreamer of dreams arises among you, . . . and if he says, 'Let us go after other gods,' which you have not known, 'and let us serve them,' you shall not listen to the words of that prophet. . . . For the Lord your God is testing you, to know whether you love the Lord your God with all your heart and with all your soul. You shall walk after the Lord your God and fear him and keep his commandments and obey his voice, and you shall serve him and hold fast to him."—I will instruct you and teach you in the way you should go; I will counsel you with my eye upon you.

Prov. 14:12; Prov. 28:26; Ps. 119:105; Ps. 17:4; Deut. 13:1–4; Ps. 32:8

MORNING

None of us lives to himself, and none of us dies to himself.

For if we live, we live to the Lord, and if we die, we die to the Lord. So then, whether we live or whether we die, we are the Lord's.—Let no one seek his own good, but the good of his neighbor.—You were bought with a price. So glorify God in your body.

Christ will be honored in my body, whether by life or by death. For to me to live is Christ, and to die is gain. If I am to live in the flesh, that means fruitful labor for me. Yet which I shall choose I cannot tell. I am hard pressed between the two. My desire is to depart and be with Christ, for that is far better.

Through the law I died to the law, so that I might live to God. I have been crucified with Christ. It is no longer I who live, but Christ who lives in me. And the life I now live in the flesh I live by faith in the Son of God, who loved me and gave himself for me.

Rom. 14:7; Rom. 14:8; 1 Cor. 10:24; 1 Cor. 6:20; Phil. 1:20–23; Gal. 2:19–20

EVENING

God gave Solomon . . . breadth of mind
like the sand on the seashore.

"Behold, something greater than Solomon is here."—Prince of Peace.

One will scarcely die for a righteous person—though perhaps for a good person one would dare even to die—but God shows his love for us in that while we were still sinners, Christ died for us.—Who, though he was in the form of God, did not count equality with God a thing to be grasped, but emptied himself, by taking the form of a servant, being born in the likeness of men. And being found in human form, he humbled himself by becoming obedient to the point of death, even death on a cross.—The love of Christ that surpasses knowledge.

Christ the power of God and the wisdom of God.—In whom are hidden all the treasures of wisdom and knowledge.—The unsearchable riches of Christ.—And because of him you are in Christ Jesus, who became to us wisdom from God, righteousness and sanctification and redemption.

1 Kings 4:29; Matt. 12:42; Isa. 9:6; Rom. 5:7–8; Phil. 2:6–8;
Eph. 3:19; 1 Cor. 1:24; Col. 2:3; Eph. 3:8; 1 Cor. 1:30

MORNING

I have loved you with an everlasting love; therefore
I have continued my faithfulness to you.

But we ought always to give thanks to God for you, brothers beloved by the Lord, because God chose you as the firstfruits to be saved, through sanctification by the Spirit and belief in the truth. To this he called you through our gospel, so that you may obtain the glory of our Lord Jesus Christ.—[God] saved us and called us to a holy calling, not because of our works but because of his own purpose and grace, which he gave us in Christ Jesus before the ages began.—Your eyes saw my unformed substance; in your book were written, every one of them, the days that were formed for me, when as yet there was none of them.

"For God so loved the world, that he gave his only Son, that whoever believes in him should not perish but have eternal life."

In this is love, not that we have loved God but that he loved us and sent his Son to be the propitiation for our sins.

Jer. 31:3; 2 Thess. 2:13–14; 2 Tim. 1:9; Ps. 139:16; John 3:16; 1 John 4:10

EVENING

"I have made, and I will bear."

But now thus says the Lord, he who created you, O Jacob, he who formed you, O Israel: "Fear not, for I have redeemed you; I have called you by name, you are mine. When you pass through the waters, I will be with you; and through the rivers, they shall not overwhelm you."—"Even to your old age I am he, and to gray hairs I will carry you."

Like an eagle that stirs up its nest, that flutters over its young, spreading out its wings, catching them, bearing them on its pinions, the Lord alone guided him.—He lifted them up and carried them all the days of old.

Jesus Christ is the same yesterday and today and forever.—I am sure that neither . . . height nor depth, nor anything else in all creation, will be able to separate us from the love of God in Christ Jesus our Lord.

"Can a woman forget her nursing child, that she should have no compassion on the son of her womb? Even these may forget, yet I will not forget you."

Isa. 46:4; Isa. 43:1–2; Isa. 46:4; Deut. 32:11–12; Isa. 63:9;
Heb. 13:8; Rom. 8:38–39; Isa. 49:15

MORNING

"I know their sufferings."

A man of sorrows, and acquainted with grief.—We do not have a high priest who is unable to sympathize with our weaknesses.

"He took our illnesses and bore our diseases."—Jesus, wearied as he was from his journey, was sitting beside the well.

When Jesus saw her weeping, and the Jews who had come with her also weeping, he was deeply moved in his spirit and greatly troubled. . . . Jesus wept.—For because he himself has suffered when tempted, he is able to help those who are being tempted.

He looked down from his holy height; from heaven the Lord looked at the earth, to hear the groans of the prisoners, to set free those who were doomed to die.—"He knows the way that I take; when he has tried me, I shall come out as gold."—When my spirit faints within me, you know my way!—He who touches you touches the apple of his eye.—In all their affliction he was afflicted, and the angel of his presence saved them.

Ex. 3:7; Isa. 53:3; Heb. 4:15; Matt. 8:17; John 4:6; John 11:33, 35;
Heb. 2:18; Ps. 102:19–20; Job 23:10 Ps. 142:3; Zech. 2:8; Isa. 63:9

EVENING

"We must work the works of him who sent me while it is day."

The soul of the sluggard craves and gets nothing, while the soul of the diligent is richly supplied.—One who waters will himself be watered.

"My food is to do the will of him who sent me and to accomplish his work. Do you not say, 'There are yet four months, then comes the harvest'? Look, I tell you, lift up your eyes, and see that the fields are white for harvest. Already the one who reaps is receiving wages and gathering fruit for eternal life, so that sower and reaper may rejoice together."—"The kingdom of heaven is like a master of a house who went out early in the morning to hire laborers for his vineyard. After agreeing with the laborers for a denarius a day, he sent them into his vineyard."

Preach the word; be ready in season and out of season.—"Engage in business until I come."—I worked harder than any of them, though it was not I, but the grace of God that is with me.

John 9:4; Prov. 13:4; Prov. 11:25; John 4:34–36;
Matt. 20:1–2; 2 Tim. 4:2; Luke 19:13; 1 Cor. 15:10

MORNING

"Look to the rock from which you were hewn, and to the quarry from which you were dug."

Behold, I was brought forth in iniquity.—"No eye pitied you, . . . but you were cast out on the open field, for you were abhorred, on the day that you were born. And when I passed by you and saw you wallowing in your blood, I said to you, . . . 'Live!'"

He drew me up from the pit of destruction, out of the miry bog, and set my feet upon a rock, making my steps secure. He put a new song in my mouth, a song of praise to our God.

While we were still weak, at the right time Christ died for the ungodly. For one will scarcely die for a righteous person—though perhaps for a good person one would dare even to die—but God shows his love for us in that while we were still sinners, Christ died for us.—But God, being rich in mercy, because of the great love with which he loved us, even when we were dead in our trespasses, made us alive together with Christ.

Isa. 51:1; Ps. 51:5; Ezek. 16:5–6; Ps. 40:2–3; Rom. 5:6–8; Eph. 2:4–5

EVENING

I will greatly rejoice in the Lord; my soul shall exult in my God.

I will bless the Lord at all times; his praise shall continually be in my mouth. My soul makes its boast in the Lord; let the humble hear and be glad. Oh, magnify the Lord with me, and let us exalt his name together!—The Lord bestows favor and honor. No good thing does he withhold from those who walk uprightly. O Lord of hosts, blessed is the one who trusts in you!—Bless the Lord, O my soul, and all that is within me, bless his holy name!—Is anyone cheerful? Let him sing praise.—Be filled with the Spirit, addressing one another in psalms and hymns and spiritual songs, singing and making melody to the Lord with your heart, giving thanks always and for everything.—Singing psalms and hymns and spiritual songs, with thankfulness in your hearts to God.

About midnight Paul and Silas were praying and singing hymns to God, and the prisoners were listening to them.—Rejoice in the Lord always; again I will say, rejoice.

Isa. 61:10; Ps. 34:1–3; Ps. 84:11–12; Ps. 103:1; James 5:13;
Eph. 5:18–20; Col. 3:16; Acts 16:25; Phil. 4:4

MORNING

*"You shall make a plate of pure gold and engrave on it,
like the engraving of a signet, 'Holy to the Lord.'"*

The holiness without which no one will see the Lord.—"God is spirit, and those who worship him must worship in spirit and truth."—We have all become like one who is unclean, and all our righteous deeds are like a polluted garment.—"Among those who are near me I will be sanctified, and before all the people I will be glorified."

"This is the law of the temple: the whole territory on the top of the mountain all around shall be most holy."—Holiness befits your house, O Lord, forevermore.

"For their sake I consecrate myself, that they also may be sanctified in truth."—Since then we have a great high priest who has passed through the heavens, Jesus, the Son of God, let us . . . with confidence draw near to the throne of grace, that we may receive mercy and find grace to help in time of need.

Ex. 28:36; Heb. 12:14; John 4:24; Isa. 64:6; Lev. 10:3;
Ezek. 43:12; Ps. 93:5; John 17:19; Heb. 4:14, 16

EVENING

My cup overflows.

Oh, taste and see that the Lord is good! Blessed is the man who takes refuge in him! Oh, fear the Lord, you his saints, for those who fear him have no lack! The young lions suffer want and hunger; but those who seek the Lord lack no good thing.—His mercies never come to an end; they are new every morning; great is your faithfulness.

The Lord is my chosen portion and my cup; you hold my lot. The lines have fallen for me in pleasant places; indeed, I have a beautiful inheritance.—Whether . . . the world or life or death or the present or the future—all are yours.—Blessed be the God and Father of our Lord Jesus Christ, who has blessed us in Christ with every spiritual blessing in the heavenly places.

I have learned in whatever situation I am to be content.—But godliness with contentment is great gain.—My God will supply every need of yours according to his riches in glory in Christ Jesus.

Ps. 23:5; Ps. 34:8-10; Lam. 3:22-23; Ps. 16:5-6; 1 Cor. 3:22;
Eph. 1:3; Phil. 4:11; 1 Tim. 6:6; Phil. 4:19

MORNING

Your word is a lamp to my feet and a light to my path.

By the word of your lips I have avoided the ways of the violent. My steps have held fast to your paths; my feet have not slipped.—When you walk, they will lead you; when you lie down, they will watch over you; and when you awake, they will talk with you. For the commandment is a lamp and the teaching a light.—Your ears shall hear a word behind you, saying, "This is the way, walk in it," when you turn to the right or when you turn to the left.

"I am the light of the world. Whoever follows me will not walk in darkness, but will have the light of life."—We have the prophetic word more fully confirmed, to which you will do well to pay attention as to a lamp shining in a dark place.—Now we see in a mirror dimly, but then face to face. Now I know in part; then I shall know fully, even as I have been fully known.—They will need no light of lamp or sun, for the Lord God will be their light, and they will reign forever and ever.

Ps. 119:105; Ps. 17:4–5; Prov. 6:22–23; Isa. 30:21;
John 8:12; 2 Pet. 1:19; 1 Cor. 13:12; Rev. 22:5

EVENING

"What do you mean, you sleeper? Arise."

This is no place to rest, because of uncleanness that destroys.—Set your minds on things that are above, not on things that are on earth.—If riches increase, set not your heart on them.—"Now set your mind and heart to seek the Lord your God. Arise."

"Why are you sleeping? Rise and pray that you may not enter into temptation."—"But watch yourselves lest your hearts be weighed down with dissipation and drunkenness and cares of this life, and that day come upon you suddenly like a trap."—"As the bridegroom was delayed, they all became drowsy and slept."—"Yet a little while, and the coming one will come and will not delay."—The hour has come for you to wake from sleep. For salvation is nearer to us now than when we first believed.—"Therefore stay awake—for you do not know when the master of the house will come, in the evening, or at midnight, or when the rooster crows, or in the morning—lest he come suddenly and find you asleep."

Jonah 1:6; Mic. 2:10; Col. 3:2; Ps. 62:10; 1 Chron. 22:19; Luke 22:46;
Luke 21:34; Matt. 25:5; Heb. 10:37; Rom. 13:11; Mark 13:35–36

MORNING

*"The accuser of our brothers has been thrown down,
who accuses them day and night before our God."*

They have conquered him by the blood of the Lamb and by the word of their testimony.—Who shall bring any charge against God's elect? It is God who justifies. Who is to condemn? Christ Jesus is the one who died—more than that, who was raised—who is at the right hand of God, who indeed is interceding for us.

He disarmed the rulers and authorities and put them to open shame.— That through death he might destroy the one who has the power of death, that is, the devil, and deliver all those who through fear of death were subject to lifelong slavery.—In all these things we are more than conquerors through him who loved us.—Put on the whole armor of God, that you may be able to stand against the schemes of the devil. . . . And take . . . the sword of the Spirit, which is the word of God.—Thanks be to God, who gives us the victory through our Lord Jesus Christ.

Rev. 12:10; Rev. 12:11; Rom. 8:33–34; Col. 2:15; Heb. 2:14–15;
Rom. 8:37; Eph. 6:11, 17; 1 Cor. 15:57

EVENING

The tree of life.

God gave us eternal life, and this life is in his Son.—"He gave his only Son, that whoever believes in him should not perish but have eternal life."—"As the Father raises the dead and gives them life, so also the Son gives life to whom he will. . . . For as the Father has life in himself, so he has granted the Son also to have life in himself."

"To the one who conquers I will grant to eat of the tree of life, which is in the paradise of God."—Through the middle of the street of the city; also, on either side of the river, the tree of life with its twelve kinds of fruit, yielding its fruit each month. The leaves of the tree were for the healing of the nations.

Blessed is the one who finds wisdom. . . . Long life is in her right hand. . . . She is a tree of life to those who lay hold of her; those who hold her fast are called blessed.—Christ Jesus, who became to us wisdom from God.

Gen. 2:9; 1 John 5:11; John 3:16; John 5:21, 26; Rev. 2:7;
Rev. 22:2; Prov. 3:13, 16, 18; 1 Cor. 1:30

MORNING

Blessed is he who trusts in the Lord.

No unbelief made [Abraham] waver concerning the promise of God, but he grew strong in his faith as he gave glory to God, fully convinced that God was able to do what he had promised.—The men of Judah prevailed, because they relied on the Lord, the God of their fathers.

God is our refuge and strength, a very present help in trouble. Therefore we will not fear though the earth gives way, though the mountains be moved into the heart of the sea.—It is better to take refuge in the Lord than to trust in man. It is better to take refuge in the Lord than to trust in princes.—The steps of a man are established by the Lord, when he delights in his way; though he fall, he shall not be cast headlong, for the Lord upholds his hand.

Oh, taste and see that the Lord is good! Blessed is the man who takes refuge in him! Oh, fear the Lord, you his saints, for those who fear him have no lack!

Prov. 16:20; Rom. 4:20-21; 2 Chron. 13:18; Ps. 46:1-2;
Ps. 118:8-9; Ps. 37:23-24; Ps. 34:8-9

EVENING

In peace I will both lie down and sleep;
for you alone, O Lord, make me dwell in safety.

You will not fear the terror of the night. He will cover you with his pinions, and under his wings you will find refuge.—"As a hen gathers her brood under her wings."—He will not let your foot be moved; he who keeps you will not slumber. Behold, he who keeps Israel will neither slumber nor sleep. The Lord is your keeper; the Lord is your shade on your right hand.

Let me dwell in your tent forever! Let me take refuge under the shelter of your wings!—Even the darkness is not dark to you; the night is bright as the day, for darkness is as light with you.

He who did not spare his own Son but gave him up for us all, how will he not also with him graciously give us all things?—You are Christ's, and Christ is God's.—"I will trust, and will not be afraid."

Ps. 4:8; Ps. 91:5, 4; Matt. 23:37; Ps. 121:3-5; Ps. 61:4;
Ps. 139:12; Rom. 8:32; 1 Cor. 3:23; Isa. 12:2

MORNING

The king . . . held out to Esther the golden scepter. . . .
Then Esther approached and touched the tip of the scepter.

"If he cries to me, I will hear, for I am compassionate."

So we have come to know and to believe the love that God has for us. God is love, and whoever abides in love abides in God, and God abides in him. By this is love perfected with us, so that we may have confidence for the day of judgment, because as he is so also are we in this world. There is no fear in love, but perfect love casts out fear. For fear has to do with punishment, and whoever fears has not been perfected in love. We love because he first loved us.—Let us draw near with a true heart in full assurance of faith, with our hearts sprinkled clean from an evil conscience and our bodies washed with pure water.— For through him we both have access in one Spirit to the Father.—We have boldness and access with confidence through our faith in him.—Let us then with confidence draw near to the throne of grace, that we may receive mercy and find grace to help in time of need.

Est. 5:2; Ex. 22:27; 1 John 4:16–19; Heb. 10:22; Eph. 2:18; Eph. 3:12; Heb. 4:16

EVENING

They said to one another, "What is it?"
For they did not know what it was.

Great indeed, we confess, is the mystery of godliness: He was manifested in the flesh.—"For the bread of God is he who comes down from heaven and gives life to the world."—"Your fathers ate the manna in the wilderness, and they died. . . . If anyone eats of this bread, he will live forever. And the bread that I will give for the life of the world is my flesh. . . . For my flesh is true food, and my blood is true drink."—The people of Israel . . . gathered, some more, some less. But when they measured it with an omer, whoever gathered much had nothing left over, and whoever gathered little had no lack. Each of them gathered as much as he could eat. . . . Morning by morning they gathered it, each as much as he could eat.—"Therefore do not be anxious, saying, 'What shall we eat?' or 'What shall we drink?' or 'What shall we wear?' . . . Your heavenly Father knows that you need them all. But seek first the kingdom of God and his righteousness, and all these things will be added to you."

Ex. 16:15; 1 Tim. 3:16; John 6:33; John 6:49, 51, 55;
Ex. 16:17–18, 21; Matt. 6:31–33

MORNING

The free gift following many trespasses brought justification.

"Though your sins are like scarlet, they shall be as white as snow; though they are red like crimson, they shall become like wool."—"I, I am he who blots out your transgressions for my own sake, and I will not remember your sins. Put me in remembrance; let us argue together; set forth your case, that you may be proved right."—I have blotted out your transgressions like a cloud and your sins like mist; return to me, for I have redeemed you.

"For God so loved the world, that he gave his only Son, that whoever believes in him should not perish but have eternal life."—But the free gift is not like the trespass. For if many died through one man's trespass, much more have the grace of God and the free gift by the grace of that one man Jesus Christ abounded for many.—And such were some of you. But you were washed, you were sanctified, you were justified in the name of the Lord Jesus Christ and by the Spirit of our God.

Rom. 5:16; Isa. 1:18; Isa. 43:25–26; Isa. 44:22; John 3:16; Rom. 5:15; 1 Cor. 6:11

EVENING

"Engage in business until I come."

"It is like a man going on a journey, when he leaves home and puts his servants in charge, each with his work, and commands the doorkeeper to stay awake."—"To one he gave five talents, to another two, to another one, to each according to his ability. Then he went away."

"We must work the works of him who sent me while it is day; night is coming, when no one can work."—"Did you not know that I must be in my Father's house?"—Leaving you an example, so that you might follow in his steps.

Preach the word; be ready in season and out of season; reprove, rebuke, and exhort, with complete patience and teaching.—Each one's work will become manifest, for the Day will disclose it.—Therefore, my beloved brothers, be steadfast, immovable, always abounding in the work of the Lord, knowing that in the Lord your labor is not in vain.

Luke 19:13; Mark 13:34; Matt. 25:15; John 9:4; Luke 2:49;
1 Pet. 2:21; 2 Tim. 4:2; 1 Cor. 3:13; 1 Cor. 15:58

MORNING

The fruit of the Spirit is . . . gentleness.

The meek shall obtain fresh joy in the Lord, and the poor among mankind shall exult in the Holy One of Israel.—"Unless you turn and become like children, you will never enter the kingdom of heaven. Whoever humbles himself like this child is the greatest in the kingdom of heaven."—The imperishable beauty of a gentle and quiet spirit . . . in God's sight is very precious.—Love does not envy or boast; it is not arrogant.

Pursue . . . gentleness.—"Take my yoke upon you, and learn from me, for I am gentle and lowly in heart."—He was oppressed, and he was afflicted, yet he opened not his mouth; like a lamb that is led to the slaughter, and like a sheep that before its shearers is silent, so he opened not his mouth.—Christ also suffered for you, leaving you an example, so that you might follow in his steps. He committed no sin, neither was deceit found in his mouth. When he was reviled, he did not revile in return . . . but continued entrusting himself to him who judges justly.

Gal. 5:22–23; Isa. 29:19; Matt. 18:3–4; 1 Pet. 3:4; 1 Cor. 13:4;
1 Tim. 6:11; Matt. 11:29; Isa. 53:7; 1 Pet. 2:21–23

EVENING

"If anyone would come after me, let him deny himself and take up his cross daily and follow me."

Through honor and dishonor, through slander and praise.—Indeed, all who desire to live a godly life in Christ Jesus will be persecuted.—The offense of the cross.

If I were still trying to please man, I would not be a servant of Christ.

If you are insulted for the name of Christ, you are blessed. . . . But let none of you suffer as a murderer or a thief or an evildoer or as a meddler. Yet if anyone suffers as a Christian, let him not be ashamed, but let him glorify God in that name.

For it has been granted to you that for the sake of Christ you should not only believe in him but also suffer for his sake.—One has died for all, therefore all have died; and he died for all, that those who live might no longer live for themselves but for him who for their sake died and was raised.—If we endure, we will also reign with him.

Luke 9:23; 2 Cor. 6:8; 2 Tim. 3:12; Gal. 5:11; Gal. 1:10;
1 Pet. 4:14–16; Phil. 1:29; 2 Cor. 5:14–15; 2 Tim. 2:12

MORNING

Wait for the Lord; be strong, and let your heart take courage.

Have you not known? Have you not heard? The Lord is the everlasting God, the Creator of the ends of the earth. He does not faint or grow weary. . . . He gives power to the faint, and to him who has no might he increases strength.—Fear not, for I am with you; be not dismayed, for I am your God; I will strengthen you, I will help you, I will uphold you with my righteous right hand.—You have been a stronghold to the poor, a stronghold to the needy in his distress, a shelter from the storm and a shade from the heat; for the breath of the ruthless is like a storm against a wall.

The testing of your faith produces steadfastness. And let steadfastness have its full effect, that you may be perfect and complete, lacking in nothing.—Therefore do not throw away your confidence, which has a great reward. For you have need of endurance, so that when you have done the will of God you may receive what is promised.

Ps. 27:14; Isa. 40:28–29; Isa. 41:10; Isa. 25:4; James 1:3–4; Heb. 10:35–36

EVENING

He makes me lie down in green pastures.

"But the wicked are like the tossing sea; for it cannot be quiet. . . . There is no peace," says my God, "for the wicked."—"Come to me, all who labor and are heavy laden, and I will give you rest."—Be still before the Lord.—Whoever has entered God's rest has also rested from his works.

Do not be led away by diverse and strange teachings, for it is good for the heart to be strengthened by grace.—So that we may no longer be children, tossed to and fro by the waves and carried about by every wind of doctrine, by human cunning, by craftiness in deceitful schemes. Rather, speaking the truth in love, we are to grow up in every way into him who is the head, into Christ.

With great delight I sat in his shadow, and his fruit was sweet to my taste. He brought me to the banqueting house, and his banner over me was love.

Ps. 23:2; Isa. 57:20–21; Matt. 11:28; Ps. 37:7; Heb. 4:10;
Heb. 13:9; Eph. 4:14–15; Song 2:3–4

MORNING

"No leaven shall be seen with you in all your territory."

The fear of the Lord is hatred of evil.—Abhor what is evil.—Abstain from every form of evil.—See to it that no one fails to obtain the grace of God; that no "root of bitterness" springs up and causes trouble, and by it many become defiled.

If I had cherished iniquity in my heart, the Lord would not have listened.—Do you not know that a little leaven leavens the whole lump? Cleanse out the old leaven that you may be a new lump, as you really are unleavened. For Christ, our Passover lamb, has been sacrificed. Let us therefore celebrate the festival, not with the old leaven, the leaven of malice and evil, but with the unleavened bread of sincerity and truth.—Let a person examine himself, then, and so eat of the bread and drink of the cup.—"Let everyone who names the name of the Lord depart from iniquity."—It was indeed fitting that we should have such a high priest, holy, innocent, unstained, separated from sinners.—In him there is no sin.

Ex. 13:7; Prov. 8:13; Rom. 12:9; 1 Thess. 5:22; Heb. 12:15; Ps. 66:18;
1 Cor. 5:6–8; 1 Cor. 11:28; 2 Tim. 2:19; Heb. 7:26; 1 John 3:5

EVENING

The serpent said to the woman, "You will not surely die. . . . Your eyes will be opened, and you will be like God, knowing good and evil."

But I am afraid that as the serpent deceived Eve by his cunning, your thoughts will be led astray from a sincere and pure devotion to Christ.

Finally, be strong in the Lord and in the strength of his might. Put on the whole armor of God, that you may be able to stand against the schemes of the devil. . . . Therefore take up the whole armor of God, that you may be able to withstand in the evil day, and having done all, to stand firm. Stand therefore, having fastened on the belt of truth, and having put on the breastplate of righteousness, and, as shoes for your feet, having put on the readiness given by the gospel of peace. In all circumstances take up the shield of faith, with which you can extinguish all the flaming darts of the evil one; and take the helmet of salvation, and the sword of the Spirit, which is the word of God.—So that we would not be outwitted by Satan; for we are not ignorant of his designs.

Gen. 3:4–5; 2 Cor. 11:3; Eph. 6:10–11, 13–17; 2 Cor. 2:11

MORNING

"Wait, my daughter."

"Be careful, be quiet, do not fear, and do not let your heart be faint."—"Be still, and know that I am God."—"Did I not tell you that if you believed you would see the glory of God?"—The haughtiness of man shall be humbled, and the lofty pride of men shall be brought low, and the Lord alone will be exalted in that day.

Mary . . . sat at the Lord's feet and listened to his teaching. . . . "Mary has chosen the good portion, which will not be taken away from her."—"In returning and rest you shall be saved; in quietness and in trust shall be your strength."—Ponder in your own hearts on your beds, and be silent.

Be still before the Lord and wait patiently for him; fret not yourself over the one who prospers in his way, over the man who carries out evil devices!

He is not afraid of bad news; his heart is firm, trusting in the Lord. His heart is steady.—"Whoever believes will not be in haste."

Ruth 3:18; Isa. 7:4; Ps. 46:10; John 11:40; Isa. 2:17; Luke 10:39, 42;
Isa. 30:15; Ps. 4:4; Ps. 37:7; Ps. 112:7–8; Isa. 28:16

EVENING

"What I am doing you do not understand now, but afterward you will understand."

"You shall remember the whole way that the Lord your God has led you these forty years in the wilderness, that he might humble you, testing you to know what was in your heart, whether you would keep his commandments or not."

"When I passed by you again and saw you, behold, you were at the age for love; . . . I made my vow to you and entered into a covenant with you, declares the Lord God, and you became mine."—"The Lord disciplines the one he loves."

Beloved, do not be surprised at the fiery trial when it comes upon you to test you, as though something strange were happening to you. But rejoice insofar as you share Christ's sufferings, that you may also rejoice and be glad when his glory is revealed.—This light momentary affliction is preparing for us an eternal weight of glory beyond all comparison, as we look not to the things that are seen but to the things that are unseen.

John 13:7; Deut. 8:2; Ezek. 16:8; Heb. 12:6;
1 Pet. 4:12–13; 2 Cor. 4:17–18

MORNING

Just as the body is one and has many members, . . . so it is with Christ.

He is the head of the body, the church.—Head over all things to the church, which is his body, the fullness of him who fills all in all.—We are members of his body.

"A body have you prepared for me."—Your eyes saw my unformed substance; in your book were written, every one of them, the days that were formed for me, when as yet there was none of them.

"Yours they were, and you gave them to me."—He chose us in him before the foundation of the world.—Those whom he foreknew he also predestined to be conformed to the image of his Son.

We are to grow up in every way into him who is the head, into Christ, from whom the whole body, joined and held together by every joint with which it is equipped . . . makes the body grow so that it builds itself up in love.

1 Cor. 12:12; Col. 1:18; Eph. 1:22–23; Eph. 5:30; Heb. 10:5;
Ps. 139:16; John 17:6; Eph. 1:4; Rom. 8:29; Eph. 4:15–16

EVENING

The fountain of living waters.

How precious is your steadfast love, O God! The children of mankind take refuge in the shadow of your wings. They feast on the abundance of your house, and you give them drink from the river of your delights. For with you is the fountain of life.

Therefore thus says the Lord God: "Behold, my servants shall eat, but you shall be hungry; behold, my servants shall drink, but you shall be thirsty."—"Whoever drinks of the water that I will give him will never be thirsty again. The water that I will give him will become in him a spring of water welling up to eternal life."—Now this he said about the Spirit, whom those who believed in him were to receive.

"Come, everyone who thirsts, come to the waters."—The Spirit and the Bride say, "Come." And let the one who hears say, "Come." And let the one who is thirsty come; let the one who desires take the water of life without price.

Jer. 2:13; Ps. 36:7–9; Isa. 65:13; John 4:14; John 7:39;
Isa. 55:1; Rev. 22:17

MORNING

Let us lift up our hearts and hands to God in heaven.

Who is like the Lord our God, who is seated on high, who looks far down on the heavens and the earth?—To you, O Lord, I lift up my soul.—I stretch out my hands to you; my soul thirsts for you like a parched land. . . . . Hide not your face from me, lest I be like those who go down to the pit. Let me hear in the morning of your steadfast love, for in you I trust. Make me know the way I should go, for to you I lift up my soul.

Because your steadfast love is better than life, my lips will praise you. So I will bless you as long as I live; in your name I will lift up my hands.—Gladden the soul of your servant, for to you, O Lord, do I lift up my soul. For you, O Lord, are good and forgiving, abounding in steadfast love to all who call upon you.

"Whatever you ask in my name, this I will do."

Lam. 3:41; Ps. 113:5–6; Ps. 25:1; Ps. 143:6–8; Ps. 63:3–4;
Ps. 86:4–5; John 14:13

EVENING

"Watchman, what time of the night?"

The hour has come for you to wake from sleep. For salvation is nearer to us now than when we first believed. The night is far gone; the day is at hand. So then let us cast off the works of darkness and put on the armor of light.

"From the fig tree learn its lesson: as soon as its branch becomes tender and puts out its leaves, you know that summer is near. So also, when you see all these things, you know that he is near, at the very gates . . . . Heaven and earth will pass away, but my words will not pass away."

I wait for the Lord, my soul waits, and in his word I hope; my soul waits for the Lord more than watchmen for the morning, more than watchmen for the morning.

He who testifies to these things says, "Surely I am coming soon." Amen. Come, Lord Jesus!

"Watch therefore, for you know neither the day nor the hour."

Isa. 21:11; Rom. 13:11–12; Matt. 24:32–33, 35; Ps. 130:5–6;
Rev. 22:20; Matt. 25:13

MORNING

Rejoice in hope.

The hope laid up for you in heaven.—If in Christ we have hope in this life only, we are of all people most to be pitied.—Through many tribulations we must enter the kingdom of God.—"Whoever does not bear his own cross and come after me cannot be my disciple."—That no one be moved by these afflictions. For you yourselves know that we are destined for this.

Rejoice in the Lord always; again I will say, rejoice.—May the God of hope fill you with all joy and peace in believing, so that by the power of the Holy Spirit you may abound in hope.—Blessed be the God and Father of our Lord Jesus Christ! According to his great mercy, he has caused us to be born again to a living hope through the resurrection of Jesus Christ from the dead.—Though you have not seen him, you love him. Though you do not now see him, you believe in him and rejoice with joy that is inexpressible and filled with glory.—Through him we have also obtained access by faith into this grace in which we stand, and we rejoice in hope of the glory of God.

Rom. 12:12; Col. 1:5; 1 Cor. 15:19; Acts 14:22; Luke 14:27; 1 Thess. 3:3;
Phil. 4:4; Rom. 15:13; 1 Pet. 1:3; 1 Pet. 1:8; Rom. 5:2

EVENING

I am poor and needy, but the Lord takes thought for me.

"For I know the plans I have for you, declares the Lord, plans for welfare and not for evil."—"My thoughts are not your thoughts, neither are your ways my ways, declares the Lord. For as the heavens are higher than the earth, so are my ways higher than your ways and my thoughts than your thoughts."—How precious to me are your thoughts, O God! How vast is the sum of them! If I would count them, they are more than the sand. I awake, and I am still with you.—How great are your works, O Lord! Your thoughts are very deep!—You have multiplied, O Lord my God, your wondrous deeds and your thoughts toward us.

For consider your calling, brothers: not many of you were wise according to worldly standards, not many were powerful, not many were of noble birth.—Has not God chosen those who are poor in the world to be rich in faith and heirs of the kingdom?—Having nothing, yet possessing everything.—The unsearchable riches of Christ.

Ps. 40:17; Jer. 29:11; Isa. 55:8–9; Ps. 139:17–18; Ps. 92:5;
Ps. 40:5; 1 Cor. 1:26; James 2:5; 2 Cor. 6:10; Eph. 3:8

MORNING

"You have been weighed in the balances and found wanting."

The Lord is a God of knowledge, and by him actions are weighed.—"For what is exalted among men is an abomination in the sight of God."—"The Lord sees not as man sees: man looks on the outward appearance, but the Lord looks on the heart."—Do not be deceived: God is not mocked, for whatever one sows, that will he also reap. For the one who sows to his own flesh will from the flesh reap corruption, but the one who sows to the Spirit will from the Spirit reap eternal life.

"What will it profit a man if he gains the whole world and forfeits his soul? Or what shall a man give in return for his soul?"—But whatever gain I had, I counted as loss for the sake of Christ.

Behold, you delight in truth in the inward being.—You have tried my heart, you have visited me by night, you have tested me, and you will find nothing.

Dan. 5:27; 1 Sam. 2:3; Luke 16:15; 1 Sam. 16:7; Gal. 6:7-8;
Matt. 16:26; Phil. 3:7; Ps. 51:6; Ps. 17:3

EVENING

Christ the firstfruits.

"Unless a grain of wheat falls into the earth and dies, it remains alone; but if it dies, it bears much fruit."—If the dough offered as firstfruits is holy, so is the whole lump, and if the root is holy, so are the branches.—But in fact Christ has been raised from the dead, the firstfruits of those who have fallen asleep.—For if we have been united with him in a death like his, we shall certainly be united with him in a resurrection like his.—The Lord Jesus Christ . . . will transform our lowly body to be like his glorious body, by the power that enables him even to subject all things to himself.

The firstborn from the dead.—If the Spirit of him who raised Jesus from the dead dwells in you, he who raised Christ Jesus from the dead will also give life to your mortal bodies through his Spirit who dwells in you.

"I am the resurrection and the life. Whoever believes in me, though he die, yet shall he live."

1 Cor. 15:23; John 12:24; Rom. 11:16; 1 Cor. 15:20; Rom. 6:5;
Phil. 3:20-21; Col. 1:18; Rom. 8:11; John 11:25

MORNING

"He has filled the hungry with good things,
and the rich he has sent away empty."

"You say, I am rich, I have prospered, and I need nothing, not realizing that you are wretched, pitiable, poor, blind, and naked. I counsel you to buy from me gold refined by fire, so that you may be rich. . . . Those whom I love, I reprove and discipline, so be zealous and repent."

"Blessed are those who hunger and thirst for righteousness, for they shall be satisfied."—When the poor and needy seek water, and there is none, and their tongue is parched with thirst, I the Lord will answer them; I the God of Israel will not forsake them.—I am the Lord your God. . . . Open your mouth wide, and I will fill it.

"Why do you spend your money for that which is not bread, and your labor for that which does not satisfy? Listen diligently to me, and eat what is good, and delight yourselves in rich food."—"I am the bread of life; whoever comes to me shall not hunger, and whoever believes in me shall never thirst."

Luke 1:53; Rev. 3:17-19; Matt. 5:6; Isa. 41:17; Ps. 81:10;
Isa. 55:2; John 6:35

EVENING

My feet had almost stumbled, my steps had nearly slipped.

When I thought, "My foot slips," your steadfast love, O Lord, held me up.

"Simon, Simon, behold, Satan demanded to have you, that he might sift you like wheat, but I have prayed for you that your faith may not fail."

The righteous falls seven times and rises again.—Though he fall, he shall not be cast headlong, for the Lord upholds his hand.

Rejoice not over me, O my enemy; when I fall, I shall rise; when I sit in darkness, the Lord will be a light to me.—"He will deliver you from six troubles; in seven no evil shall touch you."

If anyone does sin, we have an advocate with the Father, Jesus Christ the righteous.—Consequently, he is able to save to the uttermost those who draw near to God through him, since he always lives to make intercession for them.

Ps. 73:2; Ps. 94:18; Luke 22:31-32; Prov. 24:16; Ps. 37:24;
Mic. 7:8; Job 5:19; 1 John 2:1; Heb. 7:25

MORNING

"I will give them one heart and one way, that they may fear me forever, for their own good and the good of their children after them."

"I will give you a new heart, and a new spirit I will put within you."—Good and upright is the Lord; therefore he instructs sinners in the way. He leads the humble in what is right, and teaches the humble his way. All the paths of the Lord are steadfast love and faithfulness, for those who keep his covenant and his testimonies.—"That they may all be one, just as you, Father, are in me, and I in you, that they also may be in us, so that the world may believe that you have sent me."

I . . . urge you to walk in a manner worthy of the calling to which you have been called, with all humility and gentleness, . . . eager to maintain the unity of the Spirit in the bond of peace. There is one body and one Spirit—just as you were called to the one hope that belongs to your call—one Lord, one faith, one baptism, one God and Father of all, who is over all and through all and in all.

Jer. 32:39; Ezek. 36:26; Ps. 25:8-10; John 17:21; Eph. 4:1-6

EVENING

They who wait for the Lord shall renew their strength.

When I am weak, then I am strong.—My God has become my strength.—But he said to me, "My grace is sufficient for you, for my power is made perfect in weakness." Therefore I will boast all the more gladly of my weaknesses, so that the power of Christ may rest upon me.—"Let them lay hold of my protection."

Cast your burden on the Lord, and he will sustain you.—His arms were made agile by the hands of the Mighty One of Jacob.

"I will not let you go unless you bless me."

"You come to me with a sword and with a spear and with a javelin, but I come to you in the name of the Lord of hosts, the God of the armies of Israel, whom you have defied."—Contend, O Lord, with those who contend with me; fight against those who fight against me! Take hold of shield and buckler and rise for my help!

Isa. 40:31; 2 Cor. 12:10; Isa. 49:5; 2 Cor. 12:9; Isa. 27:5; Ps. 55:22; Gen. 49:24; Gen. 32:26; 1 Sam. 17:45; Ps. 35:1-2

MORNING

***Do not be conformed to this world, but be
transformed by the renewal of your mind.***

"You shall not fall in with the many to do evil."

Do you not know that friendship with the world is enmity with God?
Therefore whoever wishes to be a friend of the world makes himself an
enemy of God.—What partnership has righteousness with lawlessness? Or
what fellowship has light with darkness? What accord has Christ with Belial?
Or what portion does a believer share with an unbeliever? What agreement
has the temple of God with idols?—Do not love the world or the things in the
world. If anyone loves the world, the love of the Father is not in him. And the
world is passing away along with its desires, but whoever does the will of God
abides forever.

In which you once walked, following the course of this world, following
the prince of the power of the air, the spirit that is now at work in the sons of
disobedience.—That is not the way you learned Christ!—assuming that you
have heard about him, . . . as the truth is in Jesus.

Rom. 12:2; Ex. 23:2; James 4:4; 2 Cor. 6:14–16;
1 John 2:15, 17; Eph. 2:2; Eph. 4:20–21

EVENING

Man goes out to his work and to his labor until the evening.

"By the sweat of your face you shall eat bread, till you return to the ground."—
We would give you this command: If anyone is not willing to work, let him
not eat.—Aspire to live quietly, and to mind your own affairs, and to work
with your hands.

Whatever your hand finds to do, do it with your might, for there is no
work or thought or knowledge or wisdom in Sheol, to which you are going.—
"Night is coming, when no one can work."

Let us not grow weary of doing good, for in due season we will reap, if
we do not give up.—Always abounding in the work of the Lord, knowing that
in the Lord your labor is not in vain.

There remains a . . . rest for the people of God.—"To us who have borne
the burden of the day and the scorching heat."—"This is rest; give rest to the
weary; and this is repose."

Ps. 104:23; Gen. 3:19; 2 Thess. 3:10; 1 Thess. 4:11; Eccles. 9:10;
John 9:4; Gal. 6:9; 1 Cor. 15:58; Heb. 4:9; Matt. 20:12; Isa. 28:12

MORNING

"I have seen his ways, but I will heal him."

"I am the Lord, your healer."

O Lord, you have searched me and known me! You know when I sit down and when I rise up; you discern my thoughts from afar. You search out my path and my lying down and are acquainted with all my ways.—You have set our iniquities before you, our secret sins in the light of your presence.—All are naked and exposed to the eyes of him to whom we must give account.

"Come now, let us reason together, says the Lord: though your sins are like scarlet, they shall be as white as snow; though they are red like crimson, they shall become like wool."—"He is merciful to him, and says, 'Deliver him from going down into the pit; I have found a ransom.'"—But he was pierced for our transgressions; he was crushed for our iniquities; upon him was the chastisement that brought us peace, and with his wounds we are healed.—He has sent me to bind up the brokenhearted.—"Your faith has made you well; go in peace, and be healed of your disease."

Isa. 57:18; Ex. 15:26; Ps. 139:1–3; Ps. 90:8; Heb. 4:13;
Isa. 1:18; Job 33:24; Isa. 53:5; Isa. 61:1; Mark 5:34

EVENING

The Lord is on my side as my helper.

May the Lord answer you in the day of trouble! May the name of the God of Jacob protect you! May he send you help from the sanctuary and give you support from Zion! . . . May we shout for joy over your salvation, and in the name of our God set up our banners! . . . Some trust in chariots and some in horses, but we trust in the name of the Lord our God. They collapse and fall, but we rise and stand upright.

He will come like a rushing stream, which the wind of the Lord drives.—No temptation has overtaken you that is not common to man. God is faithful, and he will not let you be tempted beyond your ability, but with the temptation he will also provide the way of escape, that you may be able to endure it.—If God is for us, who can be against us?—The Lord is on my side; I will not fear.—"Our God whom we serve is able to deliver us, . . . and he will deliver us."

Ps. 118:7; Ps. 20:1–2, 5, 7–8; Isa. 59:19; 1 Cor. 10:13;
Rom. 8:31; Ps. 118:6; Dan. 3:17

MORNING

"If anyone thirsts, let him come to me and drink."

My soul longs, yes, faints for the courts of the Lord; my heart and flesh sing for joy to the living God.—O God, you are my God; earnestly I seek you; my soul thirsts for you; my flesh faints for you, as in a dry and weary land where there is no water. So I have looked upon you in the sanctuary, beholding your power and glory.

"Come, everyone who thirsts, come to the waters; and he who has no money, come, buy and eat! Come, buy wine and milk without money and without price."—The Spirit and the Bride say, "Come." And let the one who hears say, "Come." And let the one who is thirsty come; let the one who desires take the water of life without price.—"Whoever drinks of the water that I will give him will never be thirsty again. The water that I will give him will become in him a spring of water welling up to eternal life."—"My blood is true drink."

Eat, friends, drink, and be drunk with love!

John 7:37; Ps. 84:2; Ps. 63:1–2; Isa. 55:1; Rev. 22:17;
John 4:14; John 6:55; Song 5:1

EVENING

"You are the salt of the earth."

The imperishable.—You have been born again, not of perishable seed but of imperishable, through the living and abiding word of God.—"Whoever believes in me, though he die, yet shall he live."—"Sons of God, being sons of the resurrection."—The immortal God.

Anyone who does not have the Spirit of Christ does not belong to him. But if Christ is in you, although the body is dead because of sin, the Spirit is life because of righteousness. If the Spirit of him who raised Jesus from the dead dwells in you, he who raised Christ Jesus from the dead will also give life to your mortal bodies through his Spirit who dwells in you.—What is sown is perishable; what is raised is imperishable.

"Have salt in yourselves, and be at peace with one another."—Let no corrupting talk come out of your mouths, but only such as is good for building up, as fits the occasion, that it may give grace to those who hear.

Matt. 5:13; 1 Pet. 3:4; 1 Pet. 1:23; John 11:25; Luke 20:36;
Rom. 1:23; Rom. 8:9–11; 1 Cor. 15:42; Mark 9:50; Eph. 4:29

MORNING

"I, I am he who comforts you."

Blessed be the God and Father of our Lord Jesus Christ, the Father of mercies and God of all comfort, who comforts us in all our affliction, so that we may be able to comfort those who are in any affliction, with the comfort with which we ourselves are comforted by God.—As a father shows compassion to his children, so the Lord shows compassion to those who fear him. For he knows our frame; he remembers that we are dust.—"As one whom his mother comforts, so I will comfort you."—Casting all your anxieties on him, because he cares for you.

You, O Lord, are a God merciful and gracious, slow to anger and abounding in steadfast love and faithfulness.—"Another Helper, . . . even the Spirit of truth."—The Spirit helps us in our weakness.

"He will wipe away every tear from their eyes, and death shall be no more, neither shall there be mourning, nor crying, nor pain anymore, for the former things have passed away."

Isa. 51:12; 2 Cor. 1:3–4; Ps. 103:13–14; Isa. 66:13; 1 Pet. 5:7;
Ps. 86:15; John 14:16–17; Rom. 8:26; Rev. 21:4

EVENING

You were called into the fellowship of his Son.

He received honor and glory from God the Father, and the voice was borne to him by the Majestic Glory, "This is my beloved Son, with whom I am well pleased."—See what kind of love the Father has given to us, that we should be called children of God.

Therefore be imitators of God, as beloved children.—If children, then heirs—heirs of God and fellow heirs with Christ.

He is the radiance of the glory of God and the exact imprint of his nature.—"Let your light shine before others, so that they may see your good works and give glory to your Father who is in heaven."

Jesus, the founder and perfecter of our faith, who for the joy that was set before him endured the cross, despising the shame.—"These things I speak in the world, that they may have my joy fulfilled in themselves."—As we share abundantly in Christ's sufferings, so through Christ we share abundantly in comfort too.

1 Cor. 1:9; 2 Pet. 1:17; 1 John 3:1; Eph. 5:1; Rom. 8:17;
Heb. 1:3; Matt. 5:16; Heb. 12:2; John 17:13; 2 Cor. 1:5

MORNING

***Sin will have no dominion over you, since you
are not under law but under grace.***

What then? Are we to sin because we are not under law but under grace? By
no means!—Likewise, my brothers, you also have died to the law through the
body of Christ, so that you may belong to another, to him who has been raised
from the dead, in order that we may bear fruit for God.—Not being outside
the law of God but under the law of Christ.—The sting of death is sin, and the
power of sin is the law. But thanks be to God, who gives us the victory through
our Lord Jesus Christ.

The law of the Spirit of life has set you free in Christ Jesus from the law
of sin and death.—"Everyone who practices sin is a slave to sin. . . . So if the
Son sets you free, you will be free indeed."

Stand firm therefore, and do not submit again to a yoke of slavery.

Rom. 6:14; Rom. 6:15; Rom. 7:4; 1 Cor. 9:21; 1 Cor. 15:56–57;
Rom. 8:2; John 8:34, 36; Gal. 5:1

EVENING

He is a double–minded man, unstable in all his ways.

"No one who puts his hand to the plow and looks back is fit for the kingdom
of God."

Whoever would draw near to God must believe that he exists and that
he rewards those who seek him.—Let him ask in faith, with no doubting, for
the one who doubts is like a wave of the sea that is driven and tossed by the
wind. For that person must not suppose that he will receive anything from
the Lord.—"Whatever you ask in prayer, believe that you have received it, and
it will be yours."

So that we may no longer be children, tossed to and fro by the waves and
carried about by every wind of doctrine, by human cunning, by craftiness in
deceitful schemes. Rather, speaking the truth in love, we are to grow up in
every way into him who is the head, into Christ.

"Abide in me."—Be steadfast, immovable, always abounding in the work
of the Lord, knowing that in the Lord your labor is not in vain.

James 1:8; Luke 9:62; Heb. 11:6; James 1:6–7; Mark 11:24;
Eph. 4:14–15; John 15:4; 1 Cor. 15:58

MORNING

The Lord weighs the heart.

The Lord knows the way of the righteous, but the way of the wicked will perish.—"The Lord will show who is his, and who is holy."—"Your Father who sees in secret will reward you."

Search me, O God, and know my heart! Try me and know my thoughts! And see if there be any grievous way in me, and lead me in the way everlasting!—There is no fear in love, but perfect love casts out fear.—O Lord, all my longing is before you; my sighing is not hidden from you.—When my spirit faints within me, you know my way!—He who searches hearts knows what is the mind of the Spirit, because the Spirit intercedes for the saints according to the will of God.

God's firm foundation stands, bearing this seal: "The Lord knows those who are his," and, "Let everyone who names the name of the Lord depart from iniquity."

Prov. 21:2; Ps. 1:6; Num. 16:5; Matt. 6:4; Ps. 139:23–24;
1 John 4:18; Ps. 38:9; Ps. 142:3; Rom. 8:27; 2 Tim. 2:19

EVENING

Weeping may tarry for the night, but
joy comes with the morning.

That no one be moved by these afflictions. For you yourselves know that we are destined for this. For when we were with you, we kept telling you beforehand that we were to suffer affliction.—"In me you . . . have peace. In the world you will have tribulation. But take heart; I have overcome the world."

When I awake, I shall be satisfied with your likeness.—The night is far gone; the day is at hand.—He dawns on them like the morning light, like the sun shining forth on a cloudless morning, like rain that makes grass to sprout from the earth.

He will swallow up death forever; and the Lord God will wipe away tears from all faces.—"Death shall be no more, neither shall there be mourning, nor crying, nor pain anymore, for the former things have passed away."—We who are alive, who are left, will be caught up together with them in the clouds to meet the Lord in the air, and so we will always be with the Lord. Therefore encourage one another with these words.

Ps. 30:5; 1 Thess. 3:3–4; John 16:33; Ps. 17:15; Rom. 13:12;
2 Sam. 23:4; Isa. 25:8; Rev. 21:4; 1 Thess. 4:17–18

MORNING

"A bruised reed he will not break."

The sacrifices of God are a broken spirit; a broken and contrite heart, O God, you will not despise.—He heals the brokenhearted and binds up their wounds.—Thus says the One who is high and lifted up, who inhabits eternity, whose name is Holy: "I dwell in the high and holy place, and also with him who is of a contrite and lowly spirit, to revive the spirit of the lowly, and to revive the heart of the contrite. For I will not contend forever, nor will I always be angry; for the spirit would grow faint before me, and the breath of life that I made."

"I will seek the lost, and I will bring back the strayed, and I will bind up the injured, and I will strengthen the weak."—Therefore lift your drooping hands and strengthen your weak knees, and make straight paths for your feet, so that what is lame may not be put out of joint but rather be healed.— "Behold, your God. . . . He will come and save you."

Matt. 12:20; Ps. 51:17; Ps. 147:3; Isa. 57:15–16;
Ezek. 34:16; Heb. 12:12–13; Isa. 35:4

EVENING

Oh, taste and see that the Lord is good! Blessed is the man who takes refuge in him!

When the master of the feast tasted the water now become wine, and did not know where it came from, . . . the master of the feast called the bridegroom and said to him, "Everyone serves the good wine first, and when people have drunk freely, then the poor wine. But you have kept the good wine until now."

"The ear tests words as the palate tastes food."—"I believed, and so I spoke."—I know whom I have believed.—With great delight I sat in his shadow, and his fruit was sweet to my taste.

God's kindness.—He who did not spare his own Son but gave him up for us all, how will he not also with him graciously give us all things?

Like newborn infants, long for the pure spiritual milk, that by it you may grow up into salvation—if indeed you have tasted that the Lord is good. Let all who take refuge in you rejoice; let them ever sing for joy.

Ps. 34:8; John 2:9–10; Job 34:3; 2 Cor. 4:13; 2 Tim. 1:12;
Song 2:3; Rom. 2:4; Rom. 8:32; 1 Pet. 2:2–3; Ps. 5:11

MORNING

Open my eyes, that I may behold
wondrous things out of your law.

Then he opened their minds to understand the Scriptures.—"To you it has been given to know the secrets of the kingdom of heaven, but to them it has not been given."—"I thank you, Father, Lord of heaven and earth, that you have hidden these things from the wise and understanding and revealed them to little children; yes, Father, for such was your gracious will."—Now we have received not the spirit of the world, but the Spirit who is from God, that we might understand the things freely given us by God.—How precious to me are your thoughts, O God! How vast is the sum of them! If I would count them, they are more than the sand.— Oh, the depth of the riches and wisdom and knowledge of God! How unsearchable are his judgments and how inscrutable his ways! "For who has known the mind of the Lord, or who has been his counselor?" . . . For from him and through him and to him are all things. To him be glory forever. Amen.

Ps. 119:18; Luke 24:45; Matt. 13:11; Matt. 11:25–26;
1 Cor. 2:12; Ps. 139:17–18; Rom. 11:33–34, 36

EVENING

En–hakkore [the spring of him who called].

"If you knew the gift of God, and who it is that is saying to you, 'Give me a drink,' you would have asked him, and he would have given you living water."—"If anyone thirsts, let him come to me and drink." . . . Now this he said about the Spirit, whom those who believed in him were to receive.

"Thereby put me to the test, says the Lord of hosts, if I will not open the windows of heaven for you and pour down for you a blessing until there is no more need."—"If you then, who are evil, know how to give good gifts to your children, how much more will the heavenly Father give the Holy Spirit to those who ask him!"—"Ask, and it will be given to you; seek, and you will find."

Because you are sons, God has sent the Spirit of his Son into our hearts, crying, "Abba! Father!"—You did not receive the spirit of slavery to fall back into fear, but you have received the Spirit of adoption as sons, by whom we cry, "Abba! Father!"

Judg. 15:19; John 4:10; John 7:37, 39; Mal. 3:10;
Luke 11:13; Luke 11:9; Gal. 4:6; Rom. 8:15

MORNING

The God of all grace.

"I . . . will proclaim before you my name 'The Lord.' And I will be gracious to whom I will be gracious."—"He is merciful to him, and says, 'Deliver him from going down into the pit; I have found a ransom.'"—Are justified by his grace as a gift, through the redemption that is in Christ Jesus, whom God put forward as a propitiation by his blood, to be received by faith. This was to show God's righteousness, because in his divine forbearance he had passed over former sins.—Grace and truth came through Jesus Christ.

By grace you have been saved through faith. And this is not your own doing; it is the gift of God.—Grace, mercy, and peace from God the Father and Christ Jesus our Lord.—Grace was given to each one of us according to the measure of Christ's gift.—As each has received a gift, use it to serve one another, as good stewards of God's varied grace.—He gives more grace.

Grow in the grace and knowledge of our Lord and Savior Jesus Christ. To him be the glory both now and to the day of eternity.

1 Pet. 5:10; Ex. 33:19; Job 33:24; Rom. 3:24–25; John 1:17; Eph. 2:8;
1 Tim. 1:2; Eph. 4:7; 1 Pet. 4:10; James 4:6; 2 Pet. 3:18

EVENING

I lift up my eyes to the hills. From where does my help come? My help comes from the Lord.

As the mountains surround Jerusalem, so the Lord surrounds his people, from this time forth and forevermore.

To you I lift up my eyes, O you who are enthroned in the heavens! Behold, as the eyes of servants look to the hand of their master, as the eyes of a maidservant to the hand of her mistress, so our eyes look to the Lord our God, till he has mercy upon us.—For you have been my help, and in the shadow of your wings I will sing for joy.

"O our God, will you not execute judgment on them? For we are powerless against this great horde that is coming against us. We do not know what to do, but our eyes are on you."—My eyes are ever toward the Lord, for he will pluck my feet out of the net.—Our help is in the name of the Lord, who made heaven and earth.

Ps. 121:1–2; Ps. 125:2; Ps. 123:1–2; Ps. 63:7; 2 Chron. 20:12;
Ps. 25:15; Ps. 124:8

MORNING

Blessed is the one who finds wisdom, and the one who gets understanding.

"Whoever finds me finds life and obtains favor from the Lord."

Thus says the Lord: "Let not the wise man boast in his wisdom, let not the mighty man boast in his might, . . . but let him who boasts boast in this, that he understands and knows me, that I am the Lord."—The fear of the Lord is the beginning of wisdom.

Whatever gain I had, I counted as loss for the sake of Christ. Indeed, I count everything as loss because of the surpassing worth of knowing Christ Jesus my Lord. For his sake I have suffered the loss of all things and count them as rubbish, in order that I may gain Christ.—In whom are hidden all the treasures of wisdom and knowledge.—"I have counsel and sound wisdom; I have insight; I have strength."

Christ Jesus, who became to us wisdom from God, righteousness and sanctification and redemption.

Whoever captures souls is wise.

Prov. 3:13; Prov. 8:35; Jer. 9:23–24; Prov. 9:10; Phil. 3:7–8;
Col. 2:3; Prov. 8:14; 1 Cor. 1:30; Prov. 11:30

EVENING

Poor, yet making many rich.

You know the grace of our Lord Jesus Christ, that though he was rich, yet for your sake he became poor, so that you by his poverty might become rich.—From his fullness we have all received, grace upon grace.—My God will supply every need of yours according to his riches in glory in Christ Jesus.—God is able to make all grace abound to you, so that having all sufficiency in all things at all times, you may abound in every good work.

Has not God chosen those who are poor in the world to be rich in faith and heirs of the kingdom, which he has promised to those who love him?—Not many of you were wise according to worldly standards, not many were powerful, not many were of noble birth. But God chose what is foolish in the world to shame the wise; God chose what is weak in the world to shame the strong.

We have this treasure in jars of clay, to show that the surpassing power belongs to God and not to us.

2 Cor. 6:10; 2 Cor. 8:9; John 1:16; Phil. 4:19; 2 Cor. 9:8;
James 2:5; 1 Cor. 1:26–27; 2 Cor. 4:7

MORNING

We know that for those who love God all things work together for good.

Surely the wrath of man shall praise you; the remnant of wrath you will put on like a belt.—"You meant evil against me, but God meant it for good."

All things are yours, whether . . . the world or life or death or the present or the future—all are yours, and you are Christ's, and Christ is God's.—It is all for your sake, so that as grace extends to more and more people it may increase thanksgiving, to the glory of God. So we do not lose heart. Though our outer self is wasting away, our inner self is being renewed day by day. For this light momentary affliction is preparing for us an eternal weight of glory beyond all comparison.

Count it all joy, my brothers, when you meet trials of various kinds, for you know that the testing of your faith produces steadfastness. And let steadfastness have its full effect, that you may be perfect and complete, lacking in nothing.

Rom. 8:28; Ps. 76:10; Gen. 50:20; 1 Cor. 3:21–23;
2 Cor. 4:15–17; James 1:2–4

EVENING

The fellowship of the Holy Spirit be with you all.

"I will ask the Father, and he will give you another Helper, to be with you forever, even the Spirit of truth, whom the world cannot receive, because it neither sees him nor knows him. You know him, for he dwells with you and will be in you."—"He will not speak on his own authority. . . . He will glorify me, for he will take what is mine and declare it to you."

God's love has been poured into our hearts through the Holy Spirit who has been given to us.

He who is joined to the Lord becomes one spirit with him. Or do you not know that your body is a temple of the Holy Spirit within you, whom you have from God? You are not your own.

Do not grieve the Holy Spirit of God, by whom you were sealed for the day of redemption.—The Spirit helps us in our weakness. For we do not know what to pray for as we ought, but the Spirit himself intercedes for us with groanings too deep for words.

2 Cor. 13:14; John 14:16–17; John 16:13–14; Rom. 5:5;
1 Cor. 6:17, 19; Eph. 4:30; Rom. 8:26

MORNING

May my meditation be pleasing to him,
for I rejoice in the Lord.

As an apple tree among the trees of the forest, so is my beloved among the young men. With great delight I sat in his shadow, and his fruit was sweet to my taste.—For who in the skies can be compared to the Lord? Who among the heavenly beings is like the Lord?

My beloved is radiant and ruddy, distinguished among ten thousand.— "One pearl of great value."—The ruler of kings on earth.

His head is the finest gold; his locks are wavy, black as a raven.—Head over all things.—He is the head of the body, the church.

His cheeks are like beds of spices, mounds of sweet-smelling herbs.— He could not be hidden.—His lips are lilies, dripping liquid myrrh.—"No one ever spoke like this man!"—His appearance is like Lebanon, choice as the cedars.—Make your face shine on your servant.—"Lift up the light of your face upon us, O Lord!"

Ps. 104:34; Song. 2:3; Ps. 89:6; Song 5:10; Matt. 13:46;
Rev. 1:5; Song 5:11; Eph. 1:22; Col. 1:18; Song 5:13; Mark 7:24;
Song 5:13; John 7:46; Song 5:15; Ps. 31:16; Ps. 4:6

EVENING

"My Father, if it be possible, let this cup pass from me;
nevertheless, not as I will, but as you will."

"Now is my soul troubled. And what shall I say? 'Father, save me from this hour'? But for this purpose I have come to this hour."

"I have come down from heaven, not to do my own will but the will of him who sent me."—He humbled himself by becoming obedient to the point of death, even death on a cross.—In the days of his flesh, Jesus offered up prayers and supplications, with loud cries and tears, to him who was able to save him from death, and he was heard because of his reverence. Although he was a son, he learned obedience through what he suffered.

"Do you think that I cannot appeal to my Father, and he will at once send me more than twelve legions of angels?"—"Thus it is written, that the Christ should suffer and on the third day rise from the dead, and that repentance and forgiveness of sins should be proclaimed in his name to all nations, beginning from Jerusalem."

Matt. 26:39; John 12:27; John 6:38; Phil. 2:8;
Heb. 5:7–8; Matt. 26:53; Luke 24:46–47

MORNING

"Our God has not forsaken us."

Beloved, do not be surprised at the fiery trial when it comes upon you to test you, as though something strange were happening to you.—It is for discipline that you have to endure. God is treating you as sons. For what son is there whom his father does not discipline? If you are left without discipline, in which all have participated, then you are illegitimate children and not sons.

"The Lord your God is testing you, to know whether you love the Lord your God with all your heart and with all your soul."

"The Lord will not forsake his people, for his great name's sake, because it has pleased the Lord to make you a people for himself."—"Can a woman forget her nursing child, that she should have no compassion on the son of her womb? Even these may forget, yet I will not forget you."—Blessed is he whose help is the God of Jacob, whose hope is in the Lord his God.

"And will not God give justice to his elect, who cry to him day and night? Will he delay long over them? I tell you, he will give justice to them speedily."

Ezra 9:9; 1 Pet. 4:12; Heb. 12:7-8; Deut. 13:3;
1 Sam. 12:22; Isa. 49:15; Ps. 146:5; Luke 18:7-8

EVENING

"The one who conquers will have this heritage."

If in Christ we have hope in this life only, we are of all people most to be pitied.—As it is, they desire a better country, that is, a heavenly one. Therefore God is not ashamed to be called their God, for he has prepared for them a city.—An inheritance that is imperishable, undefiled, and unfading, kept in heaven for you.

All things are yours, . . . the world or life or death or the present or the future—all are yours.—"What no eye has seen, nor ear heard, nor the heart of man imagined, what God has prepared for those who love him"—these things God has revealed to us through the Spirit.—Watch yourselves, so that you may not lose what we have worked for, but may win a full reward.—Let us also lay aside every weight, and sin which clings so closely, and let us run with endurance the race that is set before us.

Rev. 21:7; 1 Cor. 15:19; Heb. 11:16; 1 Pet. 1:4;
1 Cor. 3:21-22; 1 Cor. 2:9-10; 2 John 8; Heb. 12:1

MORNING

For me it is good to be near God.

O Lord, I love the habitation of your house and the place where your glory dwells.—For a day in your courts is better than a thousand elsewhere. I would rather be a doorkeeper in the house of my God than dwell in the tents of wickedness.—Blessed is the one you choose and bring near, to dwell in your courts! We shall be satisfied with the goodness of your house, the holiness of your temple!

The Lord is good to those who wait for him, to the soul who seeks him.— Therefore the Lord waits to be gracious to you, and therefore he exalts himself to show mercy to you. For the Lord is a God of justice; blessed are all those who wait for him.

Therefore, brothers, since we have confidence to enter the holy places by the blood of Jesus, by the new and living way that he opened for us, . . . let us draw near with a true heart in full assurance of faith, with our hearts sprinkled clean from an evil conscience.

Ps. 73:28; Ps. 26:8; Ps. 84:10; Ps. 65:4; Lam. 3:25; Isa. 30:18; Heb. 10:19–20, 22

EVENING

You know the grace of our Lord Jesus Christ.

The Word became flesh and dwelt among us, and we have seen his glory, glory as of the only Son from the Father, full of grace and truth.—You are the most handsome of the sons of men; grace is poured upon your lips.—All spoke well of him and marveled at the gracious words that were coming from his mouth.—You have tasted that the Lord is good.—Whoever believes in the Son of God has the testimony in himself.—"Truly, truly, I say to you, we speak of what we know, and bear witness to what we have seen."

Oh, taste and see that the Lord is good! Blessed is the man who takes refuge in him!—With great delight I sat in his shadow, and his fruit was sweet to my taste.

He said to me, "My grace is sufficient for you, for my power is made perfect in weakness."—Grace was given to each one of us according to the measure of Christ's gift.—As each has received a gift, use it to serve one another, as good stewards of God's varied grace.

2 Cor. 8:9; John 1:14; Ps. 45:2; Luke 4:22; 1 Pet. 2:3; 1 John 5:10;
John 3:11; Ps. 34:8; Song 2:3; 2 Cor. 12:9; Eph. 4:7; 1 Pet. 4:10

MORNING

*And let steadfastness have its full effect, that you may
be perfect and complete, lacking in nothing.*

Now for a little while, if necessary, you have been grieved by various trials,
so that the tested genuineness of your faith—more precious than gold that
perishes though it is tested by fire—may be found to result in praise and glory
and honor at the revelation of Jesus Christ.—Not only that, but we rejoice in
our sufferings, knowing that suffering produces endurance, and endurance
produces character, and character produces hope.

It is good that one should wait quietly for the salvation of the Lord.—
You knew that you yourselves had a better possession and an abiding one.
Therefore do not throw away your confidence, which has a great reward. For
you have need of endurance, so that when you have done the will of God you
may receive what is promised.—Now may our Lord Jesus Christ himself, and
God our Father, who loved us and gave us eternal comfort and good hope
through grace, comfort your hearts.

James 1:4; 1 Pet. 1:6–7; Rom. 5:3–4; Lam. 3:26; Heb. 10:34–36; 2 Thess. 2:16–17

EVENING

God judges the secrets of men by Christ Jesus.

Therefore do not pronounce judgment before the time, before the Lord
comes, who will bring to light the things now hidden in darkness and will
disclose the purposes of the heart. Then each one will receive his commendation from God.—"The Father judges no one, but has given all judgment to the
Son . . . . And he has given him authority to execute judgment, because he is
the Son of Man."—"And to the angel of the church in Thyatira write: 'The Son
of God . . . has eyes like a flame of fire.'"

And they say, "How can God know? Is there knowledge in the Most
High?"—"These things you have done, and I have been silent; you thought
that I was one like yourself. But now I rebuke you and lay the charge before
you."—"Nothing is covered up that will not be revealed, or hidden that will
not be known."

O Lord, all my longing is before you; my sighing is not hidden from
you.—Prove me, O Lord, and try me; test my heart and my mind.

Rom. 2:16; 1 Cor. 4:5; John 5:22, 27; Rev. 2:18; Ps. 73:11;
Ps. 50:21; Luke 12:2; Ps. 38:9; Ps. 26:2

MORNING

"A God of faithfulness and without iniquity, just and upright is he."

Him who judges justly.—We must all appear before the judgment seat of Christ, so that each one may receive what is due for what he has done in the body, whether good or evil.—Each of us will give an account of himself to God.—"The soul who sins shall die."

"Awake, O sword, against my shepherd, against the man who stands next to me," declares the Lord of hosts. "Strike the shepherd."—The Lord has laid on him the iniquity of us all.—Steadfast love and faithfulness meet; righteousness and peace kiss each other.—Mercy triumphs over judgment.—The wages of sin is death, but the free gift of God is eternal life in Christ Jesus our Lord.

"A righteous God and a Savior; there is none besides me."—Just and the justifier of the one who has faith in Jesus.—Justified by his grace as a gift, through the redemption that is in Christ Jesus.

Deut. 32:4; 1 Pet. 2:23; 2 Cor. 5:10; Rom. 14:12; Ezek. 18:4; Zech. 13:7; Isa. 53:6; Ps. 85:10; James 2:13; Rom. 6:23; Isa. 45:21; Rom. 3:26; Rom. 3:24

EVENING

"Death is swallowed up in victory."

Thanks be to God, who gives us the victory through our Lord Jesus Christ.

Since therefore the children share in flesh and blood, he himself likewise partook of the same things, that through death he might destroy the one who has the power of death, that is, the devil, and deliver all those who through fear of death were subject to lifelong slavery.

Now if we have died with Christ, we believe that we will also live with him. We know that Christ, being raised from the dead, will never die again; death no longer has dominion over him. For the death he died he died to sin, once for all, but the life he lives he lives to God. So you also must consider yourselves dead to sin and alive to God in Christ Jesus.

No, in all these things we are more than conquerors through him who loved us.

1 Cor. 15:54; 1 Cor. 15:57; Heb. 2:14–15; Rom. 6:8–11; Rom. 8:37

MORNING

Humble yourselves, therefore, under the mighty hand of
God so that at the proper time he may exalt you.

Everyone who is arrogant in heart is an abomination to the Lord; be assured, he will not go unpunished.

But now, O Lord, you are our Father; we are the clay, and you are our potter; we are all the work of your hand. Be not so terribly angry, O Lord, and remember not iniquity forever. Behold, please look, we are all your people.— "You have disciplined me, and I was disciplined, like an untrained calf; bring me back that I may be restored, for you are the Lord my God. For after I had turned away, I relented, and after I was instructed, I struck my thigh; I was ashamed, and I was confounded, because I bore the disgrace of my youth."— It is good for a man that he bear the yoke in his youth.

"Affliction does not come from the dust, nor does trouble sprout from the ground, but man is born to trouble as the sparks fly upward."

1 Pet. 5:6; Prov. 16:5; Isa. 64:8–9; Jer. 31:18–19; Lam. 3:27; Job 5:6–7

EVENING

"Did God actually say . . . ?"

And the tempter came and said to him, "If you are the Son of God . . . " [Jesus] answered, "It is written, . . . it is written, . . . it is written." Then the devil left him.

"I may not return with you, . . . for it was said to me by the word of the Lord, 'You shall neither eat bread nor drink water there. . . .'" And he said to him, "I also am a prophet as you are, and an angel spoke to me by the word of the Lord, saying, 'Bring him back with you into your house that he may eat bread and drink water.'" But he lied to him. So he went back with him. . . . "It is the man of God who disobeyed the word of the Lord; therefore the Lord has given him to the lion, which has torn him and killed him, according to the word that the Lord spoke to him."—But even if we or an angel from heaven should preach to you a gospel contrary to the one we preached to you, let him be accursed.—I have stored up your word in my heart, that I might not sin against you.

Gen. 3:1; Matt. 4:3–4, 7, 10–11; 1 Kings 13:16–19, 26; Gal. 1:8; Ps. 119:11

MORNING

"So shall they put my name upon the people of Israel, and I will bless them."

O Lord our God, other lords besides you have ruled over us, but your name alone we bring to remembrance.—We have become like those over whom you have never ruled, like those who are not called by your name.

"All the peoples of the earth shall see that you are called by the name of the Lord, and they shall be afraid of you."—The Lord will not forsake his people, for his great name's sake, because it has pleased the Lord to make you a people for himself.

"O Lord, hear; O Lord, forgive. O Lord, pay attention and act. Delay not, for your own sake, O my God, because your city and your people are called by your name."—Help us, O God of our salvation, for the glory of your name; deliver us, and atone for our sins, for your name's sake! Why should the nations say, "Where is their God?"—The name of the Lord is a strong tower; the righteous man runs into it and is safe.

Num. 6:27; Isa. 26:13; Isa. 63:19; Deut. 28:10;
1 Sam. 12:22; Dan. 9:19; Ps. 79:9-10; Prov. 18:10

EVENING

The heavens declare the glory of God, and the sky above proclaims his handiwork.

His invisible attributes, namely, his eternal power and divine nature, have been clearly perceived, ever since the creation of the world, in the things that have been made.—"He did not leave himself without witness."—Day to day pours out speech, and night to night reveals knowledge. There is no speech, nor are there words, whose voice is not heard.

When I look at your heavens, the work of your fingers, the moon and the stars, which you have set in place, what is man that you are mindful of him, and the son of man that you care for him?

There is one glory of the sun, and another glory of the moon, and another glory of the stars; for star differs from star in glory. So is it with the resurrection of the dead.—Those who are wise shall shine like the brightness of the sky above; and those who turn many to righteousness, like the stars forever and ever.

Ps. 19:1; Rom. 1:20; Acts 14:17; Ps. 19:2-3; Ps. 8:3-4; 1 Cor. 15:41-42; Dan. 12:3

MORNING

By this we know love, that he laid down his life for us.

The love of Christ that surpasses knowledge.—"Greater love has no one than this, that someone lay down his life for his friends."—You know the grace of our Lord Jesus Christ, that though he was rich, yet for your sake he became poor, so that you by his poverty might become rich.—Beloved, if God so loved us, we also ought to love one another.—Be kind to one another, tenderhearted, forgiving one another, as God in Christ forgave you.—Bearing with one another and, if one has a complaint against another, forgiving each other; as the Lord has forgiven you, so you also must forgive.—"For even the Son of Man came not to be served but to serve, and to give his life as a ransom for many."—Christ also suffered for you, leaving you an example, so that you might follow in his steps.

"You also ought to wash one another's feet. For I have given you an example, that you also should do just as I have done to you."—We ought to lay down our lives for the brothers.

1 John 3:16; Eph. 3:19; John 15:13; 2 Cor. 8:9; 1 John 4:11; Eph. 4:32;
Col. 3:13; Mark 10:45; 1 Pet. 2:21; John 13:14–15; 1 John 3:16

EVENING

"Whatever the Father does, that the Son does likewise."

For the Lord gives wisdom; from his mouth come knowledge and understanding.—"I will give you a mouth and wisdom, which none of your adversaries will be able to withstand or contradict."

Wait for the Lord; be strong, and let your heart take courage.—"My grace is sufficient for you, for my power is made perfect in weakness."

Those who are called, beloved in God the Father.—He who sanctifies and those who are sanctified all have one source. That is why he is not ashamed to call them brothers.—"Do I not fill heaven and earth? declares the Lord."—The fullness of him who fills all in all.

I, I am the Lord, and besides me there is no savior.—"This is indeed the Savior of the world."

Grace and peace from God the Father and Christ Jesus our Savior.

John 5:19; Prov. 2:6; Luke 21:15; Ps. 27:14; 2 Cor. 12:9; Jude 1;
Heb. 2:11; Jer. 23:24; Eph. 1:23; Isa. 43:11; John 4:42; Titus 1:4

MORNING

"He knows the way that I take; when he has tried me, I shall come out as gold."

He knows our frame.—He does not afflict from his heart or grieve the children of men.

God's firm foundation stands, bearing this seal: "The Lord knows those who are his," and, "Let everyone who names the name of the Lord depart from iniquity." Now in a great house there are not only vessels of gold and silver but also of wood and clay, some for honorable use, some for dishonorable. Therefore, if anyone cleanses himself from what is dishonorable, he will be a vessel for honorable use, set apart as holy, useful to the master of the house, ready for every good work.

He will sit as a refiner and purifier of silver, and he will purify the sons of Levi and refine them like gold and silver, and they will bring offerings in righteousness to the Lord.—"I will . . . refine them as one refines silver. . . . They will call upon my name, and I will answer them. I will say, 'They are my people'; and they will say, 'The Lord is my God.'"

Job 23:10; Ps. 103:14; Lam. 3:33; 2 Tim. 2:19–21; Mal. 3:3; Zech. 13:9

EVENING

Make me to know your ways, O Lord; teach me your paths.

Moses said to the Lord, . . . "If I have found favor in your sight, please show me now your ways, that I may know you. . . ." And he said, "My presence will go with you, and I will give you rest."—He made known his ways to Moses, his acts to the people of Israel.

He leads the humble in what is right, and teaches the humble his way. . . . Who is the man who fears the Lord? Him will he instruct in the way that he should choose.—Trust in the Lord with all your heart, and do not lean on your own understanding. In all your ways acknowledge him, and he will make straight your paths.

You make known to me the path of life; in your presence there is fullness of joy; at your right hand are pleasures forevermore.—I will instruct you and teach you in the way you should go; I will counsel you with my eye upon you.—The path of the righteous is like the light of dawn, which shines brighter and brighter until full day.

Ps. 25:4; Ex. 33:12–14; Ps. 103:7; Ps. 25:9, 12; Ps. 3:5–6;
Ps. 16:11; Ps. 32:8; Prov. 4:18

MORNING

The fruit of the Spirit is . . . self-control.

Every athlete exercises self-control in all things. They do it to receive a perishable wreath, but we an imperishable. So I do not run aimlessly; I do not box as one beating the air. But I discipline my body and keep it under control, lest after preaching to others I myself should be disqualified.—Do not get drunk with wine, for that is debauchery, but be filled with the Spirit.

"If anyone would come after me, let him deny himself and take up his cross and follow me."

So then let us not sleep, as others do, but let us keep awake and be sober. For those who sleep, sleep at night, and those who get drunk, are drunk at night. But since we belong to the day, let us be sober.—To renounce ungodliness and worldly passions, and to live self-controlled, upright, and godly lives in the present age, waiting for our blessed hope, the appearing of the glory of our great God and Savior Jesus Christ.

Gal. 5:22–23; 1 Cor. 9:25–27; Eph. 5:18; Matt. 16:24;
1 Thess. 5:6–8; Titus 2:12–13

EVENING

We are to grow up in every way into
him who is the head, into Christ.

"First the blade, then the ear, then the full grain in the ear."—Until we all attain to the unity of the faith and of the knowledge of the Son of God, to mature manhood, to the measure of the stature of the fullness of Christ.— When they measure themselves by one another and compare themselves with one another, they are without understanding. . . . "Let the one who boasts, boast in the Lord." For it is not the one who commends himself who is approved, but the one whom the Lord commends.

The substance belongs to Christ. Let no one disqualify you, insisting on asceticism and worship of angels, going on in detail about visions, puffed up without reason by his sensuous mind, and not holding fast to the Head, from whom the whole body, nourished and knit together through its joints and ligaments, grows with a growth that is from God.

Grow in the grace and knowledge of our Lord and Savior Jesus Christ.

Eph. 4:15; Mark 4:28; Eph. 4:13; 2 Cor. 10:12, 17–18;
Col. 2:17–19; 2 Pet. 3:18

MORNING

"The goat shall bear all their iniquities on itself to a remote area, and he shall let the goat go free in the wilderness."

As far as the east is from the west, so far does he remove our transgressions from us.—"In those days and in that time," declares the Lord, "iniquity shall be sought in Israel, and there shall be none, and sin in Judah, and none shall be found, for I will pardon those whom I leave as a remnant."—You will cast all our sins into the depths of the sea. . . . Who is a God like you, pardoning iniquity?

All we like sheep have gone astray; we have turned—every one—to his own way; and the Lord has laid on him the iniquity of us all.—He shall bear their iniquities. Therefore I will divide him a portion with the many, and he shall divide the spoil with the strong, because he poured out his soul to death and was numbered with the transgressors; yet he bore the sin of many, and makes intercession for the transgressors.—"The Lamb of God, who takes away the sin of the world!"

Lev. 16:22; Ps. 103:12; Jer. 50:20; Mic. 7:19–18; Isa. 53:6; Isa. 53:11–12; John 1:29

EVENING

For who sees anything different in you?
What do you have that you did not receive?

By the grace of God I am what I am.—Of his own will he brought us forth by the word of truth.—So then it depends not on human will or exertion, but on God, who has mercy.— Then what becomes of our boasting? It is excluded.— Christ Jesus, who became to us wisdom from God, righteousness and sanctification and redemption. . . . "Let the one who boasts, boast in the Lord."

And you were dead in the trespasses and sins in which you once walked, following the course of this world, following the prince of the power of the air, the spirit that is now at work in the sons of disobedience—among whom we all once lived in the passions of our flesh, carrying out the desires of the body and the mind, and were by nature children of wrath, like the rest of mankind.—But you were washed, you were sanctified, you were justified in the name of the Lord Jesus Christ and by the Spirit of our God.

1 Cor. 4:7; 1 Cor. 15:10; James 1:18; Rom. 9:16; Rom. 3:27;
1 Cor. 1:30–31; Eph. 2:1–3; 1 Cor. 6:11

MORNING

***To him who loves us and has freed
us from our sins by his blood.***

Many waters cannot quench love, neither can floods drown it. . . . Love is strong as death.—"Greater love has no one than this, that someone lay down his life for his friends."

He himself bore our sins in his body on the tree, that we might die to sin and live to righteousness. By his wounds you have been healed.—In him we have redemption through his blood, the forgiveness of our trespasses, according to the riches of his grace.

You were washed, you were sanctified, you were justified in the name of the Lord Jesus Christ and by the Spirit of our God.—You are a chosen race, a royal priesthood, a holy nation, a people for his own possession, that you may proclaim the excellencies of him who called you out of darkness into his marvelous light.—I appeal to you therefore, brothers, by the mercies of God, to present your bodies as a living sacrifice, holy and acceptable to God, which is your spiritual worship.

Rev. 1:5; Song 8:7–6; John 15:13; 1 Pet. 2:24;
Eph. 1:7; 1 Cor. 6:11; 1 Pet. 2:9; Rom. 12:1

EVENING

There are varieties of service, but the same Lord.

Over the king's treasuries was Azmaveth the son of Adiel; and over the treasuries . . . was Jonathan the son of Uzziah; and over those who did the work of the field for tilling the soil was Ezri the son of Chelub; and over the vineyards was Shimei the Ramathite. . . . All these were stewards of King David's property.

God has appointed in the church first apostles, second prophets, third teachers, then miracles, then gifts of healing, helping, administrating, and various kinds of tongues. . . . All these are empowered by one and the same Spirit, who apportions to each one individually as he wills.

As each has received a gift, use it to serve one another, as good stewards of God's varied grace: whoever speaks, as one who speaks oracles of God; whoever serves, as one who serves by the strength that God supplies—in order that in everything God may be glorified through Jesus Christ. To him belong glory and dominion forever and ever.

1 Cor. 12:5; 1 Chron. 27:25–27, 31; 1 Cor. 12:28, 11; 1 Pet. 4:10–11

MORNING

*Moses did not know that the skin of his face shone
because he had been talking with God.*

Not to us, O Lord, not to us, but to your name give glory.—"Lord, when did we see you hungry and feed you, or thirsty and give you drink?"—In humility count others more significant than yourselves.—Clothe yourselves . . . with humility.

[Jesus] was transfigured before them, and his face shone like the sun, and his clothes became white as light.—Gazing at him, all who sat in the council saw that his face was like the face of an angel.—"The glory that you have given me I have given to them."—We all, with unveiled face, beholding the glory of the Lord, are being transformed into the same image from one degree of glory to another. For this comes from the Lord who is the Spirit.—"You are the light of the world. A city set on a hill cannot be hidden. Nor do people light a lamp and put it under a basket, but on a stand, and it gives light to all in the house."

Ex. 34:29; Ps. 115:1; Matt. 25:37; Phil. 2:3; 1 Pet. 5:5; Matt. 17:2;
Acts 6:15; John 17:22; 2 Cor. 3:18; Matt. 5:14–15

EVENING

*There are varieties of activities, but it is the same
God who empowers them all in everyone.*

Some of the men of Manasseh deserted to David. . . . They helped David against the band of raiders, for they were all mighty men of valor.—To each is given the manifestation of the Spirit for the common good.

Of Issachar, men who had understanding of the times, to know what Israel ought to do.—For to one is given through the Spirit the utterance of wisdom, and to another the utterance of knowledge according to the same Spirit.—Of Zebulun 50,000 seasoned troops, equipped for battle with all the weapons of war, to help David with singleness of purpose.—He is a double-minded man, unstable in all his ways.

That there may be no division in the body, but that the members may have the same care for one another. If one member suffers, all suffer together; if one member is honored, all rejoice together.

One Lord, one faith, one baptism.

1 Cor. 12:6; 1 Chron. 12:19, 21; 1 Cor. 12:7; 1 Chron. 12:32; 1 Cor. 12:8;
1 Chron. 12:33; James 1:8; 1 Cor. 12:25–26; Eph. 4:5

MORNING

"Call upon me in the day of trouble; I will deliver you, and you shall glorify me."

Why are you cast down, O my soul, and why are you in turmoil within me? Hope in God; for I shall again praise him, my salvation and my God.—O Lord, you hear the desire of the afflicted; you will strengthen their heart; you will incline your ear.—For you, O Lord, are good and forgiving, abounding in steadfast love to all who call upon you.

So Jacob said to his household, . . . "Let us arise and go up to Bethel, so that I may make there an altar to the God who answers me in the day of my distress and has been with me wherever I have gone."—Bless the Lord, O my soul, and forget not all his benefits.

I love the Lord, because he has heard my voice and my pleas for mercy. Because he inclined his ear to me, therefore I will call on him as long as I live. The snares of death encompassed me; the pangs of Sheol laid hold on me; I suffered distress and anguish. Then I called on the name of the Lord.

Ps. 50:15; Ps. 42:11; Ps. 10:17; Ps. 86:5; Gen. 35:2–3; Ps. 103:2; Ps. 116:1–4

EVENING

"Yet a little while, and the coming one will come and will not delay."

"Write the vision; make it plain on tablets, so he may run who reads it. For still the vision awaits its appointed time; it hastens to the end—it will not lie. If it seems slow, wait for it; it will surely come; it will not delay."

But do not overlook this one fact, beloved, that with the Lord one day is as a thousand years, and a thousand years as one day. The Lord is not slow to fulfill his promise as some count slowness, but is patient toward you, not wishing that any should perish, but that all should reach repentance.—But you, O Lord, are a God merciful and gracious, slow to anger and abounding in steadfast love and faithfulness.—Oh that you would rend the heavens and come down. . . . From of old no one has heard or perceived by the ear, no eye has seen a God besides you, who acts for those who wait for him.

Heb. 10:37; Hab. 2:2–3; 2 Pet. 2:8–9; Ps. 86:15; Isa. 64:1, 4

MORNING

"The Lord our God the Almighty reigns."

"I know that you can do all things."—"What is impossible with man is possible with God."—"He does according to his will among the host of heaven and among the inhabitants of the earth; and none can stay his hand or say to him, "What have you done?"—"There is none who can deliver from my hand; I work, and who can turn it back?"—"Abba, Father, all things are possible for you."

"Do you believe that I am able to do this?" They said to him, "Yes, Lord." Then he touched their eyes, saying, "According to your faith be it done to you."—"Lord, if you will, you can make me clean." And Jesus stretched out his hand and touched him, saying, "I will; be clean."—Mighty God.—"All authority in heaven and on earth has been given to me."

Some trust in chariots and some in horses, but we trust in the name of the Lord our God.—"Be strong and courageous. Do not be afraid or dismayed, . . . for there are more with us than with him."

Rev. 19:6; Job 42:2; Luke 18:27; Dan. 4:35; Isa. 43:13; Mark 14:36;
Matt. 9:28–29; Matt. 8:2–3; Isa. 9:6; Matt. 28:18; Ps. 20:7; 2 Chron. 32:7

EVENING

"What was it that he told you?"

He has told you, O man, what is good; and what does the Lord require of you but to do justice, and to love kindness, and to walk humbly with your God?—" . . . to keep the commandments and statutes of the Lord, which I am commanding you today for your good?"

All who rely on works of the law are under a curse; for it is written, "Cursed be everyone who does not abide by all things written in the Book of the Law, and do them." Now it is evident that no one is justified before God by the law, for "The righteous shall live by faith." . . . Why then the law? It was added because of transgressions, until the offspring should come to whom the promise had been made.

Long ago, at many times and in many ways, God spoke to our fathers by the prophets, but in these last days he has spoken to us by his Son.

"Speak, Lord, for your servant hears."

1 Sam. 3:17; Mic. 6:8; Deut. 10:13; Gal. 3:10–11, 19; Heb. 1:1–2; 1 Sam. 3:9

MORNING

He . . . teaches the humble his way.

"Blessed are the meek."

Again I saw that under the sun the race is not to the swift, nor the battle to the strong, nor bread to the wise, nor riches to the intelligent, nor favor to those with knowledge.—The heart of man plans his way, but the Lord establishes his steps.

To you I lift up my eyes, O you who are enthroned in the heavens! Behold, as the eyes of servants look to the hand of their master, as the eyes of a maidservant to the hand of her mistress, so our eyes look to the Lord our God.—Make me know the way I should go, for to you I lift up my soul.

"O our God, will you not execute judgment on them? For we are powerless against this great horde that is coming against us. We do not know what to do, but our eyes are on you."

If any of you lacks wisdom, let him ask God, who gives generously to all without reproach, and it will be given him.

"When the Spirit of truth comes, he will guide you into all the truth."

Ps. 25:9; Matt. 5:5; Eccles. 9:11; Prov. 16:9; Ps. 123:1–2;
Ps. 143:8; 2 Chron. 20:12; James 1:5; John 16:13

EVENING

*"O Lord God, . . . with your blessing shall the house
of your servant be blessed forever."*

"You, O Lord, who . . . blessed, and it is blessed forever."—The blessing of the Lord makes rich, and he adds no sorrow with it.

"Remember the words of the Lord Jesus, how he himself said, 'It is more blessed to give than to receive.'"—"When you give a feast, invite the poor, the crippled, the lame, the blind, and you will be blessed, because they cannot repay you. For you will be repaid at the resurrection of the just."—"Come, you who are blessed by my Father, inherit the kingdom prepared for you from the foundation of the world. For I was hungry and you gave me food, I was thirsty and you gave me drink, I was a stranger and you welcomed me, I was naked and you clothed me, I was sick and you visited me, I was in prison and you came to me."

Blessed is the one who considers the poor! In the day of trouble the Lord delivers him.—The Lord God is a sun and shield.

2 Sam. 7:29; 1 Chron. 17:27; Prov. 10:22; Acts 20:35;
Luke 14:13–14; Matt. 25:34–36; Ps. 41:1; Ps. 84:11

MORNING

"I will not fear; what can man do to me?"

Who shall separate us from the love of Christ? Shall tribulation, or distress, or persecution, or famine, or nakedness, or danger, or sword? No, in all these things we are more than conquerors through him who loved us.

"Do not fear those who kill the body, and after that have nothing more that they can do. But I will warn you whom to fear: fear him who, after he has killed, has authority to cast into hell. Yes, I tell you, fear him!"

"Blessed are those who are persecuted for righteousness' sake, for theirs is the kingdom of heaven. Blessed are you when others revile you and persecute you and utter all kinds of evil against you falsely on my account. Rejoice and be glad, for your reward is great in heaven."—"But I do not account my life of any value nor as precious to myself, if only I may finish my course."—I will also speak of your testimonies before kings and shall not be put to shame.

Heb. 13:6; Rom. 8:35, 37; Luke 12:4–5; Matt. 5:10–12;
Acts 20:24; Ps. 119:46

EVENING

He . . . set my feet upon a rock.

The Rock was Christ.—Simon Peter replied, "You are the Christ, the Son of the living God." . . . "On this rock I will build my church, and the gates of hell shall not prevail against it."—"And there is salvation in no one else, for there is no other name under heaven given among men by which we must be saved."

Full assurance of faith. . . . Hope without wavering.—Faith, with no doubting, for the one who doubts is like a wave of the sea that is driven and tossed by the wind.

Who shall separate us from the love of Christ? Shall tribulation, or distress, or persecution, or famine, or nakedness, or danger, or sword? . . . No, in all these things we are more than conquerors through him who loved us. For I am sure that neither death nor life, nor angels nor rulers, nor things present nor things to come, nor powers, nor height nor depth, nor anything else in all creation, will be able to separate us from the love of God in Christ Jesus our Lord.

Ps. 40:2; 1 Cor. 10:4; Matt. 16:16, 18; Acts 4:12; Heb. 10:22–23;
James 1:6; Rom. 8:35, 37–39

MORNING

"You are a God ready to forgive, gracious and merciful."

The Lord is not slow to fulfill his promise as some count slowness, but is patient toward you, not wishing that any should perish, but that all should reach repentance.—And count the patience of our Lord as salvation.

But I received mercy for this reason, that in me, as the foremost, Jesus Christ might display his perfect patience as an example to those who were to believe in him for eternal life.—Whatever was written in former days was written for our instruction, that through endurance and through the encouragement of the Scriptures we might have hope.

Or do you presume on the riches of his kindness and forbearance and patience, not knowing that God's kindness is meant to lead you to repentance?—"Rend your hearts and not your garments." Return to the Lord your God, for he is gracious and merciful, slow to anger, and abounding in steadfast love; and he relents over disaster.

Neh. 9:17; 2 Pet. 3:9; 2 Pet. 3:15; 1 Tim. 1:16; Rom. 15:4;
Rom. 2:4; Joel 2:13

EVENING

The words of the Lord are pure words.

Your promise is well tried, and your servant loves it.—The precepts of the Lord are right, rejoicing the heart; the commandment of the Lord is pure, enlightening the eyes.—Every word of God proves true; he is a shield to those who take refuge in him. Do not add to his words, lest he rebuke you and you be found a liar.

I have stored up your word in my heart, that I might not sin against you. . . . I will meditate on your precepts and fix my eyes on your ways.—Finally, brothers, whatever is true, whatever is honorable, whatever is just, whatever is pure, whatever is lovely, whatever is commendable, if there is any excellence, if there is anything worthy of praise, think about these things.—Like newborn infants, long for the pure spiritual milk, that by it you may grow up into salvation.

We are not, like so many, peddlers of God's word, but as men of sincerity, as commissioned by God, in the sight of God we speak in Christ.—We refuse to practice cunning or to tamper with God's word.

Ps. 12:6; Ps. 119:140; Ps. 19:8; Prov. 20:5–6; Ps. 119:11, 15;
Phil. 4:8; 1 Pet. 2:2; 2 Cor. 2:17; 2 Cor. 4:2

MORNING

Every family in heaven and on earth.

One God and Father of all, who is over all and through all and in all.—In Christ Jesus you are all sons of God, through faith.—As a plan for the fullness of time, to unite all things in him, things in heaven and things on earth.

He is not ashamed to call them brothers.—"Here are my mother and my brothers! For whoever does the will of my Father in heaven is my brother and sister and mother."—"Go to my brothers and say to them, 'I am ascending to my Father and your Father.'"

I saw under the altar the souls of those who had been slain for the word of God and for the witness they had borne. . . . Then they were each given a white robe and told to rest a little longer, until the number of their fellow servants and their brothers should be complete, who were to be killed as they themselves had been.—That apart from us they should not be made perfect.

Eph. 3:15; Eph. 4:6; Gal. 3:26; Eph. 1:10; Heb. 2:11; Matt. 12:49–50; John 20:17; Rev. 6:9–11; Heb. 11:40

EVENING

"Pray then like this: Our Father in heaven."

Jesus . . . lifted up his eyes to heaven, and said, "Father."—"My Father and your Father."

In Christ Jesus you are all sons of God, through faith.—You did not receive the spirit of slavery to fall back into fear, but you have received the Spirit of adoption as sons, by whom we cry, "Abba! Father!" The Spirit himself bears witness with our spirit that we are children of God.

Because you are sons, God has sent the Spirit of his Son into our hearts, crying, "Abba! Father!" So you are no longer a slave, but a son.

"In that day you will ask nothing of me. Truly, truly, I say to you, whatever you ask of the Father in my name, he will give it to you. Until now you have asked nothing in my name. Ask, and you will receive, that your joy may be full."

"I will welcome you, and I will be a father to you, and you shall be sons and daughters to me, says the Lord Almighty."

Matt. 6:9; John 17:1; John 20:17; Gal. 3:26; Rom. 8:15–16; Gal. 4:6–7; John 16:23–24; 2 Cor. 6:17–18

MORNING

Be not far from me, for trouble is near.

How long, O Lord? Will you forget me forever? How long will you hide your face from me? How long must I take counsel in my soul and have sorrow in my heart all the day?—Hide not your face from me. Turn not your servant away in anger, O you who have been my help. Cast me not off; forsake me not, O God of my salvation!

When he calls to me, I will answer him; I will be with him in trouble; I will rescue him and honor him.—The Lord is near to all who call on him, to all who call on him in truth. He fulfills the desire of those who fear him; he also hears their cry and saves them.

"I will not leave you as orphans; I will come to you."—"Behold, I am with you always, to the end of the age."

God is our refuge and strength, a very present help in trouble.—For God alone my soul waits in silence; from him comes my salvation. For God alone, O my soul, wait in silence, for my hope is from him.

Ps. 22:11; Ps. 13:1–2; Ps. 27:9; Ps. 91:15; Ps. 145:18–19;
John 14:18; Matt. 28:20; Ps. 46:1; Ps. 62:1, 5

EVENING

"Hallowed be your name."

"You shall worship no other god, for the Lord, whose name is Jealous, is a jealous God."

"Who is like you, O Lord, among the gods? Who is like you, majestic in holiness, awesome in glorious deeds, doing wonders?"—"Holy, holy, holy, is the Lord God Almighty."

Worship the Lord in the splendor of holiness.—I saw the Lord sitting upon a throne, high and lifted up; and the train of his robe filled the temple. Above him stood the seraphim. . . . One called to another and said: "Holy, holy, holy is the Lord of hosts; the whole earth is full of his glory!" . . . And I said: "Woe is me! For I am lost."—"I had heard of you by the hearing of the ear, but now my eye sees you; therefore I despise myself."

The blood of Jesus his Son cleanses us from all sin.—That we may share his holiness.—Therefore, brothers, since we have confidence to enter the holy places by the blood of Jesus, . . . let us draw near with a true heart.

Matt. 6:9; Ex. 34:14; Ex. 15:11; Rev. 4:8; 1 Chron. 16:29; Isa. 6:1–3, 5;
Job 42:5–6; 1 John 1:7; Heb. 12:10; Heb. 10:19, 22

MORNING

In Christ God was reconciling the world to himself, not counting their trespasses against them.

In him all the fullness of God was pleased to dwell, and through him to reconcile to himself all things, whether on earth or in heaven, making peace by the blood of his cross.—Steadfast love and faithfulness meet; righteousness and peace kiss each other.

"I know the plans I have for you, declares the Lord, plans for welfare and not for evil."—"Come now, let us reason together, says the Lord: though your sins are like scarlet, they shall be as white as snow; though they are red like crimson, they shall become like wool."

Who is a God like you, pardoning iniquity?—"Agree with God, and be at peace."—Work out your own salvation with fear and trembling, for it is God who works in you, both to will and to work for his good pleasure.—O Lord, you will ordain peace for us, for you have indeed done for us all our works.

2 Cor. 5:19; Col. 1:19–20; Ps. 85:10; Jer. 29:11; Isa. 1:18;
Mic. 7:18; Job 22:21; Phil. 2:12–13; Isa. 26:12

EVENING

"Your kingdom come."

"In the days of those kings the God of heaven will set up a kingdom that shall never be destroyed, nor shall the kingdom be left to another people. It shall break in pieces all these kingdoms and bring them to an end, and it shall stand forever."—"A stone was cut out by no human hand."—"Not by might, nor by power, but by my Spirit, says the Lord of hosts."—"The kingdom of God is not coming in ways that can be observed, nor will they say, 'Look, here it is!' or 'There!' for behold, the kingdom of God is in the midst of you."

"To you has been given the secret of the kingdom of God. . . . The kingdom of God is as if a man should scatter seed on the ground. He sleeps and rises night and day, and the seed sprouts and grows; he knows not how. . . . But when the grain is ripe, at once he puts in the sickle, because the harvest has come."—"Therefore you also must be ready, for the Son of Man is coming at an hour you do not expect."—The Spirit and the Bride say, "Come." And let the one who hears say, "Come."

Matt. 6:10; Dan. 2:44; Dan. 2:34; Zech. 4:6; Luke 17:20–21;
Mark 4:11, 26–27, 29; Matt. 24:44; Rev. 22:17

MORNING

"From the first day that you set your heart to understand and humbled yourself before your God, your words have been heard."

Thus says the One who is high and lifted up, who inhabits eternity, whose name is Holy: "I dwell in the high and holy place, and also with him who is of a contrite and lowly spirit, to revive the spirit of the lowly, and to revive the heart of the contrite."—The sacrifices of God are a broken spirit; a broken and contrite heart, O God, you will not despise.—Though the Lord is high, he regards the lowly, but the haughty he knows from afar.—Humble yourselves, therefore, under the mighty hand of God so that at the proper time he may exalt you.—"God opposes the proud, but gives grace to the humble." Submit yourselves therefore to God.

You, O Lord, are good and forgiving, abounding in steadfast love to all who call upon you. Give ear, O Lord, to my prayer; listen to my plea for grace. In the day of my trouble I call upon you, for you answer me.

Dan. 10:12; Isa. 57:15; Ps. 51:17; Ps. 138:6; 1 Pet. 5:6;
James 4:6-7; Ps. 86:5-7

EVENING

"Your will be done, on earth as it is in heaven."

Understand what the will of the Lord is.

"It is not the will of my Father who is in heaven that one of these little ones should perish."

This is the will of God, your sanctification.—So as to live for the rest of the time in the flesh no longer for human passions but for the will of God.—Of his own will he brought us forth by the word of truth. . . . Therefore put away all filthiness.

"You shall be holy, for I am holy."—[Jesus] said, . . . "For whoever does the will of God, he is my brother and sister and mother."—"Everyone then who hears these words of mine and does them will be like a wise man who built his house on the rock. And the rain fell, and the floods came, and the winds blew and beat on that house, but it did not fall, because it had been founded on the rock."—The world is passing away along with its desires, but whoever does the will of God abides forever.

Matt. 6:10; Eph. 5:17; Matt. 18:14; 1 Thess. 4:3; 1 Pet. 4:2; James 1:18, 21;
1 Pet. 1:16; Mark 3:34-35; Matt. 7:24-25; 1 John 2:17

MORNING

Christ died and lived again, that he might be
Lord both of the dead and of the living.

It was the will of the Lord to crush him; he has put him to grief; when his soul makes an offering for guilt, he shall see his offspring; he shall prolong his days; the will of the Lord shall prosper in his hand. Out of the anguish of his soul he shall see and be satisfied; by his knowledge shall the righteous one, my servant, make many to be accounted righteous, and he shall bear their iniquities.—"Was it not necessary that the Christ should suffer these things and enter into his glory?"—We have concluded this: that one has died for all, therefore all have died; and he died for all, that those who live might no longer live for themselves but for him who for their sake died and was raised.— "Let all the house of Israel therefore know for certain that God has made him both Lord and Christ, this Jesus whom you crucified."—He was foreknown before the foundation of the world but was made manifest in the last times for the sake of you who through him are believers in God.

Rom. 14:9; Isa. 53:10–11; Luke 24:26; 2 Cor. 5:14–15;
Acts 2:36; 1 Pet. 1:20–21

EVENING

"Give us this day our daily bread."

I have been young, and now am old, yet I have not seen the righteous forsaken or his children begging for bread.—His bread will be given him; his water will be sure.—The ravens brought him bread and meat in the morning, and bread and meat in the evening, and he drank from the brook.—My God will supply every need of yours according to his riches in glory in Christ Jesus.—Be content with what you have, for he has said, "I will never leave you nor forsake you."

"He humbled you and let you hunger and fed you with manna . . . that he might make you know that man does not live by bread alone, but man lives by every word that comes from the mouth of the Lord."—Jesus then said to them, "Truly, truly, I say to you, it was not Moses who gave you the bread from heaven, but my Father gives you the true bread from heaven. For the bread of God is he who comes down from heaven and gives life to the world." They said to him, "Sir, give us this bread always."

Matt. 6:11; Ps. 37:25; Isa. 33:16; 1 Kings 17:6; Phil. 4:19;
Heb. 13:5; Deut. 8:3; John 6:32–34

MORNING

You, O God, are my fortress.

"The Lord is my rock and my fortress and my deliverer, my God, my rock, in whom I take refuge, my shield, and the horn of my salvation, my stronghold and my refuge, my savior."—The Lord is my strength and my shield; in him my heart trusts, and I am helped; my heart exults, and with my song I give thanks to him.

He will come like a rushing stream, which the wind of the Lord drives.—We can confidently say, "The Lord is my helper; I will not fear; what can man do to me?"

The Lord is my light and my salvation; whom shall I fear? The Lord is the stronghold of my life; of whom shall I be afraid?

As the mountains surround Jerusalem, so the Lord surrounds his people, from this time forth and forevermore.—For you have been my help, and in the shadow of your wings I will sing for joy.

For your name's sake you lead me and guide me.

Ps. 59:9; 2 Sam. 22:2–3; Ps. 28:7; Isa. 59:19; Heb. 13:6;
Ps. 27:1; Ps. 125:2; Ps. 63:7; Ps. 31:3

EVENING

"Forgive us our debts, as we also have forgiven our debtors."

"Lord, how often will my brother sin against me, and I forgive him? As many as seven times?" Jesus said to him, "I do not say to you seven times, but seventy-seven times."—"'You wicked servant! I forgave you all that debt because you pleaded with me. And should not you have had mercy on your fellow servant, as I had mercy on you?' And in anger his master delivered him to the jailers, until he should pay all his debt. So also my heavenly Father will do to every one of you, if you do not forgive your brother from your heart."—Be kind to one another, tenderhearted, forgiving one another, as God in Christ forgave you.—You, . . . God made alive, . . . having forgiven us all our trespasses, by canceling the record of debt that stood against us with its legal demands. This he set aside, nailing it to the cross.—As the Lord has forgiven you, so you also must forgive.

Matt. 6:12; Matt. 18:21–22; Matt. 18:32–35; Eph. 4:32;
Col. 2:13–14; Col. 3:13

MORNING

Do not be slothful in zeal, be fervent in spirit, serve the Lord.

Whatever your hand finds to do, do it with your might, for there is no work or thought or knowledge or wisdom in Sheol, to which you are going.—Whatever you do, work heartily, as for the Lord and not for men, knowing that from the Lord you will receive the inheritance as your reward. You are serving the Lord Christ.—Whatever good anyone does, this he will receive back from the Lord.

"We must work the works of him who sent me while it is day; night is coming, when no one can work."—"Did you not know that I must be in my Father's house?"—"Zeal for your house will consume me."

Brothers, be all the more diligent to confirm your calling and election, for if you practice these qualities you will never fall.—We desire each one of you to show the same earnestness to have the full assurance of hope until the end, so that you may not be sluggish, but imitators of those who through faith and patience inherit the promises.—So run that you may obtain it.

Rom. 12:11; Eccles. 9:10; Col. 3:23–24; Eph. 6:8; John 9:4; Luke 2:49;
John 2:17; 2 Pet. 1:10; Heb. 6:11–12; 1 Cor. 9:24

EVENING

"Lead us not into temptation, but deliver us from evil."

Whoever trusts in his own mind is a fool, but he who walks in wisdom will be delivered.

Let no one say when he is tempted, "I am being tempted by God," for God cannot be tempted with evil, and he himself tempts no one. But each person is tempted when he is lured and enticed by his own desire.—"Therefore go out from their midst, and be separate from them, says the Lord, and touch no unclean thing; then I will welcome you."

Lot lifted up his eyes and saw that the Jordan Valley was well watered everywhere like the garden of the Lord. . . . So Lot chose for himself all the Jordan Valley. . . . Now the men of Sodom were wicked, great sinners against the Lord.—If he rescued righteous Lot, greatly distressed by the sensual conduct of the wicked . . . then the Lord knows how to rescue the godly from trials.—And he will be upheld, for the Lord is able to make him stand.

Matt. 6:13; Prov. 28:26; James 1:13–14; 2 Cor. 6:17;
Gen. 13:10–11, 13; 2 Pet. 2:7, 9; Rom. 14:4

MORNING

Who exult in your name all the day and in your righteousness are exalted.

"Only in the Lord, it shall be said of me, are righteousness and strength; to him shall come and be ashamed all who were incensed against him. In the Lord all the offspring of Israel shall be justified and shall glory."—Be glad in the Lord, and rejoice, O righteous, and shout for joy, all you upright in heart!

But now the righteousness of God has been manifested apart from the law, although the Law and the Prophets bear witness to it—the righteousness of God through faith in Jesus Christ for all who believe. . . . It was to show his righteousness at the present time, so that he might be just and the justifier of the one who has faith in Jesus.

Rejoice in the Lord always; again I will say, rejoice.— Though you have not seen him, you love him. Though you do not now see him, you believe in him and rejoice with joy that is inexpressible and filled with glory.

Ps. 89:16; Isa. 45:24–25; Ps. 32:11; Rom. 3:21–22, 26;
Phil. 4:4; 1 Pet. 1:8

EVENING

For yours is the kingdom and the power and the glory, forever.

The Lord reigns; he is robed in majesty. . . . Your throne is established from of old; you are from everlasting.

The Lord is . . . great in power.—If God is for us, who can be against us?— "Our God whom we serve is able to deliver us, . . . and he will deliver us."—"My Father, who has given them to me, is greater than all, and no one is able to snatch them out of the Father's hand."—He who is in you is greater than he who is in the world.

Not to us, O Lord, not to us, but to your name give glory.—"Yours, O Lord, is the greatness and the power and the glory and the victory and the majesty, for all that is in the heavens and in the earth is yours. Yours is the kingdom, O Lord, and you are exalted as head above all . . . . And now we thank you, our God, and praise your glorious name. But who am I, and what is my people, that we should be able thus to offer willingly? For all things come from you, and of your own have we given you."

Matt. 6:13; Ps. 93:1–2; Nah. 1:3; Rom. 8:31; Dan. 3:17; John 10:29;
1 John 4:4; Ps. 115:1; 1 Chron. 29:11, 13–14

MORNING

One of the soldiers pierced his side with a spear,
and at once there came out blood and water.

"Behold the blood of the covenant that the Lord has made with you."—"The life of the flesh is in the blood, and I have given it for you on the altar to make atonement for your souls."—It is impossible for the blood of bulls and goats to take away sins.—And he said to them, "This is my blood of the covenant, which is poured out for many."—He entered once for all into the holy places, not by means of the blood of goats and calves but by means of his own blood, thus securing an eternal redemption.—Peace by the blood of his cross.— Knowing that you were ransomed . . . not with perishable things such as silver or gold, but with the precious blood of Christ, like that of a lamb without blemish or spot. He . . . was made manifest in the last times for the sake of you.—I will sprinkle clean water on you, and you shall be clean, . . . from all your idols I will cleanse you.—Let us draw near with a true heart in full assurance of faith, with our hearts sprinkled clean from an evil conscience.

John 19:34; Ex. 24:8; Lev. 17:11; Heb. 10:4; Mark 14:24; Heb. 9:12;
Col. 1:20; 1 Pet. 1:18–20; Ezek. 36:25; Heb. 10:22

EVENING

Amen.

"Amen! May the Lord, the God of my lord the king, say so."—He who blesses himself in the land shall bless himself by the God of truth, and he who takes an oath in the land shall swear by the God of truth.

When God made a promise to Abraham, since he had no one greater by whom to swear, he swore by himself. . . . For people swear by something greater than themselves, and in all their disputes an oath is final for confirmation. So when God desired to show more convincingly to the heirs of the promise the unchangeable character of his purpose, he guaranteed it with an oath, so that by two unchangeable things, in which it is impossible for God to lie, we who have fled for refuge might have strong encouragement to hold fast to the hope set before us.—"The words of the Amen, the faithful and true witness."—For all the promises of God find their Yes in him. That is why it is through him that we utter our Amen to God for his glory.—Blessed be the Lord, the God of Israel, who alone does wondrous things. Blessed be his glorious name forever; . . . Amen and Amen!

Matt. 6:13; 1 Kings 1:36; Isa. 65:16; Heb. 6:13, 16–18;
Rev. 3:14; 2 Cor. 1:20; Ps. 72:18–19

MORNING

The Lord will be your confidence and will keep your foot from being caught.

Surely the wrath of man shall praise you; the remnant of wrath you will put on like a belt.—The king's heart is a stream of water in the hand of the Lord; he turns it wherever he will.—When a man's ways please the Lord, he makes even his enemies to be at peace with him.

I wait for the Lord, my soul waits, and in his word I hope; my soul waits for the Lord more than watchmen for the morning, more than watchmen for the morning.—I sought the Lord, and he answered me and delivered me from all my fears.

"The eternal God is your dwelling place, and underneath are the everlasting arms. And he thrust out the enemy before you and said, Destroy."—"Blessed is the man who trusts in the Lord, whose trust is the Lord."

What then shall we say to these things? If God is for us, who can be against us?

Prov. 3:26; Ps. 76:10; Prov. 21:1; Prov. 16:7; Ps. 130:5-6;
Ps. 34:4; Deut. 33:27; Jer. 17:7; Rom. 8:31

EVENING

Encouragement in Christ, . . . comfort from love, . . . participation in the Spirit.

"Man who is born of a woman is few of days and full of trouble. He comes out like a flower and withers; he flees like a shadow and continues not."—My flesh and my heart may fail, but God is the strength of my heart and my portion forever.

"The Father . . . will give you another Helper, to be with you forever. . . . The Holy Spirit, whom the Father will send in my name."— Blessed be the God and Father of our Lord Jesus Christ, the Father of mercies and God of all comfort, who comforts us in all our affliction, so that we may be able to comfort those who are in any affliction, with the comfort with which we ourselves are comforted by God.

Since we believe that Jesus died and rose again, even so, through Jesus, God will bring with him those who have fallen asleep. . . . And so we will always be with the Lord. Therefore encourage one another with these words.

Phil. 2:1; Job 14:1-2; Ps. 73:26; John 14:16, 26; 2 Cor. 1:3-4;
1 Thess. 4:14, 17-18

MORNING

I delight in the law of God, in my inner being.

Oh how I love your law! It is my meditation all the day.—Your words were found, and I ate them, and your words became to me a joy and the delight of my heart.—With great delight I sat in his shadow, and his fruit was sweet to my taste.—"I have treasured the words of his mouth more than my portion of food."

"I delight to do your will, O my God; your law is within my heart."—"My food is to do the will of him who sent me and to accomplish his work."

The precepts of the Lord are right, rejoicing the heart; the command-ment of the Lord is pure, enlightening the eyes. . . . More to be desired are they than gold, even much fine gold; sweeter also than honey and drippings of the honeycomb.—Be doers of the word, and not hearers only, deceiving yourselves. For if anyone is a hearer of the word and not a doer, he is like a man who looks intently at his natural face in a mirror.

Rom. 7:22; Ps. 119:97; Jer. 15:16; Song 2:3; Job 23:12;
Ps. 40:8; John 4:34; Ps. 19:8, 10; James 1:22–23

EVENING

"May the Lord your God accept you."

"With what shall I come before the Lord, and bow myself before God on high? Shall I come before him with burnt offerings, with calves a year old? Will the Lord be pleased with thousands of rams, with ten thousands of rivers of oil? Shall I give my firstborn for my transgression, the fruit of my body for the sin of my soul?" He has told you, O man, what is good; and what does the Lord require of you but to do justice, and to love kindness, and to walk humbly with your God?

We have all become like one who is unclean, and all our righteous deeds are like a polluted garment.—"None is righteous, no, not one." . . . For all have sinned and fall short of the glory of God, and are justified by his grace as a gift, through the redemption that is in Christ Jesus, whom God put forward as a propitiation by his blood, to be received by faith. . . . It was to show his righteousness at the present time, so that he might be just and the justifier of the one who has faith in Jesus.

He has blessed us in the Beloved.—You have been filled in him.

2 Sam. 24:23; Mic. 6:6–8; Isa. 64:6; Rom. 3:10, 23–26; Eph. 1:6; Col. 2:10

MORNING

From his fullness we have all received, grace upon grace.

"This is my beloved Son, with whom I am well pleased."—See what kind of love the Father has given to us, that we should be called children of God.

His Son, whom he appointed the heir of all things.—If children, then heirs—heirs of God and fellow heirs with Christ, provided we suffer with him in order that we may also be glorified with him.

"I and the Father are one. . . . The Father is in me and I am in the Father."—"My Father and your Father, . . . my God and your God."—"I in them and you in me, that they may become perfectly one."

The church, which is his body, the fullness of him who fills all in all.

Since we have these promises, beloved, let us cleanse ourselves from every defilement of body and spirit, bringing holiness to completion in the fear of God.

John 1:16; Matt. 17:5; 1 John 3:1; Heb. 1:2; Rom. 8:17; John 10:30, 38;
John 20:17; John 17:23; Eph. 1:22–23; 2 Cor. 7:1

EVENING

"A servant is not greater than his master, nor is a messenger greater than the one who sent him. If you know these things, blessed are you if you do them."

A dispute also arose among them, as to which of them was to be regarded as the greatest. And he said to them, "The kings of the Gentiles exercise lordship over them, and those in authority over them are called benefactors. But not so with you. Rather, let the greatest among you become as the youngest, and the leader as one who serves. For who is the greater, one who reclines at table or one who serves? Is it not the one who reclines at table? But I am among you as the one who serves."—"Even as the Son of Man came not to be served but to serve, and to give his life as a ransom for many."

Jesus . . . rose from supper. He laid aside his outer garments, and taking a towel, tied it around his waist. Then he poured water into a basin and began to wash the disciples' feet and to wipe them with the towel that was wrapped around him.

John 13:16–17; Luke 22:24–27; Matt. 20:28; John 13:3–5

MORNING

My heart is steadfast, O God!

The Lord is my light and my salvation; whom shall I fear? The Lord is the stronghold of my life; of whom shall I be afraid?

You keep him in perfect peace whose mind is stayed on you, because he trusts in you.—He is not afraid of bad news; his heart is firm, trusting in the Lord. His heart is steady; he will not be afraid, until he looks in triumph on his adversaries.

When I am afraid, I put my trust in you.—He will hide me in his shelter in the day of trouble; he will conceal me under the cover of his tent; he will lift me high upon a rock. And now my head shall be lifted up above my enemies all around me, and I will offer in his tent sacrifices with shouts of joy; I will sing and make melody to the Lord.

After you have suffered a little while, the God of all grace, who has called you to his eternal glory in Christ, will himself restore, confirm, strengthen, and establish you. To him be the dominion forever and ever.

Ps. 108:1; Ps. 27:1; Isa. 26:3; Ps. 112:7–8; Ps. 56:3;
Ps. 27:5–6; 1 Pet. 5:10–11

EVENING

The Lord has established his throne in the heavens, and his kingdom rules over all.

The lot is cast into the lap, but its every decision is from the Lord.—"Does disaster come to a city, unless the Lord has done it?"

"I am the Lord, and there is no other, besides me there is no God; I equip you, though you do not know me, that people may know, from the rising of the sun and from the west, that there is none besides me; I am the Lord, and there is no other. I form light and create darkness, I make well-being and create calamity, I am the Lord, who does all these things."

He does according to his will among the host of heaven and among the inhabitants of the earth; and none can stay his hand or say to him, "What have you done?"—If God is for us, who can be against us?

He must reign until he has put all his enemies under his feet.—"Fear not, little flock, for it is your Father's good pleasure to give you the kingdom."

Ps. 103:19; Prov. 16:33; Amos 3:6; Isa. 45:5–7; Dan. 4:35;
Rom. 8:31; 1 Cor. 15:25; Luke 12:32

MORNING

"One's life does not consist in the abundance of his possessions."

Better is the little that the righteous has than the abundance of many wicked.—Better is a little with the fear of the Lord than great treasure and trouble with it.—But godliness with contentment is great gain . . . . But if we have food and clothing, with these we will be content.—Give me neither poverty nor riches; feed me with the food that is needful for me, lest I be full and deny you and say, "Who is the Lord?" or lest I be poor and steal and profane the name of my God.—"Give us this day our daily bread."

"Therefore I tell you, do not be anxious about your life, what you will eat or what you will drink, nor about your body, what you will put on. Is not life more than food, and the body more than clothing?"—"When I sent you out with no moneybag or knapsack or sandals, did you lack anything?" They said, "Nothing."—Keep your life free from love of money, and be content with what you have, for he has said, "I will never leave you nor forsake you."

Luke 12:15; Ps. 37:16; Prov. 15:16; 1 Tim. 6:6, 8; Prov. 30:8–9;
Matt. 6:11; Matt. 6:25; Luke 22:35; Heb. 13:5

EVENING

"It is the Spirit who gives life."

"The first man Adam became a living being"; the last Adam became a life-giving spirit.—"That which is born of the flesh is flesh, and that which is born of the Spirit is spirit."—He saved us, not because of works done by us in righteousness, but according to his own mercy, by the washing of regeneration and renewal of the Holy Spirit.

Anyone who does not have the Spirit of Christ does not belong to him. But if Christ is in you, although the body is dead because of sin, the Spirit is life because of righteousness. If the Spirit of him who raised Jesus from the dead dwells in you, he who raised Christ Jesus from the dead will also give life to your mortal bodies through his Spirit who dwells in you.

It is no longer I who live, but Christ who lives in me. And the life I now live in the flesh I live by faith in the Son of God.—You . . . must consider yourselves dead to sin and alive to God in Christ Jesus.

John 6:63; 1 Cor. 15:45; John 3:6; Titus 3:5; Rom. 8:9–11;
Gal. 2:20; Rom. 6:11

MORNING

"I am driven away from your sight; yet I shall again look upon your holy temple."

Zion said, "The Lord has forsaken me; my Lord has forgotten me." "Can a woman forget her nursing child, that she should have no compassion on the son of her womb? Even these may forget, yet I will not forget you."—I have forgotten what happiness is; so I say, "My endurance has perished; so has my hope from the Lord."—Awake! Why are you sleeping, O Lord? Rouse yourself! Do not reject us forever!—Why do you say, O Jacob, and speak, O Israel, "My way is hidden from the Lord, and my right is disregarded by my God"?—"In overflowing anger for a moment I hid my face from you, but with everlasting love I will have compassion on you," says the Lord, your Redeemer.

Why are you cast down, O my soul, and why are you in turmoil within me? Hope in God; for I shall again praise him, my salvation and my God.—We are afflicted in every way, but not crushed; perplexed, but not driven to despair; persecuted, but not forsaken; struck down, but not destroyed.

Jonah 2:4; Isa. 49:14–15; Lam. 3:17–18; Ps. 44:23;
Isa. 40:27; Isa. 54:8; Ps. 43:5; 2 Cor. 4:8–9

EVENING

When the poor and needy seek water, and there is none, and their tongue is parched with thirst, I the Lord will answer them.

There are many who say, "Who will show us some good?"— What has a man from all the toil and striving of heart with which he toils beneath the sun? For all his days are full of sorrow, and his work is a vexation. Even in the night his heart does not rest. . . . All is vanity and a striving after wind.—"They have forsaken me, the fountain of living waters, and hewed out cisterns for themselves, broken cisterns that can hold no water."

"Whoever comes to me I will never cast out."—"I will pour water on the thirsty land."—"Blessed are those who hunger and thirst for righteousness, for they shall be satisfied."—O God, you are my God; earnestly I seek you; my soul thirsts for you; my flesh faints for you, as in a dry and weary land where there is no water.

Isa. 41:17; Ps. 4:6; Eccles. 2:22–23, 17; Jer. 2:13;
John 6:37; Isa. 44:3; Matt. 5:6; Ps. 63:1

MORNING

"Behold, I am with you always, to the end of the age."

"If two of you agree on earth about anything they ask, it will be done for them by my Father in heaven. For where two or three are gathered in my name, there am I among them."—"Whoever has my commandments and keeps them, he it is who loves me. And he who loves me will be loved by my Father, and I will love him and manifest myself to him."

"Lord, how is it that you will manifest yourself to us, and not to the world? . . ." "If anyone loves me, he will keep my word, and my Father will love him, and we will come to him and make our home with him."

Now to him who is able to keep you from stumbling and to present you blameless before the presence of his glory with great joy, to the only God, our Savior, through Jesus Christ our Lord, be glory, majesty, dominion, and authority, before all time and now and forever. Amen.

Matt. 28:20; Matt. 18:19–20; John 14:21; John 14:22–23; Jude 24–25

EVENING

The end of all things is at hand.

I saw a great white throne and him who was seated on it. From his presence earth and sky fled away.—The heavens and earth that now exist are stored up for fire, being kept until the day of judgment.

God is our refuge and strength, a very present help in trouble. Therefore we will not fear though the earth gives way, though the mountains be moved into the heart of the sea, though its waters roar and foam, though the mountains tremble at its swelling.—"You will hear of wars and rumors of wars. See that you are not alarmed."

We have a building from God, a house not made with hands, eternal in the heavens.—We are waiting for new heavens and a new earth in which righteousness dwells. Therefore, beloved, since you are waiting for these, be diligent to be found by him without spot or blemish, and at peace.

1 Pet. 4:7; Rev. 20:11; 2 Pet. 3:7; Ps. 46:1–3; Matt. 24:6;
2 Cor. 5:1; 2 Pet. 3:13–14

MORNING

The Lord reigns.

"Do you not fear me? declares the Lord. Do you not tremble before me? I placed the sand as the boundary for the sea, a perpetual barrier that it cannot pass; though the waves toss, they cannot prevail; though they roar, they cannot pass over it."—Not from the east or from the west and not from the wilderness comes lifting up, but it is God who executes judgment, putting down one and lifting up another.

He changes times and seasons; he removes kings and sets up kings; he gives wisdom to the wise and knowledge to those who have understanding.—"You will hear of wars and rumors of wars. See that you are not alarmed."

If God is for us, who can be against us?—"Are not two sparrows sold for a penny? And not one of them will fall to the ground apart from your Father. But even the hairs of your head are all numbered. Fear not, therefore; you are of more value than many sparrows."

Ps. 99:1; Jer. 5:22; Ps. 75:6-7; Dan. 2:21; Matt. 24:6;
Rom. 8:31; Matt. 10:29-31

EVENING

Guard yourselves in your spirit.

"Master, we saw someone casting out demons in your name, and we tried to stop him, because he does not follow with us." But Jesus said to him, "Do not stop him, for the one who is not against you is for you." . . . "Lord, do you want us to tell fire to come down from heaven and consume them?" But he turned and rebuked them.

"Eldad and Medad are prophesying in the camp." And Joshua the son of Nun . . . said, "My lord Moses, stop them." But Moses said to him, "Are you jealous for my sake? Would that all the Lord's people were prophets, that the Lord would put his Spirit on them!"

The fruit of the Spirit is love, joy, peace, patience, kindness, goodness, faithfulness, gentleness, self-control. . . . And those who belong to Christ Jesus have crucified the flesh with its passions and desires. If we live by the Spirit, let us also keep in step with the Spirit. Let us not become conceited, provoking one another, envying one another.

Mal. 2:15; Luke 9:49-50, 54-55; Num. 11:27-29; Gal. 5:22-26

MORNING

"He took our illnesses and bore our diseases."

"The priest shall command them to take for him who is to be cleansed two live clean birds and cedarwood and scarlet yarn and hyssop. And the priest shall command them to kill one of the birds in an earthenware vessel over fresh water. He shall take the live bird with the cedarwood and the scarlet yarn and the hyssop, and dip them and the live bird in the blood of the bird that was killed over the fresh water. And he shall sprinkle it seven times on him who is to be cleansed of the leprous disease. Then he shall pronounce him clean and shall let the living bird go into the open field."

There came a man full of leprosy. And when he saw Jesus, he fell on his face and begged him, "Lord, if you will, you can make me clean."—Moved with pity, he stretched out his hand and touched him and said to him, "I will; be clean." And immediately the leprosy left him, and he was made clean.

Matt. 8:17; Lev. 14:4–7; Luke 5:12; Mark 1:41–42

EVENING

"He whom you bless is blessed."

"Blessed are the poor in spirit, for theirs is the kingdom of heaven."

"Blessed are those who mourn, for they shall be comforted. Blessed are the meek, for they shall inherit the earth. Blessed are those who hunger and thirst for righteousness, for they shall be satisfied. Blessed are the merciful, for they shall receive mercy. Blessed are the pure in heart, for they shall see God. Blessed are the peacemakers, for they shall be called sons of God. Blessed are those who are persecuted for righteousness' sake, for theirs is the kingdom of heaven. Blessed are you when others revile you and persecute you and utter all kinds of evil against you falsely on my account. Rejoice and be glad, for your reward is great in heaven, for so they persecuted the prophets who were before you."—"Blessed . . . are those who hear the word of God and keep it!"

Blessed are those who wash their robes, so that they may have the right to the tree of life and that they may enter the city by the gates.

Num. 22:6; Matt. 5:3; Matt. 5:3–12; Luke 11:28; Rev. 22:14

MORNING

*He saw that there was no man, and wondered that there was no
one to intercede; then his own arm brought him salvation.*

In sacrifice and offering you have not delighted, but you have given me an
open ear. Burnt offering and sin offering you have not required. Then I said,
"Behold, I have come; in the scroll of the book it is written of me: I delight to
do your will, O my God; your law is within my heart."—"I lay down my life
that I may take it up again. No one takes it from me, but I lay it down of my
own accord. I have authority to lay it down, and I have authority to take it up
again."

"And there is no other god besides me, a righteous God and a Savior;
there is none besides me. Turn to me and be saved, all the ends of the earth!
For I am God, and there is no other."—"There is salvation in no one else, for
there is no other name under heaven given among men by which we must
be saved."—You know the grace of our Lord Jesus Christ, that though he was
rich, yet for your sake he became poor, so that you by his poverty might
become rich.

Isa. 59:16; Ps. 40:6–8; John 10:17–18; Isa. 45:21–22; Acts 4:12; 2 Cor. 8:9

EVENING

The enemy.

Be sober-minded; be watchful. Your adversary the devil prowls around like a
roaring lion, seeking someone to devour.—Resist the devil, and he will flee
from you.

Put on the whole armor of God, that you may be able to stand against
the schemes of the devil. For we do not wrestle against flesh and blood, but
against the rulers, against the authorities, against the cosmic powers over
this present darkness, against the spiritual forces of evil in the heavenly
places. Therefore take up the whole armor of God, that you may be able to
withstand in the evil day, and having done all, to stand firm. Stand therefore, having fastened on the belt of truth, and having put on the breastplate of
righteousness, and, as shoes for your feet, having put on the readiness given
by the gospel of peace. In all circumstances take up the shield of faith, with
which you can extinguish all the flaming darts of the evil one.

Rejoice not over me, O my enemy; when I fall, I shall rise; when I sit in
darkness, the Lord will be a light to me.

Luke 10:19; 1 Pet. 5:8; James 4:7; Eph. 6:11–16; Mic. 7:8

MORNING

He is altogether desirable.

May my meditation be pleasing to him.—My beloved is . . . distinguished among ten thousand.—"A cornerstone chosen and precious, and whoever believes in him will not be put to shame."—You are the most handsome of the sons of men; grace is poured upon your lips.—God has highly exalted him and bestowed on him the name that is above every name.—In him all the fullness of God was pleased to dwell.

Though you have not seen him, you love him. Though you do not now see him, you believe in him and rejoice with joy that is inexpressible and filled with glory.

I count everything as loss because of the surpassing worth of knowing Christ Jesus my Lord. For his sake I have suffered the loss of all things and count them as rubbish, in order that I may gain Christ and be found in him, not having a righteousness of my own that comes from the law, but that which comes through faith in Christ, the righteousness from God that depends on faith.

Song 5:16; Ps. 104:34; Song 5:10; 1 Pet. 2:6; Ps. 45:2;
Phil. 2:9; Col. 1:19; 1 Pet. 1:8; Phil. 3:8–9

EVENING

David strengthened himself in the Lord his God.

"Lord, to whom shall we go? You have the words of eternal life."—I know whom I have believed, and I am convinced that he is able to guard until that Day what has been entrusted to me.

In my distress I called upon the Lord; to my God I cried for help. From his temple he heard my voice, and my cry to him reached his ears. . . . They confronted me in the day of my calamity, but the Lord was my support. He brought me out into a broad place; he rescued me, because he delighted in me.

I will bless the Lord at all times; his praise shall continually be in my mouth. My soul makes its boast in the Lord; let the humble hear and be glad. Oh, magnify the Lord with me, and let us exalt his name together! I sought the Lord, and he answered me and delivered me from all my fears. . . . Oh taste and see that the Lord is good! Blessed is the man who takes refuge in him!

1 Sam. 30:6; John 6:68; 2 Tim. 1:12; Ps. 18:6, 18–19; Ps. 34:1–4, 8

MORNING

It is good that one should wait quietly
for the salvation of the Lord.

"Has God forgotten to be gracious? Has he in anger shut up his compassion?"—I had said in my alarm, "I am cut off from your sight." But you heard the voice of my pleas for mercy when I cried to you for help.

"Will not God give justice to his elect, who cry to him day and night? Will he delay long over them? I tell you, he will give justice to them speedily."—Wait for the Lord, and he will deliver you.—Be still before the Lord and wait patiently for him; fret not yourself over the one who prospers in his way, over the man who carries out evil devices!

"You will not need to fight in this battle. Stand firm, hold your position, and see the salvation of the Lord."

Let us not grow weary of doing good, for in due season we will reap, if we do not give up.—See how the farmer waits for the precious fruit of the earth, being patient about it, until it receives the early and the late rains.

Lam. 3:26; Ps. 77:9; Ps. 32:22; Luke 18:7-8; Prov. 20:22;
Ps. 37:7; 2 Chron. 20:17; Gal. 6:9; James 5:7

EVENING

"Catch the foxes for us, the little foxes that spoil the
vineyards, for our vineyards are in blossom."

Who can discern his errors? Declare me innocent from hidden faults.—See to it that no one fails to obtain the grace of God; that no "root of bitterness" springs up and causes trouble, and by it many become defiled.—You were running well. Who hindered you from obeying the truth?

He who began a good work in you will bring it to completion at the day of Jesus Christ. . . . Only let your manner of life be worthy of the gospel of Christ.—The tongue is a small member, yet it boasts of great things. How great a forest is set ablaze by such a small fire! And the tongue is a fire, a world of unrighteousness. The tongue is set among our members, staining the whole body, setting on fire the entire course of life, and set on fire by hell. . . . No human being can tame the tongue. It is a restless evil, full of deadly poison.—Let your speech always be gracious, seasoned with salt.

Song 2:15; Ps. 19:12; Heb. 12:15; Gal. 5:7; Phil. 1:6, 27;
James 3:5-6, 8; Col. 4:6

MORNING

"Not by might, nor by power, but by my Spirit, says the Lord of hosts."

Who has measured the Spirit of the Lord, or what man shows him his counsel?—God chose what is foolish in the world to shame the wise; God chose what is weak in the world to shame the strong; God chose what is low and despised in the world, even things that are not, to bring to nothing things that are, so that no human being might boast in the presence of God.

"The wind blows where it wishes, and you hear its sound, but you do not know where it comes from or where it goes. So it is with everyone who is born of the Spirit."—Born, not of blood nor of the will of the flesh nor of the will of man, but of God.

"My Spirit remains in your midst. Fear not."—"The battle is not yours but God's."—"The Lord saves not with sword and spear. For the battle is the Lord's."

Zech. 4:6; Isa. 40:13; 1 Cor. 1:27–29; John 3:8; John 1:13;
Hag. 2:5; 2 Chron. 20:15; 1 Sam. 17:47

EVENING

"Do as you have spoken."

Confirm to your servant your promise, that you may be feared. . . . Then shall I have an answer for him who taunts me, for I trust in your word. . . . Remember your word to your servant, in which you have made me hope. . . . Your statutes have been my songs in the house of my sojourning. . . . The law of your mouth is better to me than thousands of gold and silver pieces . . . . Forever, O Lord, your word is firmly fixed in the heavens. Your faithfulness endures to all generations.

When God desired to show more convincingly to the heirs of the promise the unchangeable character of his purpose, he guaranteed it with an oath, so that by two unchangeable things, in which it is impossible for God to lie, we who have fled for refuge might have strong encouragement to hold fast to the hope set before us. We have this as a sure and steadfast anchor of the soul, a hope that enters into the inner place behind the curtain, where Jesus has gone as a forerunner on our behalf.

Precious and very great promises.

2 Sam. 7:25; Ps. 119:38, 42, 49, 54, 72, 89–90; Heb. 6:17–20; 2 Pet. 1:4

MORNING

Blessed is the one who listens to me, watching daily at my gates, waiting beside my doors.

Behold, as the eyes of servants look to the hand of their master, as the eyes of a maidservant to the hand of her mistress, so our eyes look to the Lord our God, till he has mercy upon us.

"It shall be a regular burnt offering throughout your generations at the entrance of the tent of meeting before the Lord, where I will meet with you, to speak to you there."—"In every place where I cause my name to be remembered I will come to you and bless you."

"Where two or three are gathered in my name, there am I among them."

"The hour is coming, and is now here, when the true worshipers will worship the Father in spirit and truth, for the Father is seeking such people to worship him. God is spirit, and those who worship him must worship in spirit and truth."

Praying at all times in the Spirit, with all prayer and supplication.—Pray without ceasing.

Prov. 8:34; Ps. 123:2; Ex. 29:42; Ex. 20:24; Matt. 18:20;
John 4:23–24; Eph. 6:18; 1 Thess. 5:17

EVENING

His name shall be called Wonderful Counselor.

The Spirit of the Lord shall rest upon him, the Spirit of wisdom and understanding, the Spirit of counsel and might, the Spirit of knowledge and the fear of the Lord. And his delight shall be in the fear of the Lord.

Does not wisdom call? Does not understanding raise her voice? . . . To you, O men, I call, and my cry is to the children of man. O simple ones, learn prudence; O fools, learn sense. Hear, for I will speak noble things, and from my lips will come what is right. . . . I have counsel and sound wisdom; I have insight; I have strength.—The Lord of hosts . . . is wonderful in counsel and excellent in wisdom.—If any of you lacks wisdom, let him ask God, who gives generously to all without reproach, and it will be given him.—Trust in the Lord with all your heart, and do not lean on your own understanding. In all your ways acknowledge him, and he will make straight your paths.

Isa. 9:6; Isa. 11:2–3; Prov. 8:1, 4–6, 14; Isa. 28:29; James 1:5; Prov. 3:5–6

MORNING

Always seek to do good.

To this you have been called, because Christ also suffered for you, leaving you an example, so that you might follow in his steps. He committed no sin, neither was deceit found in his mouth. When he was reviled, he did not revile in return . . . but continued entrusting himself to him who judges justly.— Consider him who endured from sinners such hostility against himself, so that you may not grow weary or fainthearted.

Let us also lay aside every weight, and sin which clings so closely, and let us run with endurance the race that is set before us, looking to Jesus, the founder and perfecter of our faith, who for the joy that was set before him endured the cross, despising the shame, and is seated at the right hand of the throne of God.

Finally, brothers, whatever is true, whatever is honorable, whatever is just, whatever is pure, whatever is lovely, whatever is commendable, if there is any excellence, if there is anything worthy of praise, think about these things.

1 Thess. 5:15; 1 Pet. 2:21–23; Heb. 12:3; Heb. 12:1–2; Phil. 4:8

EVENING

Mighty God.

You are the most handsome of the sons of men; grace is poured upon your lips; therefore God has blessed you forever. Gird your sword on your thigh, O mighty one, in your splendor and majesty! In your majesty ride out victoriously. . . . Your throne, O God, is forever and ever. The scepter of your kingdom is a scepter of uprightness.—Of old you spoke in a vision to your godly one, and said: "I have granted help to one who is mighty."—"The man who stands next to me," declares the Lord of hosts.

"Behold, God is my salvation; I will trust, and will not be afraid; for the Lord God is my strength and my song, and he has become my salvation."— Thanks be to God, who in Christ always leads us in triumphal procession.— Now to him who is able to keep you from stumbling and to present you blameless before the presence of his glory with great joy, to the only God, our Savior, through Jesus Christ our Lord, be glory, majesty, dominion, and authority, before all time and now and forever.

Isa. 9:6; Ps. 45:2–4, 6; Ps. 89:19; Zech. 13:7; Isa. 12:2;
2 Cor. 2:14; Jude 24–25

MORNING

The ways of the Lord are right, and the upright walk in them, but transgressors stumble in them.

So the honor is for you who believe, but for those who do not believe, . . . "A stone of stumbling, and a rock of offense."—The way of the Lord is a stronghold to the blameless, but destruction to evildoers.

"He who has ears to hear, let him hear."—Whoever is wise, let him attend to these things; let them consider the steadfast love of the Lord.—"The eye is the lamp of the body. So, if your eye is healthy, your whole body will be full of light."—"If anyone's will is to do God's will, he will know whether the teaching is from God."—"To the one who has, more will be given, and he will have an abundance."—"Whoever is of God hears the words of God. The reason why you do not hear them is that you are not of God."—"You refuse to come to me that you may have life."—"My sheep hear my voice, and I know them, and they follow me."

Hos. 14:9; 1 Pet. 2:7–8; Prov. 10:29; Matt. 11:15; Ps. 107:43; Matt. 6:22; John 7:17; Matt. 13:12; John 8:47; John 5:40; John 10:27

EVENING

Everlasting Father.

"Hear, O Israel: The Lord our God, the Lord is one."

"I and the Father are one. . . . The Father is in me and I am in the Father."—"If you knew me, you would know my Father also."—Philip said to him, "Lord, show us the Father, and it is enough for us." Jesus said to him, "Have I been with you so long, and you still do not know me, Philip? Whoever has seen me has seen the Father."—"Behold, I and the children God has given me."—Out of the anguish of his soul he shall see and be satisfied.—"I am the Alpha and the Omega," says the Lord God, "who is and who was and who is to come, the Almighty."—"Before Abraham was, I am."—God said to Moses, "I AM WHO I AM." And he said, "Say this to the people of Israel, 'I AM has sent me to you.'"

Of the Son he says, "Your throne, O God, is forever and ever."—He is before all things, and in him all things hold together.—In him the whole fullness of deity dwells bodily.

Isa. 9:6; Deut. 6:4; John 10:30, 38; John 8:19; John 14:8–9; Heb. 2:13; Isa. 53:11; Rev. 1:8; John 8:58; Ex. 3:14; Heb. 1:8; Col. 1:17; Col. 2:9

MORNING

Now for a little while, if necessary,
you have been grieved by various trials.

Beloved, do not be surprised at the fiery trial when it comes upon you to test you, as though something strange were happening to you. But rejoice insofar as you share Christ's sufferings, that you may also rejoice and be glad when his glory is revealed.—The exhortation that addresses you as sons . . . "My son, do not regard lightly the discipline of the Lord, nor be weary when reproved by him."—For the moment all discipline seems painful rather than pleasant, but later it yields the peaceful fruit of righteousness to those who have been trained by it.

We do not have a high priest who is unable to sympathize with our weaknesses, but one who in every respect has been tempted as we are, yet without sin.—For because he himself has suffered when tempted, he is able to help those who are being tempted.—God is faithful, and he will not let you be tempted beyond your ability.

1 Pet. 1:6; 1 Pet. 4:12-13; Heb. 12:5; Heb. 12:11; Heb. 4:15; Heb. 2:18; 1 Cor. 10:13

EVENING

Prince of Peace.

May he judge your people with righteousness, and your poor with justice! Let the mountains bear prosperity for the people, and the hills, in righteousness! . . . May he be like rain that falls on the mown grass, like showers that water the earth! In his days may the righteous flourish, and peace abound, till the moon be no more!—"Glory to God, . . . and on earth peace among those with whom he is pleased!"

"Because of the tender mercy of our God, whereby the sunrise shall visit us from on high to give light to those who sit in darkness and in the shadow of death, to guide our feet into the way of peace."—"Peace through Jesus Christ (he is Lord of all)."

"I have said these things to you, that in me you may have peace. In the world you will have tribulation. But take heart; I have overcome the world."— "Peace I leave with you; my peace I give to you. Not as the world gives do I give to you."—The peace of God, which surpasses all understanding, will guard your hearts and your minds in Christ Jesus.

Isa. 9:6; Ps. 72:2-3, 6-7; Luke 2:14; Luke 1:78-79;
Acts 10:36; John 16:33; John 14:27; Phil. 4:7

MORNING

"Take the finest spices. . . . And you shall make
of these a sacred anointing oil."

"It shall not be poured on the body of an ordinary person, and you shall make no other like it in composition. It is holy, and it shall be holy to you."—One Spirit.—Now there are varieties of gifts, but the same Spirit.

Your God . . . has anointed you with the oil of gladness beyond your companions.—God anointed Jesus of Nazareth with the Holy Spirit and with power.—God . . . gives the Spirit without measure.

From his fullness we have all received.—But as his anointing teaches you about everything, and is true, and is no lie—just as it has taught you, abide in him.—It is God who . . . has anointed us, and who has also put his seal on us and given us his Spirit in our hearts as a guarantee.

The fruit of the Spirit is love, joy, peace, patience, kindness, goodness, faithfulness, gentleness, self-control; against such things there is no law.

Ex. 20:23, 25; Ex. 30:32; Eph. 4:4; 1 Cor. 12:4; Ps. 45:7; Acts 10:38;
John 3:34; John 1:16; 1 John 2:27; 2 Cor. 1:21–22; Gal. 5:22–23

EVENING

The present form of this world is passing away.

Thus all the days of Methuselah were 969 years, and he died.

Let the lowly brother boast in his exaltation, and the rich in his humiliation, because like a flower of the grass he will pass away. For the sun rises with its scorching heat and withers the grass; its flower falls, and its beauty perishes. So also will the rich man fade away in the midst of his pursuits.— What is your life? For you are a mist that appears for a little time and then vanishes.—The world is passing away along with its desires, but whoever does the will of God abides forever.

"O Lord, make me know my end and what is the measure of my days; let me know how fleeting I am!"—While people are saying, "There is peace and security," then sudden destruction will come upon them as labor pains come upon a pregnant woman, and they will not escape. But you are not in darkness, brothers, for that day to surprise you like a thief.

1 Cor. 7:31; Gen. 5:27; James 1:9–11; James 4:14;
1 John 2:17; Ps. 39:4; 1 Thess. 5:3–4

MORNING

When Christ who is your life appears, then you also will appear with him in glory.

"I am the resurrection and the life. Whoever believes in me, though he die, yet shall he live."—God gave us eternal life, and this life is in his Son. Whoever has the Son has life; whoever does not have the Son of God does not have life.

The Lord himself will descend from heaven with a cry of command, with the voice of an archangel, and with the sound of the trumpet of God. And the dead in Christ will rise first. Then we who are alive, who are left, will be caught up together with them in the clouds to meet the Lord in the air, and so we will always be with the Lord. Therefore encourage one another with these words.—When he appears we shall be like him, because we shall see him as he is.—It is sown in dishonor; it is raised in glory. It is sown in weakness; it is raised in power.

"If I go and prepare a place for you, I will come again and will take you to myself, that where I am you may be also."

Col. 3:4; John 11:25; 1 John 5:11–12; 1 Thess. 4:16–18;
1 John 3:2; 1 Cor. 15:43; John 14:3

EVENING

Lead me in your truth and teach me.

"When the Spirit of truth comes, he will guide you into all the truth."—You have been anointed by the Holy One, and you all have knowledge.

To the teaching and to the testimony! If they will not speak according to this word, it is because they have no dawn.—All Scripture is breathed out by God and profitable for teaching, for reproof, for correction, and for training in righteousness, that the man of God may be complete, equipped for every good work.—The sacred writings . . . are able to make you wise for salvation through faith in Christ Jesus.

I will instruct you and teach you in the way you should go; I will counsel you with my eye upon you.—"The eye is the lamp of the body. So, if your eye is healthy, your whole body will be full of light."—"If anyone's will is to do God's will, he will know whether the teaching is from God."—It shall belong to those who walk on the way; even if they are fools, they shall not go astray.

Ps. 25:5; John 16:13; 1 John 2:20; Isa. 8:20; 2 Tim. 3:16–17;
2 Tim. 3:15; Ps. 32:8; Matt. 6:22; John 7:17; Isa. 35:8

MORNING

Let them thank the Lord for his steadfast love,
for his wondrous works to the children of man!

Oh, taste and see that the Lord is good! Blessed is the man who takes refuge in him!—Oh, how abundant is your goodness, which you have stored up for those who fear you.

"The people whom I formed for myself that they might declare my praise."—He predestined us for adoption as sons through Jesus Christ, according to the purpose of his will, to the praise of his glorious grace, with which he has blessed us in the Beloved . . . so that we who were the first to hope in Christ might be to the praise of his glory.

How great is his goodness, and how great his beauty!—The Lord is good to all, and his mercy is over all that he has made. All your works shall give thanks to you, O Lord, and all your saints shall bless you! They shall speak of the glory of your kingdom and tell of your power, to make known to the children of man your mighty deeds, and the glorious splendor of your kingdom.

Ps. 107:8; Ps. 34:8; Ps. 31:19; Isa. 43:21; Eph. 1:5–6, 12;
Zech. 9:17; Ps. 145:9–12

EVENING

Behold, we consider those blessed who remained steadfast.

We rejoice in our sufferings, knowing that suffering produces endurance, and endurance produces character, and character produces hope, and hope does not put us to shame, because God's love has been poured into our hearts through the Holy Spirit who has been given to us.—For the moment all discipline seems painful rather than pleasant, but later it yields the peaceful fruit of righteousness to those who have been trained by it.—Count it all joy, my brothers, when you meet trials of various kinds, for you know that the testing of your faith produces steadfastness. And let steadfastness have its full effect, that you may be perfect and complete, lacking in nothing. . . . Blessed is the man who remains steadfast under trial, for when he has stood the test he will receive the crown of life, which God has promised to those who love him.—Therefore I will boast all the more gladly of my weaknesses, so that the power of Christ may rest upon me. . . . For when I am weak, then I am strong.

James 5:11; Rom. 5:3–5; Heb. 12:11; James 1:2–4, 12; 2 Cor. 12:9–10

MORNING

But since we belong to the day, let us be sober,
having put on the breastplate of faith and love,
and for a helmet the hope of salvation.

Therefore, preparing your minds for action, and being sober-minded, set your hope fully on the grace that will be brought to you at the revelation of Jesus Christ.—Stand therefore, having fastened on the belt of truth, and having put on the breastplate of righteousness. . . . In all circumstances take up the shield of faith, with which you can extinguish all the flaming darts of the evil one; and take the helmet of salvation, and the sword of the Spirit, which is the word of God.

He will swallow up death forever; and the Lord God will wipe away tears from all faces, and the reproach of his people he will take away from all the earth, for the Lord has spoken. It will be said on that day, "Behold, this is our God; we have waited for him, that he might save us. This is the Lord; . . . let us be glad and rejoice in his salvation."

Now faith is the assurance of things hoped for, the conviction of things not seen.

1 Thess. 5:8; 1 Pet. 1:13; Eph. 6:14, 16–17; Isa. 25:8–9; Heb. 11:1

EVENING

The people of Israel encamped before them like two little
flocks of goats, but the Syrians filled the country.

"Thus says the Lord, 'Because the Syrians have said, "The Lord is a god of the hills but he is not a god of the valleys," therefore I will give all this great multitude into your hand, and you shall know that I am the Lord.'" And they encamped opposite one another seven days. Then on the seventh day the battle was joined. And the people of Israel struck down of the Syrians 100,000 foot soldiers in one day.—Little children, you are from God and have overcome them, for he who is in you is greater than he who is in the world.

Fear not, for I am with you; be not dismayed, for I am your God; I will strengthen you, I will help you, I will uphold you with my righteous right hand.

"They will fight against you, but they shall not prevail against you, for I am with you, declares the Lord, to deliver you."

1 Kings 20:27; 1 Kings 20:28–29; 1 John 4:4; Isa. 41:10; Jer. 1:19

MORNING

"I have granted help to one who is mighty; I have exalted one chosen from the people."

"I, I am the Lord, and besides me there is no savior."—There is one God, and there is one mediator between God and men, the man Christ Jesus.—"There is no other name under heaven given among men by which we must be saved."

Mighty God.—[He] emptied himself, by taking the form of a servant, being born in the likeness of men. And being found in human form, he humbled himself by becoming obedient to the point of death, even death on a cross. Therefore God has highly exalted him and bestowed on him the name that is above every name.—We see him who for a little while was made lower than the angels, namely Jesus, crowned with glory and honor because of the suffering of death, so that by the grace of God he might taste death for everyone.—Since therefore the children share in flesh and blood, he himself likewise partook of the same things.

Ps. 89:19; Isa. 43:11; 1 Tim. 2:5; Acts 4:12; Isa. 9:6;
Phil. 2:7–9; Heb. 2:9; Heb. 2:14

EVENING

"Gather to me my faithful ones, who made a covenant with me by sacrifice!"

Christ, having been offered once to bear the sins of many, will appear a second time, not to deal with sin but to save those who are eagerly waiting for him.—He is the mediator of a new covenant, so that those who are called may receive the promised eternal inheritance, since a death has occurred that redeems them from the transgressions committed under the first covenant.

"Father, I desire that they also, whom you have given me, may be with me where I am."—"Then he will send out the angels and gather his elect from the four winds, from the ends of the earth to the ends of heaven."—"If your outcasts are in the uttermost parts of heaven, from there the Lord your God will gather you, and from there he will take you."

The dead in Christ will rise first. Then we who are alive, who are left, will be caught up together with them in the clouds to meet the Lord in the air, and so we will always be with the Lord.

Ps. 50:5; Heb. 9:28; Heb. 9:15; John 17:24; Mark 13:27;
Deut. 30:4; 1 Thess. 4:16–17

MORNING

Bearing fruit in every good work and increasing in the knowledge of God.

I appeal to you therefore, brothers, by the mercies of God, to pre-sent your bodies as a living sacrifice, holy and acceptable to God, which is your spiritual worship. Do not be conformed to this world, but be transformed by the renewal of your mind, that by testing you may discern what is the will of God, what is good and acceptable and perfect.—Just as you once presented your members as slaves to impurity and to lawlessness leading to more lawlessness, so now present your members as slaves to righteousness leading to sanctification.—Neither circumcision counts for anything, nor uncircumcision, but a new creation. And as for all who walk by this rule, peace and mercy be upon them.

"By this my Father is glorified, that you bear much fruit and so prove to be my disciples."—"I chose you and appointed you that you should go and bear fruit and that your fruit should abide, so that whatever you ask the Father in my name, he may give it to you."

Col. 1:10; Rom. 12:1–2; Rom. 6:19; Gal. 6:15–16; John 15:8; John 15:16

EVENING

I sought him, but found him not.

Return, O Israel, to the Lord your God, for you have stumbled because of your iniquity. Take with you words and return to the Lord; say to him, "Take away all iniquity; accept what is good."

Let no one say when he is tempted, "I am being tempted by God. . . ." But each person is tempted when he is lured and enticed by his own desire. . . . Do not be deceived, my beloved brothers. Every good gift and every perfect gift is from above, coming down from the Father of lights with whom there is no variation or shadow due to change.

Wait for the Lord; be strong, and let your heart take courage; wait for the Lord!—It is good that one should wait quietly for the salvation of the Lord.—"Will not God give justice to his elect, who cry to him day and night? Will he delay long over them?"

For God alone my soul waits in silence; from him comes my salvation. . . . For God alone, O my soul, wait in silence, for my hope is from him.

Song 3:1; Hos. 4:1–2; James 1:13–17; Ps. 27:14; Lam. 3:26;
Luke 18:7; Ps. 62:1, 5

MORNING

He led them in safety.

I walk in the way of righteousness, in the paths of justice.

"Behold, I send an angel before you to guard you on the way and to bring you to the place that I have prepared."—In all their affliction he was afflicted, and the angel of his presence saved them; in his love and in his pity he redeemed them; he lifted them up and carried them all the days of old.

Not by their own sword did they win the land, nor did their own arm save them, but your right hand and your arm, and the light of your face, for you delighted in them.—So you led your people, to make for yourself a glorious name.

Lead me, O Lord, in your righteousness because of my enemies; make your way straight before me.—Send out your light and your truth; let them lead me; let them bring me to your holy hill and to your dwelling! Then I will go to the altar of God, to God my exceeding joy, and I will praise you with the lyre, O God, my God.

Ps. 78:53; Prov. 8:20; Ex. 23:20; Isa. 63:9; Ps. 44:3;
Isa. 63:14; Ps. 5:8; Ps. 43:3-4

EVENING

You were washed, you were sanctified, you were justified.

The blood of Jesus his Son cleanses us from all sin.—Upon him was the chastisement that brought us peace, and with his wounds we are healed.—Christ loved the church and gave himself up for her, that he might sanctify her, having cleansed her by the washing of water with the word, so that he might present the church to himself in splendor, without spot or wrinkle or any such thing, that she might be holy and without blemish.—"It was granted her to clothe herself with fine linen, bright and pure"—for the fine linen is the righteous deeds of the saints.—Let us draw near with a true heart in full assurance of faith, with our hearts sprinkled clean from an evil conscience and our bodies washed with pure water.

Who shall bring any charge against God's elect? It is God who justifies.—Blessed is the one whose transgression is forgiven. . . . Blessed is the man against whom the Lord counts no iniquity, and in whose spirit there is no deceit.

1 Cor. 6:11; 1 John 1:7; Isa. 53:5; Eph. 5:25-27; Rev. 19:8;
Heb. 10:22; Rom. 8:33; Ps. 32:1-2

MORNING

Godly grief produces a repentance that leads to salvation without regret.

Peter remembered the saying of Jesus, "Before the rooster crows, you will deny me three times." And he went out and wept bitterly.—If we confess our sins, he is faithful and just to forgive us our sins and to cleanse us from all unrighteousness.—The blood of Jesus his Son cleanses us from all sin.

My iniquities have overtaken me, and I cannot see; they are more than the hairs of my head; my heart fails me. Be pleased, O Lord, to deliver me! O Lord, make haste to help me!

"So you, by the help of your God, return, hold fast to love and justice, and wait continually for your God."

The sacrifices of God are a broken spirit; a broken and contrite heart, O God, you will not despise.—He heals the brokenhearted and binds up their wounds.—He has told you, O man, what is good; and what does the Lord require of you but to do justice, and to love kindness, and to walk humbly with your God?

2 Cor. 7:10; Matt. 26:75; 1 John 1:9; 1 John 1:7; Ps. 40:12–13;
Hos. 12:6; Ps. 51:17; Ps. 147:3; Mic. 6:8

EVENING

"'Is all well with you? . . .'" And she answered, "All is well."

We have the same spirit of faith.—As punished, and yet not killed; as sorrowful, yet always rejoicing; as poor, yet making many rich; as having nothing, yet possessing everything.

We are afflicted in every way, but not crushed; perplexed, but not driven to despair; persecuted, but not forsaken; struck down, but not destroyed; always carrying in the body the death of Jesus, so that the life of Jesus may also be manifested in our bodies. . . . So we do not lose heart. Though our outer self is wasting away, our inner self is being renewed day by day. For this light momentary affliction is preparing for us an eternal weight of glory beyond all comparison, as we look not to the things that are seen but to the things that are unseen.

Beloved, I pray that all may go well with you and that you may be in good health, as it goes well with your soul.

2 Kings 4:26; 2 Cor. 4:13; 2 Cor. 6:9–10; 2 Cor. 4:8–10, 16–18; 3 John 2

MORNING

*Christ loved the church and gave himself up for her,
that he might sanctify her, having cleansed her by
the washing of water with the word.*

Walk in love, as Christ loved us and gave himself up for us, a fragrant offering and sacrifice to God.

You have been born again, not of perishable seed but of imperishable, through the living and abiding word of God.—"Sanctify them in the truth; your word is truth."—"Unless one is born of water and the Spirit, he cannot enter the kingdom of God."—He saved us, not because of works done by us in righteousness, but according to his own mercy, by the washing of regeneration and renewal of the Holy Spirit.—Your promise gives me life.

The law of the Lord is perfect, reviving the soul; the testimony of the Lord is sure, making wise the simple; the precepts of the Lord are right, rejoicing the heart; the commandment of the Lord is pure, enlightening the eyes.

Eph. 5:25–26; Eph. 5:2; 1 Pet. 1:23; John 17:17; John 3:5;
Titus 3:5; Ps. 119:50; Ps. 19:7–8

EVENING

Through him we both have access in one Spirit to the Father.

"I in them and you in me, that they may become perfectly one."

"Whatever you ask in my name, this I will do, that the Father may be glorified in the Son. If you ask me anything in my name, I will do it. . . . And I will ask the Father, and he will give you another Helper, to be with you forever, even the Spirit of truth, whom the world cannot receive, because it neither sees him nor knows him. You know him, for he dwells with you and will be in you."—There is one body and one Spirit—just as you were called to the one hope that belongs to your call—one Lord, one faith, one baptism, one God and Father of all, who is over all and through all and in all.—"When you pray, say: Father, hallowed be your name."

Therefore, brothers, since we have confidence to enter the holy places by the blood of Jesus, by the new and living way . . . let us draw near.

Eph. 2:18; John 17:23; John 14:13–14, 16–17; Eph. 4:4–6;
Luke 11:2; Heb. 10:19–20, 22

MORNING

You are my help and my deliverer; do not delay, O my God!

The steps of a man are established by the Lord, when he delights in his way; though he fall, he shall not be cast headlong, for the Lord upholds his hand.— In the fear of the Lord one has strong confidence, and his children will have a refuge.—"Who are you that you are afraid of man who dies, of the son of man who is made like grass, and have forgotten the Lord, your Maker?"

"I am with you to deliver you."—"Be strong and courageous. Do not fear or be in dread of them, for it is the Lord your God who goes with you. He will not leave you or forsake you."

But I will sing of your strength; I will sing aloud of your steadfast love in the morning. For you have been to me a fortress and a refuge in the day of my distress.—You are a hiding place for me; you preserve me from trouble; you surround me with shouts of deliverance.

Ps. 40:17; Ps. 37:23–24; Prov. 14:26; Isa. 51:12–13;
Jer. 1:8; Deut. 31:6; Ps. 59:16; Ps. 32:7

EVENING

"What will you do in the thicket of the Jordan?"

Now the Jordan overflows all its banks throughout the time of harvest.

The priests bearing the ark of the covenant of the Lord stood firmly on dry ground in the midst of the Jordan, and all Israel was passing over on dry ground until all the nation finished passing over the Jordan.

We see him who for a little while was made lower than the angels, namely Jesus, crowned with glory and honor because of the suffering of death, so that by the grace of God he might taste death for everyone.

Even though I walk through the valley of the shadow of death, I will fear no evil, for you are with me; your rod and your staff, they comfort me.— "When you pass through the waters, I will be with you; and through the rivers, they shall not overwhelm you."

"Fear not, I am the first and the last, and the living one. I died, and behold I am alive forevermore, and I have the keys of Death and Hades."

Jer. 12:5; Josh. 3:15; Josh 3:17; Heb. 2:9; Ps. 23:4; Isa. 43:2; Rev. 1:17–18

MORNING

God is faithful, by whom you were called into the fellowship of his Son, Jesus Christ our Lord.

Let us hold fast the confession of our hope without wavering, for he who promised is faithful.—God said, "I will make my dwelling among them and walk among them, and I will be their God, and they shall be my people."— Indeed our fellowship is with the Father and with his Son Jesus Christ.— Rejoice insofar as you share Christ's sufferings, that you may also rejoice and be glad when his glory is revealed.

That you, being rooted and grounded in love, may have strength to comprehend with all the saints what is the breadth and length and height and depth, and to know the love of Christ that surpasses knowledge, that you may be filled with all the fullness of God.

Whoever confesses that Jesus is the Son of God, God abides in him, and he in God.—Whoever keeps his commandments abides in God, and God in him.

1 Cor. 1:9; Heb. 10:23; 2 Cor. 6:16; 1 John 1:3; 1 Pet. 4:13;
Eph. 3:17–19; 1 John 4:15; 1 John 3:24

EVENING

We are his workmanship.

They quarried out great, costly stones in order to lay the foundation of the house with dressed stones.—When the house was built, it was with stone prepared at the quarry, so that neither hammer nor axe nor any tool of iron was heard in the house while it was being built.

You yourselves like living stones are being built up as a spiritual house.—Built on the foundation of the apostles and prophets, Christ Jesus himself being the cornerstone, in whom the whole structure, being joined together, grows into a holy temple in the Lord. In him you also are being built together into a dwelling place for God by the Spirit.—Once you were not a people, but now you are God's people.

You are . . . God's building.—Therefore, if anyone is in Christ, he is a new creation. The old has passed away; behold, the new has come.—He who has prepared us for this very thing is God, who has given us the Spirit as a guarantee.

Eph. 2:10; 1 Kings 5:17; 1 Kings 6:7; 1 Pet. 2:5; Eph. 2:20–22;
1 Pet. 2:10; 1 Cor. 3:9; 1 Cor. 5:17; 2 Cor. 5:5

MORNING

"Sanctify them in the truth; your word is truth."

"Already you are clean because of the word that I have spoken to you."—Let the word of Christ dwell in you richly, . . . in all wisdom.

How can a young man keep his way pure? By guarding it according to your word. With my whole heart I seek you; let me not wander from your commandments!

Wisdom will come into your heart, and knowledge will be pleasant to your soul; discretion will watch over you, understanding will guard you.

"My foot has held fast to his steps; I have kept his way and have not turned aside. I have not departed from the commandment of his lips; I have treasured the words of his mouth more than my portion of food."—I have more understanding than all my teachers, for your testimonies are my meditation.—"If you abide in my word, you are truly my disciples, and you will know the truth, and the truth will set you free."

John 17:17; John 15:3; Col. 3:16; Ps. 119:9–10; Prov. 2:10–11;
Job 23:11–12; Ps. 119:99; John 8:31–32

EVENING

Fellow citizens with the saints.

You have come to Mount Zion and to the city of the living God, the heavenly Jerusalem, and to innumerable angels in festal gathering, and to the assembly of the firstborn who are enrolled in heaven, and to God, the judge of all, and to the spirits of the righteous made perfect.

These all died in faith, not having received the things promised, but having seen them and greeted them from afar, and having acknowledged that they were strangers and exiles on the earth.—Our citizenship is in heaven, and from it we await a Savior, the Lord Jesus Christ, who will transform our lowly body to be like his glorious body, by the power that enables him even to subject all things to himself.—The Father . . . has delivered us from the domain of darkness and transferred us to the kingdom of his beloved Son.

I urge you as sojourners and exiles to abstain from the passions of the flesh, which wage war against your soul.

Eph. 2:19; Heb. 12:22–23; Heb. 11:13; Phil. 3:20–21;
Col. 1:12–13; 1 Pet. 2:11

MORNING

Your thoughts are very deep!

We have not ceased to pray for you, asking that you may be filled with the knowledge of his will in all spiritual wisdom and understanding.—That you, being rooted and grounded in love, may have strength to comprehend with all the saints what is the breadth and length and height and depth, and to know the love of Christ that surpasses knowledge, that you may be filled with all the fullness of God.

Oh, the depth of the riches and wisdom and knowledge of God! How unsearchable are his judgments and how inscrutable his ways!—For my thoughts are not your thoughts, neither are your ways my ways, declares the Lord. For as the heavens are higher than the earth, so are my ways higher than your ways and my thoughts than your thoughts.—You have multiplied, O Lord my God, your wondrous deeds and your thoughts toward us; none can compare with you! I will proclaim and tell of them, yet they are more than can be told.

Ps. 92:5; Col. 1:9; Eph. 3:17–19; Rom. 11:33; Isa. 55:8–9; Ps. 40:5

EVENING

Whatever one sows, that will he also reap.

"As I have seen, those who plow iniquity and sow trouble reap the same."—They sow the wind, and they shall reap the whirlwind.—The one who sows to his own flesh will from the flesh reap corruption.

One who sows righteousness gets a sure reward.—The one who sows to the Spirit will from the Spirit reap eternal life. And let us not grow weary of doing good, for in due season we will reap, if we do not give up. So then, as we have opportunity, let us do good to everyone, and especially to those who are of the household of faith.

One gives freely, yet grows all the richer; another withholds what he should give, and only suffers want. Whoever brings blessing will be enriched, and one who waters will himself be watered.—Whoever sows sparingly will also reap sparingly, and whoever sows bountifully will also reap bountifully.

Gal. 6:7; Job 4:8; Hos. 8:7; Gal. 6:8; Prov. 11:18;
Gal. 6:8–10; Prov. 11:24–25; 2 Cor. 9:6

MORNING

He removed them with his fierce breath in the day of the east wind.

"Let us fall into the hand of the Lord, for his mercy is great."—"I am with you to save you, declares the Lord. . . . I will discipline you in just measure, and I will by no means leave you unpunished."—He will not always chide, nor will he keep his anger forever. He does not deal with us according to our sins, nor repay us according to our iniquities. . . . For he knows our frame; he remembers that we are dust.—"I will spare them as a man spares his son who serves him."

God is faithful, and he will not let you be tempted beyond your ability, but with the temptation he will also provide the way of escape, that you may be able to endure it.—"Satan demanded to have you, that he might sift you like wheat, but I have prayed for you that your faith may not fail."—You have been a stronghold to the poor, a stronghold to the needy in his distress, a shelter from the storm and a shade from the heat; for the breath of the ruthless is like a storm against a wall.

Isa. 27:8; 2 Sam. 24:14; Jer. 30:11; Ps. 103:9–10, 14; Mal. 3:17;
1 Cor. 10:13; Luke 22:31–32; Isa. 25:4

EVENING

"I did not believe the reports until I came and my own eyes had seen it. And behold, the half was not told me."

"The queen of the South will rise up at the judgment with this generation and condemn it, for she came from the ends of the earth to hear the wisdom of Solomon, and behold, something greater than Solomon is here."—We have seen his glory, glory as of the only Son from the Father, full of grace and truth.

My speech and my message were . . . in demonstration of the Spirit and of power, so that your faith might not rest in the wisdom of men but in the power of God. . . . But, as it is written, "What no eye has seen, nor ear heard, nor the heart of man imagined, what God has prepared for those who love him"—these things God has revealed to us through the Spirit. For the Spirit searches everything, even the depths of God.

Your eyes will behold the king in his beauty.—We shall see him as he is.—"In my flesh I shall see God."—I shall be satisfied.

1 Kings 10:7; Matt. 12:42; John 1:14; 1 Cor. 2:4–5, 9–10;
Isa. 33:17; 1 John 3:2; Job 19:26; Ps. 17:15

MORNING

"You will recognize them by their fruits."

Little children, let no one deceive you. Whoever practices righteousness is righteous, as he is righteous.—Does a spring pour forth from the same opening both fresh and salt water? Can a fig tree, my brothers, bear olives, or a grapevine produce figs? Neither can a salt pond yield fresh water. Who is wise and understanding among you? By his good conduct let him show his works in the meekness of wisdom.—Keep your conduct among the Gentiles honorable, so that when they speak against you as evildoers, they may see your good deeds and glorify God on the day of visitation.

"Either make the tree good and its fruit good, or make the tree bad and its fruit bad, for the tree is known by its fruit."—"The good person out of his good treasure brings forth good, and the evil person out of his evil treasure brings forth evil."—What more was there to do for my vineyard, that I have not done in it?

Matt. 7:20; 1 John 3:7; James 3:11–13; 1 Pet. 2:12;
Matt. 12:33; Matt. 12:35; Isa. 5:4

EVENING

I will make the place of my feet glorious.

Thus says the Lord: "Heaven is my throne, and the earth is my footstool."—"But will God indeed dwell with man on the earth? Behold, heaven and the highest heaven cannot contain you, how much less this house that I have built!"

"Thus says the Lord of hosts: Yet once more, in a little while, I will shake the heavens and the earth and the sea and the dry land. And I will shake all nations, so that the treasures of all nations shall come in, and I will fill this house with glory, says the Lord of hosts. . . . The latter glory of this house shall be greater than the former, says the Lord of hosts."

I saw a new heaven and a new earth, for the first heaven and the first earth had passed away, and the sea was no more. . . . And I heard a loud voice from the throne saying, "Behold, the dwelling place of God is with man. He will dwell with them, and they will be his people, and God himself will be with them as their God."

Isa. 60:13; Isa. 66:1; 2 Chron. 6:18; Hag. 2:6–7, 9; Rev. 21:1, 3

MORNING

When I sit in darkness, the Lord will be a light to me.

"When you pass through the waters, I will be with you; and through the rivers, they shall not overwhelm you; when you walk through fire you shall not be burned, and the flame shall not consume you. For I am the Lord your God, the Holy One of Israel, your Savior."—I will lead the blind in a way that they do not know, in paths that they have not known I will guide them. I will turn the darkness before them into light, the rough places into level ground. These are the things I do, and I do not forsake them.

Even though I walk through the valley of the shadow of death, I will fear no evil, for you are with me; your rod and your staff, they comfort me.—When I am afraid, I put my trust in you. In God, whose word I praise, in God I trust; I shall not be afraid. What can flesh do to me?—The Lord is my light and my salvation; whom shall I fear? The Lord is the stronghold of my life; of whom shall I be afraid?

Mic. 7:8; Isa. 43:2–3; Isa. 42:16; Ps. 23:4; Ps. 56:3–4; Ps. 27:1

EVENING

One God, and . . . one mediator between
God and men, the man Christ Jesus.

"Hear, O Israel: The Lord our God, the Lord is one."—An intermediary implies more than one, but God is one.

We and our fathers have sinned; we have committed iniquity; we have done wickedness. Our fathers, when they were in Egypt, . . . they did not remember the abundance of your steadfast love. . . . Therefore he said he would destroy them—had not Moses, his chosen one, stood in the breach before him, to turn away his wrath from destroying them.

Therefore, holy brothers, you who share in a heavenly calling, consider Jesus, the apostle and high priest of our confession, who was faithful to him who appointed him, just as Moses also was faithful in all God's house.

The covenant he mediates is better, since it is enacted on better promises. . . . "I will be merciful toward their iniquities, and I will remember their sins no more."

1 Tim. 2:5; Deut. 6:4; Gal. 3:20; Ps. 106:6–7, 23; Heb. 3:1–2; Heb. 8:6, 12

MORNING

"Whoever comes to me I will never cast out."

"If he cries to me, I will hear, for I am compassionate."—"I will not spurn them, neither will I abhor them so as to destroy them utterly and break my covenant with them, for I am the Lord their God."—"I will remember my covenant with you in the days of your youth, and I will establish for you an ever-lasting covenant."

"Come now, let us reason together, says the Lord: though your sins are like scarlet, they shall be as white as snow; though they are red like crimson, they shall become like wool."—"Let the wicked forsake his way, and the unrighteous man his thoughts; let him return to the Lord, that he may have compassion on him, and to our God, for he will abundantly pardon."—"Jesus, remember me when you come into your kingdom." And he said to him, "Truly, I say to you, today you will be with me in Paradise."

A bruised reed he will not break, and a faintly burning wick he will not quench.

John 6:37; Ex. 22:27; Lev. 26:44; Ezek. 16:60; Isa. 1:18;
Isa. 55:7; Luke 23:42–43; Isa. 42:3

EVENING

His beloved Son.

Behold, a voice from heaven said, "This is my beloved Son, with whom I am well pleased."—Behold my servant, whom I uphold, my chosen, in whom my soul delights.—The only God, who is at the Father's side.

In this the love of God was made manifest among us, that God sent his only Son into the world, so that we might live through him. In this is love, not that we have loved God but that he loved us and sent his Son to be the propitiation for our sins. . . . So we have come to know and to believe the love that God has for us. God is love.

"The glory that you have given me I have given to them, that they may be one even as we are one, I in them and you in me, that they may become perfectly one, so that the world may know that you sent me and loved them even as you loved me."—See what kind of love the Father has given to us, that we should be called children of God.

Col. 1:13; Matt. 3:17; Isa. 42:1; John 1:18; 1 John 4:9–10, 16;
John 17:22–23; 1 John 3:1

MORNING

Praying in the Holy Spirit.

"God is spirit, and those who worship him must worship in spirit and truth."—We . . . have access in one Spirit to the Father.

"My Father, if it be possible, let this cup pass from me; nevertheless, not as I will, but as you will."

The Spirit helps us in our weakness. For we do not know what to pray for as we ought, but the Spirit himself intercedes for us with groanings too deep for words. And he who searches hearts knows what is the mind of the Spirit, because the Spirit intercedes for the saints according to the will of God.—This is the confidence that we have toward him, that if we ask anything according to his will he hears us.—"When the Spirit of truth comes, he will guide you into all the truth."

Praying at all times in the Spirit, with all prayer and supplication. To that end keep alert with all perseverance, making supplication.

Jude 20; John 4:24; Eph. 2:18; Matt. 26:39; Rom. 8:26–27;
1 John 5:14; John 16:13; Eph. 6:18

EVENING

"There is hope for a tree, if it be cut down, that it will sprout again, and that its shoots will not cease."

A bruised reed he will not break.—He restores my soul.

Godly grief produces a repentance that leads to salvation without regret, whereas worldly grief produces death.—For the moment all discipline seems painful rather than pleasant, but later it yields the peaceful fruit of righteousness to those who have been trained by it.

Before I was afflicted I went astray, but now I keep your word.—"After all that has come upon us for our evil deeds and for our great guilt, seeing that you, our God, have punished us less than our iniquities deserved and have given us such a remnant as this."

Rejoice not over me, O my enemy; when I fall, I shall rise; when I sit in darkness, the Lord will be a light to me. . . . He will bring me out to the light; I shall look upon his vindication.

Job 14:7; Isa. 42:3; Ps. 23:3; 2 Cor. 7:10; Heb. 12:11;
Ps. 119:67; Ezra 9:13; Mic. 7:8–9

MORNING

"Whoever listens to me will dwell secure and will be at ease, without dread of disaster."

Lord, you have been our dwelling place in all generations.—He who dwells in the shelter of the Most High will abide in the shadow of the Almighty.—His faithfulness is a shield and buckler.

Your life is hidden with Christ in God.—He who touches you touches the apple of his eye.—"Fear not, stand firm, and see the salvation of the Lord. . . . The Lord will fight for you, and you have only to be silent."—God is our refuge and strength, a very present help in trouble. Therefore we will not fear.

Jesus spoke to them, saying, "Take heart; it is I. Do not be afraid."—"Why are you troubled, and why do doubts arise in your hearts? See my hands and my feet, that it is I myself. Touch me, and see. For a spirit does not have flesh and bones as you see that I have."—I know whom I have believed, and I am convinced that he is able to guard until that Day what has been entrusted to me.

Prov. 1:33; Ps. 90:1; Ps. 91:1; Ps. 91:4; Col. 3:3; Zech. 2:8; Ex. 14:13–14;
Ps. 46:1–2; Matt. 14:27; Luke 24:38–39; 2 Tim. 1:12

EVENING

"My kingdom is not of this world."

But when Christ had offered for all time a single sacrifice for sins, he sat down at the right hand of God, waiting from that time until his enemies should be made a footstool for his feet.—"From now on you will see the Son of Man seated at the right hand of Power and coming on the clouds of heaven."—He must reign until he has put all his enemies under his feet.

Thanks be to God, who gives us the victory through our Lord Jesus Christ.—He raised him from the dead and seated him at his right hand in the heavenly places, far above all rule and authority and power and dominion, and above every name that is named, not only in this age but also in the one to come. And he put all things under his feet and gave him as head over all things to the church, which is his body, the fullness of him who fills all in all.—which he will display at the proper time—he who is the blessed and only Sovereign, the King of kings and Lord of lords.

John 18:36; Heb. 10:12–13; Matt. 26:64; 1 Cor. 15:25;
1 Cor. 15:57; Eph. 1:20–23; 1 Tim. 6:15

MORNING

"My mother and my brothers are those who hear the word of God and do it."

He who sanctifies and those who are sanctified all have one source. That is why he is not ashamed to call them brothers, saying, "I will tell of your name to my brothers; in the midst of the congregation I will sing your praise."—In Christ Jesus neither circumcision nor uncircumcision counts for anything, but only faith working through love.—"You are my friends if you do what I command you."—"Blessed rather are those who hear the word of God and keep it!"

"Not everyone who says to me, 'Lord, Lord,' will enter the kingdom of heaven, but the one who does the will of my Father who is in heaven."—"My food is to do the will of him who sent me."

If we say we have fellowship with him while we walk in darkness, we lie and do not practice the truth.—Whoever keeps his word, in him truly the love of God is perfected. By this we may know that we are in him.

Luke 8:21; Heb. 2:11–12; Gal. 5:6; John 15:14; Luke 11:28;
Matt. 7:21; John 4:34; 1 John 1:6; 1 John 2:5

EVENING

"What are you doing here, Elijah?"

"He knows the way that I take."—O Lord, you have searched me and known me! You know when I sit down and when I rise up; you discern my thoughts from afar. You search out my path and my lying down and are acquainted with all my ways. . . . Where shall I go from your Spirit? Or where shall I flee from your presence? . . . If I take the wings of the morning and dwell in the uttermost parts of the sea, even there your hand shall lead me, and your right hand shall hold me.

Elijah was a man with a nature like ours.—The fear of man lays a snare, but whoever trusts in the Lord is safe.—Though he fall, he shall not be cast headlong, for the Lord upholds his hand.—The righteous falls seven times and rises again.—Let us not grow weary of doing good, for in due season we will reap, if we do not give up.—"The spirit indeed is willing, but the flesh is weak."—As a father shows compassion to his children, so the Lord shows compassion to those who fear him.

1 Kings 19:9; Job 23:10; Ps. 139:1–3, 7, 9–10; James 5:17; Prov. 29:25;
Ps. 37:24; Prov. 24:16; Gal. 6:9; Matt. 26:41; Ps. 103:13

MORNING

Having been set free from sin, [you] have become slaves of righteousness.

"You cannot serve God and money."—For when you were slaves of sin, you were free in regard to righteousness. But what fruit were you getting at that time from the things of which you are now ashamed? For the end of those things is death. But now that you have been set free from sin and have become slaves of God, the fruit you get leads to sanctification and its end, eternal life.—Christ is the end of the law for righteousness to everyone who believes.

"If anyone serves me, he must follow me; and where I am, there will my servant be also. If anyone serves me, the Father will honor him."—"Take my yoke upon you, and learn from me, for I am gentle and lowly in heart, and you will find rest for your souls. For my yoke is easy, and my burden is light."

"O Lord our God, other lords besides you have ruled over us, but your name alone we bring to remembrance."—I will run in the way of your commandments when you enlarge my heart!

Rom. 6:18; Matt. 6:24; Rom. 6:20–22; Rom. 10:4; John 12:26;
Matt. 11:29–30; Isa. 26:13; Ps. 119:32

EVENING

"Everyone who calls upon the name of the Lord shall be saved."

Manasseh . . . did what was evil in the sight of the Lord, according to the despicable practices of the nations. . . . He erected altars for Baal. . . . And he built altars for all the host of heaven in the two courts of the house of the Lord. And he burned his son as an offering and used fortune-telling and omens and dealt with mediums and with necromancers. He did much evil in the sight of the Lord, provoking him to anger.—And when he was in distress, he entreated the favor of the Lord his God and humbled himself greatly before the God of his fathers. He prayed to him, and God was moved by his entreaty and heard his plea.

"Come now, let us reason together, says the Lord: though your sins are like scarlet, they shall be as white as snow; though they are red like crimson, they shall become like wool."—The Lord is . . . patient toward you, not wishing that any should perish.

Acts 2:21; 2 Kings 21:1–3, 5–6; 2 Chron. 33:12–13; Isa. 1:18; 2 Pet. 3:9

MORNING

The Lord delights in you.

"Fear not, for I have redeemed you; I have called you by name, you are mine."—"Can a woman forget her nursing child, that she should have no compassion on the son of her womb? Even these may forget, yet I will not forget you. Behold, I have engraved you on the palms of my hands; your walls are continually before me."

The steps of a man are established by the Lord, when he delights in his way.—Delighting in the children of man.—The Lord takes pleasure in those who fear him, in those who hope in his steadfast love.—"They shall be mine, says the Lord of hosts, in the day when I make up my treasured possession, and I will spare them as a man spares his son who serves him."

You, who once were alienated and hostile in mind, doing evil deeds, he has now reconciled in his body of flesh by his death, in order to present you holy and blameless and above reproach before him.

Isa. 62:4; Isa. 43:1; Isa. 49:15–16; Ps. 37:23; Prov. 8:31;
Ps. 147:11; Mal. 3:17; Col. 1:21–22

EVENING

Worldly grief produces death.

When Ahithophel saw that his counsel was not followed, he saddled his donkey and went off home to his own city. He set his house in order and hanged himself, and he died.—A crushed spirit who can bear?

Is there no balm in Gilead? Is there no physician there? Why then has the health of the daughter of my people not been restored?—The Lord has anointed me to bring good news to the poor; he has sent me to bind up the brokenhearted, . . . to comfort all who mourn; to grant to those who mourn in Zion—to give them a beautiful headdress instead of ashes, the oil of gladness instead of mourning, the garment of praise instead of a faint spirit.—"Come to me, all who labor and are heavy laden, and I will give you rest. Take my yoke upon you, and learn from me, for I am gentle and lowly in heart, and you will find rest for your souls. For my yoke is easy, and my burden is light."

Philip . . . told him the good news about Jesus.—He heals the brokenhearted and binds up their wounds.

2 Cor. 7:10; 2 Sam. 17:23; Prov. 18:14; Jer. 8:22; Isa. 61:1–3;
Matt. 11:28–30; Acts 8:35; Ps. 147:3

MORNING

"The glory that you have given me I have given to them."

I saw the Lord sitting upon a throne, high and lifted up; and the train of his robe filled the temple. Above him stood the seraphim. . . . And one called to another and said: "Holy, holy, holy is the Lord of hosts; the whole earth is full of his glory!"—Isaiah said these things because he saw his glory and spoke of him.—Seated above the likeness of a throne was a likeness with a human appearance. . . . Like the appearance of the bow that is in the cloud on the day of rain, so was the appearance of the brightness all around. Such was the appearance of the likeness of the glory of the Lord.

"Please show me your glory." . . . "But," he said, "you cannot see my face, for man shall not see me and live."—No one has ever seen God; the only God, who is at the Father's side, he has made him known.—God, who said, "Let light shine out of darkness," has shone in our hearts to give the light of the knowledge of the glory of God in the face of Jesus Christ.

John 17:22; Isa. 6:1–3; John 12:41; Ezek. 1:26, 28;
Ex. 33:18, 20; John 1:18; 2 Cor. 4:6

EVENING

My son, if sinners entice you, do not consent.

She took of its fruit and ate, and she also gave some to her husband who was with her, and he ate.—"Did not Achan the son of Zerah break faith in the matter of the devoted things, and wrath fell upon all the congregation of Israel? And he did not perish alone for his iniquity."

You shall not fall in with the many to do evil.

"The gate is wide and the way is easy that leads to destruction, and those who enter by it are many."

None of us lives to himself.—You were called to freedom, brothers. Only do not use your freedom as an opportunity for the flesh, but through love serve one another.—Take care that this right of yours does not somehow become a stumbling block to the weak. . . . Thus, sinning against your brothers and wounding their conscience when it is weak, you sin against Christ.

All we like sheep have gone astray; we have turned—every one—to his own way; and the Lord has laid on him the iniquity of us all.

Prov. 1:10; Gen. 3:6; Josh. 22:20; Ex. 23:2; Matt. 7:13;
Rom. 14:7; Gal. 5:13; 1 Cor. 8:9, 12; Isa. 53:6

MORNING

As the body apart from the spirit is dead,
so also faith apart from works is dead.

"Not everyone who says to me, 'Lord, Lord,' will enter the kingdom of heaven, but the one who does the will of my Father who is in heaven."—Holiness without which no one will see the Lord.—Make every effort to supplement your faith with virtue, and virtue with knowledge, and knowledge with self-control, and self-control with steadfastness, and steadfastness with godliness, and godliness with brotherly affection, and brotherly affection with love. For if these qualities are yours and are increasing, they keep you from being ineffective or unfruitful in the knowledge of our Lord Jesus Christ. For whoever lacks these qualities is so nearsighted that he is blind, having forgotten that he was cleansed from his former sins. Therefore, brothers, be all the more diligent to confirm your calling and election, for if you practice these qualities you will never fall.—By grace you have been saved through faith. And this is not your own doing; it is the gift of God, not a result of works, so that no one may boast.

James 2:26; Matt. 7:21; Heb. 12:14; 2 Pet. 1:5–10; Eph. 2:8–9

EVENING

Since therefore the children share in flesh and blood, he himself likewise
partook of the same things, that through death he might destroy the
one who has the power of death, that is, the devil, and deliver all
those who through fear of death were subject to lifelong slavery.

"O death, where is your victory? O death, where is your sting?" But thanks be to God, who gives us the victory through our Lord Jesus Christ.—So we do not lose heart. Though our outer self is wasting away, our inner self is being renewed day by day.

We know that if the tent that is our earthly home is destroyed, we have a building from God, a house not made with hands, eternal in the heavens. . . . So we are always of good courage. We know that while we are at home in the body we are away from the Lord. . . . We would rather be away from the body and at home with the Lord.

"Let not your hearts be troubled. Believe in God; believe also in me. In my Father's house are many rooms. If it were not so, would I have told you that I go to prepare a place for you?"

Heb. 2:14–15; 1 Cor. 15:55, 57; 2 Cor. 4:16; 2 Cor. 5:1, 6–8; John 14:1–2

MORNING

We shall be satisfied with the goodness of your house.

One thing have I asked of the Lord, that will I seek after: that I may dwell in the house of the Lord all the days of my life, to gaze upon the beauty of the Lord and to inquire in his temple.

"Blessed are those who hunger and thirst for righteousness, for they shall be satisfied."—"He has filled the hungry with good things, and the rich he has sent away empty."

He satisfies the longing soul, and the hungry soul he fills with good things.—"I am the bread of life; whoever comes to me shall not hunger, and whoever believes in me shall never thirst."

How precious is your steadfast love, O God! The children of mankind take refuge in the shadow of your wings. They feast on the abundance of your house, and you give them drink from the river of your delights. For with you is the fountain of life; in your light do we see light.

Ps. 65:4; Ps. 27:4; Matt. 5:6; Luke 1:53; Ps. 107:9; John 6:35; Ps. 36:7–9

EVENING

"Do you now believe?"

What good is it, my brothers, if someone says he has faith but does not have works? Can that faith save him? . . . Faith by itself, if it does not have works, is dead.

By faith Abraham, when he was tested, offered up Isaac, and he who had received the promises was in the act of offering up his only son. . . . He considered that God was able even to raise him from the dead.—Was not Abraham our father justified by works when he offered up his son Isaac on the altar? . . . You see that a person is justified by works and not by faith alone.

The one who looks into the perfect law, the law of liberty, and perseveres, being no hearer who forgets but a doer who acts, he will be blessed in his doing.

"You will recognize them by their fruits. Not everyone who says to me, 'Lord, Lord,' will enter the kingdom of heaven, but the one who does the will of my Father who is in heaven."—"If you know these things, blessed are you if you do them."

John 16:31; James 2:14, 17; Heb. 11:17–19; James 2:21,
24; James 1:25; Matt. 7:20–21; John 13:17

MORNING

Now may the Lord of peace himself give you peace at all times in every way. The Lord be with you all.

Peace from him who is and who was and who is to come.—The peace of God, which surpasses all understanding, will guard your hearts and your minds in Christ Jesus.

Jesus himself stood among them, and said to them, "Peace to you!"— "Peace I leave with you; my peace I give to you. . . . Let not your hearts be troubled, neither let them be afraid."

"The Helper . . . the Spirit of truth."—The fruit of the Spirit is love, joy, peace.—The Spirit himself bears witness with our spirit that we are children of God.

"My presence will go with you, and I will give you rest." And he said to him, "If your presence will not go with me, do not bring us up from here. For how shall it be known that I have found favor in your sight, I and your people? Is it not in your going with us?"

2 Thess. 3:16; Rev. 1:4; Phil. 4:7; Luke 24:36; John 14:27;
John 15:26; Gal. 5:22; Rom. 8:16; Ex. 33:14–16

EVENING

We rejoice in our sufferings.

If in Christ we have hope in this life only, we are of all people most to be pitied.

Beloved, do not be surprised at the fiery trial when it comes upon you to test you, as though something strange were happening to you. But rejoice insofar as you share Christ's sufferings, that you may also rejoice and be glad when his glory is revealed.—As sorrowful, yet always rejoicing.

Rejoice in the Lord always; again I will say, rejoice.—They left the presence of the council, rejoicing that they were counted worthy to suffer dishonor for the name.

May the God of hope fill you with all joy and peace in believing.

Though the fig tree should not blossom, nor fruit be on the vines, the produce of the olive fail and the fields yield no food, the flock be cut off from the fold and there be no herd in the stalls, yet I will rejoice in the Lord; I will take joy in the God of my salvation.

Rom. 5:3; 1 Cor. 15:19; 1 Pet. 4:12–13; 2 Cor. 6:10; Phil. 4:4;
Acts 5:41; Rom. 15:13; Hab. 3:17–18

MORNING

*Each will be like a hiding place from
the wind, a shelter from the storm.*

Since therefore the children share in flesh and blood, he himself likewise partook of the same things.—"The man who stands next to me," declares the Lord of hosts.—"I and the Father are one."

He who dwells in the shelter of the Most High will abide in the shadow of the Almighty.—There will be a booth for shade by day from the heat, and for a refuge and a shelter from the storm and rain.—The Lord is your shade on your right hand. The sun shall not strike you by day, nor the moon by night.

From the end of the earth I call to you when my heart is faint. Lead me to the rock that is higher than I.—You are a hiding place for me; you preserve me from trouble.—You have been a stronghold to the poor, a stronghold to the needy in his distress, a shelter from the storm and a shade from the heat; for the breath of the ruthless is like a storm against a wall.

Isa. 32:3; Heb. 2:14; Zech. 13:7; John 10:30; Ps. 91:1; Isa. 4:6;
Ps. 121:5–6; Ps. 61:2; Ps. 32:7; Isa. 25:4

EVENING

"Behold, I create new heavens and a new earth."

"As the new heavens and the new earth that I make shall remain before me, . . . so shall your offspring and your name remain."

But according to his promise we are waiting for new heavens and a new earth in which righteousness dwells.

Then I saw a new heaven and a new earth, for the first heaven and the first earth had passed away, and the sea was no more. And I saw the holy city, new Jerusalem, coming down out of heaven from God, prepared as a bride adorned for her husband. And I heard a loud voice from the throne saying, "Behold, the dwelling place of God is with man. He will dwell with them, and they will be his people, and God himself will be with them as their God. He will wipe away every tear from their eyes, and death shall be no more, neither shall there be mourning, nor crying, nor pain anymore, for the former things have passed away." And he who was seated on the throne said, "Behold, I am making all things new."

Isa. 65:17; Isa. 66:22; 2 Pet. 3:13; Rev. 21:1–5

MORNING

But you have been anointed by the Holy One, and you all have knowledge.

God anointed Jesus of Nazareth with the Holy Spirit and with power.—For in him all the fullness of God was pleased to dwell.—For from his fullness we have all received, grace upon grace.

You anoint my head with oil.—But the anointing that you received from him abides in you, and you have no need that anyone should teach you. But as his anointing teaches you about everything, and is true, and is no lie—just as it has taught you, abide in him.

"But the Helper, the Holy Spirit, whom the Father will send in my name, he will teach you all things and bring to your remembrance all that I have said to you."

Likewise the Spirit helps us in our weakness. For we do not know what to pray for as we ought, but the Spirit himself intercedes for us with groanings too deep for words.

1 John 2:20; Acts 10:38; Col. 1:19; John 1:16; Ps. 23:5;
1 John 2:27; John 14:26; Rom. 8:26

EVENING

With our hearts sprinkled clean from an evil conscience.

For if the blood of goats and bulls, and the sprinkling of defiled persons with the ashes of a heifer, sanctify for the purification of the flesh, how much more will the blood of Christ, who through the eternal Spirit offered himself without blemish to God, purify our conscience from dead works to serve the living God.—The sprinkled blood that speaks a better word than the blood of Abel.

In him we have redemption through his blood, the forgiveness of our trespasses, according to the riches of his grace.

For when every commandment of the law had been declared by Moses to all the people, he took the blood of calves and goats, with water and scarlet wool and hyssop, and sprinkled both the book itself and all the people. . . . And in the same way he sprinkled with the blood both the tent and all the vessels used in worship. Indeed, under the law almost everything is purified with blood, and without the shedding of blood there is no forgiveness of sins.

Heb. 10:22; Heb. 9:13–14; Heb. 12:24; Eph. 1:7; Heb. 9:19, 21–22

MORNING

"I would seek God, and to God would I commit my cause."

"Is anything too hard for the Lord?"—Commit your way to the Lord; trust in him, and he will act.—Do not be anxious about anything, but in everything by prayer and supplication with thanksgiving let your requests be made known to God.—Casting all your anxieties on him, because he cares for you.

Hezekiah received the letter from the hand of the messengers, and read it; and Hezekiah went up to the house of the Lord, and spread it before the Lord. And Hezekiah prayed to the Lord.

"Before they call I will answer; while they are yet speaking I will hear."—The prayer of a righteous person has great power as it is working.

I love the Lord, because he has heard my voice and my pleas for mercy. Because he inclined his ear to me, therefore I will call on him as long as I live.

Job 5:8; Gen. 18:14; Ps. 37:5; Phil. 4:6; 1 Pet. 5:7; Isa. 37:14–15;
Isa. 65:24; James 5:16; Ps. 116:1–2

EVENING

Our bodies washed with pure water.

"You shall . . . make a basin of bronze. . . . You shall put it between the tent of meeting and the altar, and you shall put water in it, with which Aaron and his sons shall wash their hands and their feet. When they go into the tent of meeting, . . . they shall wash with water, so that they may not die. They shall wash their hands and their feet, so that they may not die."—Your body is a temple of the Holy Spirit within you.—If anyone destroys God's temple, God will destroy him. For God's temple is holy, and you are that temple.

"In my flesh I shall see God, whom I shall see for myself, and my eyes shall behold, and not another."—But nothing unclean will ever enter it.—You who are of purer eyes than to see evil and cannot look at wrong.—I appeal to you therefore, brothers, by the mercies of God, to present your bodies as a living sacrifice, holy and acceptable to God, which is your spiritual worship.

Heb. 10:22; Ex. 30:18–21; 1 Cor. 6:19; 1 Cor. 3:17; Job 19:26–27;
Rev. 21:27; Hab. 1:13; Rom. 12:1

MORNING

"Where shall wisdom be found?"

If any of you lacks wisdom, let him ask God, who gives generously to all without reproach, and it will be given him. But let him ask in faith, with no doubting.—Trust in the Lord with all your heart, and do not lean on your own understanding. In all your ways acknowledge him, and he will make straight your paths.—The only [wise, kjv] God.—Be not wise in your own eyes.

"Ah, Lord God! Behold, I do not know how to speak, for I am only a youth." But the Lord said to me, "Do not say, 'I am only a youth'; for to all to whom I send you, you shall go, and whatever I command you, you shall speak. Do not be afraid of them, for I am with you to deliver you, declares the Lord."

"Whatever you ask of the Father in my name, he will give it to you. Until now you have asked nothing in my name. Ask, and you will receive, that your joy may be full."—"And whatever you ask in prayer, you will receive, if you have faith."

Job 28:12; James 1:5–6; Prov. 3:5–6; 1 Tim. 1:17; Prov. 3:7;
Jer. 1:6–8; John 16:23–24; Matt. 21:22

EVENING

"I would not live forever."

And I say, "Oh, that I had wings like a dove! I would fly away and be at rest. . . . I would hurry to find a shelter from the raging wind and tempest."

In this tent we groan, longing to put on our heavenly dwelling. . . . For while we are still in this tent, we groan, being burdened—not that we would be unclothed, but that we would be further clothed, so that what is mortal may be swallowed up by life.—My desire is to depart and be with Christ, for that is far better.

Let us run with endurance the race that is set before us, looking to Jesus, the founder and perfecter of our faith, who for the joy that was set before him endured the cross, despising the shame, and is seated at the right hand of the throne of God. Consider him who endured from sinners such hostility against himself, so that you may not grow weary or fainthearted.

"Let not your hearts be troubled, neither let them be afraid."

Job 7:16; Ps. 55:6, 8; 2 Cor. 5:2, 4; Phil. 1:23; Heb. 12:1–3; John 14:27

MORNING

It is good for me that I was afflicted,
that I might learn your statutes.

Although he was a son, he learned obedience through what he suffered.—We suffer with him in order that we may also be glorified with him. For I consider that the sufferings of this present time are not worth comparing with the glory that is to be revealed to us.

"But he knows the way that I take; when he has tried me, I shall come out as gold. My foot has held fast to his steps; I have kept his way and have not turned aside."

"And you shall remember the whole way that the Lord your God has led you these forty years in the wilderness, that he might humble you, testing you to know what was in your heart, whether you would keep his commandments or not. . . . Know then in your heart that, as a man disciplines his son, the Lord your God disciplines you. So you shall keep the commandments of the Lord your God by walking in his ways and by fearing him.

Ps. 119:71; Heb. 5:8; Rom. 8:17-18; Job 23:10-11; Deut. 8:2, 5-6

EVENING

"Not by might shall a man prevail."

Then David said to the Philistine, "You come to me with a sword and with a spear and with a javelin, but I come to you in the name of the Lord of hosts, the God of the armies of Israel, whom you have defied." . . . And David put his hand in his bag and took out a stone and slung it. . . . So David prevailed over the Philistine with a sling and with a stone.

The king is not saved by his great army; a warrior is not delivered by his great strength. . . . Behold, the eye of the Lord is on those who fear him, on those who hope in his steadfast love.—Both riches and honor come from you, and you rule over all. In your hand are power and might, and in your hand it is to make great and to give strength to all.

I will boast all the more gladly of my weaknesses, so that the power of Christ may rest upon me. For the sake of Christ, then, I am content with weaknesses, insults, hardships, persecutions, and calamities. For when I am weak, then I am strong.

1 Sam. 2:9; 1 Sam. 17:45, 49-50; Ps. 33:16, 18;
1 Chron. 29:12; 2 Cor. 12:9-10

MORNING

It is God who works in you.

Not that we are sufficient in ourselves to claim anything as coming from us, but our sufficiency is from God.—"A person cannot receive even one thing unless it is given him from heaven."—"No one can come to me unless the Father who sent me draws him. And I will raise him up on the last day."—"I will give them one heart and one way, that they may fear me forever."

Do not be deceived, my beloved brothers. Every good gift and every perfect gift is from above, coming down from the Father of lights with whom there is no variation or shadow due to change. Of his own will he brought us forth by the word of truth, that we should be a kind of firstfruits of his creatures.

For we are his workmanship, created in Christ Jesus for good works, which God prepared beforehand, that we should walk in them.

O Lord, you will ordain peace for us, for you have indeed done for us all our works.

Phil. 2:13; 2 Cor. 3:5; John 3:27; John 6:44; Jer. 32:39;
James 1:16–18; Eph. 2:10; Isa. 26:12

EVENING

"The spirit indeed is willing, but the flesh is weak."

In the path of your judgments, O Lord, we wait for you; your name and remembrance are the desire of our soul. My soul yearns for you in the night; my spirit within me earnestly seeks you.

For I know that nothing good dwells in me, that is, in my flesh. For I have the desire to do what is right, but not the ability to carry it out. . . . For I delight in the law of God, in my inner being, but I see in my members another law waging war against the law of my mind and making me captive to the law of sin that dwells in my members.—For the desires of the flesh are against the Spirit, and the desires of the Spirit are against the flesh, for these are opposed to each other, to keep you from doing the things you want to do.

I can do all things through him who strengthens me.—Our sufficiency is from God.—"My grace is sufficient for you."

Matt. 26:41; Isa. 26:8–9; Rom. 7:18, 22–23; Gal. 5:17;
Phil. 4:13; 2 Cor. 3:5; 2 Cor. 12:9

MORNING

For our sake he made him to be sin who knew no sin, so that in him we might become the righteousness of God.

The Lord has laid on him the iniquity of us all.—He himself bore our sins in his body on the tree, that we might die to sin and live to righteousness. By his wounds you have been healed.—As by the one man's disobedience the many were made sinners, so by the one man's obedience the many will be made righteous.

But when the goodness and loving kindness of God our Savior appeared, he saved us, not because of works done by us in righteousness, but according to his own mercy, by the washing of regeneration and renewal of the Holy Spirit, whom he poured out on us richly through Jesus Christ our Savior, so that being justified by his grace we might become heirs according to the hope of eternal life.—There is therefore now no condemnation for those who are in Christ Jesus.

"The Lord is our righteousness."

2 Cor. 5:21; Isa. 53:6; 1 Pet. 2:24; Rom. 5:19; Titus 3:4–7;
Rom. 8:1; Jer. 23:6

EVENING

I will be like the dew to Israel.

The meekness and gentleness of Christ.—A bruised reed he will not break, and a faintly burning wick he will not quench.

"The Spirit of the Lord is upon me, because he has anointed me to proclaim good news to the poor. He has sent me to proclaim liberty to the captives and recovering of sight to the blind, to set at liberty those who are oppressed, to proclaim the year of the Lord's favor." . . . And he began to say to them, "Today this Scripture has been fulfilled in your hearing." And all spoke well of him and marveled at the gracious words that were coming from his mouth.

And the Lord turned and looked at Peter. And Peter remembered the saying of the Lord, how he had said to him, "Before the rooster crows today, you will deny me three times." And he went out and wept bitterly.—He will tend his flock like a shepherd; he will gather the lambs in his arms; he will carry them in his bosom, and gently lead those that are with young.

Hos. 14:5; 2 Cor. 10:1; Isa. 42:3; Luke 4:18–19, 21–22;
Luke 22:61–62; Isa. 40:11

MORNING

Through love serve one another.

Brothers, if anyone is caught in any transgression, you who are spiritual should restore him in a spirit of gentleness. Keep watch on yourself, lest you too be tempted. Bear one another's burdens, and so fulfill the law of Christ.— My brothers, if anyone among you wanders from the truth and someone brings him back, let him know that whoever brings back a sinner from his wandering will save his soul from death and will cover a multitude of sins.—Having purified your souls by your obedience to the truth for a sincere brotherly love, love one another earnestly from a pure heart.—Owe no one anything, except to love each other, for the one who loves another has fulfilled the law.—Love one another with brotherly affection. Outdo one another in showing honor.—Likewise, you who are younger, be subject to the elders. Clothe yourselves, all of you, with humility toward one another, for "God opposes the proud but gives grace to the humble."

We who are strong have an obligation to bear with the failings of the weak, and not to please ourselves.

Gal. 5:13; Gal. 6:1-2; James 5:19-20; 1 Pet. 1:22; Rom. 13:8;
Rom. 12:10; 1 Pet. 5:5; Rom. 15:1

EVENING

The dust returns to the earth as it was.

What is sown is perishable. . . . It is sown in dishonor. . . . It is sown in weakness. . . . It is sown a natural body.—The first man was from the earth, a man of dust.

"You are dust, and to dust you shall return."—One dies in his full vigor, being wholly at ease and secure. . . . Another dies in bitterness of soul, never having tasted of prosperity. They lie down alike in the dust, and the worms cover them.

My flesh . . . dwells secure.—"And after my skin has been thus destroyed, yet in my flesh I shall see God."—The Lord Jesus Christ . . . will transform our lowly body to be like his glorious body, by the power that enables him even to subject all things to himself.

"O Lord, make me know my end and what is the measure of my days; let me know how fleeting I am!"—So teach us to number our days that we may get a heart of wisdom.

Eccles. 12:7; 1 Cor. 15:42-44; 1 Cor. 15:47; Gen. 3:19; Job 21:23, 25-26;
Ps. 16:9; Job 19:26; Phil. 3:20-21; Ps. 39:4; Ps. 90:12

MORNING

To do righteousness and justice is more
acceptable to the Lord than sacrifice.

He has told you, O man, what is good; and what does the Lord require of you but to do justice, and to love kindness, and to walk humbly with your God?—"Has the Lord as great delight in burnt offerings and sacrifices, as in obeying the voice of the Lord? Behold, to obey is better than sacrifice, and to listen than the fat of rams."—"And to love him with all the heart and with all the understanding and with all the strength, and to love one's neighbor as oneself, is much more than all whole burnt offerings and sacrifices."

"So you, by the help of your God, return, hold fast to love and justice, and wait continually for your God."—Mary . . . sat at the Lord's feet and listened to his teaching. . . . "One thing is necessary. Mary has chosen the good portion, which will not be taken away from her."—It is God who works in you, both to will and to work for his good pleasure.

Prov. 21:3; Mic. 6:8; 1 Sam. 15:22; Mark 12:33;
Hos. 12:6; Luke 10:39, 42; Phil. 2:13

EVENING

The spirit returns to God who gave it.

The Lord God formed the man of dust from the ground and breathed into his nostrils the breath of life, and the man became a living creature.—"But it is the spirit in man, the breath of the Almighty, that makes him understand."—"The first man Adam became a living being."—The spirit of man goes upward.

While we are at home in the body we are away from the Lord. . . . Yes, we are of good courage, and we would rather be away from the body and at home with the Lord.—My desire is to depart and be with Christ, for that is far better.—But we do not want you to be uninformed, brothers, about those who are asleep, that you may not grieve as others do who have no hope. For since we believe that Jesus died and rose again, even so, through Jesus, God will bring with him those who have fallen asleep.

"In my Father's house are many rooms. If it were not so, would I have told you that I go to prepare a place for you? And if I go and prepare a place for you, I will come again and will take you to myself, that where I am you may be also."

Eccles. 12:7; Gen. 12:7; Job 32:8; 1 Cor. 15:45; Eccles. 3:21;
2 Cor. 5:6, 8; Phil. 1:23; 1 Thess. 4:13-14; John 14:2-3

MORNING

"No one is able to snatch them out of the Father's hand."

I know whom I have believed, and I am convinced that he is able to guard until that Day what has been entrusted to me.—The Lord will rescue me from every evil deed and bring me safely into his heavenly kingdom.—We are more than conquerors through him who loved us. For I am sure that neither death nor life, nor angels nor rulers, nor things present nor things to come, nor powers, nor height nor depth, nor anything else in all creation, will be able to separate us from the love of God in Christ Jesus our Lord.—Your life is hidden with Christ in God.

Has not God chosen those who are poor in the world to be rich in faith and heirs of the kingdom, which he has promised to those who love him?

Now may our Lord Jesus Christ himself, and God our Father, who loved us and gave us eternal comfort and good hope through grace, comfort your hearts and establish them in every good work and word.

John 10:29; 2 Tim. 1:12; 2 Tim. 4:18; Rom. 8:37-39;
Col. 3:3; James 2:5; 2 Thess. 2:16-17

EVENING

The perfect law, the law of liberty.

"You will know the truth, and the truth will set you free. . . . Truly, truly, I say to you, everyone who practices sin is a slave to sin. . . . So if the Son sets you free, you will be free indeed."

Stand firm therefore, and do not submit again to a yoke of slavery. . . . For you were called to freedom, brothers. Only do not use your freedom as an opportunity for the flesh, but through love serve one another. For the whole law is fulfilled in one word: "You shall love your neighbor as yourself."—Having been set free from sin, [you] have become slaves of righteousness.—For a married woman is bound by law to her husband while he lives, but if her husband dies she is released from the law of marriage.

The law of the Spirit of life has set you free in Christ Jesus from the law of sin and death.—I shall walk in a wide place, for I have sought your precepts.

James 1:25; John 8:32, 34, 36; Gal. 5:1, 13-14; Rom. 6:18;
Rom. 7:2; Rom. 8:2; Ps. 119:45

MORNING

So do not let what you regard as good be spoken of as evil.

Abstain from every form of evil.—We aim at what is honorable not only in the Lord's sight but also in the sight of man.—For this is the will of God, that by doing good you should put to silence the ignorance of foolish people.

But let none of you suffer as a murderer or a thief or an evildoer or as a meddler. Yet if anyone suffers as a Christian, let him not be ashamed, but let him glorify God in that name.

For you were called to freedom, brothers. Only do not use your freedom as an opportunity for the flesh, but through love serve one another.—But take care that this right of yours does not somehow become a stumbling block to the weak.—"But whoever causes one of these little ones who believe in me to sin, it would be better for him to have a great millstone fastened around his neck and to be drowned in the depth of the sea."—"As you did it to one of the least of these my brothers, you did it to me."

Rom. 14:16; 1 Thess. 5:22; 2 Cor. 8:21; 1 Pet. 2:15; 1 Pet. 4:15–16;
Gal. 5:13; 1 Cor. 8:9; Matt. 18:6; Matt. 25:40

EVENING

"Awake, O sleeper, and arise from the dead,
and Christ will shine on you."

The hour has come for you to wake from sleep. For salvation is nearer to us now than when we first believed.— So then let us not sleep, as others do, but let us keep awake and be sober. For those who sleep, sleep at night, and those who get drunk, are drunk at night. But since we belong to the day, let us be sober, having put on the breastplate of faith and love, and for a helmet the hope of salvation.

Arise, shine, for your light has come, and the glory of the Lord has risen upon you. For behold, darkness shall cover the earth, and thick darkness the peoples; but the Lord will arise upon you, and his glory will be seen upon you.

Therefore, preparing your minds for action, and being sober-minded, set your hope fully on the grace that will be brought to you at the revelation of Jesus Christ.—"Stay dressed for action and keep your lamps burning, and be like men who are waiting for their master."

Eph. 5:14; Rom. 13:11; 1 Thess. 5:6–8; Isa. 60:1-2;
1 Pet. 1:13; Luke 12:35–36

MORNING

The Lord, is in your midst.

Fear not, for I am with you; be not dismayed, for I am your God; I will strengthen you, I will help you, I will uphold you with my righteous right hand.—Strengthen the weak hands, and make firm the feeble knees. Say to those who have an anxious heart, "Be strong; fear not! Behold, your God will come with vengeance, with the recompense of God. He will come and save you."—The Lord your God is in your midst, a mighty one who will save; he will rejoice over you with gladness; he will quiet you by his love; he will exult over you with loud singing.—Wait for the Lord; be strong, and let your heart take courage.

And I heard a loud voice from the throne saying, "Behold, the dwelling place of God is with man. He will dwell with them, and they will be his people, and God himself will be with them as their God. He will wipe away every tear from their eyes, and death shall be no more, neither shall there be mourning, nor crying, nor pain anymore."

Zeph. 3:15; Isa. 41:10; Isa. 35:3–4; Zeph. 3:17; Ps. 27:14; Rev. 21:3–4

EVENING

"Why do you cry to me? Tell the
people of Israel to go forward."

"Be strong, and let us use our strength for our people and for the cities of our God, and may the Lord do what seems good to him."—And we prayed to our God and set a guard as a protection against them day and night.

"Not everyone who says to me, 'Lord, Lord,' will enter the kingdom of heaven, but the one who does the will of my Father who is in heaven."—"If anyone's will is to do God's will, he will know whether the teaching is from God."—"Let us know; let us press on to know the Lord."

"Watch and pray that you may not enter into temptation."—Be watchful, stand firm in the faith, act like men, be strong.—Do not be slothful in zeal, be fervent in spirit, serve the Lord.

Strengthen the weak hands, and make firm the feeble knees. Say to those who have an anxious heart, "Be strong; fear not!"

Ex. 14:15; 1 Chron. 19:13; Neh. 4:9; Matt. 7:21; John 7:17; Hos. 6:3;
Matt. 26:41; 1 Cor. 16:13; Rom. 12:11; Isa. 35:3–4

MORNING

Be strengthened by the grace that is in Christ Jesus.

May you be strengthened with all power, according to his glorious might.— Therefore, as you received Christ Jesus the Lord, so walk in him, rooted and built up in him and established in the faith, just as you were taught, abounding in thanksgiving.—Oaks of righteousness, the planting of the Lord, that he may be glorified.—Built on the foundation of the apostles and prophets, Christ Jesus himself being the cornerstone, in whom the whole structure, being joined together, grows into a holy temple in the Lord. In him you also are being built together into a dwelling place for God by the Spirit.

"And now I commend you to God and to the word of his grace, which is able to build you up and to give you the inheritance among all those who are sanctified."—Filled with the fruit of righteousness that comes through Jesus Christ, to the glory and praise of God.

Fight the good fight of the faith.—And not frightened in anything by your opponents.

2 Tim. 2:1; Col. 1:11; Col. 2:6–7; Isa. 61:3; Eph. 2:20–22;
Acts 20:32; Phil. 1:11; 1 Tim. 6:12; Phil. 1:28

EVENING

For you will render to a man according to his work.

For no one can lay a foundation other than that which is laid, which is Jesus Christ. . . . If the work that anyone has built on the foundation survives, he will receive a reward. If anyone's work is burned up, he will suffer loss, though he himself will be saved, but only as through fire.—For we must all appear before the judgment seat of Christ, so that each one may receive what is due for what he has done in the body, whether good or evil.

"But when you give to the needy, do not let your left hand know what your right hand is doing, so that your giving may be in secret. And your Father who sees in secret will reward you."—"Now after a long time the master of those servants came and settled accounts with them."

Not that we are sufficient in ourselves to claim anything as coming from us, but our sufficiency is from God.—O Lord, you will ordain peace for us, for you have indeed done for us all our works.

Ps. 62:12; 1 Cor. 3:11, 14–15; 2 Cor. 5:10; Matt. 6:3–4;
Matt. 25:19; 2 Cor. 3:5; Isa. 26:12

MORNING

Give to him glorious praise!

"The people whom I formed for myself that they might declare my praise."—
"I will cleanse them from all the guilt of their sin against me, and I will forgive all the guilt of their sin and rebellion against me. And this city shall be
to me a name of joy, a praise and a glory before all the nations of the earth."—
Through him then let us continually offer up a sacrifice of praise to God, that
is, the fruit of lips that acknowledge his name.—I give thanks to you, O Lord
my God, with my whole heart, and I will glorify your name forever. For great
is your steadfast love toward me; you have delivered my soul from the depths
of Sheol.—"Who is like you, O Lord, . . . majestic in holiness, awesome in
glorious deeds, doing wonders?"—I will praise the name of God with a song;
I will magnify him with thanksgiving.—And they sing the song of Moses, the
servant of God, and the song of the Lamb, saying, "Great and amazing are your
deeds, O Lord God the Almighty!"

Ps. 66:2; Isa. 43:21; Jer. 33:8–9; Heb. 13:15; Ps. 86:12–13;
Ex. 15:11; Ps. 69:30; Rev. 15:3

EVENING

By nature children of wrath, like the rest of mankind.

For we ourselves were once foolish, disobedient, led astray, slaves to various
passions and pleasures, passing our days in malice and envy, hated by others and hating one another.—"Do not marvel that I said to you, 'You must be
born again.'"

Then Job answered the Lord and said: "Behold, I am of small account;
what shall I answer you? I lay my hand on my mouth."—And the Lord said
to Satan, "Have you considered my servant Job, that there is none like him
on the earth, a blameless and upright man, who fears God and turns away
from evil?"

Behold, I was brought forth in iniquity, and in sin did my mother conceive me.—"David, . . . of whom he testified and said, . . . 'A man after my
heart, who will do all my will.'"

Though formerly I was a blasphemer, persecutor, and insolent oppo-
nent. But I received mercy.—"That which is born of the flesh is flesh, and that
which is born of the Spirit is spirit."

Eph. 2:3; Titus 3:3; John 3:7; Job 40:3–4; Job 1:8;
Ps. 51:5; Acts 13:22; 1 Tim. 1:13; John 3:6

MORNING

Bear one another's burdens, and so fulfill the law of Christ.

Let each of you look not only to his own interests, but also to the interests of others. Have this mind among yourselves, which is yours in Christ Jesus, who, though he was in the form of God, did not count equality with God a thing to be grasped, but emptied himself, by taking the form of a servant.— "For even the Son of Man came not to be served but to serve, and to give his life as a ransom for many."—And he died for all, that those who live might no longer live for themselves but for him who for their sake died and was raised.

When Jesus saw her weeping, and the Jews who had come with her also weeping, he was deeply moved in his spirit and greatly troubled. . . . Jesus wept.—Rejoice with those who rejoice, weep with those who weep.

Have unity of mind, sympathy, brotherly love, a tender heart, and a humble mind. Do not repay evil for evil or reviling for reviling, but on the contrary, bless, for to this you were called, that you may obtain a blessing.

Gal. 6:2; Phil. 2:4–7; Mark 10:45; 2 Cor. 5:15; John 11:33, 35;
Rom. 12:15; 1 Pet. 3:8–9

EVENING

"Son, go and work in the vineyard today."

So you are no longer a slave, but a son, and if a son, then an heir through God.

So you also must consider yourselves dead to sin and alive to God in Christ Jesus. Let not sin therefore reign in your mortal body, to make you obey its passions. Do not present your members to sin as instruments for unrighteousness, but present yourselves to God as those who have been brought from death to life, and your members to God as instruments for righteousness.—As obedient children, do not be conformed to the passions of your former ignorance, but as he who called you is holy, you also be holy in all your conduct, since it is written, "You shall be holy, for I am holy."—Set apart as holy, useful to the master of the house, ready for every good work.

Therefore, my beloved brothers, be steadfast, immovable, always abounding in the work of the Lord, knowing that in the Lord your labor is not in vain.

Matt. 21:28; Gal. 4:7; Rom. 6:11–13; 1 Pet. 1:14–16;
2 Tim. 2:21; 1 Cor. 15:58

MORNING

Having loved his own who were in the world, he loved them to the end.

"I am praying for them. I am not praying for the world but for those whom you have given me, for they are yours. All mine are yours, and yours are mine, and I am glorified in them. . . . I do not ask that you take them out of the world, but that you keep them from the evil one. They are not of the world, just as I am not of the world."

"As the Father has loved me, so have I loved you. Abide in my love."—"Greater love has no one than this, that someone lay down his life for his friends. You are my friends if you do what I command you."—"A new commandment I give to you, that you love one another: just as I have loved you, you also are to love one another."

He who began a good work in you will bring it to completion at the day of Jesus Christ.—Christ loved the church and gave himself up for her, that he might sanctify her, having cleansed her by the washing of water with the word.

John 13:1; John 17:9–10, 15–16; John 15:9; John 15:13–14;
John 13:34; Phil. 1:6; Eph. 5:25–26

EVENING

The depths of God.

"No longer do I call you servants, for the servant does not know what his master is doing; but I have called you friends, for all that I have heard from my Father I have made known to you."—"To you it has been given to know the secrets of the kingdom of heaven."

Now we have received not the spirit of the world, but the Spirit who is from God, that we might understand the things freely given us by God.

For this reason I bow my knees before the Father, from whom every family in heaven and on earth is named, that according to the riches of his glory he may grant you to be strengthened with power through his Spirit in your inner being, so that Christ may dwell in your hearts through faith—that you, being rooted and grounded in love, may have strength to comprehend with all the saints what is the breadth and length and height and depth, and to know the love of Christ that surpasses knowledge, that you may be filled with all the fullness of God.

1 Cor. 2:10; John 15:15; Matt. 13:11; 1 Cor. 2:12; Eph. 3:14–19

MORNING

Give us life, and we will call upon your name!

"It is the Spirit who gives life."— Likewise the Spirit helps us in our weakness. For we do not know what to pray for as we ought, but the Spirit himself intercedes for us with groanings too deep for words. And he who searches hearts knows what is the mind of the Spirit, because the Spirit intercedes for the saints according to the will of God.—Praying at all times in the Spirit, with all prayer and supplication. To that end keep alert with all perseverance.

I will never forget your precepts, for by them you have given me life.— "The words that I have spoken to you are spirit and life."—For the letter kills, but the Spirit gives life.—"If you abide in me, and my words abide in you, ask whatever you wish, and it will be done for you."—And this is the confidence that we have toward him, that if we ask anything according to his will he hears us.

No one can say "Jesus is Lord" except in the Holy Spirit.

Ps. 80:18; John 6:63; Rom. 8:26–27; Eph. 6:18; Ps. 119:93; John 6:63;
2 Cor. 3:6; John 15:7; 1 John 5:14; 1 Cor. 12:3

EVENING

Take no part in the unfruitful works of darkness, but instead expose them.

Do not be deceived: "Bad company ruins good morals."

Do you not know that a little leaven leavens the whole lump? Cleanse out the old leaven. . . . I wrote to you in my letter not to associate with sexually immoral people—not at all meaning the sexually immoral of this world, or the greedy and swindlers, or idolaters, since then you would need to go out of the world. But now I am writing to you not to associate with anyone who bears the name of brother if he is guilty of sexual immorality or greed, or is an idolater, reviler, drunkard, or swindler—not even to eat with such a one.—That you may be blameless and innocent, children of God without blemish in the midst of a crooked and twisted generation, among whom you shine as lights in the world.

Now in a great house there are not only vessels of gold and silver but also of wood and clay, some for honorable use, some for dishonorable.

Eph. 5:11; 1 Cor. 15:33; 1 Cor. 5:6–7, 9–11; Phil. 2:15; 2 Tim. 2:20

MORNING

Let us then with confidence draw near to the throne of grace, that we may receive mercy and find grace to help in time of need.

Do not be anxious about anything, but in everything by prayer and supplication with thanksgiving let your requests be made known to God. And the peace of God, which surpasses all understanding, will guard your hearts and your minds in Christ Jesus.—For you did not receive the spirit of slavery to fall back into fear, but you have received the Spirit of adoption as sons, by whom we cry, "Abba! Father!"

"I did not say to the offspring of Jacob, 'Seek me in vain.'"—Therefore, . . . since we have confidence to enter the holy places by the blood of Jesus, by the new and living way that he opened for us through the curtain, that is, through his flesh, and since we have a great priest over the house of God, let us draw near with a true heart in full assurance of faith, with our hearts sprinkled clean from an evil conscience and our bodies washed with pure water.—So we can confidently say, "The Lord is my helper; I will not fear; what can man do to me?"

Heb. 4:16; Phil. 4:6-7; Rom. 8:15; Isa. 45:19; Heb. 10:19-22; Heb. 13:6

EVENING

"And you will know the truth, and the truth will set you free."

Where the Spirit of the Lord is, there is freedom.—For the law of the Spirit of life has set you free in Christ Jesus from the law of sin and death.—"So if the Son sets you free, you will be free indeed."

So, brothers, we are not children of the slave but of the free woman.—Yet we know that a person is not justified by works of the law but through faith in Jesus Christ, so we also have believed in Christ Jesus, in order to be justified by faith in Christ and not by works of the law, because by works of the law no one will be justified.

But the one who looks into the perfect law, the law of liberty, and perseveres, being no hearer who forgets but a doer who acts, he will be blessed in his doing.—For freedom Christ has set us free; stand firm therefore, and do not submit again to a yoke of slavery.

John 8:32; 2 Cor. 3:17; Rom. 8:2; John 8:36; Gal. 4:31;
Gal. 2:16; James 1:25; Gal. 5:1

MORNING

Light dawns in the darkness for the upright.

Who among you fears the Lord and obeys the voice of his servant? Let him who walks in darkness and has no light trust in the name of the Lord and rely on his God.—Though he fall, he shall not be cast headlong, for the Lord upholds his hand.—For the commandment is a lamp and the teaching a light.

Rejoice not over me, O my enemy; when I fall, I shall rise; when I sit in darkness, the Lord will be a light to me. I will bear the indignation of the Lord because I have sinned against him, until he pleads my cause and executes judgment for me. He will bring me out to the light; I shall look upon his vindication.

"The eye is the lamp of the body. So, if your eye is healthy, your whole body will be full of light, but if your eye is bad, your whole body will be full of darkness. If then the light in you is darkness, how great is the darkness!"

Ps. 112:4; Isa. 50:10; Ps. 37:24; Prov. 6:23; Mic. 7:8-9;
Matt. 6:22-23

EVENING

He will tend his flock like a shepherd; he will gather the
lambs in his arms; he will carry them in his bosom,
and gently lead those that are with young.

"I have compassion on the crowd because they have been with me now three days and have nothing to eat. And I am unwilling to send them away hungry, lest they faint on the way."—For we do not have a high priest who is unable to sympathize with our weaknesses.

And they were bringing children to him. . . . And he took them in his arms and blessed them, laying his hands on them.

I have gone astray like a lost sheep; seek your servant.—"For the Son of Man came to seek and to save the lost."—For you were straying like sheep, but have now returned to the Shepherd and Overseer of your souls.

"Fear not, little flock, for it is your Father's good pleasure to give you the kingdom."—"I myself will be the shepherd of my sheep, and I myself will make them lie down, declares the Lord God."

Isa. 40:11; Matt. 15:32; Heb. 4:15; Mark 10:13, 16; Ps. 119:176;
Luke 19:10; 1 Pet. 2:25; Luke 12:32; Ezek. 34:15

MORNING

He chose us in him before the foundation of the world.

That we should be holy and blameless before him.

God chose you as the firstfruits to be saved, through sanctification by the Spirit and belief in the truth. To this he called you, . . . so that you may obtain the glory of our Lord Jesus Christ.—For those whom he foreknew he also predestined to be conformed to the image of his Son, in order that he might be the firstborn among many brothers. And those whom he predestined he also called, and those whom he called he also justified, and those whom he justified he also glorified.—Elect, . . . according to the foreknowledge of God the Father, in the sanctification of the Spirit, for obedience to Jesus Christ and for sprinkling with his blood.—"And I will give you a new heart, and a new spirit I will put within you. And I will remove the heart of stone from your flesh and give you a heart of flesh."—For God has not called us for impurity, but in holiness.

Eph. 1:4; Eph. 1:4; 2 Thess. 2:13-14; Rom. 8:29-30;
1 Pet. 1:1-2; Ezek. 36:26; 1 Thess. 4:7

EVENING

"If the Lord himself should make windows in heaven, could this thing be?"

"Have faith in God."—And without faith it is impossible to please him.— "With God all things are possible."

"Is my hand shortened, that it cannot redeem? Or have I no power to deliver?"

For my thoughts are not your thoughts, neither are your ways my ways, declares the Lord. For as the heavens are higher than the earth, so are my ways higher than your ways and my thoughts than your thoughts.—"Put me to the test, says the Lord of hosts, if I will not open the windows of heaven for you and pour down for you a blessing until there is no more need."

Behold, the Lord's hand is not shortened, that it cannot save, or his ear dull, that it cannot hear.—"O Lord, there is none like you to help, between the mighty and the weak."—But that was to make us rely not on ourselves but on God who raises the dead.

2 Kings 7:2; Mark 11:22; Heb. 11:6; Matt. 19:26; Isa. 50:2; Isa. 55:8-9;
Mal. 3:10; Isa. 59:1; 2 Chron. 14:11; 2 Cor. 1:9

MORNING

And your days of mourning shall be ended.

"In the world you will have tribulation."—The whole creation has been groaning together in the pains of childbirth until now. And not only the creation, but we ourselves, who have the firstfruits of the Spirit, groan inwardly as we wait eagerly for adoption as sons, the redemption of our bodies.—For while we are still in this tent, we groan, being burdened—not that we would be unclothed, but that we would be further clothed, so that what is mortal may be swallowed up by life.

"These are the ones coming out of the great tribulation. They have washed their robes and made them white in the blood of the Lamb. Therefore they are before the throne of God, and serve him day and night in his temple; and he who sits on the throne will shelter them with his presence. They shall hunger no more, neither thirst anymore; the sun shall not strike them, nor any scorching heat. For the Lamb in the midst of the throne will be their shepherd, and he will guide them to springs of living water, and God will wipe away every tear from their eyes."

Isa. 60:20; John 16:33; Rom. 8:22–23; 2 Cor. 5:4; Rev. 7:14–17

EVENING

"Teacher, do you not care that we are perishing?"

The Lord is good to all, and his mercy is over all that he has made.

"Every moving thing that lives shall be food for you. And as I gave you the green plants, I give you everything."—"While the earth remains, seedtime and harvest, cold and heat, summer and winter, day and night, shall not cease."

The Lord is good, a stronghold in the day of trouble; he knows those who take refuge in him.—And God heard the voice of the boy, and the angel of God called to Hagar from heaven and said to her, "What troubles you, Hagar? Fear not, for God has heard the voice of the boy where he is. . . . Then God opened her eyes, and she saw a well of water. And she went and filled the skin with water and gave the boy a drink.—"Therefore do not be anxious, saying, 'What shall we eat?' or 'What shall we drink?' or 'What shall we wear?' For . . . your heavenly Father knows that you need them all."—As for the rich in this present age, charge them not to be haughty, nor to set their hopes on the uncertainty of riches, but on God, who richly provides us with everything to enjoy.

Mark 4:38; Ps. 145:9; Gen. 9:3; Gen. 8:22; Nah. 1:7;
Gen. 21:17, 19; Matt. 6:31–32; 1 Tim. 6:17

MORNING

Your work of faith.

"This is the work of God, that you believe in him whom he has sent."

So also faith by itself, if it does not have works, is dead.—Faith working through love.—For the one who sows to his own flesh will from the flesh reap corruption, but the one who sows to the Spirit will from the Spirit reap eternal life.—For we are his workmanship, created in Christ Jesus for good works, which God prepared beforehand, that we should walk in them.—Who gave himself for us to redeem us from all lawlessness and to purify for himself a people for his own possession who are zealous for good works.

We ought always to give thanks to God for you, brothers, as is right, because your faith is growing abundantly, and the love of every one of you for one another is increasing. . . . To this end we always pray for you, that our God may make you worthy of his calling and may fulfill every resolve for good and every work of faith by his power.—For it is God who works in you, both to will and to work for his good pleasure.

1 Thess. 1:3; John 6:29; James 2:17; Gal. 5:6; Gal. 6:8; Eph. 2:10;
Titus 2:14; 2 Thess. 1:3, 11; Phil. 2:13

EVENING

"Where is the promise of his coming?"

It was also about these that Enoch, the seventh from Adam, prophesied, saying, "Behold, the Lord comes with ten thousands of his holy ones, to execute judgment on all."—Behold, he is coming with the clouds, and every eye will see him, even those who pierced him, and all tribes of the earth will wail on account of him.

For the Lord himself will descend from heaven with a cry of command, with the voice of an archangel, and with the sound of the trumpet of God. And the dead in Christ will rise first. Then we who are alive, who are left, will be caught up together with them in the clouds to meet the Lord in the air, and so we will always be with the Lord.

For the grace of God has appeared, bringing salvation for all people, training us to renounce ungodliness and worldly passions, and to live self-controlled, upright, and godly lives in the present age, waiting for our blessed hope, the appearing of the glory of our great God and Savior Jesus Christ.

2 Pet. 3:4; Jude 14–15; Rev. 1:7; 1 Thess. 4:16–17; Titus 2:11–13

MORNING

"Or let them lay hold of my protection, let them make peace with me."

"For I know the plans I have for you, declares the Lord, plans for welfare and not for evil."—"There is no peace," says the Lord, "for the wicked."

But now in Christ Jesus you who once were far off have been brought near by the blood of Christ. For he himself is our peace.

For in him all the fullness of God was pleased to dwell, and through him to reconcile to himself all things, whether on earth or in heaven, making peace by the blood of his cross.—Christ Jesus, whom God put forward as a propitiation by his blood, to be received by faith. This was to show God's righteousness, because in his divine forbearance he had passed over former sins . . . so that he might be just and the justifier of the one who has faith in Jesus.—If we confess our sins, he is faithful and just to forgive us our sins and to cleanse us from all unrighteousness.

Trust in the Lord forever, for the Lord God is an everlasting rock.

Isa. 27:5; Jer. 29:11; Isa. 48:22; Eph. 2:13-14; Col. 1:19-20; Rom. 3:24-26; 1 John 1:9; Isa. 26:4

EVENING

God gave us eternal life, and this life is in his Son.

"For as the Father has life in himself, so he has granted the Son also to have life in himself. . . . For as the Father raises the dead and gives them life, so also the Son gives life to whom he will."

"I am the resurrection and the life. Whoever believes in me, though he die, yet shall he live, and everyone who lives and believes in me shall never die."—"I am the good shepherd. The good shepherd lays down his life for the sheep. . . . No one takes it from me, but I lay it down of my own accord. I have authority to lay it down, and I have authority to take it up again. This charge I have received from my Father."—"No one comes to the Father except through me."—Whoever has the Son has life; whoever does not have the Son of God does not have life.—For you have died, and your life is hidden with Christ in God. When Christ who is your life appears, then you also will appear with him in glory.

1 John 5:11; John 5:26, 21; John 11:25-26; John 10:11, 17-18; John 14:6; 1 John 5:12; Col. 3:3-4

MORNING

For if you live according to the flesh you will die, but if by the
Spirit you put to death the deeds of the body, you will live.

Now the works of the flesh are evident: sexual immorality, impurity, . . . and things like these. I warn you, as I warned you before, that those who do such things will not inherit the kingdom of God. But the fruit of the Spirit is love, joy, peace, patience, kindness, goodness, faithfulness, gentleness, self-control; against such things there is no law. And those who belong to Christ Jesus have crucified the flesh with its passions and desires. If we live by the Spirit, let us also keep in step with the Spirit.

For the grace of God has appeared, bringing salvation for all people, training us to renounce ungodliness and worldly passions, and to live self-controlled, upright, and godly lives in the present age, waiting for our blessed hope, the appearing of the glory of our great God and Savior Jesus Christ, who gave himself for us to redeem us from all lawlessness.

Rom. 8:13; Gal. 5:19, 21–25; Titus 2:11-14

EVENING

The commanders of the Philistines said,
"What are these Hebrews doing here?"

If you are insulted for the name of Christ, you are blessed, because the Spirit of glory and of God rests upon you. But let none of you suffer as a murderer or a thief . . . or as a meddler.

So do not let what you regard as good be spoken of as evil.—Keep your conduct among the Gentiles honorable.

Do not be unequally yoked with unbelievers. For what partnership has righteousness with lawlessness? Or what fellowship has light with darkness? . . . For we are the temple of the living God; . . . "Therefore go out from their midst, and be separate from them, says the Lord, and touch no unclean thing."

But you are a chosen race, a royal priesthood, a holy nation, a people for his own possession, that you may proclaim the excellencies of him who called you out of darkness into his marvelous light.

1 Sam. 29:3; 1 Pet. 4:14–15; Rom. 14:16; 1 Pet. 2:12;
2 Cor. 6:14, 16–17; 1 Pet. 2:9

MORNING

The goodness and loving kindness of God our Savior appeared.

"I have loved you with an everlasting love."

In this the love of God was made manifest among us, that God sent his only Son into the world, so that we might live through him. In this is love, not that we have loved God but that he loved us and sent his Son to be the propitiation for our sins.

But when the fullness of time had come, God sent forth his Son, born of woman, born under the law, to redeem those who were under the law, so that we might receive adoption as sons.—And the Word became flesh and dwelt among us, and we have seen his glory, glory as of the only Son from the Father, full of grace and truth.—Great indeed, we confess, is the mystery of godliness: He was manifested in the flesh.

Since therefore the children share in flesh and blood, he himself likewise partook of the same things, that through death he might destroy the one who has the power of death, that is, the devil.

Titus 3:4; Jer. 31:3; 1 John 4:9-10; Gal. 4:4-5; John 1:14;
1 Tim. 3:16; Heb. 2:14

EVENING

Thanks be to God for his inexpressible gift!

Make a joyful noise to the Lord, all the earth! Serve the Lord with gladness! Come into his presence with singing! . . . Enter his gates with thanksgiving, and his courts with praise! Give thanks to him; bless his name!—For to us a child is born, to us a son is given; and the government shall be upon his shoulder, and his name shall be called Wonderful Counselor, Mighty God, Everlasting Father, Prince of Peace.

He . . . did not spare his own Son but gave him up for us all.—"He had still one other, a beloved son. Finally he sent him."

Let them thank the Lord for his steadfast love, for his wondrous works to the children of man!—Bless the Lord, O my soul, and all that is within me, bless his holy name!

"My soul magnifies the Lord, and my spirit rejoices in God my Savior."

2 Cor. 9:15; Ps. 100:1-2, 4; Isa. 9:6; Rom. 8:32; Mark 12:6;
Ps. 107:21; Ps. 103:1; Luke 1:46-47

MORNING

Be steadfast, immovable, always abounding in the work of the Lord.

Knowing that in the Lord your labor is not in vain.—As you received Christ Jesus the Lord, so walk in him, rooted and built up in him and established in the faith, just as you were taught, abounding in thanksgiving.—"But the one who endures to the end will be saved."—"As for that in the good soil, they are those who, hearing the word, hold it fast in an honest and good heart, and bear fruit with patience."

For you stand firm in your faith.

"We must work the works of him who sent me while it is day; night is coming, when no one can work."

For the one who sows to his own flesh will from the flesh reap corruption, but the one who sows to the Spirit will from the Spirit reap eternal life. And let us not grow weary of doing good, for in due season we will reap, if we do not give up. So then, as we have opportunity, let us do good to everyone, and especially to those who are of the household of faith.

1 Cor. 15:58; 1 Cor. 15:58; Col. 2:6-7; Matt. 24:13; Luke 8:15;
2 Cor. 1:24; John 9:4; Gal. 6:8-10

EVENING

He is able to save to the uttermost those who draw near to God through him.

"I am the way, and the truth, and the life. No one comes to the Father except through me."—"And there is salvation in no one else, for there is no other name under heaven given among men by which we must be saved."

"My sheep hear my voice, and I know them, and they follow me. I give them eternal life, and they will never perish, and no one will snatch them out of my hand."—He who began a good work in you will bring it to completion at the day of Jesus Christ.—"Is anything too hard for the Lord?"

Now to him who is able to keep you from stumbling and to present you blameless before the presence of his glory with great joy, to the only God, our Savior, through Jesus Christ our Lord, be glory, majesty, dominion, and authority, before all time and now and forever. Amen.

Heb. 7:25; John 14:6; Acts 4:12; John 10:27-28;
Phil. 1:6; Gen. 18:14; Jude 24-25

MORNING

We look not to the things that are seen but to the things that are unseen. For the things that are seen are transient, but the things that are unseen are eternal.

For here we have no lasting city.—You knew that you yourselves had a better possession and an abiding one.

"Fear not, little flock, for it is your Father's good pleasure to give you the Kingdom."—Now for a little while, if necessary, you have been grieved by various trials.—"There the wicked cease from troubling, and there the weary are at rest."

For while we are still in this tent, we groan, being burdened.—"He will wipe away every tear from their eyes, and death shall be no more, neither shall there be mourning, nor crying, nor pain anymore, for the former things have passed away."

The sufferings of this present time are not worth comparing with the glory that is to be revealed to us.—For this light momentary affliction is preparing for us an eternal weight of glory beyond all comparison.

2 Cor. 4:18; Heb. 13:14; Heb. 10:34; Luke 12:32; 1 Pet. 1:6; Job 3:17;
2 Cor. 5:4; Rev. 21:4; Rom. 8:18; 2 Cor. 4:17

EVENING

For he himself is our peace.

In Christ God was reconciling the world to himself, not counting their trespasses against them. . . . For our sake he made him to be sin who knew no sin, so that in him we might become the righteousness of God.—Through him to reconcile to himself all things, whether on earth or in heaven, making peace by the blood of his cross. And you, who once were alienated and hostile in mind, doing evil deeds, he has now reconciled in his body of flesh by his death, in order to present you holy and blameless and above reproach before him.—By canceling the record of debt that stood against us with its legal demands. This he set aside, nailing it to the cross.—By abolishing the law of commandments expressed in ordinances, that he might create in himself one new man in place of the two, so making peace.

"Peace I leave with you; my peace I give to you. Not as the world gives do I give to you. Let not your hearts be troubled, neither let them be afraid."

Eph. 2:14; 2 Cor. 5:19, 21; Col. 1:20–22; Col. 2:14;
Eph. 2:15; John 14:27

MORNING

"Your sins are forgiven."

"For I will forgive their iniquity, and I will remember their sin no more."—"Who can forgive sins but God alone?"

"I, I am he who blots out your transgressions for my own sake, and I will not remember your sins."—Blessed is the one whose transgression is forgiven, whose sin is covered. Blessed is the man against whom the Lord counts no iniquity, and in whose spirit there is no deceit.—Who is a God like you, pardoning iniquity?

God in Christ forgave you.—The blood of Jesus his Son cleanses us from all sin. If we say we have no sin, we deceive ourselves, and the truth is not in us. If we confess our sins, he is faithful and just to forgive us our sins and to cleanse us from all unrighteousness.

As far as the east is from the west, so far does he remove our transgressions from us.—For sin will have no dominion over you, since you are not under law but under grace. . . . And, [you] having been set free from sin, have become slaves of righteousness.

Mark 2:5; Jer. 31:34; Mark 2:7; Isa. 43:25; Ps. 32:1–2; Mic. 7:18;
Eph. 4:32; 1 John 1:7–9; Ps. 103:12; Rom. 6:14, 18

EVENING

"Sir, we wish to see Jesus."

O Lord, we wait for you; your name and remembrance are the desire of our soul.

The Lord is near to all who call on him, to all who call on him in truth.

"For where two or three are gathered in my name, there am I among them."—"I will not leave you as orphans; I will come to you."—"And behold, I am with you always, to the end of the age."

Let us run with endurance the race that is set before us, looking to Jesus, the founder and perfecter of our faith.

For now we see in a mirror dimly, but then face to face.—My desire is to depart and be with Christ, for that is far better.

Beloved, we are God's children now, and what we will be has not yet appeared; but we know that when he appears we shall be like him, because we shall see him as he is. And everyone who thus hopes in him purifies himself as he is pure.

John 12:21; Isa. 26:8; Ps. 145:18; Matt. 18:20; John 14:18; Matt. 28:20;
Heb. 12:1–2; 1 Cor. 13:12; Phil. 1:23; 1 John 3:2–3

MORNING

Understand what the will of the Lord is.

For this is the will of God, your sanctification.—"Agree with God, and be at peace; thereby good will come to you."—"And this is eternal life, that they know you the only true God, and Jesus Christ whom you have sent."—And we know that the Son of God has come and has given us understanding, so that we may know him who is true; and we are in him who is true, in his Son Jesus Christ. He is the true God and eternal life.

We have not ceased to pray for you, asking that you may be filled with the knowledge of his will in all spiritual wisdom and understanding.—The God of our Lord Jesus Christ, the Father of glory, . . . give you the Spirit of wisdom and of revelation in the knowledge of him, having the eyes of your hearts enlightened, that you may know what is the hope to which he has called you, what are the riches of his glorious inheritance in the saints, and what is the immeasurable greatness of his power toward us who believe, according to the working of his great might.

Eph. 5:17; 1 Thess. 4:3; Job 22:21; John 17:3; 1 John 5:20;
Col. 1:9; Eph. 1:17–19

EVENING

Draw near to God, and he will draw near to you.

Enoch walked with God.—"Do two walk together, unless they have agreed to meet?"—It is good to be near God.

"The Lord is with you while you are with him. If you seek him, he will be found by you, but if you forsake him, he will forsake you. . . . But when in their distress they turned to the Lord, the God of Israel, and sought him, he was found by them."

"For I know the plans I have for you, declares the Lord, plans for welfare and not for evil, to give you a future and a hope. Then you will call upon me and come and pray to me, and I will hear you. You will seek me and find me, when you seek me with all your heart."

Therefore, brothers, since we have confidence to enter the holy places by the blood of Jesus, by the new and living way, . . . and since we have a great priest over the house of God, let us draw near with a true heart in full assurance of faith.

James 4:8; Gen. 5:24; Amos 3:3; Ps. 73:28; 2 Chron. 15:2, 4;
Jer. 29:11–13; Heb. 10:19–22

MORNING

Guiltless in the day of our Lord Jesus Christ.

And you, who once were alienated and hostile in mind, doing evil deeds, he has now reconciled in his body of flesh by his death, in order to present you holy and blameless and above reproach before him, if indeed you continue in the faith, stable and steadfast, not shifting from the hope of the gospel.—That you may be blameless and innocent, children of God without blemish in the midst of a crooked and twisted generation, among whom you shine as lights in the world.

Therefore, beloved, since you are waiting for these, be diligent to be found by him without spot or blemish, and at peace.—Pure and blameless for the day of Christ.

Now to him who is able to keep you from stumbling and to present you blameless before the presence of his glory with great joy, to the only God, our Savior, through Jesus Christ our Lord, be glory, majesty, dominion, and authority, before all time and now and forever.

1 Cor. 1:8; Col. 1:21–23; Phil. 2:15; 2 Pet. 3:14; Phil. 1:10; Jude 24–25

EVENING

"He will guard the feet of his faithful ones."

If we say we have fellowship with him while we walk in darkness, we lie and do not practice the truth. But if we walk in the light, as he is in the light, we have fellowship with one another, and the blood of Jesus his Son cleanses us from all sin.—"The one who has bathed does not need to wash, except for his feet, but is completely clean."

I have taught you the way of wisdom; I have led you in the paths of uprightness. When you walk, your step will not be hampered, and if you run, you will not stumble. . . . Do not enter the path of the wicked, and do not walk in the way of the evil. Avoid it; do not go on it; turn away from it and pass on. . . . Let your eyes look directly forward, and your gaze be straight before you. Ponder the path of your feet; then all your ways will be sure. Do not swerve to the right or to the left; turn your foot away from evil.

The Lord will rescue me from every evil deed and bring me safely into his heavenly kingdom. To him be the glory forever and ever. Amen.

1 Sam. 2:9; 1 John 1:6–7; John 13:10; Prov. 4:11–12, 14–15, 25–27;
2 Tim. 4:18

MORNING

*"The Lord your God carried you, as a man carries his son,
all the way that you went until you came to this place."*

"I bore you on eagles' wings and brought you to myself."—In his love and in his pity he redeemed them; he lifted them up and carried them all the days of old.—Like an eagle that stirs up its nest, that flutters over its young, spreading out its wings, catching them, bearing them on its pinions, the Lord alone guided him.

"Even to your old age I am he, and to gray hairs I will carry you. I have made, and I will bear; I will carry and will save."—This is God, our God forever and ever. He will guide us forever.

Cast your burden on the Lord, and he will sustain you.—"Do not be anxious about your life, what you will eat or what you will drink, nor about your body, what you will put on. . . . For . . . your heavenly Father knows that you need them all.

"Till now the Lord has helped us."

Deut. 1:31; Ex. 19:4; Isa. 63:9; Deut. 32:11–12; Isa. 46:4; Ps. 48:14;
Ps. 55:22; Matt. 6:25, 32; 1 Sam. 7:12

EVENING

"There remains yet very much land to possess."

Not that I have already obtained this or am already perfect, but I press on to make it my own, because Christ Jesus has made me his own.

"You therefore must be perfect."—Make every effort to supplement your faith with virtue, and virtue with knowledge, and knowledge with self-control, and self-control with steadfastness, and steadfastness with godliness, and godliness with brotherly affection, and brotherly affection with love.

And it is my prayer that your love may abound more and more, with knowledge and all discernment.

"What no eye has seen, nor ear heard, nor the heart of man imagined, what God has prepared for those who love him"—these things God has revealed to us through the Spirit.

So then, there remains a Sabbath rest for the people of God.—Your eyes will behold the king in his beauty; they will see a land that stretches afar.

Josh. 13:1; Phil. 3:12; Matt. 5:48; 2 Pet. 1:5–7; Phil. 1:9;
1 Cor. 2:9–10; Heb. 4:9; Isa. 33:17

THE MORNING HOUR

A List of Daily Texts Arranged in Bible Order

Genesis

13:10, 11	Mar. 22
15:6	Mar. 24
16:13	Jan. 29
21:1	April 24
22:14	Mar. 10
24:63	Mar. 30
28:16	May 2
32:26	April 5
32:28	May 31
39:3	June 8
41:52	Mar. 2

Exodus

2:9	June 20
3:7	Aug. 24
12:11	June 2
12:43	July 2
13:7	Sept. 3
19:6	July 16
25:21, 22	June 18
28:12	May 23
28:36	Aug. 26
30:23, 25	Nov. 5
33:14	July 12
34:29	Oct. 4

Leviticus

1:3, 4	April 22
1:4	Mar. 17
4:12	Feb. 17
16:22	Oct. 2
17:11	May 29
20:8	Feb. 21

Numbers

6:24	Mar. 11
6:25, 26	Mar. 12
6:27	Sept. 28
10:33	June 24
23:19	Aug. 20
31:23	June 12
33:55	Jan. 31

Deuteronomy

1:31	Dec. 31
3:24	Aug. 18
8:10	Feb. 7
12:9	Jan. 4
13:17	April 20
17:16	Feb. 4
18:18	April 18
29:29	June 15
32:4	Sept. 26
33:25	Jan. 28

Joshua

1:18	Mar. 28

Ruth

3:18	Sept. 4

1 Samuel

7:3	April 2
12:24	April 29

1 Chronicles

4:10	Feb. 2
4:10	June 26
22:5	Aug. 16

Ezra
9:9	Sept. 23

Nehemiah
5:19	Jan. 7
8:10	Aug. 14
9:17	Oct. 9

Esther
5:2	Aug. 30

Job
5:8	Dec. 3
19:25	June 28
23:10	Sept. 30
28:12	Dec. 4

Psalms
9:10	Jan. 8
18:18	April 23
22:11	Oct. 11
25:9	Oct. 7
25:12	Feb. 22
27:14	Sept. 2
31:19	May 25
31:22	April 16
40:17	Nov. 14
48:14	Jan. 22
50:15	Oct. 5
50:23	April 17
51:2	May 19
59:9	Oct. 15
60:4	Jan. 9
63:5, 6	April 14
65:1	Jan. 11
65:4	Nov. 29
66:2	Dec. 14
73:28	Sept. 24
78:53	Nov. 11
80:18	Dec. 17
85:10	May 6
89:16	Oct. 17
89:19	Nov. 9
90:17	Jan. 6
92:5	Nov. 17
99:1	Oct. 26
104:34	Sept. 22
107:7	Jan. 3
107:8	Nov. 7
108:1	Oct. 22
112:4	Dec. 19
119:18	Sept. 18
119:25	Jan. 15
119:57	Aug. 21
119:71	Dec. 5
119:105	Aug. 27
119:130	Mar. 20

Proverbs
1:33	Nov. 23
2:6	Feb. 19
2:8	Mar. 6
3:5, 6	Mar. 3
3:9	April 13
3:12	Aug. 6
3:13	Sept. 20
3:26	Oct. 19
4:18	Aug. 8
8:34	Nov. 1
10:19	April 11
11:18	Mar. 27
16:20	Aug. 29
20:9	Feb. 15
21:2	Sept. 16
21:3	Dec. 9
27:1	Feb. 29

Song of Solomon
1:3	Feb. 16
1:5	April 10
2:6	April 26
4:7	Aug. 9
5:16	Oct. 29
7:10	July 13

Isaiah

9:6	Jan. 20
26:3	Jan. 13
27:5	Dec. 23
27:8	Nov. 18
32:2	Dec. 1
38:14	Mar. 5
38:14	Mar. 18
38:17	Jan. 17
38:17	Mar. 8
42:10	Jan. 2
43:1	April 9
51:1	Aug. 25
51:12	Sept. 14
53:10	May 8
53:11	Feb. 20
54:5	Mar. 7
57:18	Sept. 12
59:1	May 4
59:16	Oct. 28
60:20	Dec. 21
62:4	Nov. 26
64:1	July 29

Jeremiah

15:20	July 11
17:7	Feb. 18
31:3	Aug. 23
32:39	Sept. 10
50:34	April 15

Lamentations

3:26	Oct. 30
3:31, 32	Aug. 12
3:40	Feb. 26
3:41	Sept. 6

Ezekiel

1:26	Feb. 13
20:19	May 17
36:37	Feb. 24

Daniel

5:27	Sept. 8
10:12	Oct. 13

Hosea

14:9	Nov. 3

Jonah

2:4	Oct. 24
4:2	July 17

Micah

7:8	Nov. 20

Nahum

1:7	May 27

Zephaniah

3:15	Dec. 12
3:17	June 6

Haggai

2:4	Feb. 3
2:9	June 4

Zechariah

3:4	July 9
4:6	Oct. 31

Malachi

3:16	Feb. 11
3:17	Feb. 12

Matthew

1:21	April 25
3:15	Feb. 14
4:1	July 7
5:48	May 3
6:10	July 15
6:31, 32	May 5
7:20	Nov. 19
8:17	Oct. 27
10:24	July 10
12:20	Sept. 17

12:34	July 14	15:4	June 13
24:6	May 7	15:15	Feb. 8
25:13	June 3	17:15	Aug. 10
25:14, 15	Mar. 26	17:16	July 20
25:34	Mar. 29	17:17	Nov. 16
28:20	Oct. 25	17:22	Nov. 27
		19:30	Aug. 4
Mark		19:34	Oct. 18
2:5	Dec. 28		
		Acts	
Luke		3:26	Mar. 19
1:49	July 19	20:19	Jan. 19
1:50	Aug. 3		
1:53	Sept. 9	**Romans**	
8:21	Nov. 24	1:1	May 16
11:34	Feb. 10	3:1	July 21
12:15	Oct. 23	3:22	Jan. 25
15:13	June 10	5:5	Jan. 23
15:20	June 11	5:14	Jan. 18
16:25	Feb. 9	5:16	Aug. 31
17:10	June 5	6:4	Aug. 5
18:1	June 7	6:10	July 22
		6:11	Feb. 27
John		6:14	Sept. 15
1:16	Oct. 21	6:18	Nov. 25
1:29	April 28	7:22	Oct. 20
3:16	Feb. 28	8:3	April 12
5:26	May 18	8:13	Dec. 24
6:37	Nov. 21	8:17	July 3
7:37	Sept. 13	8:28	Sept. 21
7:46	June 9	12:2	Sept. 11
10:3	July 18	12:11	Oct. 16
10:7	April 19	12:12	July 24
10:10	Feb. 5	12:12	Sept. 7
10:29	Dec. 10	14:7	Aug. 22
13:1	Dec. 16	14:9	Oct. 14
13:23	July 4	14:16	Dec. 11
14:16, 17	June 23		
14:26	Aug. 7	**1 Corinthians**	
14:27	May 22	1:5	April 8
14:28	Jan. 14	1:8	Dec. 30
15:2	Jan. 21	1:9	Nov. 15

7:29 — April 27
12:12 — Sept. 5
15:24 — July 23
15:34 — May 11
15:58 — Dec. 26

2 Corinthians

1:5 — June 14
4:4 — July 27
4:18 — Dec. 27
5:19 — Oct. 12
5:21 — Dec. 7
6:10 — April 7
7:10 — Nov. 12

Galatians

5:13 — Dec. 8
5:22 — Mar. 1
5:22 — April 1
5:22 — May 1
5:22 — June 1
5:22 — July 1
5:22 — Aug. 1
5:22 — Sept. 1
5:22 — Oct. 1
6:2 — Dec. 15

Ephesians

1:4 — Dec. 20
3:15 — Oct. 10
4:30 — May 24
5:2 — July 28
5:15, 16 — June 16
5:17 — Dec. 29
5:25, 26 — Nov. 13
6:10 — May 21

Philippians

2:13 — Dec. 6
3:10 — May 14
3:13, 14 — Jan. 1
3:20 — May 28

4:1 — April 21
4:5 — Jan. 24
4:6 — June 17
4:19 — Mar. 31

Colossians

1:10 — Nov. 10
1:19 — Jan. 16
3:1 — July 30
3:2 — Mar. 4
3:3 — June 22
3:4 — Nov. 6
4:6 — July 6

1 Thessalonians

1:3 — Dec. 22
5:8 — Nov. 8
5:15 — Nov. 2
5:23 — Jan. 10

2 Thessalonians

3:16 — Nov. 30

1 Timothy

1:14 — Feb. 6
2:5 — Mar. 13
2:8 — May 13
4:16 — May 20
6:17 — Mar. 9

2 Timothy

2:1 — Dec. 13
2:3 — July 31

Titus

2:10 — Mar. 14
3:4 — Dec. 25

Hebrews

2:10 — Mar. 15
2:14 — Aug. 11
4:3 — Jan. 5
4:11 — May 30

4:16	Dec. 18
7:25	April 6
11:1	May 9
11:8	July 26
11:16	Aug. 13
12:1, 2	Jan. 30
12:14	June 19
12:24	Feb. 23
13:5	Mar. 25
13:6	Oct. 8
13:13, 14	Jan. 26
13:20	May 26
13:20, 21	Aug. 15

James

1:4	Sept. 25
2:26	Nov. 28
4:7	Feb. 25
4:14	Mar. 16
5:16	Aug. 17

1 Peter

1:6	Nov. 4
1:8	Feb. 1
1:15	Aug. 19
2:21	June 21
5:6	Sept. 27
5:10	Sept. 19

2 Peter

3:8, 9	April 3

1 John

1:9	July 8
2:5	April 30
2:20	Dec. 2
3:2	June 25
3:5	Jan. 27
3:8	May 10
3:14	July 25
3:16	Sept. 29
4:7	May 12
4:16	July 5
5:3	June 29

Jude

20	Nov. 22
25	Jan. 12

Revelation

1:5	Oct. 3
1:17	April 4
3:2	Mar. 21
3:19	June 30
4:8	Mar. 23
6:17	June 27
12:10	Aug. 28
13:8	Aug. 2
19:6	Oct. 6
21:4	May 15

THE EVENING HOUR

List of the Daily Texts Arranged in Bible Order

Genesis

1:27	Feb. 17
2:9	Aug. 28
3:1	Sept. 27
3:4, 5	Sept. 3
3:15	Jan. 14
5:3	Feb. 18
5:22	April 22
6:9	Mar. 20
17:1	June 3
49:11	Jan. 24
49:15	Mar. 4

Exodus

12:42	June 26
14:15	Dec. 12
16:15	Aug. 30
17:15	Mar. 1
20:11	Mar. 15
33:18	Feb. 12

Numbers

18:20	Feb. 14
22:6	Oct. 27

Deuteronomy

30:19	Jan. 27
31:8	Jan. 1
32:9	Jan. 20

Joshua

1:5	Jan. 7
13:1	Dec. 31
14:12	Mar. 22

Judges

6:24	April 1
15:19	Sept. 18

Ruth

3:1	June 23

1 Samuel

2:9	Dec. 5
2:9	Dec. 30
2:25	Jan. 31
2:30	Aug. 3
3:17	Oct. 6
7:12	July 1
29:3	Dec. 24
30:6	Oct. 29

2 Samuel

7:25	Oct. 31
7:29	Oct. 7
23:5	Aug. 14
24:23	Oct. 20

1 Kings

4:29	Aug. 22
10:7	Nov. 18
19:9	Nov. 24
20:27	Nov. 8

2 Kings

4:26	Nov. 12
7:2	Dec. 20

2 Chronicles

6:18	Jan. 10

Nehemiah
4:9 — July 16

Esther
6:1 — May 23

Job
2:10 — Feb. 24
7:4 — Jan. 12
7:16 — Dec. 4
14:7 — Nov. 22
20:5 — June 9
23:3 — Feb. 25
34:3 — July 15
38:19 — Aug. 11

Psalms
4:8 — Aug. 29
9:10 — April 6
12:6 — Oct. 9
13:1 — Mar. 30
16:5 — June 2
16:7 — May 16
16:11 — July 25
18:16 — Aug. 4
18:39 — July 27
19:1 — Sept. 28
23:2 — Sept. 2
23:5 — Aug. 26
24:1 — Aug. 6
25:4 — Sept. 30
25:5 — Nov. 6
25:7 — June 29
25:18 — June 7
26:3 — July 6
27:11 — April 11
30:5 — Sept. 16
31:15 — Mar. 7
34:8 — Sept. 17
38:10 — May 13
40:2 — Oct. 8
40:17 — Sept. 7

41:3 — April 7
42:6 — Mar. 13
50:5 — Nov. 9
51:12 — April 14
55:6 — May 29
61:2 — April 4
61:5 — July 29
62:12 — Dec. 13
69:20 — May 12
69:26 — Feb. 4
69:26 — May 7
71:14 — April 28
73:2 — Sept. 9
77:8 — Mar. 21
78:20 — Feb. 10
86:12 — Jan. 29
86:13 — April 22
89:19 — May 17
90:11 — Feb. 23
91:15 — April 16
93:3 — Feb. 15
94:19 — Jan. 22
94:20 — July 8
97:11 — Feb. 21
97:12 — July 26
102:27 — Feb. 29
103:4 — Jan. 11
103:14 — June 5
103:15, 16 — Aug. 17
103:19 — Oct. 22
104:16 — Feb. 11
104:23 — Sept. 11
105:39 — May 5
107:9 — July 11
118:7 — Sept. 12
119:28 — Mar. 19
119:50 — Feb. 13
121:1, 2 — Sept. 19
133:3 — July 19
139:3 — June 20

139:12	Feb. 3	40:31	Sept. 10
141:2	Jan. 2	41:17	Oct. 24
141:3	Jan. 5	45:11	Aug. 19
143:2	June 27	46:4	Aug. 23
145:10	June 17	53:6	Jan. 19
145:15	April 24	53:6	April 23
		60:13	Nov. 19

Proverbs

		60:18	Feb. 8
1:10	Nov. 27	61:10	Aug. 25
3:24	Feb. 22	62:6	May 8
14:12	Aug. 21	63:3	Aug. 2
14:29	April 30	63:4	Feb. 19
15:15	July 20	63:7	April 9
20:27	Feb. 28	65:17	Dec. 1
23:26	July 10		
24:10	Aug. 20	**Jeremiah**	
27:24	Mar. 29	2:13	Aug. 9
29:25	Aug. 10	2:13	Sept. 5
		12:5	Nov. 14

Ecclesiastes

1:2	May 10	20:9	April 19
5:2	June 30	23:6	Feb. 1
12:7	Dec. 8	45:5	April 15
12:7	Dec. 9		

Lamentations

Song of Solomon		3:27	Jan. 30
1:4	April 17		
2:15	Oct. 30	**Ezekiel**	
2:16	Mar. 10	48:35	May 1
3:1	Nov. 10		
4:16	Jan. 28	**Hosea**	
5:6	June 21	2:14	Aug. 15
6:10	April 26	5:15	May 24
		14:5	Dec. 7

Isaiah

9:6	Nov. 1	**Amos**	
9:6	Nov. 2	4:11	April 3
9:6	Nov. 3		
9:6	Nov. 4	**Jonah**	
21:11	Sept. 6	1:6	Aug. 27
34:16	July 13		
40:11	Dec. 19	**Zechariah**	
		13:7	June 25

Malachi

2:15	Oct. 26
3:15	Jan. 21

Matthew

1:23	June 1
5:13	Sept. 13
6:9	Oct. 10
6:9	Oct. 11
6:10	Oct. 12
6:10	Oct. 13
6:11	Oct. 14
6:12	Oct. 15
6:13	Oct. 16
6:13	Oct. 17
6:13	Oct. 18
14:14	Feb. 7
17:20	June 18
20:28	July 7
21:28	Dec. 15
22:42	Aug. 7
26:39	Sept. 22
26:41	Dec. 6
26:42	Aug. 5
26:44	July 2
27:46	Mar. 6
27:51	July 21

Mark

2:8	June 8
4:38	Dec. 21
6:30	Jan. 6
14:8	July 18

Luke

5:5	Mar. 25
9:23	Sept. 1
10:19	Oct. 28
10:41	June 14
10:42	Jan. 9
18:8	April 2
18:41	Jan. 3

19:13	Aug. 31
24:29	Mar. 23

John

1:38, 39	June 24
5:19	Sept. 29
6:20	May 9
6:63	Mar. 14
6:63	Oct. 23
7:50	July 30
8:32	Dec. 18
9:4	Feb. 9
9:4	Aug. 24
9:35	June 13
10:27	May 11
11:11	Mar. 28
11:35	Mar. 11
11:36	June 22
11:42	May 30
12:21	Dec. 28
13:7	Sept. 4
13:16	Oct. 21
16:31	Nov. 29
17:4	May 4
18:36	Nov. 23
20:16	May 20

Acts

2:21	Nov. 25
26:15	April 20

Romans

2:16	Sept. 25
3:23	April 12
4:20	July 24
5:3	Nov. 30
8:15	Jan. 25
8:26	May 22
8:27	June 15
10:13	Aug. 8
12:3	Jan. 15
12:3	Mar. 26

12:16	July 5	6:7	Nov. 17
13:12	June 4		

1 Corinthians		**Ephesians**	
1:9	May 21	2:3	Dec. 14
1:9	Sept. 14	2:6	May 15
1:27	Aug. 12	2:10	Nov. 15
1:28	Aug. 13	2:14	Dec. 27
1:28	July 3	2:18	Nov. 13
1:31	Aug. 18	2:19	Nov. 16
2:10	Dec. 16	4:3	July 31
3:13	July 9	4:15	Oct. 1
4:7	Oct. 2	4:26	Jan. 13
6:11	Nov. 11	5:11	Dec. 17
7:31	Nov. 5	5:14	Dec. 11
7:32	May 27		
9:24	May 28	**Philippians**	
10:13	Mar. 27	1:5	May 19
12:5	Oct. 3	2:1	Oct. 19
12:6	Oct. 4	3:14	Mar. 3
14:15	Mar. 16	3:20, 21	Jan. 26
15:23	Sept. 8	4:6	July 28
15:35	May 6		
15:41	Feb. 2	**Colossians**	
15:54	Sept. 26	1:13	Nov. 21
15:55	Jan. 4	1:17	Aug. 16
		3:13	June 10

2 Corinthians		**1 Thessalonians**	
5:4	Feb. 16	2:12	Mar. 24
5:10	Feb. 5	5:25	July 23
6:10	Sept. 20		
6:14	Mar. 31	**2 Thessalonians**	
7:1	May 3	2:13	July 17
7:10	Nov. 26	2:16	April 18
8:9	April 25		
8:9	Sept. 24	**1 Timothy**	
9:15	Dec. 25	2:5	Nov. 20
13:14	Sept. 21	4:1	June 28
		6:12	Mar. 5

Galatians		**2 Timothy**	
5:11	Jan. 23	1:12	Mar. 8
5:26	May 18	3:12	April 10

Titus

2:13	April 29

Hebrews

2:14, 15	Nov. 28
3:8	Feb. 20
4:9	Mar. 2
4:15	Mar. 17
7:25	Dec. 26
10:20	June 6
10:22	Dec. 2
10:22	Dec. 3
10:24	July 12
10:37	Oct. 5
12:2	April 5

James

1:5	Feb. 27
1:8	Sept. 15
1:25	Dec. 10
4:8	Dec. 29
5:11	Aug. 1
5:11	Nov. 7

1 Peter

2:24	June 12
4:7	Oct. 25

2 Peter

3:4	Dec. 22

1 John

2:1, 2	July 4
2:28	May 31
3:22	Mar. 12
5:11	Dec. 23
5:21	May 2

3 John

14	July 14

Jude

21	July 22

Revelation

1:19	Jan. 16
1:19	Jan. 17
1:19	Jan. 18
2:17	April 27
2:18	May 25
3:11	June 16
3:18	June 19
4:3	Feb. 26
12:11	May 14
14:3	Mar. 9
14:5	Jan. 8
21:5	June 11
21:7	Sept. 23
21:23	May 26
21:25	April 13
22:4	Mar. 18
22:4	April 8
22:16	Feb. 6